December's child: a
book of Chumash oral
narratives. 1975

December's Child

For the Simi Valley Library
on the occasion of the
dedication of the Chumash
Mural —

Tom Blackburn

December's Child

A Book of Chumash Oral Narratives

Edited, with an Analysis, by

Thomas C. Blackburn

UNIVERSITY OF CALIFORNIA PRESS
BERKELEY • LOS ANGELES • LONDON

UNIVERSITY OF CALIFORNIA PRESS
BERKELEY AND LOS ANGELES, CALIFORNIA
UNIVERSITY OF CALIFORNIA PRESS, LTD.
LONDON, ENGLAND
COPYRIGHT © 1975 BY THE REGENTS OF
THE UNIVERSITY OF CALIFORNIA
ISBN: 0-520-02930-5
LIBRARY OF CONGRESS CATALOG CARD
NUMBER: 74-27284
PRINTED IN THE UNITED STATES OF AMERICA
DESIGNED BY DAVE COMSTOCK

DEDICATION

To Fernando, María, Luisa, Lucrecia, Juan,
Simplicio, and so many others, who lived and
remembered a vanished way of life—and to
John P. Harrington, who did so much to
preserve it for us all—this book is
respectfully and affectionately dedicated.

Contents

Preface

*O*ne of the more intriguing aspects of anthropology's
development as an academic discipline (and one that
will doubtless engage the attention of some future
historian of the field) must be the curious fact that there seems
to have been the greatest lag in theoretical maturation in those
areas where one would expect it least—the interfaces between
anthropology and the other social sciences. Part of the reason
probably lies in the fact that until recently the need for "two
skills in one skull," resulting from conflicting or divergent
paradigms, required a professional commitment of time and
energy that many scholars were reluctant to give. But whatever the reason, interdisciplinary methods and models have
tended to receive less attention from anthropologists than
those more closely identified with anthropology *per se*. This
has certainly been the case with folkloristic studies in anthropology. Although many ethnographers have faithfully collected myths and folktales along with more conventional data
on social, economic, or political behavior, only a few have

utilized the materials they have obtained in any kind of theoretical context (see Hallowell, 1947:544-546). Fewer still have attempted to deal with the fundamental issue of the inter-relationships between oral narratives and other aspects of culture—with what might be termed the mythic problem *par excellence*. How—and how well—do oral narratives relate to other forms of social behavior, and what are their social functions? How can the anthropologist best utilize these materials to elucidate the problems that concern him, and how is he to resolve apparent conflicts? Do oral narratives reflect significant aspects of cultural behavior, and, if so, to what extent and in what fashion? As Bascom has pointed out,

> the problem of the "cultural context" or the relationship between folklore and other aspects of culture . . . has two distinct facets, the first of which concerns the extent to which folklore, like language, is a mirror of culture and incorporates descriptions of the details of ceremonies, institutions and technology, as well as the expression of beliefs and attitudes. . . . The second aspect of the problem . . . has to do with the fact that characters in folktales and myths may do things which are prohibited or regarded as shocking in daily life. . . . The striking contrasts between folklore and actual conduct raise new problems of wider theoretical significance concerning the relations between folklore and culture. Over many centuries folklorists and other scholars have attempted to explain them, or to explain them away. Most of the earlier explanations are unacceptable today, but the problem itself remains with us as one of the most intriguing and basic of all the problems of folklore (1954:336-338).

The present book, a revised and somewhat condensed version of my doctoral dissertation, addresses this basic issue directly, and is intended to clarify some of the difficulties, as well as potential rewards, awaiting anyone who ventures into what all too often has been a theoretical no—man's—land. But I should like to emphasize that I make no particular claim to being either methodologically or theoretically innovative in this study. I have simply returned, albeit with a different perspective, to an anthropological research tradition which I believe is in danger of being buried under the obfuscating verbiage of structuralist approaches to oral narratives. The central focus of attention remains ethnographic—illuminating previously obscure facets of the extinct, fascinating, and possibly unique culture of the Chumash Indians of southern California. Attaining this objective has necessarily entailed the adoption of certain basic assumptions about the nature of oral traditions and their interrelationships with other aspects of cultural behavior, since research can never be pursued in a theoretical vacuum. Such a procedure, of course, would appear to lead inevitably to the same kind of circularity that has so often plagued other attempts to relate mythology to culture. The scholar who believes that myths are constructed in terms of philosophical oppositions, for example, will undoubtedly find what he is looking for in the material he examines:

> If I read a myth, select certain elements from it, and arrange them in a pattern, that "structure" is bound to be in the material unless I have misread the text or demonstrably misrendered it. The fact of its being there does not, however, indicate that my arrangement is anything more than my personal whim. . . . A myth is therefore bound to have a number of possible "structures" that are both in the material and in the eye of the beholder. The problem is to decide between them and to determine the significance of any of them (Maybury-Lewis, 1969: 118-119).

Fortunately, any "structure" or set of data derived from an analysis of oral narratives can be at least partially evaluated in terms of such criteria as internal consistency, consistency with alternate data, applicability to specific needs and objectives, and general explanatory usefulness. This in turn opens the way for a judicious reexamination of the initial assumptions upon which the original analysis was based, thus enabling the researcher to avoid a logical snare of his own making. It is imperative, therefore, that the fundamental assumptions underlying a study such as this be made explicit, and expressed as hypotheses to be tested in terms of their success in generating data capable of satisfying the criteria mentioned above.

Parenthetically, it should be noted that the basic approach followed here represents something of a departure from that normally pursued, in that oral narratives are being used to obtain information on other aspects of culture, rather than the reverse. Most previous anthropological studies concerned with the interrelationships between mythology and culture have been solidly based upon extensive ethnographic data, and have focused on the extent to which the oral narratives faithfully reflected these previously gathered data (e.g., Boas, 1935; Benedict, 1935; Ehrlich, 1937; Opler, 1938; Spencer, 1957; Herskovitz and Herskovitz, 1958; Berndt, 1966; and Lessa, 1966). While such a procedure is certainly immune to many of the criticisms often directed at folkloristic studies in general, it might be suggested that it also fails to exploit fully the unique potentialities for cultural insight inherent in the data, for the researcher is always constrained by the ethnographic facts he has previously gathered—and these facts must, in part at least, predetermine his results by implicitly directing his attention along certain lines. Thus the ethnographer who knows that conflict arising out of matrilineal inheritance is of major concern to his society will inevitably expect to find this reflected in oral narratives to some extent, and as a consequence he may unconsciously overlook or overemphasize other data. Ideally, of course, oral narratives should provide the anthropologist with data that complement rather than supplement data from other sources; that they have not normally done so may explain some of the neglect of what often seems a "floating segment of culture" (Hallowell, *op. cit.*). But by utilizing a procedure in which the narratives themselves constitute the primary data, in turn suggesting potentially testable hypotheses concerning the nature of Chumash culture, I hope that some of the circularity and limitations of earlier attempts to relate mythology and culture have been avoided, and that it has now become possible to evaluate pragmatically certain cherished assumptions about a fascinating but not easily understood facet of human behavior.

As was previously mentioned, the analysis of Chumash oral traditions, which comprises the bulk of Chapter Three, is clearly an extension of an important research tradition to which a number of prominent anthropologists have contributed over the years, and obviously it has depended heavily upon—and profited greatly by—their pioneering explorations and insights. Methodologically speaking, the present study is patterned most closely after Katherine Spencer's seminal work on Navaho mythology (1947; 1957). The theoretical assumptions underlying the analysis, on the other hand, are based to a considerable extent on John Fischer's highly useful summary of anthropological approaches to the study of folklore (1963). These assumptions may be summarized as follows:

1. Narratives are meaningful and reflect important aspects of culture.
2. Some types of narratives are more factual than others, but where distortion exists it is non-random and subject to analysis.
3. Employing the largest and most diverse corpus of narratives possible will accentuate both consistencies and inconsistencies—and inconsistencies are more apt to be indicative of distortion.
4. Distortion will usually involve either exaggeration or inversion.
5. Individual behavior involving social roles and expectations will tend to be most subject to distortion.
6. The presence of distortion or fantasy is an indication of cultural stress or concern.

These, then, are the initial assumptions which guided the analysis that constitutes the major portion of Part I. Now we must ask ourselves, in light of that analysis, how valid these assumptions appear in retrospect, and what conclusions might be drawn from this study of Chumash oral traditions that could be of benefit to others pursuing similar lines of research in the future.

To begin with, if this study can be seen as contributing in a meaningful way to our understanding of Chumash culture, the validity of the first two assumptions must be considered virtually self-evident, even though that has never been seriously at issue anyway. Oral narratives *are* meaningful and *do* reflect varying facets of cultural belief and practice, some of which complement rather than simply supplement data obtained through more usual channels, and any deviations from a strict depiction of "reality" *are* culturally patterned and hence potentially analyzable through proper methodological procedures. The problem remains one of recognizing and interpreting such deviations when they occur—although here again certain kinds of narratives can be initially accepted at face value (just as some statements by informants can be considered factual observations in ethnographic contexts) and thus can serve as points of reference in studying other types of narratives. The third assumption is therefore of crucial importance to the present study, for it represents a suggested solution to the problem—central to a number of previous anthropological analyses of folklore—of identifying and separating actual from fictitious behavior or norms.

At first glance, the indiscriminate gathering together of diverse narrative forms into a single heterogeneous conglomeration might seem a dangerous analytic procedure, and one highly susceptible to criticism. All societies, after all, distinguish between sacred myths which relate vital events involving important supernatural beings, and whose truth is axiomatic, and secular tales which are told primarily for entertainment or instruction, and which are not necessarily regarded by the members of the society as factual descriptions of real occurrences. Nevertheless, how can the fantastic adventures or creative acts of powerful supernatural beings or of ancestors, or the picaresque escapades of a character like Coyote, be of help in elucidating the mundane behavior of real people in a real world—people who themselves must have considered such adventures or escapades extraordinary in the first place? As the analysis in Chapter Three clearly shows, the dangers inherent in a comparison of divergent narrative types are self-correcting, for it is precisely through such a process of comparison and contrast that it becomes possible eventually to distinguish between the ordinary and the extraordinary in narrative action—and only then can certain norms and standards be inferred.

The remaining assumptions are less easily dealt with, for all involve the complex issue of distortion in one form or another. As the extended discussion of this topic in Chapter Three should demonstrate, the very use of terms such as "distortion" or "fantasy" is suspect, for it implies an implicit acceptance of a specific philosophical paradigm that may well be ethnocentric and culture-specific, and hence dangerously obfuscating in a theoretical sense. However, the depiction of unusual, infrequent, or seemingly improbable behavior or reactions in oral narratives remains a very real difficulty in utilizing folklore to answer anthropological questions, even if one manages to avoid facile labeling. Once again, however, the use of a corpus of narratives as the unit of study places such forms of behavior in context, and facilitates the identification of clear patterning in what might otherwise be seen as exercises in imagination or as the products of largely individual psychic processes.

The regularities that emerge from this approach appear to conform to certain general principles. First, much of the unusual behavior that occurs in the narratives seems to be the result of a dramatic requirement for conflict that disrupts the status quo. This kind of "distortion" is easily identified in most cases by the way in which positive or negative sanctions are subsequently brought into operation during plot development. (It might be suggested that in the future one way of isolating and characterizing these initial conflict situations more systematically than was attempted in the present study would be to utilize the kind of eidochronic analysis recently proposed by Colby [1973]). Second, a great deal of the dramatic effect in oral narratives, distinguishing them from more prosaic kinds of ethnographic statements, results from the use of exaggeration or inversion to highlight events and themes important in narrative structure. Again, only a comparison of many different narratives will enable the analyst to distinguish one form of emphasis from another, although the distinction is obviously one of crucial importance in properly interpreting any body of myths or folktales. Third, a significant number of the apparent expressions of fantasy in narratives can more profitably be considered symbolic representations of actual shamanic experiences and beliefs than as products of psychological mechanisms, so that the narratives themselves are perhaps best characterized as shamanic allegories. Thus, while the fourth and fifth assumptions seem well supported by the present study, the sixth appears to require serious reevaluation.

For some thirty years, discrepancies between real and depicted behavior in oral narratives have been generally accepted as revealing indications of tension or stress in the fabric of social life, and therefore the conflicting conclusions outlined above represent a considerable departure from earlier points of view. While there has been an admitted bias in this study in favor of cognitive or symbolic interpretations as opposed to those of a more purely affective or "psychological" nature, the results certainly appear to justify such a theoretical emphasis. Whether or not similar conclusions would be derived from studies of other bodies of folklore must remain a moot question for the time being. But the considerable benefits of a cognitive approach reinforce the belief that oral narratives have been left for too long to the dubious mercy of psychoanalytic interpretations, and will doubtless prove to be of even greater value when placed within the context of symbolic anthropology.

Of the many conclusions one might draw from a study such as this, perhaps none is more obvious (or more trite) than that oral narratives are richly complex, multivocal phenomena capable of communicating a variety of information on several levels simultaneously. Thus no single explanation or interpretation of myths or folktales is necessarily either right or wrong. As in the parable of the blind men and the elephant, wherein each was possessed of a portion of the truth, we are often unable to transcend our paradigms long enough to apprehend the holistic nature of our subject matter. Narratives *are* reflections of culture, social charters, storehouses of adjustive responses, expressions of socially thwarted needs, reflections of organizational pressures within a social structure, cultural models for coping with subjective stress, and perhaps even logical models for mediating unwelcome contradictions—but they are many other things as well, and in choosing to emphasize one particular facet rather than another, we almost inevitably sacrifice some of the potentially valuable insights into major cultural processes afforded by oral narratives. In concentrating on a thread of a particular color, we lose sight of the elaborate tapestry of which the thread is an integral and essential part. Only by means of many more eclectic studies of the kind presented here will the rich potential of oral narratives for anthropology be realized, for these narratives constitute a virtually untapped resource of considerable theoretical promise.

One final point that seems worth emphasizing here is that oral narratives form part of a *structured cultural subsystem*, firmly linked to time and place, dynamically interacting with other subsystems, and subject to the same processes of change and adaptation as any other aspect of culture. Any specific narrative, it might be suggested, is thus only fully meaningful (or interpretable) in the context of the system as a whole, and the attributes of the system are not predictable from the study of a single narrative. Thus Lévi-Strauss's suggestion (1967:213) that a myth actually consists of all its versions may contain a germ of truth, in that no single narrative will codify more than a small portion of the information contained in a corpus of narratives. Additionally, one would expect a narrative to be transmitted from one society to another only when it is congruent with the narrative subsystem as a whole, although the nature of the congruency (and hence the "meaning" of the narrative to the members of the society) might be quite different in the two cases. Structuralist studies of single myths, or folkloristic studies of particular themes or types of stories, are therefore handicapped from the start in their attempts to elucidate the meaning of oral narratives or comprehend their role in the complex web of social and spiritual life. The only approach that seems to offer any hope of ultimately understanding the richly varied tapestry of meanings that myths or folktales represent is one that, like the present study, emphasizes the systemic and synergetic nature of the subject matter, and views narratives as rare opportunities for glimpses into the inner workings of unique cultural universes.

A book such as this is seldom a product of the sole efforts of one individual. I would therefore like to take this opportunity to thank some of the many people who have contributed, either directly or indirectly, to my investigation of the Chumash and their oral traditions. The members of my doctoral committee—Drs. Johannes Wilbert, William Bright, James Hill, Henry Nicholson, and Stanley Robe—provided wise counsel, sound criticism, and expert guidance in the writing of my dissertation, and I am most grateful for their perseverance in the face of what occasionally became adverse circumstances. Dr. Joan Greenway and David Lord, my colleagues at California State Polytechnic University, Pomona, also read many portions of the manuscript and discussed them with me, and contributed in innumerable other ways to the success of this study. My fellow Californianist, Dr. Lowell Bean, first encouraged me to reenter the lists against the academic windmill, and I have since profited greatly from our many discussions on the finer nuances of California ethnology. I have also learned a great deal over the years from Chester King, archaeologist and Chumash enthusiast *extraordinaire,* who first initiated me into the rich and complex world of the Harrington notes. Margaret Blaker, ex-archivist of the National Anthropological Archives, and her staff were most helpful and supportive of my research, and offered every assistance during my visits to the Smithsonian Institution. Dr. Mary Haas of the Department of Linguistics, University of California, Berkeley, was also extremely helpful in providing access to the Harrington material stored there. Dr. Richard Applegate provided me with translations of several crucial Chumash texts, and Manuel Vizcaino clarified a number of archaic and idiomatic Spanish phrases—I am grateful to them both. Dr. Madison Beeler was kind enough to supply me with personal data on certain Harrington informants which I could not otherwise have obtained. I also wish to express my sincere appreciation to my typist, Pat Harrell, who labored diligently and expertly over what must often have seemed a refractory and most exotic text. Portions of my research were supported by grants from the Smithsonian Institution, Washington, D.C., and the Archaeological Survey Office, University of California, Los Angeles—I would like to acknowledge my indebtedness to both for their very kind assistance, and particularly thank the Smithsonian Institution for its permission to publish this small portion of the incredibly rich Harrington collection. Finally, I am very grateful to the following individuals and institutions for generously providing otherwise unobtainable illustrative materials: Travis Hudson of the Santa Barbara Museum of Natural History; the Lompoc Valley Historical Society; the Santa Ynez Valley News; Harry Lawton of Malki Press; and John, Josephine and Angela Yee of Goleta, the grandchildren of Lucrecia García. William Setzer of the Brooks Institute did an exceptional job of copying photographs that were often badly faded by time, while James Platt very kindly utilized his cartographic skills on my behalf. I extend my most heartfelt appreciation to them all.

T.C.B.

Part I: *The Analysis*

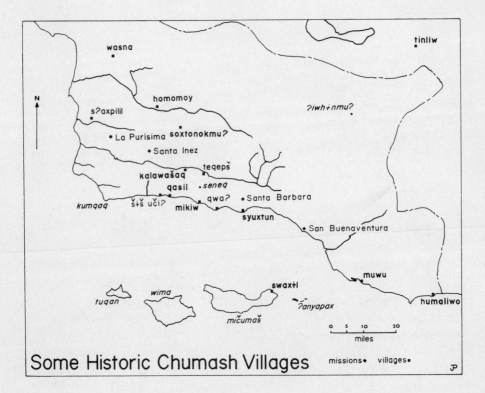

Some Historic Chumash Villages

missions◆ villages■

Chapter One

Background of the Study

lthough the Chumash Indians seem to have engen-
dered greater interest and respect among early explorers and missionaries than perhaps did any other
group in California, they remain to this day a people shrouded
in relative obscurity—an obscurity scarcely warranted by their
obvious technological sophistication and general level of cultural complexity. Some forty-five years ago A. L. Kroeber
lamented the paucity of data available for a reconstruction of
Chumash culture, stating that "there is no group in the State
that once held the importance of the Chumash concerning
which we know so little" (Kroeber, 1953:550). In many ways
the situation has changed little since Kroeber's *Handbook of the
Indians of California* first appeared in 1925, at least in terms of
published data; fortunately, however, future analysis of the
wealth of information contained in the ethnographic and linguistic notes compiled by John P. Harrington (from which the
narratives utilized for this study are derived) will surely result

in a remarkable expansion of our knowledge of many aboriginal California societies, including that of the Chumash.

The brief sketch of Chumash culture presented in this chapter does not, however, reflect the added insight afforded by the data in the Harrington notes, although these will be utilized to some extent in a later chapter to test the validity of the analysis. Since a primary objective of this study is to explore the feasibility of deriving important ethnographic data from oral narratives without prior reference to more conventional sources of information, I feel it best simply to present the kind of cultural sketch possible with the data now available. But since the purpose of this study is not a complete ethnographic description of the Chumash, nor is it the sorely needed analysis of all of Harrington's notes on the group, the cultural sketch included here will perforce be brief and sparingly documented. The interested reader who wishes a detailed or extensive treatment of the historic or standard ethnographic sources should consult Kroeber (1953), or the more recent descriptions of Landberg (1965) or Grant (1965), while Anderson's "A Bibliography of the Chumash and Their Predecessors" (1964) is particularly valuable for bibliographic references.

SOURCES OF INFORMATION

Sources of information on Chumash culture fall generally into four categories corresponding to major chronological periods: (1) the period of Spanish exploration (1542-1770); (2) the Mission period (1772-1834); (3) the period of initial ethnographic interest (1860-1900); and (4) the period of modern anthropological research (1900-present). Unfortunately, while these sources are voluminous, they are largely secondary— and the primary sources are all too brief or superficial. Only the future promise of Harrington's material brightens an otherwise dismal situation.

The period of Spanish exploration opens with the voyage of Juan Cabrillo in 1542 and ends with the founding of the first mission in Chumash territory some 230 years later. The Cabrillo expedition spent several months in the Santa Barbara Channel area and presumably wintered on San Miguel Island, where Cabrillo died and is thought to be buried. This initial voyage was succeeded by those of Cermeño in 1595 and Vizcaino in 1602, both of which passed through the Channel, but neither of them contributed more than brief observations to the sparse ethnographic data contained in the surviving records of the Cabrillo expedition. The accounts of these voyages are typical of most written by Spanish explorers and missionaries in that most of the information that can be derived from them concerns material culture items such as dress, housing, boats and utensils—in other words, those things most apparent to the superficial observer. Seldom does one find in the diaries any data on social organization, economic or political behavior, or religious beliefs or practices, a circumstance perhaps not unexpected in light of the fact that the Spanish as a rule considered aboriginal cultures to be of little interest or significance *per se*, and certainly unable to contribute substantively to scientific knowledge. The diaries kept by various members of the Portolá expedition of 1769-70 and the Anza expedition of 1775 represent some improvement over earlier accounts in that they are considerably more detailed, and are based on explorations by land with the consequent opportunities for closer observations of daily life, but there is still an ethnocentric bias to the observations that results in fleeting or impressionistic sketches of scenes recorded in passing, much like those one might expect from a passenger in a train who takes a few moments to jot down on paper the activities he can observe from his window during a brief stop. Again there is the same attention to material culture and the surface expression of daily life, but there is little interest in the deeper meanings beneath the surface.

With the establishment of the Franciscan missions of San Luis Obispo (1772), San Buenaventura (1782), Santa Barbara (1786), La Purísima (1787), and Santa Inés (1808), the Spanish had an unparalleled opportunity to observe and record Chumash culture as never before. Unfortunately, though, there was neither a Boscana nor an Arroyo de la Cuesta among the missionaries stationed in Chumash territory, and the accounts of native life stemming from this period of massive acculturation come primarily from sources external to the mission system itself. The extraordinary botanist José Longinos Martínez passed through Santa Barbara in 1792 and wrote a fascinating description of the local Indians, and the following year another botanist, Archibald Menzies, also made ethnographic observations while the Vancouver expedition was briefly anchored at Santa Barbara. The only data from this period recorded by the missionaries themselves (with the exception of the mission books recording births, baptisms, marriages, and so on) were in the form of brief answers to the *Interragatorio* of 1811, a questionnaire sent to each of the missions by the civil authorities in Mexico, or in sparse comments in letters, or in such rare documents as the *confesionario* of José Señán (Beeler, 1967).

The effects of missionization on the California Indians have been amply documented (see Cook, 1943), and certainly the effects on the Chumash were no exception to the rule. The combination of repeated epidemics, deliberate abortion, and destructive acculturation during the Mission period, followed by dispossession of their lands and a general exodus upon the secularization of the missions in 1834, led to a massive decrease in population and a virtual end to Chumash culture as a living entity by the time scholars began to interest themselves in the reconstruction of California's aboriginal past. Although some vestiges of Chumash political and economic organization may have survived as late as the 1860s (see Blackburn, 1974), only a few scattered survivors were still available for questioning by the time competent ethnographers began investigating aboriginal cultural patterns. The period of time between the secularization of the missions in 1834 and the initiation of ethnographic research in the 1870s still represents a major unfilled gap in our knowledge of Chumash acculturation and assimilation.

The beginnings of ethnographic research in California are clearly discernible in Alexander Taylor's famous collection of journalistic miscellany, published between 1860 and 1863 as a series of newspaper articles under the rubric of "The Indianology of California," although a real flowering of interest in aboriginal cultures does not occur for another decade. During the 1870s anthropological research in California proliferated, and much of it was centered upon the Chumash and their neighbors. The Wheeler Survey, for example, collected archaeological, ethnographic, and linguistic data in the Santa Barbara region, and men such as Paul Schumacher, Stephen Bowers, and Léon de Cessac vied with one another in accumulating vast quantities of archaeological materials. In addition, Cessac also apparently recorded a considerable amount of ethnographic data from informants like Rafael Solares. Unfortunately, most of his ethnographic notes have been misplaced, although the archaeological materials have recently been discovered in Paris (see Reichler and Heizer, 1964). From 1880 to 1888 H. W. Henshaw collected linguistic and some ethnographic data from surviving Indians for the Bureau of American Ethnology, and it is interesting to note that one of his major Chumash informants was Juan Estévan Pico, a half-breed who seems in turn to have obtained much of *his* data from Fernando Librado, Harrington's most valuable Ventureño informant. Between 1887 and 1896, Lorenzo Yates published a series of articles on Chumash archaeological and ethnographic materials, using data derived in some cases from living informants.

Almost all of the data collected during this period of initial ethnographic research are either archaeological or linguistic, and are most useful in reconstructing aspects of Chumash material culture. The ethnographic data, for the most part, are sparse, isolated from context, and recorded by people whose primary interest was not the explication of Chumash social organization. Only the notes recorded by Cessac might have differed in this respect, and they have yet to be recovered. Few of the scholars who concerned themselves in one way or another with Chumash culture at this time had either the training or the inclination to exploit systematically the knowledge possessed by the elderly Indians still living who provided a direct link with an aboriginal way of life. By the time such a man did appear it was nearly too late.

John Peabody Harrington, ethnologist and linguist, was born on April 29, 1884, and died on October 21, 1961, after a career nearly as remarkable for eccentricity as for its productivity. After his death the Smithsonian Institution began the task of locating and assembling his scattered field notes, which were eventually to fill over 400 large boxes and provide significant data on virtually every aboriginal linguistic group in North America. Although this mass of material may very well represent the greatest collection of linguistic and ethnographic information about North American Indians ever compiled by one man, Harrington's predilection for privacy and his complete indifference to the rewards of scholarly recognition make it difficult even now to provide more than the merest outline of his career, especially as the bulk of his collection has not as yet been adequately catalogued. It is to be hoped that a biography of this extraordinary man will some day be published, but until then Harrington's few published writings, the recollections of others (see Stirling and Glemser, 1963), and the internal evidence in his notes will have to suffice as sources of information about his research.

Harrington seems to have begun his research with the Chumash sometime in 1912. At first he worked with the aid of an interpreter conversant with Spanish, but within a few months he had become fluent enough to dispense with an intermediary. He apparently spent almost all of his available time during the next four years with the few elderly Chumash still fluent in the language, and the data collected during this period are perhaps the most valuable that he obtained. On February 20, 1914, he formally joined the staff of the Smithsonian Institution (from which he had already received financial support) as Ethnologist, a position he was to hold until his retirement in 1954. He continued his work in the field until September, 1917, returning to his Chumash research from August, 1918, until May, 1919, and from July, 1921, until May, 1922. The deaths of key informants at this time may have discouraged him temporarily, for he turned his attention to archaeological research between 1923 and 1926, excavating a number of sites in Chumash territory, including that of Burton Mound or *Syuxtun* at Santa Barbara. The period from September, 1927, to March, 1928, was once again devoted to linguistic and ethnographic research, apparently with Lucrecia García as informant, although most of his energy went into rechecking earlier transcriptions with his informants. Harrington does not seem to have ever again worked with a primary Chumash informant, although he did spend some time towards the end of his life checking the accuracy of earlier transcriptions with Lucrecia's daughter, and he also seems to have attempted the monumental task of organizing his own material in order to write a history and ethnography of the Chumash.

It would appear that no group in North America held a greater fascination for Harrington than the Chumash, to whom his prodigious energies were turned so often throughout his life. Certainly no other group is represented as massively or as consistently in his notes. However, with the exception of brief notices of ongoing field work in the Bureau of American Ethnology *Annual Reports*, Harrington's only ethnographic publication on the Chumash was the Culture Element Distributions trait list (1942) that he filled out at the urging of Kroeber—probably with reluctance and under duress, in the belief that only in this way could he keep others from invading what he apparently felt to be his own private ethnographic preserve. Although the C.E.D. report is probably fairly accurate in most respects, it must be used and evaluated with certain qualifications clearly in mind. First, it is far removed in spirit and style from the research methodology that Harrington seems to have found most congenial, and it is quite probable that he had little real interest in the project from start to finish. Second, he was using notes that he himself had probably not glanced at for over twenty years, and there are occasional discrepancies between the C.E.D. list and the notes, which indicate an unfamiliarity with his own material that should come as no surprise to anyone aware of the state of monumental disorganization in which the collection was found after his death. Third, the necessity of fitting a great mass of often disjointed data into the rather procrustean form of the C.E.D. trail list occasionally seems to have resulted in an omission or distortion of essential facts. This seems to be especially true in the sensitive areas of social organization and religion. In sum, the C.E.D. report can best be likened to a block of ice perched upon the tip of the proverbial iceberg: far more exists than meets the eye.

Since Harrington's death in 1961, improved access to his notes has resulted in the appearance of several papers based on some aspect or portion of the data that he collected on Chumash culture. Craig (1966 and 1967) has published papers on Ventureño basketry and related topics, drawing heavily on Harrington notes at Berkeley. Linda King (1969) has utilized similar materials in her report on excavations at Medea Creek, providing an ethnographic dimension to her archaeological data. Heizer (1970b) has published a brief Harrington notebook discovered among the Merriam papers, Chester King (1971) has combined historic and ethnographic data with extracts from the Harrington notes in order to describe Chumash economic interaction, and Blackburn (1974) has used similar materials to discuss social integration throughout Southern Califor-

nia. Thus an increasing number of scholars are becoming
familiar with the potentialities inherent in Harrington's linguistic and ethnographic notes, although what little has been
published so far gives but the barest indication of the wealth of
information available.

THE STATUS OF CHUMASH CULTURE

Aboriginally, of course, the Chumash were neither a cultural nor a linguistic entity *per se*. Rather, theirs was a large and
probably diverse population occupying numerous relatively
autonomous but contiguous settlements scattered irregularly
across a rich and ecologically varied habitat. They shared many
important cultural traits, and spoke a number of languages and
dialects belonging to a single branch of the Hokan language
family. The territory held by Chumashan peoples extended
along the California coast from Topanga Canyon in the south
to Estero Bay in the north, and included the three islands of
Santa Cruz, Santa Rosa and San Miguel. To the northeast it
ranged as far inland as the edge of the San Joaquin Valley.
Within this region of islands, coasts, foothills, valleys and
mountains lived a population variously estimated to have
numbered anywhere from 8,000 to over 20,000, although a
figure of perhaps 15,000 seems most reasonable in view of the
evidence (Brown, 1967). The largest portion of this population
was clustered along the shores of the Santa Barbara Channel,
where the combination of exceptionally rich marine fauna and
a relatively sheltered coastline favored maritime adaptation
and promoted a degree of cultural complexity which would be
of interest to anyone attempting to delineate evolutionary
mechanisms underlying indigenous cultural change.

The Chumashan languages have been relatively unstud-
ied compared to many other language families in California, at
least by modern standards. In 1925 Kroeber distinguished at
least eight Chumash "dialects": Obispeño, Purismeño, Inezeño, Barbareño, Ventureño, Island, Cuyama, and Emigdiano
(1953:552). Recent studies have demonstrated that most of
these were distinct languages rather than dialects, and that
each in turn had a number of dialectical subdivisions. Obispeño and the Island dialects seem to have been the most divergent, while Barbareño and Inezeño were quite similar to one
another. Additional information from Harrington's unpub-

lished notes indicates that there were two major Barbareño dialects (Dos Pueblos and Santa Barbara-Rincon), two island dialects (Santa Cruz and Santa Rosa-San Miguel), and several Ventureño dialects (Ventura, Mugu, Malibu, and Castaic Lake or kaštek). The dialect spoken at San Emigdio (corresponding to Kroeber's Cuyama dialect) was said to be very similar to Barbareño—what was spoken in the area labelled Emigdiano in Plate I of Kroeber's *Handbook* was actually kaštek Ventureño. There may also have been an Ojai dialect of Ventureño, and perhaps two major dialects of Inezeño, but a detailed analysis of Harrington's linguistic material must be carried out before any firm conclusions about the internal relationships of the Chumashan languages can be drawn.

Chumash villages varied considerably in population. A number of the pueblos or "towns" described by early explorers may have contained as many as a thousand people, although communities of one to two hundred were probably more typical. Each village consisted of a number of hemispherical or conical houses constructed of poles covered with thatching. In some of the larger pueblos the houses seem to have been arranged in orderly rows along streets, and there is some evidence along the northwestern part of the Santa Barbara Channel of a bipartite division of communities perhaps indicative of social institutions peculiar to that area (Brown, 1967:5). The typical house was approximately twenty feet in diameter and contained a single family, although some reached a diameter of over fifty feet and housed a number of apparently related families. These latter houses almost certainly belonged to chiefs or other distinguished men, and may have contained a single extended family consisting of a man, his wives and immature children, and his married sons and their families. In addition to houses, each village also contained one or more temescals or sweathouses, a gaming field for playing shinny or hoop–and–pole, a stockaded cemetery, and a shrine containing an offertory pole where sacrifices of food or money were made and ceremonies were held on ritual occasions.

The material culture of the Chumash, with the exception of specific technological items associated with a maritime adaptation, differed little from that of their neighbors to the north or east. Their most striking technological innovation, of course, was the *tomol* or plank canoe that so impressed the

Spanish explorers. This was made of fitted planks sewn together and then caulked with asphaltum. It was generally about twenty feet in length, carried three to four men, and was propelled by double-bladed paddles. The Chumash used the *tomol* for hunting sea mammals, fishing, and trading back and forth between the mainland and the islands. Sea mammals were hunted with tridents or harpoons, while fish were taken in nets, or caught on hooks of three different kinds, or speared. Hunting techniques on land were little different from those used by most California Indians. Both the self-bow and the sinew-backed bow were used, as well as a variety of traps, but it is uncertain whether the atlatl or the curved throwing stick were used, though it is possible. Freshwater fish were caught in traps or speared.

Chumash basketry was diverse and finely made, though not exceptionally so, and resembled that made by adjacent Uto-Aztecan groups (Dawson and Deetz, 1965). It was used for collecting, carrying, and storing the wide variety of vegetable foods utilized, and it was also used for the cooking, leaching, or other preparation of such foods. Most personal belongings, too, were stored in baskets. Exceptionally fine bowls and plates were carved from wood, and steatite from Santa Catalina Island was obtained through trade and used to make such objects as paint mortars, bowls, digging stick weights, comales, pipes, beads, and effigies. Many of these items were probably manufactured by full-time specialists, and were often traded as far away as the San Joaquin Valley.

The Chumash economic system was complex and involved intensive interaction over a wide geographic area (Chester King, 1971). Manufactured goods were produced primarily by occupational specialists who belonged to "brotherhoods" or gremios, sodality-like organizations that cross-cut localized affiliations and had a kinship-based charter. Most manufactured goods were produced on the islands (where resources were scarcer) and exported to the mainland, while the mainland exported food stuffs and goods manufactured from materials not present on the islands. Most exchange appears to have been based upon an individual profit motivation, and apparently operated according to the law of supply and demand. A form of currency based upon shell beads was widely used, and the Chumash appear to have been the pri-

mary source of currency for the southern half of the state.
There were standards of measurement for both money and
other goods, based either on length or on volume, and there
were also standard rates of exchange for trading purposes. The
Chumash thus had an essentially monetized market economy
in which food, manufactured goods, and some services were
exchanged or purchased. Fiestas and other ceremonial occasions seem to have been important contexts for economic
exchange, and there is little doubt that there were significant
interrelationships between the economic system of the Chumash and the political and religious hierarchy typified by the
ʔantap cult (Blackburn, 1974).

Perhaps the least understood facet of Chumash culture
involves their kinship and marriage patterns. In his C.E.D.
paper (1942) Harrington notes that the Chumash had three
types of kinship groups: (1) moieties, (2) nonlocalized "patri-
clans," and (3) patrilineages. But Harrington's own field notes
on the subject are brief, cryptic, and contradictory, and certainly open to differing interpretations. Practically all of the
data were supplied by a single informant, María Solares, who
had visited among the southern Yokuts and was partially of
Yokuts descent, a fact that must be kept in mind when evalu-
ating her information. The presence of moieties among most
Chumash groups is highly unlikely, although the bipartite
arrangement of villages along the northwest coast of the
channel, referred to earlier, may indicate the presence of some
kind of dichotomous organization in that area. The "clans,"
which were almost certainly Yokuts-like "totem groups" (see
Kunkel, 1962), may very well have been differentially ranked
either in terms of wealth and prestige or in terms of the pur-
ported power of the animal helper or totem, but there is good
reason to believe that the Chumash did not have a moiety system in historic times such as those described for some other
California groups.

Chumash social organization seems to have most closely
resembled that of some of the Yokuts tribelets of the San
Joaquin Valley to the north. Harrington's "clans," as was mentioned above, were apparently composed of people sharing
common animal helpers, and both group and helper were
referred to as škalukš. An individual inherited the škalukš of
both father and mother, though that of the father was con-

sidered the stronger. The *škalukš* does not seem to have been exogamous, and may not in fact have acted as a corporate group. The lineages reported by Harrington were probably equivalent to, or the basis for, virilocal extended families similar to those that among the Yokuts occupied either multi-family dwellings or nuclear family neighborhoods. Certainly, the available data suggest such a pattern for the Chumash. Most of the Chumash lived in houses suitable for nuclear families only, but chiefs and other influential or wealthy people apparently occupied houses large enough for six or seven related families. Marriage was probably regulated most by the general ban against marriage to a close relative of any kind. There have been some suggestions that village endogamy may have been practiced among some of the Chumash (see Landberg, 1965:29-33), but there is considerable evidence of intermarriage between villages in the Santa Monica Mountains in the mission records (Brown, 1967:7). The problem has yet to be resolved. Apparently only chiefs were allowed more than a single spouse at a time, with a majority of marriages being monogamous.

The political organization of the Chumash achieved a complexity surprising even for California. Although a situation involving multiple chiefs has been described by most authorities, there is a strong possibility that this may be an erroneous supposition resulting from attempts by the Spanish to explain indigenous patterns in ethnocentric terms, and from a general application of the word *capitán* to anyone occupying a political office. The primary political unit was the village, presided over by the *wot* or chief, whose duties included caring for visitors and the poor, furnishing ceremonial property and personnel for fiestas, arranging for fiestas and other ceremonies, and representing the village on such occasions. Chieftainship was hereditary and usually involved primogeniture, although a chief's younger son or a sister or daughter could be named to succeed him if the community felt it best. The chief was assisted by a *paxa* or ceremonial leader, and two *ksen* or messengers. The *paxa* was the most important political figure in the village after the *wot*. He made announcements and gave orations at fiestas, collected offerings and fines, and presided over ceremonies. He was probably also the major link between the political hierarchy represented by the *wot* and the religious net-work of the *ʔantap* cult.

Chumash villages were linked in a number of loose federations that might possibly have been coterminous with the dialect groupings mentioned earlier. These federations may have been based on kinship relationships between the *wot*s of the component villages, on membership in the *ʔantap* cult, or both. They seem to have been organized around a principal village (Malibu, Mugu, Santa Barbara, Dos Pueblos, etc.) whose *wot* was recognized as having some degree of authority over the villages in the federation. There is historic evidence that in some cases the son of the *wot* of the principal village was himself *wot* of another (Brown, 1967:48). Interaction also occurred in other contexts as well, and it is possible that much of the political integration observed between Chumash villages was based on mechanisms other than kinship:

> Although the Chumash had the usual variety of herb and suck-ing doctors, rattlesnake, bear and weather shamans, and many individuals with limited powers derived from possession of an *ʔatiswin* (a dreamhelper or talisman), there was also a formal cult organization homologous to the Chingishnish cult as it proba-bly existed among the Gabrielino and Luiseño. Members of this cult were referred to as *ʔantap*, and their primary responsibility seems to have been the performance of dances and other rituals at large public ceremonies. Members were baptized into the cult as children, and through a period of apprenticeship learned the esoteric language, sacred songs and dances, and other aspects of ritual that characterized it. The parents of chilren who became members apparently had to pay a considerable sum of money for the privilege; presumably, only high-status families could af-ford this, and it is interesting to note that the chief and all mem-bers of his family were required to belong. There were appar-ently at least twelve *ʔantap* in every major village, many of whom participated from time to time in ceremonies held in widely-scattered locations; since the chiefs, other important offi-cers, and shamans were all members of what essentially was a ubiquitous, far-flung religious elitist society, the *ʔantap* cult acted as an important integrative mechanism throughout the Chumash area (Blackburn, 1974:104-105).

In discussing Chumash religious beliefs and practices, it may be useful to distinguish between those that were essentially private and those involving the community as a whole. Private ceremonies, primarily of interest to a few individuals or families, were performed on such occasions as birth, giving a child a name, adolescence, the taking of *Datura*, marriage, illness and recovery from illness, and wakes, while occasions calling for public observance included a chief's birthday, the appearance of rattlesnakes from hibernation, a mourning anniversary, completion of the summer harvest, and the summer and winter solstices. Perhaps the most significant ceremony as far as the individual was concerned was the drinking of *Datura*, for it was during the subsequent coma and hallucinatory state that the boy or girl established the special relationship with a dream helper (represented by the *ʔatišwin* or talisman) and received prognostications concerning his or her future from the *alčuklaš* or administering official. The great public ceremonies (the mourning anniversaries, the September harvest fiesta, and the winter solstice ceremony) involved performances by dancers and singers associated with the *ʔantap* cult, shamans' contests, the construction of a *siliyik* or sacred enclosure, and sacrifices of money, food or down to the sun and the earth (which is called either *xutaš* or *šup*) at the *šawil* or shrines. They also involved complex social, economic, and political interaction between villages over a wide geographical area (see Blackburn, 1974). Chumash religious beliefs have been summarized as follows:

> Chumash religious beliefs, and their more important public (as opposed to private) rituals, revolved around the esoteric and metaphorical worship of two sacred celestial "bodies," earth and sun. The sun was regarded as perhaps supreme, a vivifying male force or entity that was also vaguely threatening, a possible bringer of death; the earth, on the other hand, was the generally maternal provider of food and other necessities of life, to be worshipped in her three aspects of wind, rain and fire. A fairly precise twelve-month lunar calendar, semi-annually adjusted by reference to the solar solstices, was employed in determining the proper times to observe a variety of occasions; the importance of such astronomical cycles to the Chumash is demonstrated by the fact that there was even a kind of astrologer called an *alčuklaš* whose duties included the naming of new-born children according to their birth-month, the administering of toloache, and the reporting of illnesses or other social problems to the chief. When two of the most important ceremonial occa-

sions, the late September harvest fiesta and the Winter Solstice ceremony, were held was directly determined by the phases of earth and sun (Blackburn, 1974:104).

Chumash cosmography and mythology will not be discussed here, since they are treated extensively elsewhere in this study, but it should be pointed out that no other facets of Chumash culture have been more shrouded in obscurity. Only two Chumash narratives (collected by Yates) have ever been published (Heizer, 1955b).

The Harrington Papers

As was previously mentioned, the Smithsonian Institution began the task of locating, organizing and cataloging Harrington's manuscripts and field notes shortly after his death, an undertaking that has yet to be completed. Of the several hundred boxes of materials now available, approximately sixty or so contain notes on the Chumash Indians of southern California. Unfortunately, somewhat less than half of these sixty boxes are presently in the National Anthropological Archives at the Smithsonian, or have even been catalogued; the remainder are on loan to the Department of Linguistics, University of California, Berkeley. This has made the examination and use of the Chumash materials exceptionally difficult and has necessitated several trips to both Washington, D.C., and Berkeley, although the great helpfulness of various staff personnel, access to a Xerox copier and small grants from both the Smithsonian Institution and the UCLA Archaeological Survey have ensured a successful conclusion to the research that has culminated in this study.

Since Harrington carried out research on the Chumash from time to time throughout his long career, his notes reflect varying stages of organization, ranging from rambling notes jotted down in pencil on odd scraps of paper to drafts of manuscripts that were never published. The original field notes were usually written in pen or pencil on both sides of letter-sized paper. These were then copied, either by hand or by typewriter, sometimes verbatim and sometimes in the form of brief extracts. Extracts were usually placed on small cards which were then filed according to an elaborate system apparently clear only to Harrington himself. The same data will thus appear in a variety of places, and it is often difficult to deter-

mine which informant supplied the data originally. Much of
the bulk that makes the materials so difficult to work with
stems from the fact that so many copies and extracts were
made and variously filed that one is practically overwhelmed
by the apparent mass of information. This, in fact, may explain
Harrington's own seeming inability to achieve an overview in
spite of the repeated attempts that are evidenced by the
various rough drafts of manuscripts scattered throughout his
papers.

The narratives and traditions presented here have been
drawn from this mass of materials after a careful examination
of all the relevant boxes at both Berkeley and Washington,
D.C. They probably represent well over ninety-five percent of
the narratives collected by Harrington from his Chumash
informants, although there is the obvious possibility that more
will be discovered in the future when the materials have been
adequately organized and catalogued. Harrington apparently
intended at one time to gather together all of the stories that he
had collected and publish them as part of a book of California
Indian folklore, for many of the narratives exist in the form of
neatly typed, translated, and rewritten copies needing little
subsequent attention. There is also a brief reference to such a
project in some of his early correspondence. But like so many
of Harrington's intentions, the book never materialized.

Although many of the narratives were put into semi-final
form by Harrington himself, the rest required varying degrees
of translation and editing. Some narratives appeared in the
form of Chumash texts with interlinear Spanish or English
translations, while many had been recorded in the rather
colloquial Spanish spoken by the informants. But even those
narratives rewritten by Harrington required partial editing of
incomplete, awkward, or extraneous sentences, as well as the
occasional translation of terms or reorganization of para-
graphs. In addition, a few of the "narratives" in Section A of
Part II were in a sense created by the editor, in that short comments by an informant on a particular subject were brought
together in the form of a coherent statement, with a great deal
of extraneous material being deleted. However, during translation and editing, the primary objective was always faithful
adherence to the detail and flavor of the original without sacri-
ficing either readability or grammatical integrity. Such a proce-

dure is of course subject to criticism, because of the possible
introduction of inaccuracies and an insensitivity to the nuances
of Chumash narrative style, but the fact remains that that facet
of Chumash oral literature will be illuminated only through a
careful linguistic analysis of original texts—a project far beyond the scope of this study. In addition, many of the narratives were first recorded in Spanish rather than Chumash, so
that a serious obfuscation of stylistic elements has already
occurred. Most of the narratives presented few real problems
in terms of translation from Spanish, although there were
several that contained passages which were either obscure in
meaning or which had not been translated from Chumash by
Harrington (practically all of which were told by Fernando
Librado). Some were recorded in English and must remain
obscure, but future linguistic analysis may well clarify the rest.
The informant, location, and original form of each narrative are
listed in the Appendix.

THE INFORMANTS

Perhaps nowhere was Harrington's passion for privacy
more evident than in the manner in which the identity of his
informants was hidden. They were never referred to by name
even in the field notes; instead, Harrington usually applied
either a cryptic abbreviation of his own devising such as
"qub.," "sa.," or "lc.," or else simply jotted down "inf. says"
or "according to inf." For this reason it has been difficult to
determine the identities of his informants and to obtain bio-
graphical information on them, although a careful cross-
checking of notes and examination of scattered references has
made some progress possible. The data that follow are brief
and should be considered tentative—a careful search of various mission records would probably turn up more data than
are included here, although they are often disappointing in
terms of permitting the identification of specific individuals,
due in part to an unfortunate habit among the priests of using
first names only when referring to the neophytes. The inform-
mants discussed here are only those that supplied narratives
used in the study (although a full list of Harrington's informants would be valuable and may someday be compiled and
published elsewhere).

Fernando Librado

Fernando was probably born sometime in 1804, in the village of *swaxɨl* on Santa Cruz Island, and was brought to the mainland shortly thereafter. Most of his early years were spent in Ventura, but he later spent many years as a vaquero on ranches near Las Cruces. During the last twenty years of his life he was a handyman for the Loustalot family at the Las Cruces stage—station. He died in Santa Barbara on June 19, 1915, and was buried in the poor ground at Calvary Cemetery. He never married.

Fernando's father was José Antonio Mamerto, son of Ambrosio, captain of the village of *swaxɨl*. His paternal uncles were Andrés and Baltazar *sulupsiauset*. Fernando's father, paternal grandfather, and great-grandfather were all born at *swaxɨl*, and all had the Indian name *kitsepawit*, as did Fernando. Fernando's mother was Juana María Alifonsio, daughter of José Raymundo *tɨʔmi* of *simoʔmo* and a Santa Cruz Island woman. Fernando's father died in Santa Barbara and his mother in Ventura.

Fernando's primary language was Ventureño, but he was also familiar with Cruzeño (the Santa Cruz Island dialect), Inezeño, and some Purismeño. He was Harrington's most important Ventureño informant, and supplied perhaps the best data on aboriginal political organization and ritual that Harrington ever obtained. He apparently supplied Juan Estévan Pico, Henshaw's informant, with much of his data also. Harrington usually used the abbreviation "F." when referring to Fernando, and he may also have used either "quc." or "quic." when Fernando supplied Purismeño data.

María Solares

María's date of birth has not been determined, although she was born at Mission Santa Ynez and lived in the Santa Ynez Valley most of her life. In 1868, after her mother's death, she visited relatives at *tinliw* on the Tejon Ranch, at a time when that village contained people of diverse origins. María married several times, and her daughter Clara Miranda was born in 1875. María died in 1922 at Santa Ynez, at an advanced age.

María's father was Bienvenuto and her paternal grandfather Estévan *qiliqutayɨwit*, both of *kalawašaq* village in the

Santa Ynez Valley. Estevan was married to Eularia, and was the uncle of Ignacio *tilinawit* of *kalawašaq*. María's mother was Brigida, who was born at *tinliw* and was half Yokuts. Her maternal grandfather was Ygnacio, a Chumash from *sxenen* or La Paleta, who was married to a Yokuts woman. Brigida's half-brother was Juan Moynal, a Tachi Yokuts who at one time was captain of *tinliw*.

María was Harrington's primary Inezeño informant, and appears to have been the informant most knowledgeable on the subject of mythology. Her relationship to Rafael Solares, Cessac's informant and the *ʔantap* whose photograph was published by Reichler and Heizer (1964), is uncertain, but he was apparently her father-in-law. Harrington used the abbreviations "qu." or "qub." to designate María.

Luisa Ygnacio

Luisa was born at Mission Santa Barbara, probably in 1830, and lived in the Santa Barbara area all her life. She died on December 7, 1922, and was buried at Calvary Cemetery.

Luisa's father was Antonino, who was baptized and raised at Santa Barbara although all of his relatives were from *kuyam* near Dos Pueblos. Her mother was María Joaquina. Luisa had the Indian name *nutʔu* (a species of bird). She married Policarpio in 1851, and then after his death married José Ygnacio *tumyalatset* in 1856. Her daughter Lucrecia was born in Santa Barbara in 1877, and José Ygnacio died in 1880.

Luisa was probably Harrington's best Barbareño informant, and was the mother and grandmother of two other Harrington informants. Harrington used the abbreviations "la.," "sa.,," or "λ" when referring to her.

Lucrecia García

Lucrecia was born in Santa Barbara on June 29, 1877, and died on May 5, 1937. She was the daughter of José Ygnacio and Harrington's informant Luisa Ygnacio. She married a Yaqui Indian by the name of Florentín García. Her daughter María or Mary acted as an informant for both Harrington and Madison Beeler.

Lucrecia was a Barbareño informant and was most valuable in supplying linguistic data. Harrington used the abbreviations "lc." or "luc." to designate her.

Juan de Jesús Justo

Juan Justo was born in Santa Barbara on November 16, 1858, and lived in the Santa Barbara area all his life. He was a well-known character and seems to have supplied information to a number of early ethnographers at one time or another. He died on May 5, 1941, and was buried at Calvary Cemetery.

Juan Justo's father was Justo, chief of *mikiw* or Dos Pueblos, and son of Andrés and Sevarina. Justo died in Santa Barbara in 1895. Juan Justo's mother was Cecilia, daughter of Segundo and Petra, who died in Santa Barbara in 1903.

Juan Justo was a Barbareño informant and a noted raconteur. Most of the narratives having a Latin American source were told by him. Harrington used the abbreviations "ju." or "J.J.J." when referring to him.

Simplicio Pico

Simplicio was born in Ventura in May, 1839, and died in Ventura on February 12, 1918. His father was Vicente Pico, and he was probably related to Juan Estévan Pico, Henshaw's informant. Little else is known about him. He was an important Ventureño informant, but does not seem to have known many narratives. Harrington used the abbreviations "Sp." or "pama" to designate him.

Chapter Two

Descriptive Summary
of the Collection

GENERAL CHARACTERISTICS

The collection of oral traditions presented here is exceptionally diverse, and includes materials ranging from timeless myths to anecdotes about relatively recent or even contemporary events. Some of the materials, in fact, might not be considered truly "folkloric" by those preferring a strict interpretation of the term, but I have chosen in general to ignore purely definitional arguments as irrelevant to my specific concerns, and I have included any story or anecdote which seems to me to either illustrate or illuminate a portion of Chumash behavior and the belief system underlying it, and which appears to fall clearly within the bounds of oral tradition. The Chumash themselves distinguished between a *tišipiš* or "story," such as one might tell a child for amusement or diversion, and a *timoloqinaš* or "history" that presumably dealt with real events occurring long ago (whether or not other emic categories were also recognized is as yet unknown). But I have not made any serious attempt to distinguish between such familiar narrative types as "myths," "legends," or "folktales"—and even "narrative" is employed in a wider sense than is normally done by folklorists, to designate "any story or description of actual or fictional events" (*American Heritage Dictionary*, 1969:873).

The several categories into which the collection has been subdivided reflect pragmatic choices selected more for the convenience of the reader than for any specific theoretical purpose. Section A, for example, is comprised of explanatory statements concerning the structure and nature of the cosmos, its inhabitants and their history, and their relationships. It provides a helpful introduction to the narratives that follow by explaining the setting and introducing some of the important members of the cast. Section B is comprised of several narratives belonging to a single important family of myths, all concerned with the adventures of the grandson(s) of the rich old woman, Momoy (*Datura meteloides*). Section C includes a variety of narratives in which Coyote is the central character— as hero or villain, as trickster or victim. Some are extensive and important myths, while others appear to be nothing more than humorous stories that were probably told simply for enjoyment. Section D is comprised of narratives which do not involve Coyote but generally are placed in the distant, mythical past, and which would therefore normally be classified as either myths or legends. Section E includes stories and anecdotes about events within historic or protohistoric time. Magic and the supernatural play a prominent role here, and the opportunity is afforded of acquiring a valuable perspective on shamanistic practices and beliefs among the Chumash and their neighbors. Section F, finally, contains stories borrowed from European or Latin American sources during the historic period and recast into indigenous forms. The changes occurring in the process are both interesting and illuminating.

Although there is considerable variation in plot from one narrative to the next, hero tales and trickster stories make up the bulk of the purely fictional narratives in the collection. The adventures and narrow escapes of a protagonist who encounters dangerous monsters or malevolent, powerful supernatural beings and overcomes them seem to have been favorite subjects for Chumash storytellers. Similarly, tales in which the protagonist (who is usually Coyote) either gains or loses a desired objective through cunning and deceit were apparently as popular among the Chumash as they were elsewhere in North America. Often, of course, the two narrative types are combined into a single story, with a hero who escapes from a dangerous or embarrassing situation by the use of trickery and deception. Another characteristic of many narratives (and one that is widespread in California) is their composite quality: several distinct incidents from various sources may be combined to create a new story, or used to modify or expand an old one. Thus two different narratives may share one or more incidents, yet not really be variants of the same story at all; or variants of a story can be quite different in certain sections, or in the inclusion or order of specific incidents, yet remain versions of the same narrative.

Magic and the supernatural play a prominent role in most of the narratives in the collection, as might be expected in this type of material, and are often pivotal factors in the development of the plot. But there is a surprising variety of such elements from one tale to the next, and the way in which they are woven into the plot tells a great deal about aboriginal shamanism. For example, a significant number of the stories are concerned in one way or another with conflicts between innate and acquired powers—between innately powerful and dangerous creatures such as monsters or supernatural beings, and protagonists who depend upon acquired magical helpers or power—objects. Occasionally, however, the conflict is between one form of innate or acquired power and another. Usually the individual with acquired power is ultimately successful, but not always, or perhaps only as a consequence of superior deceit. The basic dichotomy between innate and acquired power seems to have been of fundamental concern to the Chumash, and was undoubtedly reflected in actual shamanistic practices as clearly as it is in the folktales. It also seems to have been subject to some ambiguity, and it is not always clear whether a particular manifestation of shamanistic abilities is due to innate or acquired powers, or both. Bear shamans, for example, are depicted sometimes as individuals capable of actual physical transformations and sometimes as individuals who simply possess special equipment endowed with power.

Another common plot device is the death (and later revivification) of a protagonist early in the story, as a consequence of being overconfident or of using poor judgment in a first encounter with a malevolent being. The death of the character is never irrevocable, and the revivification is usually accomplished by the use of a "medicine" or the application of a power–object. Supernatural birth and exceptionally rapid growth also occur in a number of stories and usually involve the use of the same medicine employed for revivification.

An exhaustive treatment of the stylistic features of Chumash oral narratives must await a detailed linguistic analysis, but a number of comments are possible at this time. Certain stock phrases occur frequently at the beginning or ending of a narrative, and correspond roughly to our own "once upon a time," and "they lived happily ever after." Many of the stories, for example, begin with such phrases as "it is a *timoloqinaš*," "when animals were people," or "when Coyote was human." Sometimes, however, the narrative dispenses with a statement of time and begins with a statement of place, action or character, such as "Coyote was at *syuxtun*," "Coyote was hungry," or "Momoy was a rich widow." Stories traditionally ended with the phrase *sutiwayan ulʔatuts?*, an idiomatic expression meaning "I am finished, it is the end." Another common storytelling device, and one found in many folktales throughout the world, is the repetition of a particular description or incident over and over again during the course of the story so as to prolong an otherwise brief narrative. This device is particularly evident in the stories told by Juan de Jesús Justo, a noted raconteur. Again, the depiction of emotion in Chumash narratives is characteristically weak, and the motivations underlying the action (as in most North American Indian folktales) are seldom explicit or obvious. The actions taken by the characters in a story are an inevitable outgrowth of their fundamental nature—they do what they do because they must, rather than as a consequence of having made deliberate choices between viable alternatives. It may very well be that the apparent absence of motivation in many American Indian stories reflects a basic philosophical attitude toward human nature distinct from that prevalent in Western society.

The cast of characters appearing in the various narratives is surprisingly large, even though the stories extant represent

only a portion of the original corpus of Chumash oral literature. Three distinct groups of characters can be distinguished
in the narratives: the First People, supernatural beings, and
nunašiš or monsters. The First People—who at the time of the
Flood became transformed into the present animals, birds or
plants—are the people who occupied the world long ago. They
live and talk and act very much as people do today, although
they are ambiguously depicted as having both human and
animal traits on occasion. In terms of popularity and frequency
of appearance, Coyote seems to have been the most important
of the First People, either as culture hero or trickster. The category of supernatural beings includes characters such as Sun,
the two Thunders, and the *ʔelyeʔwun*, who existed in mythical
times and who still exist today. Although they are usually
depicted as having a generally human form, they are endowed
with exceptional abilities and normally do not impinge on
human affairs except peripherally. Since they are extremely
powerful, they may also be dangerous if so inclined (a characteristic that typifies the ambiguity with which "power" was
regarded in aboriginal California). The category of *nunašiš* or
monsters includes various malevolent beings, some of them
still living and others killed before the Flood, who are dangerous to human beings because of their intrinsic nature and
innate powers. They are generally depicted as somewhat
deformed or misshapen, nocturnal, and basically evil.

A frequent characteristic of the narratives, and one that
certainly contributes to whatever quality of fantasy is present,
is *inversion*, the reversal of what might be considered normal or
expectable responses or behavior. Quite often the inversion is
readily apparent in terms of context, as when the protagonist
ignores the dictates of common sense, or as a symbolic
reversal, as when supernatural beings ingest only toxic or
noxious substances, or when the activities of day and night are
inverted in the Land of the Dead. On other occasions the
inversion is more subtle, and can only be detected or verified
by observing the operation of sanctions or carefully comparing
several narratives. This characteristic is of considerable interest, since it is present in some descriptions of ethnographic
behavior as well as in the oral narratives, and may very well be
part of a generally widespread but poorly understood phenomenon involving, for example, such things as "rituals of

conflict" (Norbeck, 1963). Because of its theoretical interest and significance in terms of the proper interpretation of the narratives in the collection, inversion will be discussed in detail in a later chapter.

The aboriginal context in which narration took place is obscure where the Chumash are concerned, but the frequency of restrictions with regard to storytelling elsewhere in California makes it seem likely that similar concepts existed among the Chumash as well. There is certainly evidence that at least some kinds of narratives (the *timoloqinaš*?) were normally related only in the winter months, and that most storytelling occurred at night. Tales seem to have been narrated primarily by older people, perhaps as part of their general function of enculturating the young. Whether there were also professional raconteurs at one time is impossible to say, though it does not seem particularly unlikely in view of other aspects of Chumash culture. Storytelling, as in many primitive societies, was undoubtedly an important and valued activity during the long winter nights, and the skillful narration of some of the complex myths (which may have taken two or three evenings to relate) probably required considerable ability and an excellent memory. As Fernando Librado's grandfather José Raymundo expressed it, the words of a story were frequently "metaphorical and enigmatic"—perhaps a consequence of the fact that there was a special ceremonial language used within the *siliyɨk* and on other ritual occasions. Some of the myths were almost certainly part of an esoteric ritual complex, and had implications, ramifications, and hidden meanings fully comprehensible only to the privileged few who were ʔantap or baptized members of the *siliyɨk*. Many of the stories undoubtedly served a primarily didactic function, communicating important social norms and values in an entertaining form, while still others were told for their entertainment value alone.

Another characteristic of the narratives that is difficult to control in any systematic or detailed manner is variability. Obviously, much of the variation between one story and the next is a function of the cultural context and purpose underlying each narrative. But these factors (which were discussed above) are not the only source of variation in the collection. There is also variation due to the individual background and personality of each informant, geographical or subcultural differences between different Chumash groups, and the presence in the collection of different versions of the same story. Unfortunately, it is impossible in most cases to separate one source of variability from another in terms of any specific informant, since that informant is usually the only source of information on a particular group or topic. María Solares, for example, was one of Harrington's most valuable informants and virtually his only source of data on the Inezeño, but she was a woman and does not seem to have been privy to some of the more esoteric aspects of the political and religious hierarchy, even though her data on cosmography and mythology is perhaps the best of any informant. In addition, María was part Yokuts and had visited among the Yokuts, and some of her stories obviously reflect this fact. Juan de Jesús Justo, a Barbareño informant, was perhaps the best storyteller of all, but he does not seem to have been very knowledgeable about Chumash culture in general, and appears to have been quite acculturated. On the other hand, Fernando Librado, Harrington's major Ventureño and Isleño informant, seems to have been a rather poor storyteller even though the myths he knew were apparently quite important and he seems to have had access to considerable data on all facets of his culture, including ritual and politics. But what is impressive, in spite of the differences among informants due to such factors as age, sex, social rank, marital status, travel experiences, residence, occupation, and other life experiences, is the degree to which their data tend to supplement and reinforce one another in spite of occasional contradictions or discrepancies. There is a strong impression that, regardless of linguistic variation, the intensive interaction between diverse social groups suggested by the ethnographic data for the protohistoric and historic periods (Blackburn, 1974) resulted in a unity of outlook and custom traditionally considered unusual for California. Thus in most cases it is probable that whenever differences do exist between narratives related by different informants, they can be attributed to individual rather than cultural differences, although the use of local settings for specific stories will introduce some changes.

A comparison of the present collection of narratives with those obtained previously in other areas of California reveals both predictable similarities and surprising differences. In spite of a number of broad correspondences and occasional

duplications of detail, Chumash stories seem to be characterized by a striking degree of individuality. Most do not appear
in cognate form in any previous collection of folktales from
California, even though many such collections exist, and those
that do appear elsewhere tend to be stories so widely distributed throughout the state that their absence would be more
significant than their presence. As might be expected, a majority of the cognate stories are from Yokuts sources, although
even here the only two narratives that have not been reported
elsewhere as well ("Mikiti," or "Falcon Kills Bear," and
"Falcon Captured By Water People"; Gayton and Newman,
1940:23, 67-72, 81) are almost certainly of Chumash origin. In
addition, the cognates normally occur in the form of single
incidents that are combined with others to create a composite
narrative, and the incidents thus combined are seldom the
same from one society to the next. For example, the incident in
which Coyote kills a flock of geese by trickery in "Coyote and
His Sons" is cognate to the Wintu story "Why Duck's Eyes Are
Pink" (Demetracopoulou and DuBois, 1932: 494), even though
the rest of the narrative is completely unrelated. Thus the Chumash storyteller, like his counterparts elsewhere, did not hesi-
tate to borrow a theme or incident that appealed to him and in-
corporate it into an "original" narrative whose seams might be
scarcely visible with the passage of time. This process is readily
apparent in the case of the several stories borrowed from European sources that are presented here (some have been combined with aboriginal incidents or themes, and all are com-
patible with indigenous values and attitudes). The main protagonists are animals (usually Coyote) whose fortunes or misfortunes are generally a consequence of the operation of guile
or deceit. All of these stories have virtually identical cognates
in Mexico or other parts of Latin America (see Robe, 1970).

The idiosyncratic quality of Chumash mythology can be
seen not only in the scarcity of folktales with cognates elsewhere, but in the cosmography and general structure of the
collection as well. Although Chumash oral narratives belong
quite clearly within the general central California mythological
region delineated by Gayton (1935a) and others, some of the
definitive myths of that region (such as Earth-Diver, the Theft
of Sun, and the Theft of Fire) are not represented here. Chumash mythology is definitely not the southerly extension of

Yokuts mythology that one might expect on geographic and ethnographic grounds, even though most of the folktales that are cognate to stories in this collection occur among the Yokuts, and Yokuts and Chumash mythologies share such features, among others, as the Orpheus myth, a rather unformulated creation of man, numerous tales in which Falcon and Eagle play important roles (with Eagle as chief), and a similar conception of the Land of the Dead. But Yokuts cosmography and mythology seem quite different in most other respects from those of the Chumash.

The closest parallels in terms of general structure are to be found not between the Chumash and such adjacent groups as the Yokuts, Kitanemuk or Gabrielino, but between the Chumash and the Pomo of northern California. Even though there are almost no specific folktales common to both groups, Pomo and Chumash mythologies seem amazingly alike in general outline, and there are some interesting correspondences in detail as well. As described by Barrett (1933), the Pomo universe consists of three superimposed worlds occupied by a considerable number of supernatural beings, many of them malevolent and highly dangerous. The existence of this universe is largely assumed, so that there is no real creation story such as is found elsewhere in central California. The being described as creator, Madumda, is often identified with Coyote, who as either culture hero or trickster is the chief protagonist in the tales. The stories mostly concern the adventures of the bird-people, who became transformed into the present animals and plants prior to the creation of human beings, and their conflicts with the supernatural beings. Many of the stories are of a composite nature, and include both trickster and etiological elements. The various supernatural beings include Tsikolkol (cf. Chumash *Xolxol*), Madumda's younger brother who wears a feather suit; Sun-man, who often eats human beings, and the Sun-maidens, who have pubes fashioned from rattlesnakes; the Gilaks, bird-like beings who also eat people, live in a house surrounded by a shining white mountain formed from the bones of their victims, and offer food to their visitors consisting of human flesh and blood; and Thunder, who in one myth is described as living in a crystal house beneath the sea. The striking and fundamental parallels with Chumash mythology are impressive despite the many superficial differences, and certainly indicate a need for further investigation. The existence of such broad parallels in cosmography between two widely separated but linguistically related social groups raises interesting questions regarding the dynamics of ideological change and the role of oral narratives in communication between interacting cultural systems. In addition, it calls into question the all too frequent practice of basing conclusions on the distribution of individual motifs or folktales. A corpus of oral narratives, as part of a larger cultural system, may very well have a significance *as a subsystem* that is greater than the total significance of its component parts.

CONTENT

The Chumash universe, like that of the Pomo, consists of a series of worlds placed one above the other. Usually three such worlds are described, but one myth mentions five as the proper number, and there is some confirmation in the fact that the neighboring Kitanemuk also had a conception of five superimposed and progressively smaller worlds. In any case, the middle world is that of normal human events, occupied now by human beings; the first world below is occupied by the *nunašiš*, dangerous creatures who enter our world after dark and wander around; and the first world above is the home of such supernatural beings as Sun, the giant eagle *Slo?w*, and *Šnilemun*, the Coyote of the Sky. The middle world is supported in the great abyss by two gigantic serpents, whose movements are the cause of earthquakes, while the upper world is held up by the great wings of *Slo?w*. The middle world, *?itiašup*, is generally flat and circular in shape, and consists primarily of ocean in which float a number of islands. The largest island of all is located at the center of the world, and is occupied by the Chumash and their neighbors. Contact between the middle and upper worlds is difficult and infrequent, but it can occur if one wishes to search for the trail to the Sky that is said to begin near Huasna, north of Santa Maria. Far to the west is the Land of the Dead, where the souls of those who have died await rebirth. There are three different places there—*wit*, *?ayaya* and *Šimilaqša*—which are described by María Solares as being somewhat like purgatory, hell and heaven. The final destination of good souls, *Šimilaqša*, can only be reached by crossing a long pole or bridge that alternately rises and falls above a body of water containing the transformed souls of people undergoing punishment for various sins.

The Chumash universe is an orderly but uncertain place, where the major causative factors underlying most important natural phenomena are animate beings of great power. These beings do not normally concern themselves with everyday human affairs, but their involvement in such fundamental matters as the passage of seasons, the fall of rain, or the growth of animals and plants, results in their activities indirectly affecting the lives—and deaths—of everyone. Like all who possess power, they are regarded ambiguously, for they are capable of both benevolent and malevolent behavior on occasion, and their course of action may follow no discernible rules. Thus life, for the Chumash, is generally predictable within narrow limits, but there is always an element of uncertainty due to the fact that man's fate depends ultimately on the actions of remote and occasionally whimsical supernatural beings. This uncertainty is symbolically expressed in one of the narratives through the medium of a gambling game between Sun and Šnilemun in which the two sides represent forces either favorable or inimical to man. Thus, both natural and supernatural events exist in an uneasy balance between the order that results from the operation of rules intrinsic to rational behavior, and the disorder that results from the operation of chance or the unpredictable malevolent impulse conceived of as an equally intrinsic part of all human (and superhuman) nature.

It is difficult to place the narratives in this collection in any precise chronological order, and the sequence of events occurring in them is not always very clear, but that was undoubtedly of little concern to the Chumash, who seem to have had only a slight interest in time *per se* anyway. This lack of interest in the past *as past* apparently extended to problems of origin as well, for there is no myth in the collection explaining or describing the creation of the world, and the creation of man is barely touched upon. In fact, there is a notable dearth of the etiological elements usually found in collections of this kind. The only exceptions to this generalization are found in some of the stories narrated by Fernando Librado, in which the protagonist of one is referred to as a kinsman of the protagonist of another, and it is possible that these stories may reflect either a greater integration of mythology and religion in the past than is now evident or differential access to esoteric knowledge on the part of the informant. But, as a general rule, there is little apparent interest in chronology or etiology, and the past is rendered in a rather flat perspective.

The relatively timeless past, however, can be subdivided to a certain extent by reference to two major events: the mythical Flood, which covered the earth and brought about the transformation of the *molmoloqʔiqu* or First People into the present animals and plants, and European colonization, the cultural deluge that began in 1769 and ended with the virtual extinction of Chumash culture perhaps a hundred years later. Most of the narratives in this collection take place before the Flood, and can properly be termed myths; they relate the adventures of the First People in their dealings with the supernatural beings, the *nunašiš* and monsters, and each other. The cause of the Flood is never explained—it simply occurs—but it brings the old world of myth to an end, and the First People are transformed. After the Flood the present human beings are created by the supernatural beings of the upper world, with *Šnilemun* apparently playing a central role in the drama (although he is frustrated in his intention to model the human hand after his own by Lizard's prompt action). Death is also instituted at this time, when overpopulation is shown to be the inevitable consequence of continual rejuvenation. After the creation of man there is a period of time preceding the arrival of Europeans during which some of the stories in Section D take place; this period might be called that of legendary time, and is presumably of rather short duration. Finally, there is the period of historic time that follows the establishment of the various missions, and during which the events described in Section E presumably occur.

Chumash eschatological concepts are surprisingly detailed in comparison to those of many other California groups, yet they are also occasionally either contradictory or ambiguous. Some of the contradictions may very well reflect either subcultural differences or the personal background of the informants (including acculturative influences); the ambiguity is probably inherent, since assumptions about death and the nature of the soul inevitably involve the complex issues of cosmography and shamanistic belief as well. The soul is apparently conceived of as an eternal entity with an existence quite separate from that of the body, capable on occasion of independent action. Although the soul does not normally leave the body until three days after death, it may on occasion be seen elsewhere (either in the form of a ball of light or having the appearance of the living person) as a sign of imminent death. If, however, the affected individual takes an infusion of *momoy* or toloache (*Datura meteloides*), death may sometimes be averted. Consequently, death or sickness may sometimes be explained as due to the loss or separation of the soul. After death, the soul stays at the grave either three or five days, overseeing the destruction of personal property and visiting familiar places known in life; then it leaves and travels to Point Conception, and from there to the Land of the Dead far across the ocean to the west. On the way it may be seen as a shining ball of light travelling through the air.

It is interesting to note that the soul's journey to Šimilaqša (and the perils and difficulties encountered on the way) is described in considerably greater detail than the destination itself, and that there are definite moralistic overtones discernible in the description. A number of particular motifs are widespread (the clashing rocks, the rising and falling bridge, etc.), but the complexity of the overall concept seems unusual. The soul arrives first at a place occupied only by widows, who rejuvenate themselves by bathing in a spring and obtain nourishment by simply smelling food and drink. The soul then enters a deep ravine where it must first pass two clashing rocks and then two giant ravens—the rocks kill any living person who tries to pass, while the ravens peck out the eyes of the soul, which subsequently replaces them with poppy flowers. Next the soul encounters a tall woman with a scorpion-like tail who attracts attention by clapping and then tries to sting anyone who approaches. Once past this peril, the soul reaches a body of water that separates this world and Šimilaqša. On the near shore are evil souls that have turned to stone from the neck down. A bridge consisting of an immense pole that steadily rises and falls stretches across the water to the shore of Šimilaqša, but as the soul is crossing two monsters arise from the water and attempt to frighten it. The soul of anyone of insufficient knowledge or power falls into the water and is transformed into a fish or amphibian, but a soul of someone strong in spirit reaches the far side safely. Šimilaqša itself is a land of plenty, where there is nothing to do but eat, sleep, dance, and play games. An old man who lives in a crystal house is chief. Here the soul stays forever, or until it is reincarnated.

The ultimate fate of the soul appears subject to some controversy, and it is possible that the variation of opinion that exists may reflect differences between exoteric and esoteric dogma. According to María Solares, the Inezeño believe that the souls of both children and adults reach Šimilaqša, where they remain forever, never growing older. But the Ventureño, according to Fernando Librado, believe that the souls of people who have drowned, or of babies, do not reach Šimilaqša at all, and that those that do reach it are reincarnated at the end of twelve years. The doctrine of reincarnation seems well established, at least for the Ventureño, and is certainly of considerable interest in terms of philosophical implications.

Another apparent contradiction that seems to exist in Chumash eschatology involves the role of Sun in death. Although there are elaborate descriptions of the soul's journey to Šimilaqša, it is evident from several accounts that Sun, his two daughters, and Sloʔw are all conceived of as beings who live on human flesh and blood. Sun brings people home every day for him and his daughters to eat, and the house of Sloʔw is surrounded by a mountain of bleached white bones. In addition, there are ethnographic descriptions, for both the Chumash and the Kitanemuk, of people staying indoors all day at the time of the winter solstice in the belief that the sun is especially angry at this time and might take them into his house were they to venture out. The great importance of the sun in Chumash myth and ritual is significant and will be discussed in detail at a later time.

As was previously mentioned, three major classes of beings can be distinguished in the narratives: the First People, supernatural beings, and the nunašiš. The list of species comprising the First People is rather interesting, for many of the animals that one might suppose would figure prominently in Chumash stories—such as bears, rattlesnakes, mountain lions, whales, deer, and elk—are either not mentioned at all or briefly touched upon in passing. Most of the First People mentioned by name are birds of one kind or another, although several mammals, reptiles, insects, and plants also appear as characters from time to time. Fish, with the exception of the ?ely?wun (swordfish), are not mentioned. There is no simple or readily apparent explanation for the presence or absence of particular species in the cast of characters—important food sources, major carnivores, or species with unusual characteristics may or may not appear. *Datura*, for example, is a major character in the stories, but tobacco is simply a useful and important plant used either for food or as a narcotic.

But although more of the First People are birds than mammals, at least as specific characters, the most important of them by far is Coyote, who as either culture-hero or trickster plays the central role in Chumash oral literature. Coyote, it might be suggested, represents man himself in all his variety—alternately wise and foolish, brash and cautious, good and evil—and exemplifies in exaggerated form the virtues and vices with which the Chumash invest human nature. Like most of the important and powerful figures in Chumash mythology, he is usually depicted as an old man in appearance, although his apparent age never seems to hinder his activity or agility in important moments. His place in the social universe of the First People is a curious one, for although his power and knowledge seem generally recognized, he is never really part of the wealthy clique of high-born families surrounding the chief, *Slo?w*. Perhaps his uncertain status is symbolic of the ambivalence with which the shaman was frequently regarded in aboriginal California—respected and feared for his possession of supernatural powers, but lacking in the moral authority that could only be acquired by birth.

The social order of the First People is dominated by a number of wealthy families headed by *Slo?w* (eagle) and his relatives *Xelex* (falcon), *?Anič?apapa* (sharp-shinned hawk), and *?Atimasɨq* (another hawk species). *Slo?w* is the wise and powerful chief, but he seldom figures in the narratives as anything but an important offstage presence. *Xelex*, on the other hand, appears in many of the narratives and is usually described as second only to *Slo?w* in social status. Occasionally he also seems to occupy a distinct political office, perhaps that of sub-chief. Most of the other First People who appear in the narratives are not consistently cast in any particular role or appear only sporadically as minor characters. However, *Hew* (pelican) and *Mut* (cormorant) are mariners and fisherman, *Muhu* (horned owl) is a shaman, and *Ksen* (mudhen) is a messenger. As might be expected, the daily life of the First People—their occupations (and preoccupations), material goods, social life, and habitat—is in most respects essentially that of the Chumash themselves.

Perhaps the most unusual of the First People, and in many ways certainly one of the most interesting, is the old woman *Momoy*, who becomes the narcotic plant *Datura meteloides* at the time of the Flood. Its presence as a central character in several of the most important Chumash myths suggests a long and extensive involvement with *Datura* on the part of the Chumash, and the fact that it does not appear, as far as is known, to any significant extent in the mythology of any other group in California lends added weight to its inclusion in Chumash mythology. *Momoy* is always described as a very wealthy old widow, living by herself or with a daughter in a remote place, and ultimately playing the role of fostering grandmother or adoptive mother. Although she herself does not seem to have the power to affect directly the outcome of events or overcome malevolent beings, she has both the wisdom and ability to foresee the future, partially at least, and warn others of the probable consequences of their actions. By drinking water in which she has washed her hands, other people can share this ability to a certain extent, falling into a coma in which they see visions that seem to be portents of things to come or that provide access to sources of supernatural powers.

The cast of supernatural beings is, of course, headed by Sun and his two daughters, who live in a quartz-crystal house in the upper world. Sun is depicted as an extremely old widower, wearing nothing but a feathered headband in which he sometimes tucks the bodies of little children, and carrying a torch of tightly rolled bark with which he lights the world below. His two daughters, who have never married, wear aprons made of live rattlesnakes with their tails intertwined. Each day Sun takes his torch and follows a trail around the world, returning each evening with the bodies of people he has brought home for him and his daughters to eat. The crystal house in which they live is filled with tame animals of every kind. Every night for a year, in a special house built for the purpose, Sun plays peon with other inhabitants of the upper world. Sun and the great eagle *Sloʔw* are on one side, Šnilemun (the Coyote of the Sky) and Morning Star are on the other, and Moon is referee. At the time of the winter solstice they decide who has won the game for that year. If *Šnilemun*'s side wins it is a rainy year in the world below and there is plenty of food, but if Sun's side wins the debt is paid in human lives.

With the exception of Sun, the supernatural beings living in the upper world are poorly described. Moon is a single woman who lives in a house near that of Sun, and Morning Star is presumably male. *Sloʔw* is a giant eagle who supports the upper world with his wings, and lives in a place surrounded by hills of white bones that can be seen shining from afar. He seldom speaks or moves—he is just there, thinking. *Šnilemun* has the form of a great coyote, and it is he who champions man's well-being and looks out for the welfare of all in the world below him. According to María Solares, the Inezeño regard him as a father and pray to him. There are two brothers, the Thunders, who also live in the upper world. One is older than the other, and thunders very heavily; the younger thunders quite violently and frightens people. The sound is caused by their playing the hoop—and—pole game. They roll their hoops and run after them and then pierce them with their poles. They also have devices with which they throw a light they have, and when the lightning hits the ground it makes flint. *Xoy* is still another supernatural being, but he lives all alone in the last upper world.

The *ʔelyeʔwun* (swordfish) are the most prominent of the various supernatural beings inhabiting the middle world of the Chumash. They are described as having the appearance of powerful old men with long beards, long white eyebrows, and with either plumes or bone swords projecting from their heads. There are eight of them living in a crystal house under the sea, where they hunt whales for food. When they catch a whale they play ball with it, throwing the whale back and forth. They have prodigious appetites and terrible manners, for they tear a whale apart with their hands and teeth and eat it raw. Like many supernatural beings, they tend to be malevolent by nature, even though they benefit the Chumash by driving whales ashore for people to eat.

There are other supernatural beings beside the *ʔelyeʔwun*

that are associated with water. For example, there is a village of people living very much like normal human beings at the bottom of Zaca Lake near Santa Ynez, and there are beings resembling old men with long flowing hair that inhabit and control certain springs. Serpents constitute another class of important supernatural beings. There are, first of all, the *masaqsiqʔitašup*, the two giant serpents that support the middle world and cause earthquakes when they stir. Then there are the various serpent people who have the power to transform themselves into something resembling humans. They inhabit or frequent certain dangerous and very special places that the Chumash normally avoid, and their tracks can sometimes be seen leading to or from these places.

The third major category of characters appearing in Chumash narratives is comprised of the various ogres, monsters and other malevolent beings that are generically referred to as *nunašɨš*. The term *nunašɨš* can have the general meaning of "animal," though it is usually applied primarily to such creatures as bears or rattlesnakes as an expression meaning "dangerous or inimical animal"—and hence by extension "devil" or "demon" in the present context. The *nunašɨš*, like other supernatural beings, existed during the time of the First People, and many still exist today. They live in *cʔoyinašup*, the world below, and come out after dark to travel around the middle world. Most of the *nunašɨš* have a generally human form, but they are usually misshapen or deformed in one way or another. The *haphap* or sucking monster is the most dangerous of the *nunašɨš*, for he can swallow trees and rocks and people with the greatest of ease and has a voracious appetite. The *yowoyow* or *lewelew* is also dangerous, particularly to children, for he tosses them into the carrying basket on his back and takes them home to eat. Some other *nunašɨš* are the *ququ*, whose body is covered with pus; the *xolxol*, a big animal covered with feathers; the *pakaʔs asʔɨl*, or lame devil; the *maxulaw*, who looks like a cat; the *ʔašixuč*, an old woman who rolls a burning tray at people; the *malaxšišinɨš*, the woman with a tail like a scorpion; and *ʔalʔheleqeč*, the old woman with the basket of hot tar on her back.

Perhaps the single most frequently occurring element in the narratives is, as might be expected, magic and supernaturalism in one form or another. As was mentioned earlier, the dichotomy between innate and acquired supernatural power seems to constitute a topic of considerable interest to the Chumash, and the conflict between *nunašïš* and protagonists dependent upon an *ʔatišwïn* or talisman is a frequent story device. It is interesting to note that individuals possessing innate powers are normally depicted as naturally malevolent to a certain degree—a characteristic most strikingly pronounced, of course, in the *nunašïš*—while those individuals with acquired powers are regarded much more ambivalently. The primary focus of acquired power is the *ʔatišwïn* or sacred talisman that symbolizes the special relationship existing between a person and his tutelary animal or dream-helper, a relationship developed during the hallucinatory state induced by *Datura* and cultivated thereafter in dreams and through prayers and offerings. The term *ʔatišwïn* thus refers both to the tutelary and to the material object symbolizing (and perhaps activating) that tutelary.

A particularly important point to note about the depiction of supernatualism in the narratives is the apparent fidelity (if apparent elements of fantasy are excluded) with which actual shamanistic beliefs and practices are incorporated. In several stories, for example, Coyote utilizes his *takulšoxšinaš* (a cord with interwoven bird down) to accomplish some objective magically—and it is apparent from the descriptions in Section E of actual shamanistic practices during historic times that such a cord was a standard part of the shaman's stock in trade. The numerous magical transformations that occur in the myths are not simply expressions of fantasy: the historic narratives again make it abundantly clear that many such transformations are accepted as completely feasible if one has the requisite power or knowledge. The importance of the *ʔatišwïn*—mentioned time and again in every type of narrative—has already been commented on. Even those magical devices which seem most clearly rooted in fantasy may have their origin in fact. The "medicine" used to revive the dead in several stories did not exist, of course, but apparently no one doubted the ability of a really powerful shaman to return a dead person to life. The feather down used by a protagonist in one myth to escape the *haphap* has its counterpart in the down incorporated in the *takulšoxšinaš* and prominent in ethnographic descriptions of prayers and offerings at shrines. And the flute used by

Momoy's grandsons as a magical helper is kin to the flute played in the *siliyik* and on other ceremonial occasions, and which obviously had an important role in Chumash ritual. Only the device of traveling long distances by echo—a local version of the "magical flight" motif—is clearly fantasy.

One of the more interesting expressions of supernatural power in the narratives is the phenomenon of transformation or transmorphism, involving an actual modification or creation of physical form. A belief in the existence of were-animals— people capable of transforming themselves at will into such dangerous animals as bears or wolves—is of course common not only in California but elsewhere as well. But the beliefs of the Chumash are considerably more varied and complex, for they are convinced of the existence not only of were-animals but were-people as well—animals capable of assuming human form or imitating the semblance of specific persons—and in magically-vitalized simulacra. Like most groups in California, the Chumash believe in the existence of individuals with the ability to assume the form of bears, although there is a certain amount of confusion between those bear shamans capable of actual transmorphism and those who utilize a special costume with exceptional powers. There is no evidence that, among the Chumash, people ever assume the form of animals other than bears. But serpents, bears and coyotes are all mentioned as animals apparently capable of assuming human form on occasion—the serpents and bears simply transforming themselves into people, and coyotes assuming the likeness of specific living people who in order to avoid illness or death must then take *Datura*. And shamans are capable of creating or inducing the creation of human simulacra, children that seem normal but have only a brief life span.

The Chumash belief in transmorphism, it might be suggested, is part of a complex series of philosophical assumptions and postulates concerning the relationship between supernatural power and human nature on the one hand, and man's interactions with his environment on the other. Transformation, it would seem, is regarded as a kind of natural phenomenon, an inherent part of the structure of reality potentially available to all. The present animals, birds, and plants are transformations of the First People, just as human patterns of behavior today are simply extensions of those followed long ago. Thus no real dichotomy separates man from his environment, or distinguishes man from beast, for transformation renders each potentially equivalent to the other. The ecological and philosophical implications of such an ideological structure are of considerable interest, and have been partially delineated for such other groups as the Yokuts, Luiseño and Cahuilla (Gayton, 1946; White, 1963; and Bean, 1972).

Quite a variety of religious practitioners are referred to either directly or indirectly in the narratives—the bear shamans, *ʔatišwinic*, diviners, *ʔalšuqlaš*, weather shamans, pipe and singing doctors—a fact that tends to confirm ethnographic reconstructions which emphasize the unexpected complexity of aboriginal sociopolitical organization (see Blackburn, 1974). Most such practitioners seem to derive their powers from the possession of several *ʔatišwin* or an *ʔatišwin* of exceptional strength, and in fact *ʔatišwinic* often seems to be used as a kind of generic term for shaman. Whether all such practitioners ultimately derive their power from *ʔatišwin* can not be determined at this time, although it does not seem unlikely. It is also impossible to say whether or not there are hereditary factors involved in the acquisition of shamanistic powers. But the acquisition of several *ʔatišwin* almost certainly involves a personal drive for power motivated by ambition or idiosyncratic personality factors. And the particular expression of shamanistic ability—in curing illness by singing or blowing smoke or administering herbs, in foretelling the future or discovering the location of lost objects, or in controlling the weather—is almost certainly a function of whatever *ʔatišwin* one acquires. Bear shamans, however, are anomalous in several ways, for unlike other types of shamans they seem to have no readily apparent socially approved function. The source of their power is likewise obscure, for sometimes they seem to draw on innate abilities and sometimes they depend upon a specially constructed device with powers of its own.

In any case, shamans, regardless of type, seem to be regarded with a great deal of ambivalence by the Chumash, and one gets the impression that they are viewed as a kind of necessary evil. As the narratives make abundantly clear—and as Gayton (1930) has shown with respect to the neighboring Yokuts—shamans serve a vital function in a society plagued by uncertainty, where illness and death may stem from the natural malevolence of supernatural beings or even one's fellow man. But shamans must be treated with considerable circumspection, for their powers are amoral and can be used for evil purposes as well as for good, causing sickness as well as curing it. And shamans are in some senses outside the social system, no longer responsive to the same claims of kinship or sentiment that motivate and control the average person. Their shamanistic contests and demonstrations serve to reinforce their prestige (and of course their psychological effectiveness) while dramatizing the gulf that divides them inevitably from the rest of society.

Chapter Three

Structure and Content
of the Narratives

One of the more obvious conclusions to be drawn from
a historical survey of the literature in our field is that
there has been among anthropological folklorists an
increasing appreciation of the complexity of oral narratives,
and a growing realization that myths are often—to use a term
suggested by Victor Turner (1969b)—"multivocal" in nature,
capable of multiple meanings and referents and simultaneously interpretable on several distinct levels. One consequence of this fact is that mythological analysis may often take
on some of the flavor of archaeological excavation, as the
exposure of successive strata leads to an accumulation of new
data, as well as to the generation of new hypotheses based
upon these data. And like the archaeologist, the analyst of
myth begins at the level of manifest, overt content, hoping to
arrive eventually at a level of latent, covert structure. But the
analogy can only be carried so far, for the levels involved in the
analysis of oral narratives are always levels of interpretive
abstraction, each of which is dependent upon (and to a certain

extent includes) the preceding conceptual level, rather than units that can presumably be distinguished objectively in the real world. However, the analyst of oral narratives has one great advantage over his archaeological counterpart, as Otis T. Mason once remarked (1891:99), in that his primary data are not affected by the process of analysis, and are always available for restudy by more adequate techniques or more knowledgeable scholars.

The analysis of Chumash oral narratives presented below involves a number of different conceptual levels which have been chosen more for convenience than theoretical stringency. Beginning with a consideration of face-value manifest content or "cultural reflection," the analysis proceeds by means of a process of increasing abstraction to a presentation of latent norms and postulates. This is followed by a discussion of contradictions, exaggerations, and inversions in the narratives that may represent points of stress in the normative structure of Chumash culture. Finally, an attempt is made to compare the various preceding insights and hypotheses with one another and with data external to the study itself.

MATERIAL CULTURE

The attention devoted by early anthropologists such as Boas to descriptions of material culture items in mythology is readily understandable, for probably no other facet of culture is more readily or objectively derivable from the study of oral narratives. For reasons given earlier, descriptions of the material bases of daily life can generally be assumed to be reasonably factual in nature, and there is seldom any great ambiguity in the descriptions to puzzle the analyst. It seems logical, therefore, to begin the analysis of Chumash narratives with a consideration of the material background that forms the context or setting for the dramatic action of the stories themselves, and then of the specific items of material culture mentioned in the narratives. These items, placed in their narrative context, are listed in Table 1.

As might be expected, the world depicted in the narratives is that inhabited in historic times by the Chumash themselves. With the exception of incidents occurring in the world above or in the Land of the Dead, narratives almost invariably involve

Table 1. Material Culture Items and
Traits Mentioned in Narratives

ITEM	NARRATIVE NUMBER
A. Implements and tools	
Axe	17, 20, 48
Knife	20
Awl	40
Flesher	20
Dibble	97
Throwing stick	37
Mortar and pestle	15, 40
Fire-sticks	16, 21, 24
Comb	23, 54
B. Hunting and fishing gear	
Backed bow	15, 17, 67, 84
Arrow	
point	18, 67, 84
foreshaft	20, 38
Quiver	15, 19, 20
Shaft straightener	15
Harpoon	26
Fishhook	23
Spear	32
Trap	35, 56, 62
Canoe	13, 15, 19, 29, 32
Litter	20
C. Hunting and fishing techniques	
Fire-drive	102
Trapping	35, 56, 62
Achery	19, 20
Harpooning	26
Handline fishing	23, 26
D. Containers	
Wooden bowl	2, 15, 29, 40, 86
Sack	40, 102
Carrying net	5, 31, 32
Tobacco tube	21, 24, 84
Basketry	
general	15, 17
cradle	29
tray	10, 15, 20, 85, 86, 91
water bottle	87
burden basket	16, 94
storage basket	20
trinket basket	32
basket hat	54
E. Materials	
Bark	2
Cordage	15, 32, 86

	NARRATIVE
ITEM	NUMBER
Leather	20
Chert	32
Wood	32
Shell	2, 32

F. *Foods*
Plant foods

acorns	2, 15, 19, 55
islay	2, 12, 33, 55
chia	2, 15, 18, 19, 20, 33
lily bulbs	12, 31, 36, 57
huxminas	20
yucca, agave	20, 29
cactus fruit	106
greens	57
tule roots	52, 57
pine nuts	18, 102

Animal foods

deer	2, 17, 18, 29, 37
rabbit	18, 102
squirrel	20
gopher	20
badger	20
fish	15, 48
whale	27
shellfish	21
duck	2, 20, 56
goose	2, 20
quail	20
bird (gen.)	20

G. *Food preparation*

Roasting meat	15, 20, 24, 32, 48, 56, 57
Drying meat	18, 20, 32
Baking food	20, 21, 36, 48
Seed grinding	15, 32
atole	15, 18, 19, 20
Butchering	20, 37
Food storage	55

H. *Settlement and structures*

House	16, 24, 26
bed	20, 32
mat	20, 32, 88
door	18, 26, 29, 32
fireplace	26
smokehole	15, 24
Temescal	33
Game field	28, 54
Cemetery	
grave	12, 59, 69, 75
Shrine	12
Dance enclosure	93

	ITEM	NARRATIVE NUMBER
I.	*Dress*	
	Ordinary dress	65
	loin cloth	17
	woman's apron	2, 14, 54
	belt	2, 15
	sandals	16
	basket hat	54
	cloak	28
	blanket	38
	Ceremonial dress	
	headdress	27, 35
	headband	2, 18
	feathered banner	2, 15, 18
	dance skirt	27
	Hair styles	18, 71
	Body painting	12, 15
	Tobacco tubes	21, 24, 84
	Ornaments	
	necklace	54
	bracelet	54
	earrings	54
J.	*Ritual gear*	
	Bullroarer	93, 102
	Rattle	15, 26, 27, 69, 73, 84
	Flute and whistle	15, 17, 21, 61, 93
	Dance Stick	73
	Charmstone	39, 76
	Talisman	25, 72, 75, 78
	Feathered pole	91
	Downy cord	15, 30, 86, 87
K.	*Drugs*	
	Datura	12, 19, 20, 29, 78, 93, 97, 98
	Tobacco	16, 20, 26, 84
L.	*Money and bead types*	
	General	13, 18, 19, 29, 32
	Bead types	
	ʔikʔimiš	15, 63, 86
	sqilmoy	15
	ʔapɨ	15
	mucucu	63
M.	*Games and races*	
	Hoop–and–pole	18, 28, 63
	Shinny	54
	Footrace	15, 26
	Gomi	21
	Walpiʔy	25
	Pole climbing	30
	Peon	2, 39

local settings familiar to everyone, with many events occurring in or near such important historic villages as *syuxtun* (Santa Barbara) or *mikiw* (Dos Pueblos). Daily life is normally village life, and the villages—with their gaming fields, cemeteries, shrines, work areas, houses, and temescals—are those familiar to the storyteller and his audience. Similarly, the environment in which the protagonists live, and the resources and exploitative techniques utilized by them, are essentially the same as those known and utilized every day by the Chumash themselves.

The same is true of the various material culture items listed in Table 1. With the possible exception of certain games (which may reflect shamanistic themes such as "magical flight" rather than actual social practice), almost all of the items mentioned in the narratives have some ethnographic confirmation in the form of historical accounts, ethnographic reconstructions, or archaeological discoveries. Unfortunately, this ethnographic reliability is partially nullified by the fact that Chumash narratives seem generally characterized by a paucity of descriptive detail, thus many items of material culture are simply mentioned in passing, with no attempt made to provide adequate descriptions of what were undoubtedly all-too-familiar objects. It is interesting to note, however, that over half of the items listed in Table 1 are referred to in two or more narratives, and that most of the major categories of Chumash artifacts known do seem to be represented in the collection.

One final point with regard to the items in Table 1 is worth emphasizing. In a number of cases the information provided by the narratives actually complements rather than simply supplements our knowledge of aboriginal material culture, or it confirms the presence or usage of items whose existence was only suspected on the basis of distributional evidence or fragmentary historical accounts. Many of the data on containers, foods and food preparation, structures, dress, ritual gear, and games, for example, would probably fall under the heading of significant additions to present knowledge of Chumash culture. Thus the narratives not only provide what appears to be an accurate if not overly detailed picture of the material aspects of Chumash daily life already known from other sources, they also supply some completely new data and furnish fresh insights into the social contexts of old data.

SOCIAL ORGANIZATION

The major outlines of the social structure of the First People seem reasonably consistent (as one might expect) with what little is presently known about this facet of Chumash culture. As is the case with items of material culture, a detailed exposition of social behavior cannot be readily derived from the narratives, and certain aspects of that behavior are almost totally absent or are presented so ambiguously as to be uninterpretable at this time. Nevertheless, the overall organization of social behavior emerges clearly and consistently from the narratives, so that many aspects of the social structure of the First People (and hence by implication the Chumash) can be portrayed with some confidence.

The First People live in an orderly, highly structured society, characterized by a considerable differentiation of statuses, most of which are apparently ascribed or partially ascribed by birth. For example, specific political, ritual, and economic statuses are numerous and well-defined, and are consistently associated with pronounced variations in wealth, prestige, and social prerogatives. Society is hierarchically structured, and there exists a palpable feeling of class consciousness that permeates most social relationships. Families or households appear to be the only prominent corporate units, and there is a notable absence of the large, corporate social groups based primarily on kinship that are so important in many societies. It is the status rather than the group that is ranked, so that the inheritance of rights to statuses is more important than membership in specific social groups, and the individual occupying a significant status is the nucleus around which a group is organized.

Somewhat surprisingly, the facet of social life least readily derivable from the narratives is that involving patterns of kinship and marriage, although certain general conclusions can be drawn. For the First People marriage is the normal adult state, and young people are encouraged to marry whenever possible (nos. 20, 24). Considerable premarital sexual freedom is depicted as existing for both girls and boys, and many marriages probably develop from casual liaisons (nos. 15, 20, 28). The change in status involved in marriage occurs easily and is primarily an individual matter (nos. 28, 32). Similarly, adultery and the dissolution of marriage are not uncommon and occur with equal facility (nos. 22, 25, 28, 56, 57, 88). Although marriage often develops from a romantic liaison, there is an explicit preference for young women to marry older, established men who can support them economically (no. 24), or for men to marry wealthy women (nos. 24, 29, 32). Thus arranged marriages may occur frequently, particularly when the individuals involved are members of wealthy or prestigious families, or one party is attempting to enhance his opportunities for social mobility.

Since marriage is invariably depicted as monogamous, and postmarital residence usually appears to involve virilocality, the fact that the typical household contains a single nuclear family is not unexpected. A more complex residential unit is described in only one narrative (no. 24), although the description is one that presents a number of interesting possibilities in interpretation. Perhaps the likeliest interpretation is that the particular residential group depicted represents an avunculocal extended family resulting from avunculocal residence and marriage to MBD (see Murdock, 1960:35). However tenuous this interpretation, it is strengthened by the fact that there is corroborative evidence elsewhere in the narratives for the existence of a certain degree of matrilaterality in at least some facets of society. The relationship between uncle and nephew, for example, figures prominently in a number of the stories—in fact, far more prominently than the relationship between father and son. In addition, *Xelex*, who is in a position of authority second only to *Slo?w*, the chief, is usually described as being the nephew of *Slo?w* (nos. 26, 28, 32). Accession to political office might therefore be interpreted as being matrilineally inherited.

Another factor worth mentioning in this connection is the status of women. Women are described on occasion as independently wealthy and capable of a considerable degree of autonomy (nos. 29, 32). A chief's daughter seems to be accorded great respect, and may even occupy a position of authority herself (nos. 21, 60). Thus while the society of the First People cannot be described as markedly lateral in nature as a whole, it might reasonably be hypothesized that some goods and statuses are matrilineally inherited, and that occasionally large residential groups coalesce around those individuals inheriting rights in such properties. Such a situation is not unlike that described ethnographically for some

Pomo tribelets (Kunkel, 1962). As a cautionary note, however, the statement in no. 21 that "the Indians always gave the derecho to men and not to women" should be kept in mind, although that particular passage can be variously interpreted and may refer more to spiritual qualities than to the determination of descent or inheritance rights.

Regardless of the specific mode of transmission of various social prerogatives, there is good reason to believe that most are inheritable, and that ascription rather than personal achievement is the factor most frequently involved in the recruitment of personnel for important statuses. A variety of both political and economic statuses is described in the narratives, and the invariable association of these statuses with specific First People is undoubtedly significant. The political role of chief, for example, is always played by *Slo?w*, with *Xelex* as his assistant, while the economic roles of canoe owner and fisherman are consistently attributed to the characters of *He?w* and *Mut* (nos. 19, 26, 32). Even ritual services are apparently owned; in no. 29, for instance, Coyote is called upon to administer *Datura* to all of the eight-year-old boys in the village, and the implication is that this is a task that only he can perform.

The society of the First People is characterized by considerable variations in wealth and social prestige, as well as by a surprising degree of social, political, and economic role diversification. There would appear to be an incipient class system based upon wealth, with a great deal of social distance between rich and poor families (nos. 18, 28, 29, 31, 32). Money is the standard by which social prestige is measured, and money figures prominently in most kinds of transactions (nos. 19, 29, 32, 41, 61). In addition, numerous occupational specializations or professions are referred to in the narratives, and they appear to be differentially ranked, as are the various political and ritual roles. The more important of these specialized roles are listed in Table 2.

The political structure of the First People seems generally consistent with those described ethnographically for other areas of California. In most narratives Eagle is depicted as being the primary political authority, with Falcon occupying a subsidiary position. In some narratives, however, only Eagle is mentioned, while in at least one (no. 35) both Eagle and Falcon appear to have equal authority. In addition, one narrative (no.

38) depicts Raven as a political figure also. Perhaps the most
logical interpretation of what seems to be a curious situation
would be that the political differentiation depicted depends to
some degree on the size of the settlement involved; thus small
villages are characterized by a single chief, while larger towns
such as *mikiw* or *syuxtun* are controlled by a primary chief with
one or more secondary chiefs.

Table 2. Social Roles Mentioned in Narratives

ROLE	NARRATIVE NUMBER
A. *Economic roles*	
Canoe owner	19, 26, 31, 32
Fisherman	19, 26, 31, 32, 88
Hunter	31, 37, 56
Cordage maker	31, 32
Bead maker	31, 41
Tobacco maker	31
Net maker	31
Basket maker	31
Leather worker	31
Bow and arrow maker	31
Bowl maker	31
Mortar maker	31
Flint worker	32
Board maker	32
Headdress maker	31
Mortician	75
B. *Political roles*	
Chief	18, 19, 21, 26, 28, 29, 32, 33, 35, 37, 38, 45
Assistant chief	29, 32, 35, 38
Ceremonial leader	15, 28, 30, 102
Messenger	18, 33
Chief's daughter	21, 23, 24, 60
C. *Ritual roles*	
Astrologer priest	13, 29, 53, 84
Diviner	80, 85, 86, 87
Sacrificer	31
Curing shaman	73, 74, 75
Singer	69, 73, 88, 89, 90
Cult member	93
Weather shaman	77
Bear shaman	67, 68, 69, 70, 71
Sorcerer	74, 76, 78, 79, 81, 83

The role played by the chief, Eagle, in the narratives is a
significant one, although he is seldom directly involved in the
events that occur. He is often an influential if unseen presence,

an embodiment of normative values and an expression of social equilibrium. He is usually depicted as both wise and good (no. 21), with great prestige and moral authority if little overt power (no. 33). He is wealthy, capable of buying rare or costly items (nos. 16, 27), providing hospitality to guests (nos. 19, 28), supporting the expenses of fiestas (no. 29), and rewarding services rendered to him (nos. 26, 33). In addition, he maintains a store of food and other goods for the benefit of the community (nos. 26, 33), and is in turn maintained by the productive activities of others (no. 37). He does not play an active role in warfare, but sends others to do so (nos. 33, 38). Even his house is sacrosanct, a place where frivolous or unseemly activities should not occur (no. 26). However, he is not uniformly depicted in a positive light. Some of the darker aspects of chieftainship in California that have been described ethnographically (see Gayton, 1930; Blackburn, 1974) are certainly present in no. 29, for example, where Eagle and Falcon first employ sorcerers to try to kill Coyote's son and then threaten him with death if he cannot adequately assist them in defraying the expenses of a fiesta.

Although the chief is the ultimate political authority, there are other politically significant individuals in the society who assist him in one way or another. *Xelex* or Falcon, Eagle's nephew, is an assistant or secondary chief with considerable authority of his own (nos. 32, 35). There is a *ksen* or messenger, who delivers messages and makes public announcements (nos. 18, 33), and there is a *paxa* or ceremonial leader, who acts as a kind of master of ceremonies at fiestas and may also serve on occasion as the chief's spokesman (nos. 28, 102). Economic specialists and the wealthy heads of families undoubtedly have political influence as well, and may very well function as a kind of informal council (no. 32). In addition, there is little doubt that some of the individuals occupying ritual roles are, to some extent at least, politically significant, although the relation of these people to the bureaucratic hierarchy is seldom alluded to except indirectly (no. 29). Nonetheless, the considerable power attributed to them is attested to in almost every narrative, and the existence of formalized roles and an organized cult group that almost certainly has close ties to the political bureaucracy seems clearly indicated (nos. 13, 29, 31, 53, 93, 102).

While warfare is not a particularly prominent thematic element in the narratives, there is an occasional allusion to it, and it seems to constitute an acceptable if infrequent factor in the life of the First People. Usually warfare seems to involve only a portion of the population of two feuding villages (nos. 33, 34), although sometimes people from a number of widely scattered villages may become embroiled in the conflict, apparently as a consequence of the formation of military alliances (no. 38). Smoke signals are used to transmit information about the forthcoming battle (no. 38), and the principal weapon is the bow and arrow (nos. 33, 34, 38). The time and place of battle is decided by mutual agreement beforehand (no. 33). The fighting continues until one side surrenders or withdraws from the field (no. 33).

Legal mechanisms are not as clearly formalized as those involving warfare. The more serious crimes such as homicide and witchcraft (no. 12) are crimes against the individual, and self-help appears to be the victim's primary legal recourse (no. 25). However, the chief as community spokesman can become involved in a conflict situation, and seems capable of applying both formal (nos. 29, 35, 45) and informal (no. 29) sanctions to the nonconforming individual. Anyone who commits a serious crime risks death unless he leaves the community at once— and other members of his family may still be held liable for his actions (no. 25).

Life crises do not play as prominent a role, or at least as explicit a role, in the narratives as one might perhaps expect. Birth apparently takes place in the home (no. 15), whereupon the infant is wrapped in wildcat skins (no. 18) and placed in a cradle (nos. 29, 55). Prior to puberty boys are given *Datura* to drink by an official appointed for that purpose (nos. 19, 20, 29)—whether or not girls also receive the drug is not clear. The transition to adulthood is marked by changes in both dress and hair-styling (no. 18), and apparently occurs soon after puberty. Marriage is relatively informal (nos. 28, 32, 54), and usually involves virilocality (nos. 16, 29, 54). When someone dies, a wake is held over the body (nos. 10, 25, 34, 75). The body is then buried (nos. 10, 59, 69, 72, 75) by women who are professional morticians (no. 75), and the house and personal belongings of the deceased are burned (no. 72).

Certain aspects of the behavior of the First People that are not covered in preceding sections deserve mention, if only in passing. Games both of skill and of chance are popular, and gambling plays a prominent role in daily life (nos. 2, 15, 18, 21,

25, 26, 28, 30, 39, 63). Hospitality is highly valued (nos. 15, 16, 18, 19, 21, 28, 32, 36, 40, 45, 60), and good manners on the part of both host and guest are emphasized (nos. 20, 26, 36, 60). A refusal of hospitality, in fact, is not to be taken lightly (nos. 19, 36, 40). People get up early in the morning and bathe before sunrise (nos. 3, 15, 103). Laziness is frowned upon. The sweathouse is apparently used only by the men and older boys (nos. 33, 57), who occasionally sleep there (no. 57). Wood for the sweathouse is gathered in turn by the users (no. 33). Most activities around the home, such as drying meat, preparing hides, or making clothing, are the responsibility of the women (nos. 17, 20), but the men do all the roasting of meat and fowl (nos. 56, 57). Finally, hand clapping is used as a means of attracting attention (nos. 12, 15), or as a signal (no. 26).

Interpersonal Relationships

As indicated earlier, the aspect of social behavior perhaps least amenable to clear and unambiguous interpretation involves the normative structure of family and kinship relationships. Part of the difficulty stems from the fact that psychological motivations and the dynamics of interpersonal relationships are seldom explicitly described or analyzed in American Indian oral narratives—a characteristic certainly present in the corpus under consideration here. The linguistically imprecise texts available for analysis, in conjunction with the unknown nature of Chumash kinship terminology, constitute still another obstacle to the direct interpretation of certain aspects of the narratives. Such terms as "uncle" or "grandfather" (or their Spanish equivalents), for example, may very well be inaccurate or misleading translations of the original Chumash kin terms. In addition, in a number of narratives kin terms are used by non-kin in order to elicit desired forms of behavior or to establish specific relationships (e.g., nos. 26, 30, 36, 40, 57). Thus the precise relationship existing between two characters cannot always be immediately determined or assumed on the basis of the terms present in the text.

Perhaps the greatest difficulty in deriving the normative structure of interpersonal relationships from the narratives, however, arises from the fact that such relationships seem especially subject to the operation of distortion and exaggeration. The depiction of household structure is a good illustration. Although "typical" households involving complete nuclear families are described occasionally (nos. 24, 25, 31, 46, 53, 54, 55), a large number of narratives involve what seem to be rather unusual combinations of personnel: a widower or single man and his children (nos. 2, 15, 18, 29, 52); a widow or deserted woman and her children or grandchildren (nos. 15, 17, 18, 19, 20, 45, 52, 56); two or more siblings (nos. 4, 15, 26, 27, 32); two unrelated men (nos. 33, 34, 35, 42); and either a single man or single woman (nos. 2, 15, 20, 24, 30, 40). While some of this "distortion" or exaggeration in the depiction of behavior may very well indicate the existence of some degree of stress in the relationships or institutions involved, as a number of scholars have suggested, much of it seems clearly a consequence of the requirements of plot development and narrative action in stories that may, in fact, be primarily concerned with reaffirming the value of normative relationships. In many cases, it is the existence of an atypical initial situation or relationship that triggers all subsequent dramatic events and gives the narrative its dramatic impetus. Fortunately, distortion or exaggeration in the depiction of a relationship or role can often be discerned through careful analysis of plot development and the observation of positive or negative sanctions in operation, so that it usually becomes possible to distinguish between normative and atypical role behavior in the narratives. Once this has been accomplished, the way is open to an elucidation of both the normative structure of interpersonal relationships and the subtle stresses to which those relationships are subjected.

Male and female

Relationships between the sexes appear to revolve around two major and partially conflicting themes: (1) the relatively high status of women and (2) a covert antagonism or tension between men and women. Neither of these primary themes is normally explicit in the narratives, but both clearly influence the kinds of interaction depicted.

While there is evidence that a wife's attitude toward her husband should properly involve both respect and obedience (e.g., nos. 32, 45), it is abundantly clear that women are not totally subservient to men, particularly within the context of family life. Women are frequently depicted as independently owning or controlling either property or wealth (nos. 15, 18, 24, 29, 32, 63), and the indirect evidence for at least some matrilateral inheritance of certain goods and statuses has already been commented upon. Women are often depicted as actively (or even aggressively) initiating a sexual relationship (nos. 19, 20, 28, 29), and it is a boy's mother rather than his father who acts as go-between in arranging a marriage (nos. 54, 59). Although residence seems to be most frequently virilocal, there are a number of indications that it is the husband, rather than the wife, who is normally peripheral to family structure. Thus on every occasion in which a household is described as containing extra personnel, it is a relative of the wife that is present—her mother (nos. 27, 65), her father (no. 24), or her aunt (no. 88). In addition, the single example of a relatively complex household (no. 24) is most reasonably interpreted as involving avunculocal residence and marriage to MBD. Further confirmation of the woman's importance in family life lies in the fact that it is the wife, rather than the husband, who retains the children following the dissolution of a marriage (nos. 56, 57).

In spite of a well-developed concept of romantic love, as evidenced by such themes as marriage for love (nos. 21, 25, 28, 32, 47) and the following of a deceased spouse to the land of the dead (nos. 25, 59), a strong element of latent hostility or tension appears to pervade relationships between the sexes. The marriage relationship is seemingly quite brittle, and divorce or abandonment (usually as a result of infidelity on the part of the husband) occurs frequently (nos. 22, 25, 28, 56, 57, 65, 88, 89). In a significant number of narratives an individual suffers death or misfortune as a consequence of the accidental or deliberate actions of a spouse (nos. 15, 18, 25, 31, 47, 56, 74, 76). Female sexuality seems to be subject to some ambivalence— malevolent beings, for instance, are frequently female in the narratives (nos. 12, 15, 63, 94, 95), and on numerous occasions women are depicted as dangerous or potentially dangerous to men and male activities (nos. 15, 18, 25, 56, 74). Finally, a woman's loyalty is more often to her own kin or children than to her husband or affines (nos. 16, 17, 31, 47).

An examination of specific narratives will provide more detailed illustrations of the tension seemingly inherent in the male—female relationship. In nos. 15 and 18, for example, a girl is first wooed and then killed by her supernatural lover (a theme that expresses the axiom, found also in no. 78, that supernatural power and those having such power are amoral and unresponsive to ties of kinship or other social norms that usually constrain behavior). In nos. 16 and 17, a woman assists her brothers/nephews in escaping from her evil husband. In no. 18, a man rejects his wife because he suspects that she is responsible for his loss of gambling skill. In no. 22, Coyote's attempted infidelity brings his wife's curses down upon him, and in no. 56 a man's infidelity to his wife and cruelty to his son result in his death at the hands of the wife. Wives are abandoned by their husbands in nos. 88 and 89, while in no. 65 a wife who flirts with other men at a fiesta is beaten by her jealous husband. A wife poisons her husband in no. 74, and in no. 76 a rejected suitor poisons a girl who has turned him down. In no. 31, Coyote's excesses anger his wife, who effectively punishes him for his behavior, and in no. 25 Coyote's misbehavior brings about his wife's death.

In summary, then, the male−female relationship, while often emotionally rewarding and personally satisfying, is apparently not as structurally important in Chumash society as it might be. The husband seems peripheral to family life in certain ways, and the household as a structural unit may very well be based upon a dyadic relationship other than that of husband/wife—one that is not as brittle, or as susceptible to covert stress. Males receive deference and respect from females, but women are not in a particularly subservient status and may indeed have a great deal of influence within the context of family life, or over the course of their own lives and activities. Female sexuality (as opposed to the female sex) seems to be a source of some anxiety, and to be viewed on occasion as vaguely threatening to males and their activities, although women past menopause are frequently cast in benign and protective roles.

Parents and children

One of the more surprising aspects of the depiction of interpersonal relationships in the narratives is the lack of attention paid to the relationship between parents and children. The fact that this relationship does not figure at all prominently in the stories seems all the more surprising in view of ethnohistoric statements to the effect that the Chumash are exceptionally fond of children and allow them considerable latitude in behavior. One possible explanation might be that the parent−child relationship, while emotionally significant to the individual participants, is not one of great structural concern to the society as a whole. This interpretation would be in accord with the evidence cited above indicating that the father/husband roles are not necessarily vital to the normal functioning of a complex household containing more than a single nuclear family. A complementary interpretation might be that the individuals of immediate relevance in a child's life are not his parents (who may be too concerned with subsistence or other productive activities), but other kin—such as grandparents, uncles or aunts, or older siblings—who may play a more active role in childrearing, discipline, and enculturation. Whatever the explanation, the interactions of parents and children occupy little space in the narratives, and then only in the context of the operation of negative sanctions. It is only in the breach of a norm that the parent-child relationship becomes a motivating factor in a narrative plot.

The relationship between father and son depicted in the narratives seems mutually supportive if not overly close in an emotional sense. A good father is one who provides for his children and looks out for their welfare (nos. 2, 15, 24, 29, 31, 56, 57). He is also responsible for their behavior (no. 32). In turn a son is respectful and obedient to his father, following his advice and honoring his wishes whenever possible (nos. 25, 29, 31). A son is concerned for his parents' welfare when they are elderly, and provides for them just as they once did for him (nos. 24, 29).

The relationship between a man and his daughter hardly figures in the narratives at all, although in the two cases where it does appear the context is perhaps significant. In no. 24, an older man ashamedly admits to an outsider his sexual interest in his married daughter. In no. 53, a daughter's pregnancy leads a man to suspect an incestuous relationship between the daughter and one of her brothers—and when the father discovers his error, his shame is such that he leaves home. Unless one adopts a purely psychological interpretation, the fairly open occurrence of the incest theme here might again reflect certain parameters of family structure—perhaps sociological distance between father and daughter.

The relationships between a mother and her son and daughter are poorly delineated, although respect and deference to age are undoubtedly important elements here, just as they are in the father-son relationship. A mother is concerned for her child's well-being (nos. 15, 24, 31, 56), and wants him to marry well (nos. 24, 54, 59). A son or daughter is in turn obedient and respectful (nos, 15, 18, 54, 55, 56).

The operation of negative sanctions in the narratives provides further insight into the parent-child relationship, and seems to indicate that (1) the maintenance of a normative relationship is considered to be of at least some importance to the society, and (2) the relationship is subject to a certain degree of stress. It is interesting to note that in practically every case where a breach of norm occus, it is the parent rather than the child who is the primary offender, and the breach results in a serious negative sanction. In no. 31, for example, Coyote's greed and stinginess toward his sons arouse his wife's wrath, and she brings about his downfall. In no. 52, a mother exasperated by her daughter's laziness and gluttony commits infanticide, but then suffers such mental anguish that she becomes an animal. In no. 56, a man who has abandoned his wife and remarried treats his son cruelly when the boy comes to visit, and in revenge the wife attacks and kills him. In no. 57, the indifference of their mothers and step-fathers causes several boys first to leave home and then to turn into geese; and when their mothers realize what is happening, they are grief-stricken and try to make amends, but to no avail. In each of these narratives, the importance of normative parental behavior is emphasized by the operation of stringent negative sanctions. The existence of stress, on the other hand, can reasonably be inferred from narratives such as nos. 18, 45, 56, and 67, with their malevolent paternal figures and themes of patricide or supernaturalism.

Siblings

No relationship described in the narratives seems stronger or less subject to stress than that between siblings, and there can be little doubt that siblings are linked by a close and rather special bond that rivals in some ways that between husband and wife. An older brother or sister is clearly a kind of surrogate parent to a younger sibling, giving advice, administering discipline, providing moral and material support, and acting as an example of proper behavior (nos. 15, 16, 17, 29, 52). The older sibling is frequently given sole responsibility for the care and welfare of a younger child when adults are busy with

other activities (nos. 52, 55, 87). The sibling bond is emotionally close as well—in fact, siblings will risk death or suffer
privation in order to help or succor one another (nos. 17, 52,
87). Also siblings are sometimes closer to one another emotionally than a mother and daughter (no. 52) or a husband and
wife (nos. 16, 75). The importance of the sibling relationship is
such that even sexual jealousy must not disturb it—an incident in
no. 15 involving Thunder and his brother Fog, for example,
can reasonably be interpreted as a tacit allowance of sexual
access to a sibling's spouse, or an acceptance of the sexual
equivalence of siblings.

While the sibling bond is perhaps closest between siblings
of the same sex, it is by no means unimportant or weakly
developed between opposite—sex siblings. In no. 32, for
example, the social irresponsibility of a girl's two "tramp"
brothers is emphasized by their failure to provide properly for
their sister. In no. 75, a shaman leaves his personal talisman
with his older sister, rather than with his wife or son, and in
no. 74 the same man destroys his shamanic gear when a niece
is unable to replace her mother as his assistant. Thus the special
bond between siblings seems to extend to the children of
siblings as well.

Siblings' children and parents' siblings

As has been mentioned previously, the relationship between uncle and nephew figures prominently in the narratives, and it seems reasonable to assume that this represents an
extension of the very strong bond linking siblings. A parent's
siblings certainly appear to be rather significant actors in an
individual's life, and are almost invariably shown in a highly
favorable light. While an uncle or aunt is rarely depicted as a
member of the protagonist's immediate household, he or she is
usually on hand in time of need and frequently plays a crucial
role in the sequence of narrative events. An uncle, like an older
brother, can be called upon for assistance in emergencies, for
advice, and for expert guidance in dangerous undertakings
(nos. 5, 19, 26). An aunt, like an older sister, is a sympathetic,
maternal figure, ready to provide what help she can, even at
the expense of other relationships (nos. 15, 16, 17). In summary, a warm and very close bond seems to exist between an
individual and his parents' siblings, and they are often cast in

the role of parental surrogates—helping, guiding, advising, and being generally supportive.

Grandparents and grandchildren

The degree of formality or emotional distance that seems to be a part of the relationship between parents and children is not, apparently, also present in the relationship between grandparents and grandchildren. Relations between alternate generations appear to be close and relatively warm, and to have many of the qualities present in the relationship between an individual and his parents' siblings. While older siblings play an important role in supervising a child's daily activities, it is a grandparent who assumes much of the responsibility for educating and socializing the child (nos. 9, 15, 17, 18, 19, 20, 103). A grandfather trains a boy in both practical and esoteric lore, while a grandmother acts as a nurturing, maternal figure. The closeness of the bond between alternate generations is emphasized in nos. 21 and 24, where it is suggested that a man will tend to have important spiritual qualities similar to those evidenced by a grandfather.

Affines and other kin

Affinal relationships, as in so many societies, seem rather stressful, a characteristic that again might reasonably be expected in view of the tension inherent in the bond between husband and wife. But such relationships do not figure very prominently in the narratives, a fact that might be interpreted as an indication that affines normally have little significant social contact with one another. Where affinal relationships do appear in the narratives, it is usually in a somewhat negative context. The relationship between same—sex siblings-in-law is probably reasonably congenial under normal circumstances, but with some covert stress in evidence. In no. 16, for example, two boys are greeted hospitably by their sister's husband, although he secretly plots their death, and in no. 32, Coyote's new brothers-in-law are tramps and are somewhat contemptuously sent on errands. In no. 54, the embarrassing comments of her sister-in-law cause a girl to run away in shame. The relationship between opposite—sex siblings-in-law, on the other hand, seems to be characterized by considerable interpersonal freedom, including sexual access—in no. 15 a man makes love to his brother's wife and the brother tacitly accepts the situation. As indicated earlier, this can reasonably be interpreted as evidence that, sexually, siblings are considered equivalent, a fact that in turn suggests the hypothesis that the institution of the levirate is present.

The relationship between a man and his mother-in-law is depicted in only one narrative. In no. 47, when Coyote's mother-in-law persists in making insulting remarks about his eating habits, he kills her in a fit of rage, only to lose his wife as a result. While this might be viewed simply an an indication of stress in the relationship, a more reasonable interpretation might be that this particular narrative represents a mythological rationalization for a certain degree of mother-in-law avoidance, especially restrictions on verbal behavior. This interpretation seems consistent with ethnographic data from other areas in California.

The step-parent relationship, as might be expected, seems to be viewed as particularly difficult and susceptible to disruption. In no. 45, the evil stepfathers' indifference to their stepsons causes the boys to leave home. Another possibly difficult relationship depicted in the narratives is that between half-siblings, as indicated in no. 73—however, the apparently contrary evidence in no. 72 makes this a moot point.

SANCTIONS, POSTULATES, AND WORLD VIEW

While there has been a steadily growing interest in recent years in such cognitive aspects of human behavior as belief systems, values, and symbols, there has not been a concomitant development of rigorous methods or theories. Terms such as "configuration," "theme," "postulate," or "value-orientation" are often used interchangeably, and even a concept as basic as that of world view is subject to fundamental disagreements and seemingly antithetical definitions (see Jones, 1972). In the analysis that follows, therefore, no attempt will be made to be either rigorous or innovative—world view, in the present context, will be considered to be simply the explicit and implicit beliefs held by a society about the nature of man, of the universe, and of man's relations to the universe and to his fellow man. Within this general frame of reference two major types of postulates or basic assumptions can then be distinguished that apparently provide the members of the society with criteria for choosing between alternative courses of action. Existential postulates are statements about the nature of things, the what and how of existence, while normative postulates are concerned with desirable states and goals, with what "should be" rather than with what "is." Existential and normative postulates are for the most part mutually consistent and reinforcing; in fact, one set should logically be derivable from the other through careful analysis.

The existential and normative postulates presented below have been abstracted from the narratives by means of the detailed study of three primary kinds of evidence: (1) explanatory elements of the sort found in Section A, (2) characteristic features of plot development, and (3) the operation of positive and negative sanctions in the dramatic action. Explanatory elements have proven to be most useful in the isolation of existential postulates, while normative postulates have been most readily derivable from an analysis of plot and sanctions.

The abstraction of norms and standards from the operation of sanctions in the narratives has presented certain difficulties similar to those previously noted by Spencer in her analysis of Navaho chantway myths (1957:51-53). First, positive sanctions are seldom as clearly or unambiguously formulated as negative ones, so that positively valued norms are usually only implicit in actions to be avoided rather than explicitly stated. Second, it is sometimes difficult to tell in a specific case whether a particular action is the expression of a socially recognized sanction or the impulsive reaction of an individual actor. Third, it is often difficult to judge the significance of success or failure in particular narratives: "When may success be attributed to virtuous conduct; when is failure due to displeasure or punishment by gods or men? . . . If a bold and rebellious action meets with success, does this represent a fantasied wish fulfillment of desired but forbidden impulses? Or does it mean that the rebellious act is thereby condoned or approved?" (Spencer, 1957:52). Fortunately, these problems of analysis have not been insurmountable. The detailed comparison of many narratives has usually provided firm answers in cases involving what might otherwise have been irresolvable ambiguities.

The various existential and normative postulates presented in Table 3 represent, of course, theoretical abstractions far

Table 3. Existential and Normative Postulates
in Narratives

A. *Existential Postulates*
   1. Assumption of a personalized universe
   2. Assumption of the kinship of sentient beings
   3. Assumption of the existence and potentialities of power
   4. Assumption of determinism
   5. Assumption of negative-positive integration
   6. Assumption of a dangerous universe
   7. Assumption of unpredictability
   8. Assumption of inevitable and inherent inequality
   9. Assumption of affectability
   10. Assumption of entropy
   11. Assumption of mutability and spatial proximity
   12. Assumption of a closed and finite universe
   13. Assumption of a dynamic equilibrium of oppositions
   14. Assumption of centricity
B. *Normative Postulates*
   1. Knowledge
   2. Age and seniority
   3. Prudence
   4. Self-constraint
   5. Moderation
   6. Reciprocity
   7. Honesty
   8. Industriousness
   9. Dependability and responsibility
   10. Self-assertion and self-respect
   11. Pragmatism
   12. Etiquette
   13. Language

---

removed in kind from the verifiable reality of material life, and the accuracy of the analysis cannot be judged by equivalent standards. However, certain criteria can be applied: (1) replicability, (2) explanatory power, (3) internal consistency, and (4) external comparisons. Although application of the first criterion must await further research, the others provide a useful gauge of the validity of the postulates abstracted from the narratives, and in fact strongly support the analysis in most respects. Not surprisingly, the world view of the Chumash that emerges from the narratives has many features in common with those ascribed to other North American Indian societies. The greatest similarities, of course, are to nearby California groups such as the Cahuilla, Luiseño, Pomo, or Wintu (see Bean, 1972; White, 1963; Aginsky, 1940; Halpern, 1953; Lee, 1938), but there are even extensive parallels with the world view of tribes as geographically distant as, for example, the Navaho or Pueblo Indians (see Kluckhohn, 1949; Ladd, 1957; Ortiz, 1972a). The existence of these apparent homologies among so many geographically and culturally distinct groups suggests both the validity of the several analyses and the value of further research on the social and cognitive processes involved.

Assumption of a personalized universe

The Chumash, in common with many other societies throughout the world, tend to personify aspects of their natural environment and attribute to the beings thus depicted the same qualities of sentience, will, rationality, and emotionality that characterize man himself. Thus plants, animals and birds, celestial bodies, and various natural forces are all part of the social universe to which man belongs, and their activities and interests may vitally affect the course of human events. There are also various beings that are less clearly identifiable with the natural environment, but who nonetheless play equally significant roles in the interacting community of sentient creatures. However, the members of that community are neither equally powerful nor equally active, especially at the present time. Many have been transformed into other shapes since the Flood, or are no longer actively concerned with human affairs. But all events and phenomena are the result of actions taken by specific sentient beings, rather than the product of impersonal forces.

Assumption of the kinship of sentient beings

Not only are the causative agencies in the Chumash universe personified, they are interrelated as well. Like the Cahuilla (Bean, 1972:165), the Chumash assume that they are part of an interacting system, but it is a highly personalized system, the component elements of which share reciprocal rights and responsibilities with respect to one another and comprise the membership of a structured community reinforced by bonds of kinship and mutual dependency. Thus all sentient beings are related (no. 14), and each has a task to do according to its nature (nos. 1, 2, 14), however humble that nature may be (no. 13).

Assumption of the existence and potentialities of power

Perhaps no postulate is of greater importance in properly understanding the world view of the Chumash—or, for that matter, that of any other group in native California—than that recognizing the existence and potentialities of power. The value of the concept of power (or mana, as it is usually referred to in the anthropological literature) as an explanatory device is attested to by its nearly universal distribution and its presence in disguised form in even the most complex of modern theological systems. In California, power seems to be inextricably associated with sentience and will, and all beings with the capacity for rational existence possess at least the potentiality for obtaining and exercising power. Everything in the universe is thus placed into one of two major categories: (1) those beings whose possession of rationality and potential for action make them part of the social universe and therefore kin to man, and (2) inanimate objects lacking both "personality" and power. Power is an incorporeal force that can be used for either good or evil (nos. 73, 75). It can be inherent in either an object or a person, or it can be inherited or deliberately acquired by someone (nos. 15, 20, 25, 39, 53, 81, 84). It allows one to transcend the normal parameters of time and space or to modify and transform the shape of objects (nos. 18, 25, 26, 30, 32, 51, 63, 67, 97). While the concept of power is not explicitly developed in the narratives, practically every page bears witness to its central position in the belief system, and there is every reason to suspect as sophisticated a development of the concept among the Chumash as that described ethnographically for the Luiseño (White, 1957; 1963) or the Cahuilla (Bean, 1972).

Assumption of determinism

Since power and the potential for action are inseparable from rationality and will, all actions and events are explainable in terms of specific causative agencies, and there is virtually no development of the concept of fortune or chance in human affairs. Success or failure in any endeavor depends upon the relative power and knowledge of the participants—there is neither luck nor accident. Aginsky (1940:3) has commented on the relevance of this assumption for Pomo conceptions of death and illness, and Kluckhohn's remarks concerning this aspect of Navaho philosophy seem equally applicable to the world view of the Chumash:

> The conception of "good luck" is hard to translate into the Navaho language. In their scheme of things one is not "lucky" or "unlucky." One has the requisite knowledge (sacred or profane) or one hasn't. Even in what European languages call "games of chance" the Navaho depends upon medicines, rites, and verbal formulas. The same is true with hunting. Getting a deer is never a matter of good fortune; it is a matter of ritual knowledge and of one's relations with supernaturals which, again, are controllable (Kluckhohn, 1949:362).

Thus the success in gambling enjoyed by Momoy's grandson in no. 18 is implicit evidence of his exceptional power, while his subsequent losses are due to Coyote's bewitchment (significantly, however, the boy blames his failure on the behavior of his wife). Coyote's deliberate actions also affect the outcome of contests in other narratives as well (nos. 15, 26, 30). The great game of peon, described in no. 2 as determining life and death during the course of the year for so many, is therefore probably best viewed as an expression of the balance of opposing forces and powers rather than as a reification of the concept of fortune, as was suggested earlier.

Assumption of negative-positive integration

For the Chumash, good and evil are not mutually exclusive categories, nor is the sharp dichotomy between the two, familiar to Western society, of any great relevance to daily life. Any being capable of action has the potential of behaving in either a negative or a positive manner on any occasion, depending on impulse and self-interest. Morality is egoistic and essentially situational in nature (see Ladd, 1957). No being is either purely good or purely evil; rather, each has the potential for being both simultaneously, although one end of the continuum may predominate most of the time. Sun brings warmth and light to man, but he also brings death (no. 2). Coyote can be wise, helpful, and good (nos. 2, 15, 26, 29, 30, 32), but he is equally capable of stupidity, deceit, and malevolence (nos. 25, 30, 31, 33, 34, 45). Being impersonal and amoral, power can be wielded for either negative or positive purposes, to kill or to cure (nos. 30, 73, 75). At the same time, power does seem to be regarded as generally more negative than positive, since those beings with exceptional power are characterized most often as dangerous or antipathetic to man rather than helpful or sympathetic (nos. 2, 18, 26, 76, 78, 79). Because of this fact, and because of the combination of positive and negative elements in all phenomena, the universe is considered to be both dangerous and unpredictable.

Assumption of a dangerous universe

Given the nature of the preceding postulates, it is virtually inevitable that the universe should be considered to be filled with dangers to be avoided or circumvented if possible. The most important causative agencies in the universe, for example, are powerful beings that are more frequently inimical or indifferent to man than supportive (nos. 2, 8, 18, 29, 58). After dark one might meet any of a variety of hostile *nunašiš* (nos. 3, 63, 65, 66, 94, 95), or even a spirit or ghost (nos. 98, 99, 100). One might also be accosted by some kind of were-being (nos. 15, 18, 67, 70, 97). And after death, the journey to the Land of the Dead is full of dangers to be surmounted (nos. 12, 15, 59). It is not surprising, therefore, to find in narrative after narrative the strong implication that anyone departing from the security of familiar surroundings or accepted procedures will almost invariably encounter danger or misfortune in the form of a powerful supernatural being. The universe, in short, is fraught with peril, full of dangers that one can only hope to avoid through a judicious combination of knowledge and prudence.

Assumption of unpredictability

Because all causative agencies in the universe are personalized and endowed with such human qualities as will, intelligence, and emotionality, and because the beings so conceptualized are considered to have the potentiality for either positive or negative action, unpredictability is an essential aspect of all events and all phenomena. In addition, with sufficient power, form can be modified at will (nos. 15, 18, 25, 26, 29, 57, 62, 63, 67, 69, 85, 97), death can be reversed (nos. 15, 16, 17, 18, 26, 30, 51, 75, 84), and even the normal boundaries of time and space overcome (nos. 15, 18, 20, 25, 30, 32, 51, 86, 101). Theoretically, then, nothing is immutable in the face of sufficient power—although such power may not always be available in actuality to any one being. The universe is thus subject to sudden changes that are neither foreseeable nor predictable. A good deed may be repaid by evil (nos. 21, 45, 107), or an evil deed by good; a winner may inexplicably lose (nos. 15, 18, 30), or an ineffectual man succeed (no. 21). Form is mutable, and behavior uncertain.

Assumption of inevitable and inherent inequality

Since success or failure in any enterprise is a function of either power or knowledge (which is itself a form of power), and power is unevenly distributed throughout the universe, inequalities in abilities, potentialities, and social prerogatives are assumed to be both innate and inevitable. Some beings are simply inherently superior to other beings. Similarly, differences in social rank and prestige are proper and natural, since they are based on biologically and socially inheritable differences in supernatural power and esoteric knowledge. A person inherits his status in a hierarchical society and universe just as he inherits the skills and qualities necessary to the proper performance of the role. However, the rigidity of such a status quo is partially ameliorated by the leavening of knowledge, which stands in a kind of symbolic, balanced opposition to innate supernatural power.

Assumption of affectability

Because of the personalization of causative agencies, it is possible for man to affect or influence these agencies directly. He is not at the mercy of completely impersonal, unaffectable forces obeying inexorable laws. Beings in the upper world like Sun and Slo?w, for example, are subject to influence, and can be moved to action by cajolery (no. 18), entreaty (nos. 5, 29, 30), or insult (no. 18). They are also capable of such human emotions as pity (nos. 5, 52), anger (no. 6), or pride (no. 29). Lesser beings are even more susceptible to influence or control, and are easily deceived·as well (nos. 15, 16, 17, 18, 19, 26, 27, 30, 53, 65, 66).

Assumption of entropy

One of the least explicit postulates in the narratives is the assumption that power is gradually diminishing through time in both quantity and availability, so that the forms of power and subtlety of knowledge accessible to man today are significantly less effective than those wielded by people in mythological times. As Bean has pointed out regarding the Cahuilla, power "was very intense in the beginning, but it has constantly and elusively diminished through time. Its presence and availability to man throughout history, however, have testified to its earlier potency, and it has continued to account for phenomena in the present" (Bean, 1972:161). This assumption of entropy can be seen most clearly in the device of a medicine used to revive the dead, the secret of which has since been lost or forgotten (nos. 15, 17, 18, 20), and in the disappearance of sacred places once inhabited by powerful supernatural beings (no. 62).

Assumption of mutability and spatial proximity

The fundamental postulate presented above regarding the existence of power and its potentialities has certain corollaries that involve assumptions about the nature of matter, time, and space. Thus form is not invariant or immutable, but rather is a function of power in an almost Einsteinian sense—with sufficient power, one form of matter can be converted into another, even though the conversion is normally only temporary (nos. 15, 18, 23, 25, 26, 28, 29, 56, 57, 62, 63, 67, 69, 97).

Time is another apparently variable dimension of reality for the Chumash. Subjective time in the realm of the sacred may be quite different from that normally experienced by man (no. 51), or it may be virtually meaningless to any structured reality. Thus some mythological beings and events have their primary existence outside of time, in a dimension where such concepts as past, present, or future can have little significance. Specific nunašiš are destroyed in myth after myth, yet they still exist (no. 3) and probably always will.

Normal spatial parameters also can, with sufficient power, be transcended. In fact, the ability to travel great distances rapidly is an almost certain indication of the possession of exceptional powers (nos. 15, 19, 20, 21, 25, 30, 67, 101). This seems to be a corollary of the principle that spatial proximity is a necessary adjunct to causality, which has also been ascribed to the Navaho (Ladd, 1957:221-222). Another corollary involves the belief that spatially remote power is not particularly dangerous, so that one can escape peril by running away from it or by not going to meet it (nos. 15, 16, 17, 18, 19, 20, 21, 25, 26, 27, 51, 53, 62, 63, 65, 66, 78, 94, 96, 99, 102). Action at a distance is impossible, although spatially separated parts of a whole can still affect one another (nos. 75, 89).

Assumption of a closed and finite universe

Implicit in the narratives is a conception of the universe as a finite and essentially closed system, where causation is determinate and boundaries are sharply definable. The entire universe consists of three flat, circular worlds floating in a great abyss, and supported by powerful supernatural beings (nos. 1, 10). Astronomical objects are either supernatural beings living in the world above (nos. 1, 2, 6, 9, 15, 18, 29, 30, 52, 57) or sparks from the torch carried by Sun (no. 21). Each of the three worlds is limited in scope, and can be circumnavigated quickly (nos. 15, 30). Death had to be instituted so that the earth would not be overcrowded (no. 7), but life and death are simply stages in an endlessly recurring cycle of reincarnation (nos. 10, 11, 21). The souls of the dead simply occupy a distant portion of the same world as the living. Thus matter is neither created nor destroyed, but simply transformed; and there are no forces, beings, or places beyond man's ken.

Assumption of a dynamic equilibrium of oppositions

For the Chumash, the great forces of nature are in a constant state of balanced opposition to one another, with none possessing an ultimate superiority that might irrevocably alter the proper condition of dynamic equilibrium that should normally prevail in the universe. This equilibrium of oppositions is graphically expressed by the gambling game in no. 2 between those forces sympathetic to man and those antithetical to him. (It might equally be viewed as a symbolic expression of the continual struggle between life and death, or between good and evil.) This idea of dynamic balance is strikingly similar to what Kluckhohn, in reference to the Navaho, has somewhat misleadingly called "a basic quest for harmony":

> In the Navaho conception of the relationship between their divinities there is the mechanical notion of a balance of opposing forces. No one divine being has unfettered control over the others. Each is limited by the powers of others as well as by the remorseless working out of processes beyond the control of the

whole pantheon. In this equilibrium of forces human effort in the form of observance of taboos and in the performance of compulsive rituals can play its part. Individually acquired knowledge can assist in the restoration of harmony in one person's life, in that of the community, in that of the whole universe (Kluckhohn, 1949:362).

Among the Chumash, the emphasis is certainly less on harmony than on balanced oppositions between contrasting forces, categories, and states of being. Some of the more important oppositions implicit in the narratives that should be mentioned here are those between good and evil, between male and female, between innate power and acquired knowledge/power, and between the forces of social continuity and the possessors of power, individuals who are basically amoral and antisocial (nos. 78, 79). Certain of these oppositions have already been commented upon in other contexts.

Assumption of centricity

The final existential postulate to be discussed involves the assumption that the structure of reality is fundamentally concentric in nature, with man, both specifically and generically, at the center. This assumption is seen most readily in the Chumash conception of a circular world, interstratified between two other worlds, in which the Chumash themselves form the geographic and cultural center (no. 1). But it is implicit in other beliefs as well. For example, powerful (and hence dangerous) beings are usually encountered only when one deliberately forsakes the security of the known and the familiar and travels *outward* into the unknown and unpredictable region at the periphery of one's accustomed sphere of activity. Thus even limited travel is virtually synonomous with some degree of peril (nos. 3, 12, 15, 16, 17, 18, 19, 26, 27, 29, 30, 51, 53, 62, 63, 65, 66, 79, 78, 86, 87, 92, 93, 94, 95, 96, 97, 102). On the other hand, one is relatively safe from even the most powerful of sorcerers while indoors or in camp (no. 78). The farther one travels from home, the greater the likelihood of encountering increasingly powerful and malevolent beings or people— hence the belief, seemingly so common in California, that people in neighboring groups are more warlike and more adept at witchcraft than individuals in one's own society. Each Chumash is at the center of a series of concentric circles,

ranging outward from the individual first to his immediate
family and then to his kin, affines, neighbors, and fellow Chumash, and ending finally with the most distant peoples known
to anyone. Thus centripetality is associated with security, pre-
dictability, sociality, and the realm of the profane, while centri-
fugality clearly means danger, unpredictability, and powers
associated with nature and the realm of the sacred. The
concept of centricity, parenthetically, probably underlies the
Pomo distinction between the Inside and the Outside that
Halpern (1953) characterizes as a dichotomy rather than a continuum. It may also be a major parameter in Wintu thought, as
Lee's often quoted statement suggests: "The Wintu has a small
sphere wherein he can choose and do, can feel and think and
make decisions. Cutting through this and circumscribing it, is
the world of natural necessity wherein all things that are
potential and probable are also inevitable, wherein existence is
unknowable and ineffable" (Lee, 1938:102). The Chumash,
too, cling to a small core of partial security in the midst of an
unpredictable, perilous, and all too often hostile world.

Knowledge

Given the existential postulates presented above, it is easy
to understand the emphasis that the Chumash place upon
knowledge as a normative value. In common with other North
American Indians, the Chumash feel that knowledge is virtue
and ignorance vice, for only through wisdom can one achieve
security, age, or respect—which, after all, are the only depend-
able measures of morality. The importance of knowledge is
nicely expressed in no. 12, where the waters surrounding
Šimilaqša are described as being filled with the transformed
souls of people "who merely lived in ignorance," and had "no
ʔatišwin or who did not know about the old religion and did
not drink toloache." In addition, in narrative after narrative,
failure to heed good advice brings misfortune or disaster,
while success invariably attends those who listen to wise
counsel (nos. 15, 16, 17, 18, 21, 24, 29, 30, 50, 59, 62, 69, 75, 78,
92, 96, 99, 102, 104).

Age and seniority

Age, like knowledge, is highly valued in Chumash society,
and the two are, in fact, highly correlated. Age presumably

brings wisdom, and only wisdom (and the power stemming from it) can ensure one's survival to a respectable age in a mostly hostile universe. Significantly, powerful characters (with certain interesting exceptions) are always described in the narratives as elderly (nos. 2, 13, 15, 16, 18, 19, 20, 26, 27, 30, 36, 51, 59, 91, 92, 93, 94, 95). Sun, presumably the most powerful of all, is depicted as a *very* old man (no. 2). Also, older siblings are characterized as cautious, knowledgeable, and responsible, while younger siblings are normally described as mischievous, impulsive, and irresponsible (nos. 15, 16, 17). Power and authority are thus a direct function of maturity and seniority.

Prudence

In a generally dangerous and unpredictable world, the wise man is cautious and serious, and keeps his own counsel to the point of secrecy. A man who is careful is held in esteem by others (no. 13). He follows good advice (nos. 15, 17, 21, 24, 92), and avoids displays that might arouse envy in others (nos. 18, 29, 30, 33). He minds his own business and expects others to do likewise (nos. 32, 35, 39, 47). Above all, he is careful in both word and deed to avoid anything that might arouse enmity in others or bring him to the attention of potentially hostile forces, for a lack of prudence can have serious consequences (nos. 15, 16, 17, 18, 22, 23, 25, 29, 30, 31, 32, 33, 35, 38, 39, 47, 58, 62, 63, 69, 74, 75, 76, 78, 99, 102, 104).

Self-constraint

Personal control is an important facet of prudent behavior, for a loss of such control seems to be a major factor in precipitating dangerous or unpleasant situations. Acting in haste or in anger, without giving thought to the consequences, is apt to lead to misfortune (nos. 17, 18, 23, 25, 29, 33, 34, 35, 38, 47, 52, 72). Impulsive speech or behavior of any kind must be avoided.

Moderation

Considerable stress is placed upon the necessity of avoiding excesses of any kind, an emphasis that again reflects the importance of prudent behavior as a normative standard— although the existential postulate of balanced opposition may also be a factor here. Killing game in excess of one's actual need for food is regarded unfavorably (no. 20). Gluttony is also frowned upon, and is in fact a common characteristic imputed to such unpleasant and dangerous beings as the *Hap* and the *ʔelyeʔwun* (nos. 17, 20, 26, 31). Another area of concern involves the maintenance of balanced reciprocal relationships. Excessive generosity or profligacy is not encouraged (nos. 32, 63), but then neither is stinginess (nos. 31, 35, 36, 45, 56, 57). Moderate, controlled behavior is the ideal for which people strive.

Reciprocity

As Bean (1972:174) emphasizes in his discussion of Cahuilla norms and values, behavior involving the ethic of reciprocity has frequently been described in the anthropological literature as being founded on ordinary generosity, when in fact the analyst has often simply observed one segment of a complex cycle of material exchanges which the participants are careful to keep in balance. The treatment of hospitality in the narratives is a case in point—in story after story, there are extensive descriptions of visitors expecting (and receiving) food and shelter—even when the host is a malevolent being who fully intends to kill the guest before the night is through (nos. 15, 16, 17, 26, 27, 29), or when the host fears his guest's intentions (no. 45). The great stress placed on hospitality by the Chumash cannot be doubted, but it involves more than simple generosity. A failure to offer hospitality is regarded quite seriously (no. 36), but so is a demand or open request for it (nos. 29, 40, 45). A refusal of profferred hospitality is even worse, for it is tantamount to an overt expression of hostility (nos. 19, 40). Offering a guest food and shelter is thus simply one expression of a pattern of reciprocal relationships that is deeply ingrained in Chumash behavior. Other expressions of this ethic of reciprocity involve such things as having to match gesture for gesture (nos. 27, 29), repaying a debt in an equivalent manner (nos. 18, 32, 33, 40, 81), and honoring the ties of kinship (nos. 31, 56, 57, 78).

Honesty

Honesty is one of the more obviously sanctioned normative postulates in the Chumash value system. Whenever there is an example of theft, lying, or deceit in the narratives, a negative reaction normally results that is both immediate and severe. Property rights are apparently quite important in Chumash society, for stealing is never condoned—and a thief usually receives immediate punishment for his actions (nos. 15, 17, 24, 27). Telling lies or being deliberately deceitful are other forms of dishonesty that also normally receive short shrift (nos. 18, 21, 22, 25, 29, 33, 35, 45). Additionally, they are characteristic of evil beings or other wrongdoers (nos. 15, 16, 17, 26, 27, 29, 31, 34). However, lying and deceit are apparently subject to some ambivalence, for there are certain occasions when a resort to such behavior is regarded as not only necessary but even commendable (nos. 15, 16, 17, 18, 20, 26, 29). Dishonesty is bad, but overcoming superior or hostile forces with wit and guile is admirable (indeed, Odysseus might have been Chumash).

Industriousness

A good person is industrious as well as honest. He rises and bathes early in the morning (nos. 3, 15, 18, 103). He works hard during the day, and provides for his family (nos. 18, 19, 20, 29, 32). Laziness must be avoided, for it is reprehensible and dangerous behavior (nos. 31, 32, 52, 103). This postulate is nicely expressed in no. 103: "María's grandfather . . . told her to get up early in the morning, for he said that if the sun saw her lying in bed he would spit on her and make her ill. Everyone used to bathe before sunrise in the morning. . . . If a person is lazy in the summer and omits the bath, his blood will be warm and he will be bitten by a rattlesnake. But if your blood is cool . . . the rattlesnake will hiss and give warning."

Dependability and responsibility

Irresponsible and undependable behavior is generally frowned upon in any society, but it is particularly unfortunate when a society is located in a universe believed to be characterized by instability and unpredictability. Such forms of irresponsible behavior as infidelity, failing to fulfill obligations to kin, and ignoring the dictates of common sense and prudence typically meet with negative sanctions (nos. 17, 21, 22, 25, 31, 33, 39, 56, 57, 63, 88, 111). The individual who meets his responsibilities, provides for his family and kin, responds appropriately in social situations, and can be depended upon to behave seriously and prudently, is the kind of person esteemed in Chumash society.

Self-assertion and self-respect

Another important element in Chumash behavior involves the need to assert oneself and avoid losing face publicly. Although braggadocio and personal displays should be minimized, a certain amount of self-assertion is necessary for the proper maintenance of reciprocal relationships: the self-respecting individual receives as well as gives. "August is named . . . the 'month of fiesta'. A man born in this month will stand in the middle of a festive gathering and take everything he can that properly belongs to him and take it home. And he is very saving, too. He is good to his neighbors" (no. 13). Maintaining face is a most important facet of self-respect, also. An individual is anxious to sustain a good public image, and will sometimes go to great lengths to do so (nos. 26, 27, 29, 32, 33, 73). Conversely, loss of face is a serious matter (nos. 15, 18, 22, 35, 54, 60, 63, 75, 76)—hence the typical reaction to an insult or a slight (nos. 23, 29, 38, 45, 47, 60, 69, 75, 76).

Pragmatism

The narratives are pervaded by an attitude that could be characterized as fatalistic, but is probably best described as one of complete practicality or pragmatism. Thus there is a general acceptance (without resignation) of the fact that man is capable of evil as well as good, so that one should not expect too much of others or be overly dependent upon them, as human nature is as unpredictable as everything else in the universe. A good deed, for example, may be met with evil (nos. 21, 45, 107)—and one should never count one's chickens before they hatch (nos. 15, 16, 17, 48, 50, 106, 107, 108). One should be as pragmatic in choosing a spouse as in anything else (nos. 24, 29). There is no point in trying to alter the inevitable—in fact, such behavior can be dangerous (nos. 25, 59). Accepting the *status quo* is the only sensible thing to do (nos. 6, 7, 15, 33, 46, 51, 63), unless, of course, a practical solution exists.

Etiquette

A concern for good manners, expressed in several of the narratives, provides an unexpected insight into certain aspects of Chumash social behavior. Food and its consumption is apparently of considerable interest, judging by the emphasis placed upon it in story after story, and a lack of proper manners marks a character as intrinsically suspect. Coyote's comment in no. 26 on the eating habits of the ʔelyeʔwun provides an amusing illustration of the emphasis on etiquette: "How ugly these people are when they eat, what pigs they are, how different from the way we eat our acorn soup with two fingers." Similarly, the gluttony and boorishness of the father in no. 56 simply underlines the reprehensible nature of his behavior, while in nos. 47 and 54 the misfortunes of the protagonists are a direct result of their improper eating habits. Verbal behavior is another facet of social life that illustrates the Chumash concern for proper etiquette. Insults or improper verbal responses characteristically elicit dramatic reactions from other people (nos. 23, 27, 29, 34, 35, 38, 45, 47, 54, 58, 75). Language, for the Chumash, thus appears to be more than simply a neutral medium of communication.

Language

Language appears to play an interesting and significant role in Chumash culture. Verbal behavior certainly seems to be as structured as any other aspect of life depicted in the narratives, a fact that is not overly surprising in view of the emphasis on precise and rational discourse apparently so characteristic of many North American Indian cultures (see Ladd, 1957). The impact of language on a particular character or plot situation in the stories has already been commented upon in other contexts, with special reference to certain forms of misbehavior such as telling lies or insulting someone. But another form of verbal behavior occurs in the narratives which has not been previously discussed: silence. As Basso has pointed out with particular reference to Apache culture, refraining from speech may be as significant in some ways as speaking. Silence as a form of verbal behavior occurs in several of the narratives, and the particular contexts in which it occurs (nos. 15, 17, 18, 51, 69) tend to support Basso's hypothesis that silence is a reaction to uncertainty and unpredictability in social relations (Basso, 1970:227). A somewhat unusual type of silent behavior is depicted in nos. 32 and 35, in which Coyote pretends to be mute; here the apparent inability to speak may be either a device to emphasize Coyote's exceptional nature (as in the inversions of normal behavior attributed to the more powerful supernatural beings) or a way of underlining his condition of isolation and separateness from the social system he is attempting to join (as a contrast, perhaps, between Man and Nature—*à la* Lévi-Strauss). For the Chumash, as for ourselves, language is a unique and vital element in any conception of rational existence.

Distortion, Inversion, and Fantasy

Although the problem of an unrealistic depiction of behavior in folk narratives has been considered a major stumbling block in the path of anyone wishing to utilize such stories for the purpose of obtaining specific ethnographic insights, it has become, I hope, increasingly obvious in the course of this study that even such a potentially serious obstacle is not insurmountable if properly approached. In a preceding section, for example, it was pointed out that much of the distortion or exaggeration of behavior that occurs in the narratives is clearly a result of the dramatic prerequisite for an initial contradiction or conflict situation necessitating resolution, easily identifiable as such through the prompt operation of negative or positive sanctions in plot development. Thus behavior that in many of the narratives seems at first glance contrary to any reasonable social norms becomes readily understandable as part of a dramatic reaffirmation of community standards, while the narratives themselves can in many cases be interpreted simply as heuristic media serving a primarily didactic function. In fact, a major portion of the discrepancy between real and depicted behavior occurring in the narratives under consideration here can undoubtedly be explained as just such a consequence of the necessity for an initial conflict requiring subsequent dramatic resolution—however, certain contradictions still remain that can not be interpreted in this manner.

Perhaps the most interesting category of departures from realistic behavior involves what has been referred to in an earlier chapter as *inversion*, the reversal or transcendence of normative standards and constraints in the narratives by individuals who thus demonstrate their exceptional nature vis-à-vis mankind as a whole. Almost all of the inversions of normal behavior in the present collection occur in the context of narratives 15 through 20, and are easily distinguishable from the discrepancies discussed earlier by the absence or suspension of the sanctions that would usually be operative in such cases. It is readily apparent from a careful analysis of specific examples that inversion, like exaggeration, serves the dual functions of emphasizing desirable standards of normative behavior while simultaneously stressing the distinctiveness of certain individuals closely associated with the realm of the sacred (such as Sun, *Momoy*, and *Momoy*'s kin). Such characters violate the canons of expectable behavior with virtual impunity, or else behave in ways that distinguish them sharply from others. They may be characterized by some kind of miraculous birth (nos. 15, 18, 20, 29, 53), or demonstrate supernatural growth or abnormal strength (nos. 18, 19, 20). They may be cannibalistic, or eat only tobacco or other noxious substances (nos. 2, 18, 19, 20). They usually live in isolation (nos. 17, 18, 19, 20, 29, 33, 35, 40, 45), and are frequently depicted as widows or widowers (nos. 2, 15). They may also shun sex and marriage (no. 20). Unlike other people, they are immune to the effects of *Datura* (nos. 19, 20). They seemingly fly in the face of common sense, and deliberately court danger (nos. 15, 16, 17, 18, 19, 20). In addition, they may violate such other normative standards as respect for age (nos. 15, 17), hospitality (no. 19), honesty (nos. 15, 17), etiquette (no. 20), moderation (no. 20), and language (nos. 32, 35).

The use of inversion to distinguish the sacred from the profane is not, of course, characteristic of Chumash narratives alone. A common eschatological theme in many parts of the world, for example, is the belief that events and activities in the hereafter are often a reversal of those experienced during life. This is nicely expressed in the present collection by the inversion of food and feces in nos. 12 and 15, and by the equivalence of the living protagonist's slumber in the Land of the Dead (symbolic death) with his return to the world of the living (symbolic rebirth) in no. 59. But inversion as a form of symbolic emphasis seems to be a phenomenon present in other contexts than simply that of folk narrative, and one well worthy of greater attention than it has hitherto received. Although there has been extensive ethnographic documentation of inversions in the context of ritual, the major theoretical treatment touching upon the subject has been in relation to African rituals of conflict (Norbeck, 1963; Turner, 1969a), and explanation has been in terms of sociological and psychological factors only. Thus inversion, where recognized, has been primarily explained as a psychological outlet for stresses induced by frustrations and inequalities inherent in a cultural system, a safety valve that ensures the continuance of the system by affording an opportunity for emotional catharsis to those individuals who might otherwise disrupt it. While such an explanation may be perfectly valid from a psychological point of view, it overlooks the symbolic significance of inversion as an alternate means of stressing culturally important norms and postulates. There are, after all, only two primary means of stressing or emphasizing any theme—by exaggerating salient characteristics, and extrapolating from the known to the unknown, or by inverting major traits, so that the known and unknown contrast isomerically. Exaggeration as a form of stress is essentially quantitative in nature, while inversion is qualitative; thus the effectiveness lost through familiarity with one, it might be suggested, could be restored through recourse to the second. This might very well explain such apparently anomalous behavior as ritualized clowning, "rituals of conflict," and the abeyance of certain mores during festivals or important public ceremonies (see Crumrine, 1969, 1974; Hieb, 1972; and Makarius, 1970, for complementary data and similar conclusions).

Specific examples of behavioral inversions in ritual contexts can be found in Harrington's ethnographic notes on the Chumash and Kitanemuk, and the information provided (in conjunction with data already obtained) suggests that such behavior had wide distribution aboriginally, both in California and elsewhere (see Steward, 1931). Members of the ʔantap cult, for example, are reported to have used excessively insulting language to one another while within the confines of the ceremonial enclosure or siliyik, and to have demanded food and drink from the attending populace—both forms of behavior which are, of course, contrary to Chumash norms under ordinary circumstances. Again, during one particular night of the important Winter Solstice ceremony, a woman was required to submit sexually to anyone who approached her, although adultery was apparently dealt with rather severely on other occasions. Among the Kitanemuk (and probably the Chumash as well), certain dancers would perform a burlesque of others during serious rites and attempt to make the audience laugh. Anyone doing so, however, had to pay a monetary fine. Similar ritual clowning has been reported in many areas of the state, and comparisons have been drawn with certain elements of Pueblo Indian ceremonialism. Until very recently, however, discussion has been primarily in terms of historical diffusion (Loeb, 1934a, 1934b; Steward, 1931). In addition, the suspension of normal standards of behavior at the time of the winter solstice seems broadly analogous to particular features of such diverse occasions as the World Renewal ceremonies of Northwest California, the Saturnalia of ancient Rome, or contemporary festivals such as Mardi Gras.

Inversion may also explain the Contrary societies of the Plains Indians, in that a reversal of normal behavior symbolically identifies or aligns the individual with the sacred, and hence more easily affords him access to supernatural power. While a burlesque of the sacred may in many cases provide a psychological release for culturally induced tensions, ritual clowning (and inversion) is often motivated by far more serious concerns than humor alone, as Steward's comments (1931:199-200) clearly indicate: "Among the Pomo and Patwin the clown was primarily an antinatural being, a ghost, and the grotesque dress, strange behavior and contrary nature were as much an attempt actually to represent such a being as to produce a ludicrous impression. Moreover, within these tribes an atmosphere of sacred unnaturalness, even in regard to the buffoonery of the clowns, is attested by the fact that the audience was prohibited from laughing."

Although it can be legitimately argued that much of the inversion present in the Chumash narratives serves primarily to symbolically emphasize the exceptional quality of specific individuals or incidents, the hypothesis that such "distortions" of reality represent points of stress in the social fabric must not be neglected altogether. And if this frame of reference is adopted, two related themes can be derived from the stories that can logically be construed as expressions of wish fulfillment. One such theme involves youth excelling those with greater age and experience (nos. 15, 16, 17, 18, 19, 20, 50, 53, 57, 66), while the other involves an open flaunting of authority (nos. 28, 29, 32, 38, 53). Both themes, it might be suggested, are expectable expressions of the normal stresses, conflicts, and frustrations encountered universally during the process of maturation, particularly in a society in which age, experience, knowledge, seniority, and adherence to authority are especially emphasized. Thus while many of the narratives explicitly reaffirm the necessity of conforming to community standards of behavior, and reinforce the norms and postulates so vital to the smooth functioning of society, they may also provide a psychological outlet through emotional catharsis for the individual frustrations inevitably generated during socialization by external demands for conformance and compromise.

A consideration of themes such as those discussed above leads inevitably to the topic of fantasy, a major *bête noire* of many contemporary folklorists interested in behavioral interpretations. The term itself, of course, implies more than just a distortion of reality—illusion and imagination, involving a considerable departure from realism, must be present as well. And certainly at first glance the Chumash narratives seem replete with elements that could justifiably and unambiguously be identified as pure fantasy. The existence of heroes who eat only tobacco (nos. 18, 19, 20) and travel by echo (nos. 19, 20), the revival of the dead through an application of "medicine" (nos. 15, 16, 17, 18, 20, 26, 29, 30, 52, 75), the transformation of one's physical form (nos. 15, 18, 23, 25, 28, 29, 31, 32, 45, 47, 52, 56, 57, 63, 69, 71, 97), the existence of beings who live underwater (nos. 26, 27, 86), the *nunašiš* themselves—all of these appear to be typical examples of the operation of fantasy and imagination. Yet applying the term fantasy to elements such as these, and interpreting them accordingly, may be dangerously misleading: it is a basic truism in anthropology that one man's simple statement of fact may be considered the wildest fiction by someone else. To label a belief or statement of fact as fantasy is to assume that the element is primarily a consequence of psychological processes and can most profitably be interpreted as such—a procedure highly susceptible to ethnocentric bias, and perhaps hopelessly obfuscating as well. Is the fundamental Christian belief in the resurrection of Jesus, for example, best interpreted as a significant indication of certain kinds of psychological stresses in contemporary Christian societies?

The detailed examination of specific recurrent themes or motifs in the narratives may help to clarify certain of the difficulties just alluded to by placing them in some kind of perspective. The treatment of food, for example, seems clearly a consequence of psychological (or ecological) factors operative in Chumash culture. The consumption of food is continually mentioned in narrative after narrative. Eating, in fact, is probably the most frequently depicted activity of all. The various monsters encountered by the protagonists inhale, swallow, bite, bake or suck blood from them, and are often prodigious eaters (nos. 15, 16, 17, 18, 26, 30, 37, 66). Characters with exceptional supernatural powers are cannibals (nos. 2, 18), or eat only tobacco (nos. 18, 19, 20). Similarly, food in the realm of the sacred fades away (no. 25) or is inverted to feces (nos. 12, 15). Thus food is of considerable concern to the Chumash (as would be expected in a hunting and gathering society), and this concern is clearly reflected in the narratives. Feces are symbolically associated with food as well, but the treatment they receive in the narratives indicates a closer identification with the individual personality and hence a higher cognitive than affective content. Thus feces can identify someone (nos. 31, 46, 106), or be animated into a surrogate of that individual (no. 26). In addition, food and feces clearly stand in a relationship of symbolic inversion to one another— the feces of supernatural beings cure (i.e., "feed") a mortal (no. 51), while their food becomes feces or fades away when examined (nos. 12, 15, 25).

The treatment of water in the narratives is an even better example of the dangers of facile labelling. Such concepts as a flood that destroys the world (nos. 5, 18), rejuvenation through submersion (nos. 7, 12, 15, 18), springs or other bodies of water that are focal points for danger (nos. 3, 15, 18, 58, 62, 91, 102) or exits from the realm of the supernatural (no. 51), and water as an antidote for poison (nos. 26, 79), seem at first disconnected elements that clearly reflect the operation of fantasy. But closer examination reveals the existence of certain basic ideas that are logically consistent and congruent with ethnographic data from both California and elsewhere. Water, then, can be said to be (1) a substance by means of which symbolic inversion can be accomplished, and (2) a substance that represents an active interface between the realms of the sacred and the profane. Throughout much of the state, for example, the world is believed to have been created by a drawing forth of matter or substance from the primeval sea through an exercise of supernatural power (i.e., power, through the medium of water, is symbolically transformed into non-power), while individuals seeking supernatural power, such as bear or other shamans, are thought to be able to achieve their ends by plunging into certain springs or lakes (i.e., non-power is symbolically transformed into power). Similarly, supernatural power can be neutralized by water through inversion to non-power, as in the use of water for curing poisoning (nos. 26, 79), or the belief that a deceased shaman's kit can only be safely disposed of in a stream or lake. In addition, through submersion in water age is transformed into youth (nos. 7, 12, 15, 18), and the world itself is rejuvenated (nos. 5, 18). But water is also a particularly labile boundary between the sacred and the profane, and hence bodies of water are peculiarly susceptible to dangerous manifestations of the supernatural (nos. 3, 15, 18, 58, 91, 102). Plunging into water is like passing through a doorway into another world (nos. 26, 27, 86), one can also return from the realm of the sacred in this way (no. 51). In summary, then, it seems that the treatment of water in the stories reflects rather widespread postulates concerning the nature of reality rather than psychological processes involving fantasied "distortions" of that reality.

This conclusion leads inevitably to one of the major hypotheses suggested by the preceding analysis of Chumash oral narratives: that a significant number of myths and tales can be profitably interpreted, at one level of abstraction, as allegorical expressions of shamanic concepts and experiences, many of them having a virtually universal distribution. As Mircea Eliade demonstrates so convincingly in his exhaustive study of the subject (*Shamanism: Archaic Techniques of Ecstasy*), such seeming expressions of fantasy as death and rebirth, ascents to the sky and magical flight, and the recovery of souls after arduous and dangerous ordeals involving combat with supernatural beings, are all clearly part of the shamanic tradition (whose ubiquity and apparent antiquity suggest that *culture-specific* psychologically and sociologically oriented interpretations are probably both futile and specious). While the intimate linkage between myth and ritual has been recognized for many years, anthropological attention has been directed primarily at myth in relationship to sociocentric rather than egocentric ritual, which has resulted in the relative neglect of the mythic and symbolic bases of much shamanic behavior. Recently, however, there has been a resurgence of interest in shamanism as an increasing number of scholars have realized that cavalier dismissals of the shaman as a neurotic or borderline psychotic, whose dreams and fantasies are only amenable to psychoanalytic interpretation, have been seriously in error, and have therefore begun to devote greater time and energy to a study of the subject. Consequently, there has been a growing awareness of the considerable shamanic content present in many myths, rituals and artistic productions from around the world. In fact, the present suggestion that oral narratives are often thinly disguised shamanic allegories is implicit in Eliade's discussion of North American shamanism:

> Here as everywhere else, the shamanic ideology (or, more precisely, that part of the traditional ideology that was assimilated and largely developed by shamans) is also found in myths and legend in which shamans properly speaking do not figure. Such is the case, for example, with what has been called the "North American Orpheus Myth". . . . All the recorded versions of this myth display an amazing similarity. The bridge, the rope on which the hero crosses the infernal river, the kindly person (old woman or old man, Lord of the Underworld), the animal guardian of the bridge, and so on—all the classic motifs of the descent to the underworld are present in nearly all the variants. . . . What is "shamanic" in all these myths is the descent to the underworld to bring back the soul of the beloved woman. For shamans are believed capable not only of bringing back the strayed souls of the sick but also of restoring the dead to life; and they who are thus restored, on their return from the underworld, tell the living what they have seen—exactly like those who have gone down to the land of the dead "in spirit," those who have visited the nether worlds and paradise in ecstasy and have nourished the multimillenary visionary literature of the entire world. It would be going too far to regard such myths as solely creations of shamanic experiences; but it is certain that they use and interpret such experiences (Eliade, 1964:310-313).

The North American Orpheus Myth to which Eliade refers in the passage just cited exists in the present collection of Chumash narratives in two different versions (nos. 25, 59), but shamanic motifs are perhaps even more strikingly evident in such narratives, for example, as nos. 30 and 51, both of which

seem unambiguously to be allegorical expressions par excellence of classic shamanic experiences. The initiatory "death" at
the hands of the older shaman, the ascent of a pole to the sky
world (an ordeal involving conflicts with supernatural beings
and the reduction of the initiate to bare bones), the initiate's
rescue by his sponsor, their ultimate return to earth, and the
new shaman's resurrection of the sponsor—all of these elements in "Coyote and Centipede" are standard and virtually
universal shamanic themes (Eliade, 1964). "The Story of
ʔAxiwalič," with its illness and despair, descent to the underworld, eventual giving of aid by supernaturals who are initially
hostile, and return to earth with restored health, is similarly
clear in symbolic intent. Many of the other narratives also contain obvious shamanic themes, although they are not always as
sharply delineated as in the examples just given. It is also clear
from a comparison of narratives in different sections of the collection that the various magical devices utilized by protagonists were an essential feature of actual shamanic practice.
There is abundant ethnographic confirmation for the shamanic
use of such items as the down-covered string (nos. 15, 30, 80,
86, 87), the flute (nos. 15, 16, 17, 21, 26, 61, 92, 93), the charmstone (nos. 39, 76), drugs (nos. 12, 16, 18, 19, 20, 21, 26, 29, 33,
84, 91, 93, 97, 98), and ʔatišwɨn (nos. 12, 17, 20, 25, 28, 52, 62,
65, 72, 75, 78), while revival of the dead (nos. 15, 16, 17, 18, 20,
26, 29, 30, 52, 75) and ability to travel great distances rapidly
(nos. 19, 20, 30, 32, 67) are again characteristics universally
attributed to shamans. Finally, it might be mentioned in
passing that pole-climbing was an integral element of many of
the rituals associated with the Kuksu cults of central California
(Loeb, 1934a,b), and was also part of the Luiseño *Notush* ceremony (Kroeber, 1953:676).

In conclusion, the hypothesis that many apparently fantastic elements in the narratives are best interpretable as allegorical or symbolic expressions of actual shamanic beliefs and
experiences seems well supported by the evidence, and certainly sheds greater light on important aspects of Chumash
culture than would a strict adherence to psychological
explanations.

John P. Harrington in the field, 1927 (courtesy of Harry Lawton).

Another picture of Harrington (courtesy of Josephine and John Yee).

Fernando Librado (courtesy of Lompoc Valley Historical Society).

(L. to R.) Rafael Solares, María Solares, Jaspar Miranda, Clara Miranda, and Isabel Miranda at Santa Ynez *Circa* 1890 (courtesy of Santa Ynez Valley News).

Louisa Ygnacio (courtesy of Josephine and John Yee).

Lucrecia García (courtesy of Angela and John Yee).

Juan de Jesús Justo (courtesy of Santa Barbara Museum of Natural History).

Part II: *The Narratives*

A.

The Three Worlds

1 THE THREE WORLDS There is this world in which we live, but there is also one above us and one below us. The world below is cʔoyinašup, the other world. That is where the nunašɨš live. This world here is ʔitiašup, and the world above is ʔalapay, although one can also say mišupašup and ʔalapayašup. Here where we live is the center of our world—it is the biggest island. And there are two giant serpents, the maʔaqsiqʔitaʔšup, that hold our world up from below. When they are tired they move, and that causes earthquakes. The world above is sustained by the great Sloʔw, who by stretching his wings causes the phases of the moon. And the water in the springs and streams of this earth is the urine of the many frogs who live in it.

2 THE SKY PEOPLE There is a place in the world above where Sun and Sloʔw, Morning Star and Šnilemun (the Coyote of the Sky—not the Coyote of this world) play peon. There are two sides and two players on each side, and Moon is referee. They play every night for a year, staying up till dawn. The game is played in a special house—not in Sun's house, but in a place where they only play peon. On Christmas eve they make the count of six to see which side has won the game. When Šnilemun's side comes out ahead there is a rainy year. Sun stakes all kinds of harvest products—acorns, deer, islay, chia, ducks, and geese—and when Šnilemun is the winner he cannot wait for the stakes to be distributed, but pulls open the door so that

everything falls down into this world. And we humans are involved in that game, for when Sun wins he receives his pay in human lives. He and Šnilemun then have a dispute, for Šnilemun wants to pay his debt with old people who are no longer of any use. But once in a while Sun wins the argument and a young person may be picked out to die.

Each one of those beings has a task to perform: Sun lights the day, Morning Star the dawn, and Moon the night. Moon is a single woman. She has a house near that of Sun. She and Sun and the others never get older; they are always there. Šnilemun was like God to the old people, María thinks. They had great faith in him. Sun is our uncle, but Šnilemun is our father—that is why he works for us, giving us food and sparing our lives. He watches over us all the time from the sky. Šnilemun has the form of a coyote—a *big* coyote.

And Sloʔw is up there watching the whole world too. He never moves; he is always in the same spot. When he gets tired of sustaining the upper world, he stretches his wings a little, and this causes the phases of the moon. When there is an eclipse of the moon it is because his wings cover it completely. María thinks that Sun and Sloʔw are partners in the peon game, for it was said that both ate people. The place where Sloʔw lives is surrounded by hills and hills of bleached white bones that can be seen from afar. They are the bones of people of this world that Sloʔw has eaten. Sloʔw has neither wife nor family. He is never referred to as a relative, only as wot—he who commands. He is very patient. He is always there in the sky, thinking.

Sun is an *old* man. He is naked, with a cuqeleʔ on his head, and he carries a fire-brand in his hand. The fire-brand is made from the inner bark of a tree that grows only in the sky—not a cottonwood, such as women's aprons were once made from, but a tree in the sky with a similar kind of inner bark. The brand is made from a bundle of that fiber, tightly rolled so that it doesn't burn too quickly. Sun uses his thumbnail as a measure to adjust the height of the fire-brand. In the early morning he carries his firebrand at a certain height, and then lowers it one measure at a time to adjust the heat. On very hot days he lowers it a measure or two more. Sun has three resting places on his trail around the world. At about ten o'clock he reaches the first place and rests there a while. At midday he rests longer. At about three o'clock he reaches his third resting spot, where there is a spring. When he reaches the west he takes his fire-brand and returns home very quickly, going around far to the south.

Sun is a widower. He lives alone with his pets and his two daughters, who have never married. They have aprons made of live rattlesnakes like the haphap's daughters. The snakes have woven their tails together voluntarily at the top of the aprons so that they seem deliberately made that way. Sun's house is very big, and it is full of all kinds of animals—bears, lions, elk, deer, wolves, rattlesnakes, birds—all of them tame. The house is made of xɨlɨw, a kind of crystal that people once used to inlay around the edges of wooden bowls.

When Sun returns home in the evening he takes along whatever people he wants. If they are big he tucks them under his belt, but if they are babies he tucks them under the ciwin on his head. He arrives home in time for supper, and at first when he enters the house there is a dense fog. He throws the adults down in the doorway and then takes the babies from his ciwin and throws them down too. And when the fog clears away, there stands Sun with his firebrand. He and his two daughters just pass the people through the fire two or three times and then eat them half-cooked. And they don't drink water like we do, but blood. Every day Sun carries people from this world off this way—every day.

3 THE NUNAŠɨŠ The nunašɨš are creatures of the other world that come out soon after nightfall and travel all around. The old people used to say that you should bathe early before they return from going around the world, for later the water is steaming because they bathe in it. The haphap is nunašɨš—he has the form of a man, but he is very dangerous and very devilish. When he inhales he draws trees and rocks and everything toward himself and swallows them. Ququ, lewelew, yowoyow, and the manunašɨš paka?s as?ɨl— the lame devil whose leg is broken and who goes hopping around the world—all have human form also. Ququ and lewelew have bodies covered with pus, and their facial skin is loose. The yowoyow is similar. He lives at a certain place down near Ventura, and the people there see his smoke rising some times. And the people around here believe in La Llorona, the

maxulaw or mamismis, that cries up in the trees like a newborn baby. Once a man saw one: it looks like a cat, but with skin like leather or rawhide. When you hear it someone is going to die. It is strange that you don't see La Llorona anymore. And the xolxol are big animals covered with feathers, and the feathers make a noise when they move. The late Rafael wrestled with the lewelew once. He was with his wife at the time. He jumped out of bed suddenly and his wife lit a candle. He was swaying and staggering around the room. He finally fell down exhausted, and his wife asked, "What's wrong with you, are you crazy?" At first he couldn't answer, but he finally got his breath back and said, "What else can you expect, wrestling with the lewelew?" What a thing to happen!

4 THE SEA PEOPLE The ʔelyeʔwun are men. They have no wives or children or anything. When they catch a whale they throw it out of the water. They just toss it—and you know how big a whale is. The ʔelyeʔwun are called swordfish in English. And María has also heard of the siren. In the old days otter hunters used to see her. Once a party of otter hunters was way down by San Diego and saw the siren down there. She has beautiful hair and the body of a woman. She was so hungry that she came close to the boat, and they tossed her a biscuit and she indicated where the otters were.

5 THE FLOOD Maqutikok, Spotted Woodpecker, was the only one saved in the flood. He was Sun's nephew. María doesn't know why the flood came or how it started, but it kept raining and the water kept rising higher and higher until even the mountains were covered. All the people drowned except Maqutikok, who found refuge on top of a tree that was the tallest in the world. The water kept rising until it touched his feet, and the bird cried out, "Help me, Uncle, I am drowning, pity me!" Sun's two daughters heard him and told their father that his kinsman was calling for help. "He is stiff from cold and hunger," they said. Sun held his firebrand down low and the water began to subside. Maqutikok was warmed by the heat. Then Sun tossed him two acorns. They fell in the water near the tree and Maqutikok picked them up and swallowed them. Then Sun threw two more acorns

down and the bird ate them and was content. That is why he likes acorns so much—they are still his food. And after the water was gone only Maqutikok remained. María has seen rocks in the mountains that are the exact shape of human arms and hands: they are the remains of the people who died in the flood. Those first people, the molmoloqʔiku, were very tall. They used to wade across the channel without needing boats, taking chia and acorns and other things to the islanders in carrying nets. The *very* old men told María that people had found bones on Santa Rosa Island and at Mikiw which were human, but which were yards long.

6 **THE MAKING OF MAN** After the flood Šnilemun (the Coyote of the Sky), Sun, Moon, Morning Star, and Sloʔw (the great eagle that knows what is to be) were discussing how they were going to make man, and Sloʔw and Šnilemun kept arguing about whether or not the new people should have hands like Šnilemun. Coyote announced that there would be people in this world and they should all be in his image since he had the finest hands. Lizard was there also, but he just listened night after night and said nothing. At last Šnilemun won the argument, and it was agreed that people were to have hands just like his. The next day they all gathered around a beautiful table-like rock that was there in the sky, a very fine white rock that was perfectly symmetrical and flat on top, and of such fine texture that whatever touched it left an exact impression. Šnilemun was just about to stamp his hand down on the rock when Lizard, who had been standing silently just behind, quickly reached out and pressed a perfect hand-print into the rock himself. Šnilemun was enraged and wanted to kill Lizard, but Lizard ran down into a deep crevice and so escaped. And Sloʔw and Sun approved of Lizard's actions, so what could Šnilemun do? They say that the mark is still impressed on that rock in the sky. If Lizard had not done what he did, we might have hands like a coyote today.

7 **THE ORIGIN OF DEATH** Simplicio heard only that Coyote wanted to make people with hands like his but that Lizard wanted them to look like his hands instead, and Lizard won the argument. And later during the same conference Coyote proposed throwing man

into a lake when he got old and making him young again. But the matavenado said no, the earth will get too full of people and there will be no room to stand. So Coyote lost out in this proposition also. The matavenado is therefore also talked to and killed by the Ventureño, who tell it that it caused death.

8 ELEMENTS The Indians adored three sacred "bodies"—earth, air, and water. The sun was their chief god. They adored the sun. The sun was male and the moon was female. There were men among the old Indians to whom it was a pleasure to listen when they gave their views on this world. They were men of great ideas. They said that this earth was on top of the waters of the ocean, and that there were three elements concerning which we must be cautious— wind, rain, and fire. The rainbow is the shadow of these three elements that compose the world, and therefore it has three colors. The white is wind, the red is fire, and the blue is rain. The wind was sometimes called cenhes heʔišupʔ, "breath of the world." And whenever there was lightning the old men would say, "Now beware, that is an element from the hand of a power that caused us to see this world." An old man told Fernando that thunder was the wind. All the winds get together up above. And sometimes there are whirlwinds so strong that they take the water and convert it into hail.

9 THE SUN Fernando's grandfather told him that we say "the sun is made this way or that," but all we have are our ideas. He said that he and others before him had tried to figure out how the sun was made, but how could they? The sun is the beauty of the world—it is born in the east, giving the world beautiful light. They used to say that they had no idea as to who it was that created the sun. The morning and evening stars were the wives of the sun, for before sunrise the morning star comes first, then the dawn, and then the sun. The sun goes to rest in this hole (of the sand dollar) and leaves its rays outside while it rests inside. The sun was like a man. Whenever the dawn of morning comes be careful not to be misguided, for that is the breath of the sun who is a man. Fernando's grandfather used to tell him and other boys that when they heard a story they should listen carefully to the wording, which was metaphorical and enigmatic, so that they would get

the substance of the story. Dawn is the sigh of the sun. The real name of the sun was kaqunup?mawa. This was its metaphorical name, and really meant "the radiance of the child born on the twenty-fourth of December."

10 THE SOUL

The old men when winnowing chia told Fernando that this world is merely a great flat winnowing tray. Some men move up and some down. And there is much chaff mixed through it all. The dead go west and are born again in this world. It is all a circle, an eddy within the abyss (?alampauwauhani). The Indians did absolutely nothing at the moment of death. They believed that the soul stayed around the old living place for five days after death, and that is why they fed it every night. But the soul of someone who was cremated went west with the flames and did not stay around for five days like the others. The soul of a drowned person always stayed in the sea, wandering, and never reached the land in the west or was born again. The soul of a baby that died before or after birth went west also, but it never reached the place that souls of adults did. They explained that the small surf fish never reached the place that the deep-water fish did. Fernando was told that the soul is eternal. The soul went to the west and at the end of twelve years it would return and live here reincarnated, born again. When Fernando was a boy and went out hunting the Indians used to tell him to be careful about shooting because the time was going to come—to be careful because there would be many young children. Those were pure spirits. They never slept. They were constantly on guard, watching and waiting for the spirits that were coming. Some spirits would go about the world, observing the nature of all others during those twelve years they inhabited another sphere, far in the west, very far from here. People would place food on the grave of a newly-buried person. They would celebrate for five days. They would cook meals early and at about four o'clock in the afternoon they would sit down to mourn and to scatter food. They scattered it with their hands, they scattered it to the four winds. Fernando's grandfather used to say that the "white people are a reincarnation of the souls that had gone west. They had a different color, were reincarnated in a lighter color, and spoke a different language. The color and language of whites and Indians

are different, but the noble principles of the soul are the same.
For this world is a single congregation."

11 REINCARNATION Silverio qonoyo of
Santa Inez, whose ancestors were all from Santa Rosa
Island, once told Fernando the following story. The
old men who understood such things once gathered together
to discuss the nature of he who watches over us: Sun. Sun sees
everything. "And those who die—how do they come to be
born again?" asked one of that assembly. The wise man who
was their leader answered, "They follow the sun. Every day
they enter the portal of the sun. All over the world they die
when the time comes for them to do so. He who dies will
resurrect with the same feelings in his heart, but different in
one respect—color." There was a sand dollar in that place that
was lying mouth down, and the old man showed it to his companions and said, "Look at this—here in the middle" (between
the tip of the middle petal of the flower and the rim). "The sun
rises from the east and goes to the west, and all the spirits follow him. They leave their bodies. The sun reaches the door
and enters, and the souls enter too. When it is time for the sun
to fulfill his duty he emerges, for he lights the abysses with his
eye, and all who are in the dusk resurrect."

12 THE SOUL'S JOURNEY TO
ŠIMILAQŠA Three days after a person has
been buried the soul comes up out of the grave in the
evening. Between the third and fifth day it wanders
about the world visiting the places it used to frequent in life.
On the fifth day after death the soul returns to the grave to
oversee the destruction of its property before leaving for
Šimilaqša. The soul goes first to Point Conception, which is a
wild and stormy place. It was called humqaq, and there was no
village there. In ancient times no one ever went near humqaq.
They only went near there to make sacrifices at a great šawil.
There is a place at humqaq below the cliff that can only be
reached by rope, and there is a pool of water there like a basin,
into which fresh water continually drips. And there in the
stone can be seen the footprints of women and children. There
the spirit of the dead bathes and paints itself. Then it sees a

light to the westward and goes toward it through the air, and thus reaches the land of Šimilaqša.

Sometimes in the evening people at La Quemada (Šišácʔiʔi) village would see a soul passing by on its way to Point Conception. Sometimes these were the souls of people who had died, but sometimes they were souls that had temporarily left the body. The people of La Quemada would motion with their hands at the soul and tell it to return, to go back east, and they would clap their hands. Sometimes the soul would respond and turn back, but other times it would simply swerve a little from its course and continue on to Šimilaqša. When the people of La Quemada saw the soul it shone like a light, and it left a blue trail behind it. The disease from which the person had died was seen as a fiery ball at its side. When the soul turned back, as it sometimes did, anyone at La Quemada who might have recognized it would hurry to the village where the man whose soul it was lived, and if the sick man then drank a lot of toloache he might recover and not die. María heard that a short time after the soul passed La Quemada the people there would hear a report like a distant cannon shot, and know that that was the sound of the closing of the gate of Šimilaqša as the soul entered.

The old people said that there were three lands in the world to the west: wit, ʔayaya, and Šimilaqša. These were somewhat like purgatory, hell, and heaven. When the soul leaves Point Conception and crosses the sea, it first reaches the Land of Widows. When the women there get old their friends dip them in a spring and when they awake they are young again. And they never eat, though they have all kinds of food there. They merely take a handful of food and smell it and throw it away, and as soon as they do so it turns to feces. And when they are thirsty they just smell the water and their thirst is quenched. Once past the Land of Widows the soul comes to a deep ravine through which it must pass. The road is all cut up and consists of deep, fine earth as a result of so many souls passing over it. In the ravine are two huge stones that continually part and clash together, part and clash together, so that any person who got caught between them would be crushed. Any living person who attempted to pass would be killed, but souls pass through unharmed.

Once past the clashing rocks the soul comes to a place

where there are two gigantic qaq perched on each side of the trail, and who each peck out an eye as the soul goes by. But there are many poppies growing there in the ravine and the soul quickly picks two of these and inserts them in each eye-socket and so is able to see again immediately. When the soul finally gets to Šimilaqša it is given eyes made of blue abalone. After leaving the ravine the soul comes to La Tonadora, the woman who stings with her tail. She kills any living person who comes by, but merely annoys the soul who passes safely.

Just beyond this woman lies a body of water that separates this world from the next, with a bridge that the soul must cross to reach Šimilaqša. The souls of murderers and poisoners and other evil people never reach the bridge, but are turned to stone from the neck down. They remain there on the near shore forever, moving their eyes and watching other souls pass. When the pole begins to fall the soul starts quickly across, but when it reaches the middle two huge monsters rise from the water on either side and give a loud cry, attempting to frighten it so that it falls into the water. If the soul belongs to someone who had no ʔatišwɨn or who did not know about the old religion and did not drink toloache—someone who merely lived in ignorance—it falls into the water and the lower part of the body changes to that of a frog, turtle, snake, or fish. The water is full of these beings, who are thus undergoing punishment. When they are hungry they crawl out of the water and wander through the hills nearby looking for cacomites to eat. The old people used to say that someone who drank toloache always passed the pole safely for they were strong of spirit.

Once the soul has crossed the bridge it is safe in Šimilaqša. There are two roads leading from the bridge—one goes straight ahead and the other goes to the left. María knows nothing about souls being born again in this world. Souls live in Šimilaqša forever and never get old. It is packed full of souls. They harvest islay, sweet islay, and there is no end of it. Every kind of food is there in abundance. When children die they take the same route as adults. The qaq peck out their eyes, but they have no other troubles on the journey. They pass the bridge easily, for the monsters that try to frighten other souls do not appear.

13 ASTROLOGY The Ventura Indians did not baptize their children; they were named according to the month in which they were born. ʔAlšuqlaš, "astrologer," was the title of an officer who gave names to children. He was an old man, and he could judge the destiny of the child. He always started his count from the first month, January. The year was divided into twelve lunar months, all of which had names. The month of January was called hesiqʔmomoy momoy, "month of toloache." A man born in January will have a great deal of self-respect. When a man knows how to use virtues properly he succeeds. Toloache has virtues also, but it must be properly used. It has the best qualities of any plant. Hesiqʔmomoy ixša cpuʔun was the name of February, the "month when things begin to grow." The rain, finding a place where the soil is nicely pulverized, brings forth whatever is there. If a person is born in February he is the victim of uncertainty—he is never sure of anything. People born in this month are sometimes unreliable. He is brave when he sees the other person humble, and he is very meek when he encounters sternness. And when he finds that all is going his way he watches over opening plants waiting for a chance to take them for himself. March was called hesiqʔmomoy sqapuni, the "month of spring." Spring leaves do not all come out equally strong, and the same is true of people born in this month. Some of them might be strong and healthy, but many are sickly. Very seldom is there a person born in this month who is happy. He may be happy for a while, but sadness soon overtakes him. The name of April was hesiqʔmomoy ʔan capipquees, "month when flowers are already in bloom." A person born in this month is cheerful and works for the community. He is pleasant to the world, for the flower season is pleasant. May was called hesiqʔmomoy ʔan maišaxuc̓, "month when carrizo is abundant." A person born in May is knowledgeable in fundamental things for the good of man, such as medicine. June was named hesiqʔmomoy ʔan spʔatata, "month when things are divided in half," because it is time to go out in different directions, although they are eventually reunited. A person born in June is said to be sensitive, serious, careful, and held in esteem by other people.

July was called hesiqʔmomoy ʔan ciwolhoyoyo, "month when everything blows away." All the plants with leaves commence to shed them at this time, and the wind blows away those that have not been shed. The man born in this month is never at peace—he is always stirring things up. August is named hesiqʔmomoy ʔan smaxaʔtam, the "month of fiesta." A man born in this month will stand in the middle of a festive gathering and take everything he can that properly belongs to him and take it home. And he is very saving, too. He is good to his neighbors. September is called hisiqʔmomoy ʔan ciyam loqayiʔalaxsɨw, "month when those that are dry come down." All creatures who fear cold and water must come down to a warmer place, for they have already stored what they need for the year. A man born in this month is careful and watchful of dangers. The month of October was called hesiqʔmomoy quwue sulupiauset, the "month of sulupiauset." All canoemen were ordered not to go out at this time. Sulupiauset was the great-grandfather of Fernando's uncle. When the first canoe was made, he was the first to enter it. There had been canoes before, but the ends had been round. He was the first to make one with ends such as they have now, and with rods for the inside of the ribs. He taught people the use of the canoe, how to sail out to sea and when. A man born in October would be very rich in beads, and he would make beads much as a silversmith does now. He will always be roaming from place to place, but the world will protect him. The month of November was called hesiqʔmomoy ʔan tuhui pimaam, "month when rain keeps one indoors." A man born in this month is never satisfied. December is named hesiqʔmomoy ʔan hushununa qa qunupʔmawa, "month when the sun's brilliance begins." A man born in this month is like a baby in an ecstatic condition, but he leaves this condition. When a man reaches a certain age he comes out of his lethargy and enters the action of life. The sun gives strength to man to comprehend that man also is a god in the world. For what would this world be without man? The sun comes out of his lethargy too.

14 ANIMALS

Fernando's grandfather told him that all animals are related. The horned toad is wot of all beasts, the swordfish of all fish, and the sloʔw of all birds. The bear is the older sibling of all the animals. The

eagle, condor, and buzzard are said to remove the foulness of
the world. I told Fernando of the San Gabriel belief that the
condor rips up carcasses for the buzzard—that they are first
cousins. Fernando replied that an old man told him that we are
all brothers, and our mother is one: this mother earth. He has
always believed what the old people told him when he was a
boy—that the world is God.

B.

Old Woman Momoy

15 SIXʔUSUS AND SUMIWOWO (I)

Momoy was a very rich woman, a widow, and she had a daughter of whom she was very fond. The daughter used to go to the river to bathe every morning before sunrise, and Momoy warned her not to stay by the water too long. But one time the girl stayed there for a long time looking into the pool. Suddenly she saw a figure reflected on the surface of the water and when she turned around she saw a young man standing there. He was really a bear transformed into a young man. He was tall, with big arms. She began to think about what her mother had said—that something might happen to her if she stayed by the water too long. Finally the man came and had intercourse with her there. The old woman was worried and waited for the girl all day. The girl finally came home late in the afternoon, very sad. When it got dusk the bear came to the house, this time in animal rather than in human form. The next morning the girl went to bathe again, and the bear killed and chewed her to pieces. Some of her blood fell on a sycamore tree nearby.

Later that day Momoy came looking for her daughter, but all she found were some bones and a little blood. She took some of the blood home and put it in a wooden bowl and added some water. She had medicine for reviving the dead, and she added this medicine to the contents of the bowl and then covered everything with a basket. After a while she heard a little noise coming from the bowl, and when she looked in it she found a little girl lying there. It was her granddaughter.

She took the child out and washed it and then wrapped it in a wildcat skin. She painted it (they used to paint the body in those days). She brought the little girl up, and she became a beautiful woman just as her mother had been. The granddaughter began to go and bathe in the river, and Momoy warned her not to stay too long by the water. But one day she stayed too long and saw a shadow fall on the water. When she turned around she saw Thunder standing there with a cuqele? on his head, dressed in all the fine clothing of old, and holding a tokoy in his hand (it is with that that he makes the thunder). The girl bowed her head as soon as she saw him, but he told her not to be afraid, that he would not harm her. When she raised her head again she was already in the sky. She began to cry, and Thunder said, "Don't cry. Here you have everything. This house and everything in it are yours. This is not a bad thing that is happening to you. When you want to see your grandmother Momoy just look down into the world below."

Thunder had a brother, Fog, who lived there with him. That night the two brothers made a bed for the girl, and in the morning they got up and fixed breakfast for her. They told her that they had to leave to go around the world each day, but that she was to remain at home until they returned in the evening. On the first day, when the brothers were half of the way around the world, Fog said that he had forgotten his belt and had to return for it, but that was just an excuse to go back and kiss his sister-in-law who was such a beautiful girl. Old Thunder knew what was going on but he didn't say anything. So Fog hurried back to the house and kissed his sister-in-law, and then caught up with Thunder again. And the two proceeded on together on their journey around the world. But this same thing happened every day—Fog would forget his belt and have to return for it—and eventually the girl became pregnant. When the time came for her to give birth, it began to thunder in her belly more and more, until at last the child was born. Thunder took the baby and wrapped it up. Then there came a fog so thick that one could not see, and Fog was afraid that the second child would look just like him, and sure enough it did. Fog himself went and wrapped the child up, for it was his. The next day the two went around the world again and left the woman with their two children. Fog did not forget his belt this time. He went with his brother properly. The two

children began to grow up. One was a little thunder and the
other a little fog. And Old Thunder and Old Fog made their
daily trips around the world as they had always done.

One morning little Thunder (whose name was Six?usus)
and little Fog (whose name was Sumiwowo) were talking, and
Six?usus (who was the older of the two) said, "I wonder where
the old ones go? They start out early and return late. Let's you
and I go traveling too!" After breakfast the brothers started off.
Six?usus said, "Follow me." When they had gone some distance he said, "Stop." He shaped sand in the form of the
boards of a canoe, with milkweed fiber and all, and then
recited an incantation and turned it into a real canoe. Sumiwowo just watched. His brother said, "Leave it now until
tomorrow morning." The next morning after breakfast Six-
?usus said, "Now let's start." He took his flute and they went to
where they had made the canoe. "Get in," said Six?usus to his
younger brother. He took the paddle and they traveled until
they reached syuxtun, where they tied the canoe up and rested
for a while. Then Six?usus said, "Little brother, now we have
rested. Now let's get in the canoe and travel and see the world.
We shall go the same as Old Thunder and Old Fog, only they
travel above and we travel here in this world."

Now the two boys knew they had an aunt living at a place
called seneq in the mountains west of Santa Barbara, and they
decided to visit her first. When they were halfway up the grade
there came a hot wind. Sumiwowo asked, "What is this?" His
brother replied, "Keep quiet, something is going to happen.
Hold on to my belt and don't let go!" They saw a woman
approaching them who had locks of hair hanging down in
such a way as to cover her eyes. She was carrying a tray under
her right arm and she had little bells hanging all over her that
jingled as she walked. When she saw the boys she rolled the
batea on the ground toward them, and it came rolling like fire
and was going to burn them up. Six?usus took his flute and
stuck it in the ground and then gave a spring with the flute still
in his hand, and the two brothers came down on the far side of
a broad canyon. Momoy's brother Woy happened to see all
this, and he called out to Old Thunder and Old Fog, saying
that the boys were in danger there at seneq mountain. Then
how it thundered! It seemed the world was about to end. The
boys reached their aunt's house, which was in a gigantic

mescal bush, and she opened the door and let them in so that they were safe. And Old Thunder shot a lightning bolt and killed the old woman, who was called ʔašiqutč, La Quemadora.

The boys stayed with their aunt for five days, resting, and then they bade her goodbye and started off again. "Whenever anything threatens you, think of me and come back here," she told them. When the boys left they headed north. They had gone a little way when Sumiwowo said, "There is an old man coming." "Keep quiet," said his brother. The old man had a sinew-backed bow and two arrows, and his quiver was all tattered to pieces. He approached the boys with drawn bow, but lowered it when he saw who they were. It was Coyote, xuxaw, the Coyote of this world (for Šnilemun never descends into this world—he is another Coyote, the Coyote of the Sky). "Grandsons, I know what has befallen you," said Coyote. "Why didn't you ask me for aid? I am going to accompany you now so that nothing will happen to you even if I should die. I am a man!" And Sumiwowo laughed, for he wondered what this funny old man could do. Coyote turned and said to him, "Be silent, say nothing, I will tell you everything that is going to happen." Then he stood up and asked, "My grandsons, in which direction are you going?" Sixʔusus answered, saying, "We have started out to travel all around the world." "Don't worry," said Coyote. "I know every place in this world, if you're going to travel around it."

They went along together for a while, and then Coyote stopped and said, "Boys, stop for a minute. There is an old witch woman here on this trail. But don't be afraid, just follow me." They went a little distance farther and heard the old woman pounding in a mortar, pounding, pounding. Coyote passed by without stopping, but he had his bow drawn. Sixʔusus passed also, but as Sumiwowo went by he noticed that there were piles of ground chia by the mortar. He stole a handful and ate it, and then he stole a second handful. The old witch-woman was blind, but noticing that the quantity of ground chia was diminishing, she suddenly grabbed Sumiwowo by the wrist as he put his hand into the mortar and said, "Tell me who you are!" The boy was ashamed to tell her that he was the son of Fog and Momoy's granddaughter and so he remained silent. "Tell me who you are or I won't let go!" she said. Coyote noticed that the old woman had Sumiwowo by

the wrist, and he said to Six?usus, "It will be a long time before
the old woman will let him go." After the old woman had held
Sumiwowo by the wrist for a long time and only the sinews of
his wrist remained, Coyote came and kicked her in the ribs and
shot her with an arrow so that she fell dead. Coyote stroked
Sumiwowo's wrist and healed it. "Be cautious, and as long as
you travel with me and mind me, nothing will happen to you,"
he told the boys.

Coyote and the two boys traveled on for a while, and they
came at last to the cave that opens and shuts at five-year inter-
vals. Lots of people lived in the cave—it was like a village—
and it was hung with all kinds of regalia such as rattles, head-
dresses, and so forth. The cave was open when they approached, and Coyote said, "That's my home! And that's my
rattle hanging there!" Coyote entered the cave but the boys
stayed outside. He approached the rattle slowly and put out
his hand very gradually so that the rattle would make no noise.
But when he touched it it made a sound and the cave shut with
Coyote inside. The boys heard his cries get fainter and fainter
as his strength gave out until finally they ceased. At last Sumiwowo said, "We might as well go, for we won't see him
anymore." But Six?usus replied, "No, let's wait for a while
longer." At last the cave opened and the paxa of that place
threw Coyote out, dead and stinking. "Let's go. See, he's dead
and stinking," said Sumiwowo. "No," said Six?usus. "But
he's wormy! Don't you smell him?" Sumiwowo replied. Six-
?usus pulled out his flute and began to play it, and as he
played Coyote began to move his thumb back and forth. Then
he suddenly jumped up alive and said, "I was sleeping!"
(Coyote never would admit that he was dead—he was just
"asleep").

They traveled on until at last Coyote said, "There is something here more dangerous than anything we have met. You
must do everything I tell you and you'll come through all
right." They descended a very steep mountain. "At the base of
that mountain is the house of the haphap," said Coyote. "You
two wish to travel and see the world. I can't stop at that house
but you can. I am too old and have seen everything. That man
has two daughters, and he is a great assassin. You must be
very careful." Coyote had a takulšoxšinaš, a downy string, in
his belt and he gave it to the boys, saying, "In case there is any

danger throw this string in my direction and all will be well."
He also gave Six?usus a powder and told him to put the powder in the fire so that the haphap would fall asleep and allow
the boys to escape. And Coyote said that when the haphap
came home he would cover the house tightly with skins so that
the boys couldn't get away, but that Six?usus should erect his
flute and say, "hoyo por hoyo, hoyo por hoyo," and all the
skins would fall.

When the boys reached the house the haphap's daughters
received them well. But the girls were wearing aprons of rattlesnakes with their heads hanging down so that the boys were
afraid to get near them. Then the girls put on otter-skin
aprons. They told the boys not to be afraid when the old man
arrived because they would protect them. They said that when
he came rocks would hurl in their faces, but they were to get
behind the girls and they would be protected from injury. In a
little while they heard what sounded like a storm coming—
rocks, wind, trees, and dirt were flying, and each boy got
behind a girl. When the storm subsided the boys saw the
haphap seated there with his face buried in his folded arms.
One of the girls told the old man that they had visitors, and he
said, "Good, treat them well!" But he said that to throw them
off guard so that he could devour them that night. The old man
said each girl could take a boy and lie down with him, and he
hurried to prepare accommodations for them. They went to
bed, and Sumiwowo stayed close to Six?usus. Six?usus looked
around carefully and noticed two big logs in a corner. The boys
began to snore and pretended to be asleep, although they were
wide awake. Coyote had told them to go to bed with their arms
folded so that they wouldn't touch the girls, for if they did
something would go wrong. As soon as the haphap thought
the boys were asleep he got up and went outside and placed
chunks of wood and rocks all around the house. He then put
skins over the smokehole. But Six?usus erected his flute and
said, "hoyo por hoyo" five or six times, and the skins fell
down. He then put some powder on a log in the fire and lay
down again.

When the old man came back in he poked the fire, and
pretty soon he said he felt sleepy and thought he would lie
down and watch the boys from there, and then he went right
to sleep. "He is fast asleep," Six?usus told his brother. He took

a log and placed it next to one girl, and then got the other log and put it in his brother's place. Then they climbed out through the smokehole. About midnight the haphap woke up and said to himself, "It's getting late. It's about time they were in my stomach!" He took a deep breath and inhaled one of his daughters and the log beside her, and then inhaled again and swallowed the other daughter and the log beside her. But then he looked around and saw no daughters, logs or boys, and he realized he'd been deceived. He told himself that he should have devoured the boys when they first arrived. He went outside, furious, and at each inhalation he swallowed rocks, logs, and trees. He even swallowed part of the house. Then he said to himself, "The boys must be in that direction." He followed them.

Six?usus said to Sumiwowo, "Don't let go of my belt, for if you do we are lost. Let us go as fast as we can." They hurried straight toward where Coyote was waiting. The haphap followed, inhaling, and at every inhalation the boys were sucked nearer. At the third inhalation Six?usus said, "Hold tight, little brother, we are in danger!" The haphap inhaled again, but Six?usus placed his flute crosswise in haphap's mouth and one boy sat on each end. Coyote was aware of what was happening, and he shouted out, "Come in this direction and throw one end of the string to me!" Six?usus threw one end of the string to Coyote, and they started toward him. Every time the haphap would be about to swallow them they would place the flute across his mouth and sit on it. Then Coyote shouted, "Remember the tree!" Now there was a very thorny tree there—in all the world there was no tree like that one. The boys pulled the tree out of the ground and when the haphap inhaled the next time Six?usus threw it right into his mouth and the haphap swallowed it. The thorns stuck clear through him and he died.

The boys and Coyote proceeded on their way and finally arrived at Coyote's house where they rested for a while. Then they started out again, and in a little while Coyote told them, "Now, my children, here is another danger. We shall meet an old woman who will try to make you believe that you are her nephews, that your father is her brother. She has a basket of hot tar, and when she catches someone she puts him in it and burns him to death." It happened just as Coyote had foretold.

The old woman came along and tried to grab the boys. She had her back open between the shoulder-blades and her heart was visible. Coyote reached in and pinched her heart and the old woman fell dead. There is a lot of tar over there in the Tulare country still, over towards the valley, where the old woman, Pohono, died.

After much traveling the three reached the top of a mountain where they found lots of women. Coyote said, "These are all widows, and they never die. Don't eat anything you see." They were getting close to Šimilaqša now. Coyote went on ahead and paid no attention to the women, who came out crying, "Do not pass through, there are no people living beyond." Now Sumiwowo was always a little mischievous, and he saw some fish and acorn mush and other food lying there and he started to pick it up and eat it, but Coyote said, "Don't eat it, it's feces!" Sumiwowo threw the food away and smelled his hand, and it was true. Then he washed his hands, and they brought them some good roast fish and acorn mush, which the three travelers ate. The women in that place never get old, for when they start to age they dip themselves in a shallow spring and they are young again. And when they eat they just smell the food and they are nourished.

After Coyote and the brothers had eaten there at the place of the widows they went on. After they had gone a short distance Coyote told them that there was trouble ahead. "We are going to arrive at a place where we'll meet malaxšišiniš, she who thunders. She is a tall woman, white, with a long tail. While she is talking with you she'll sting you with the end of her tail, which is very poisonous." In a little while they reached the place where the woman was, and she clapped her hands and told them to come in, that there was plenty of good food and fine clothing for them there. Coyote and Sumiwowo kept their distance, but Sixʔusus was confident that he could handle the situation and he approached her. She came out and tried to shake his hand. As she got close Sixʔusus was ready for her. He had a fine arrow-straightener in the suqele on his head, and as her tail made a dive for him he shoved the stone into the open mouth at the end of the tail and broke the teeth off. The woman gasped, "You have hurt me sorely!" And she fell dead.

The three travelers went on and were soon in Šimilaqša.

The chief of Šimilaqša was Šaq (Turtle). He was still a man
then and a great runner. Coyote challenged Šaq to a race
around the world. Šaq wanted to run the race right away, but
Coyote wanted to wait until the following day. That night the
three made camp some distance away from everyone, and
Coyote told the two boys what should be done. He said that
his grandson Six?usus was to run·the race with Šaq and that he
was going to be the referee himself. Šaq had not wanted
Coyote to be referee at first because he was too tricky, but Šaq
had at last consented because he was so confident of winning
the race anyway. Each of the two racers was to have a separate
track—that was the way they used to run races in the old days.
Coyote told Six?usus, "Šaq can beat you, yet through my
power you will win. Don't be afraid." Coyote asked the
gophers to aid him. Their captain came and Coyote told him,
"These are my grandsons. They are from a good family. I want
you to work underground tonight beneath Šaq's trail, for I
have pity for my grandsons and do not want Šaq to win over
them." So the gophers hollowed out the ground under the trail
Šaq was to follow the next morning, and that night Coyote laid
a string all the way around the world. In the morning they got
ready for the race. Coyote said, "It's time," and Šaq answered,
"Very well." Then Coyote said to Šaq, "If we win, your neck
will pay the penalty and if you win my grandsons will be the
ones to suffer. Here there will be no money compensation and
no small business. Life itself will be the penalty for losing."

Then the race began, and first one and then the other was
leading. But then Coyote began to help Six?usus. He inhaled
deeply and pulled Six?usus towards him quickly—but it
wasn't really Six?usus that Šaq was racing, just a counterfeit of
him. Coyote had hidden the real Six?usus, who appeared at
the end of the race just in time to win. Šaq wanted to pay a
fine—he got a lot of ?ik?imɨš, qilmoy, and ?apɨ and offered it all
to Coyote—but Coyote insisted on the death penalty. They had
already decided how they were going to do it. They put Šaq on
top of a big pile of wood and tied him down, and then started
the wood burning. But Šaq urinated and extinguished the fire.
They got together a new pile of wood and tied Šaq to it, but
again he urinated and put it out. But the third time they started
a fire under Šaq he couldn't urinate, and so he died.

16 SIX?USUS AND SUMIWOWO (II)

There were two brothers, Six?usus and Sumiwowo, and Six?usus was the older of the two. Their father was Thunder and their mother was Fog. They had a sister, ?anix?ex?ehe?e, who was married to the Hap, and one day Six?usus said, "Let us go and see our sister—she is married to the Hap." The two boys traveled to the house of the Hap, and when their sister saw them she began to cry. "Why does sister cry?" asked Sumiwowo. His brother said, "Because the Hap is going to try to kill us!" The Hap was out catching deer for dinner when they arrived, so they sat down and waited for him to come home. The Hap arrived home that evening and said, "My brothers-in-law have come to visit!" He bathed the two boys (so that they would be clean to eat) and then went to sleep with an arm around each boy, telling them that he wanted to keep them warm (but he really wanted to make sure that they didn't escape). He also put a number of deer hides over the smoke-hole on the pretext of keeping the house warm, but Six?usus bewitched them as he did so and the arrow-holes were on top of one another. Six?usus then gave his sister some pespibata to give to the Hap in order to make him sleep soundly.

As soon as her husband was asleep the girl put rocks in the boys' places and helped them escape. When the Hap woke up he began to eat the rocks, and when he discovered the deception he was so angry that he kicked his wife. "Why didn't you tell me?" he demanded. He grabbed the buckskins and told her that he was going to give them to the boys as a present. The Hap yelled to the boys, "Stop! Take these hides with you!" Sumiwowo said, "Listen, the Hap says he is going to give us those buckskins." His brother replied, "Hurry! The Hap is a liar!" The Hap was sucking in air, and the boys were being drawn closer and closer in spite of all their running. Their aunt, Woy (a type of hawk), saw their predicament and told Thunder, "Look, the Hap is about to catch your children!" Thunder came quickly, and as the Hap sucked in again Thunder filled him full of water. But the Hap kept on inhaling. Then Thunder kicked the Hap, but he still didn't die. Finally, Thunder filled the Hap's mouth with sharp pieces of flint, and

this killed the Hap at last. The place where the Hap was killed
is in Laurel Canyon. There are lots of big, cracked rocks there.

After the Hap's death the two brothers traveled all around
the world. The older brother wore sandals and the younger
brother went barefoot: that is the origin of shoes. There is a
place in the Tulare country where Six?usus's tracks can be seen
still. The boys killed two other creatures as well—the yowoyow
and xolxol. The yowoyow was a great singer, and he would
travel around the world singing the following song:

> yowoyow he
> sipyototon
> heq?eleq?
> yowoyow
>
> yowoyow
> my carrying-basket is boiling
> yowoyow

He had a basket on his back into which he would throw
people, both children and adults. Sumiwowo heard the yowoyow singing this song and said to his brother, "Didn't you tell
me there were no people around here? I hear someone singing!" Six?usus answered, "He is not a human being, he is an
animal. He will try to eat us, but let's go and see him." They
went on to where the yowoyow was, and when he saw them
he began to chase them. They ran as fast as they could, but he
caught them. But when the yowoyow threw them into his
basket of boiling tar, Six?usus put his flute across the mouth of
the basket and the two boys sat on it. Then Six?usus took out
his firesticks and began to sing:

> weletepet?
> weletepet?
> qwilimiye
>
> fire-sticks
> fire-sticks
> I am making fire

Pretty soon the tar caught fire. The two boys waited until it
was burning furiously, and then they jumped off and ran. The
yowoyow burned up and turned to stone. You can still see the
tar on the ground where this happened, over in the Tulare
country.

The brothers kept traveling, and pretty soon they met the xolxol who was out hunting game. This was in open country, and the xolxol bewitched the boys and killed them and took them home with him to eat. Their grandfather, Coyote, missed them. He cried, thinking that they were dead. He went to look for them and pretty soon he came in sight of the xolxol's house. The xolxol was just coming home, and when he saw Coyote coming he tried to reach his house first, but Coyote got there ahead of him. As the xolxol approached he tried to bewitch Coyote, for he was a very good sorcerer, but Coyote was better. As soon as xolxol finished his attempts to bewitch him, Coyote said, "Now it is my turn—I will bewitch you!" He began to bewitch the xolxol, and at last the xolxol fell dead. No one excelled Coyote. Coyote thought that he would take the xolxol's feathers and sell them to the captain, Slo?w, but he found the xolxol's body so heavy that he couldn't lift it, so he had to leave the feathers behind. He then went up to the xolxol's house, which he found to be a big iron house without a door. He said, "I don't see any doors. The four corners must be doors." He bewitched the house and made the four corners doors. He then peeked in and saw that the xolxol had killed and eaten his grandsons and filled their skins with sand, and that the two stuffed skins were standing in opposite corners of the house. Coyote used his sorcery and revived the two boys. Six?usus said, "My poor grandfather—he knew that we were dead and he saved us!" The boys were very grateful that Coyote had rescued them. Coyote noticed that there were many other dead people there in the house, and he revived them all. They all went home, and Coyote took his grandsons home with him to recuperate. They had many more adventures, but Luisa can't remember any more of the story. But Sumiwowo was very mischievous and kept getting killed—he didn't believe everything his brother told him and so he got into trouble.

17 SIX?USUS AND SUMIWOWO (III)

There were two brothers who lived with Momoy, but Luisa can't remember their names or how the story started. These boys were big—Momoy didn't raise them from infancy as she did the Tupnekč—but the younger brother was very mischievous. The older brother shot game and the younger brother

carried it home, and they took everything they killed to Momoy. That was how they passed their time. One day Momoy
said, "Don't go very far away—only as far as that hill over
there." But the younger brother said to the older, "Why don't
we hunt in that far canyon? There are lots of deer there."
"Well, grandmother said not to go that far," replied the older
boy. "No, we'll go there tomorrow," said the younger brother.
"Don't let the old woman know. Let's just go!" So the next day
they left the house and went to the canyon, and the older
brother killed a deer. Now Momoy kept a close watch on them,
and she saw where they went. When they returned carrying
the deer she said, "Ah, you went too far away this time!" They
didn't say a word. The following day Momoy said, "Don't go
in that canyon again—there is an ʔɨhɨy there that will kill you if
you do!" The younger brother said, "What can he do to me? I
can run and dodge, and if he shoots an arrow at me I'll dodge
it!" Momoy replied, "You're wrong. You have no sense. Look,
I'm going to tell you just what he's like. He's a kinsman, and
he's going to kill you!" "No, he won't get me, he won't get
me!" exclaimed the boy. "His name is Monsow, weasel,"
Momoy continued. The younger brother began to laugh, and
said, "The monsow is tiny. What can he do to me?" She said,
"He'll get you—he'll get you today!" The boy laughed and
replied, "How can he? He's tiny. If I watch out carefully, how
can he get me?"

The two brothers left to go hunting and they entered the
canyon that Momoy had warned them about. They became
separated, and the younger boy decided to look for Monsow.
But he didn't see him anywhere, and he thought to himself,
"My grandmother was lying—there isn't any Monsow, there
isn't anything!" After a while he came to a cave that was nice
and clean inside. It was the Monsow's door. The boy decided
to defecate there in the cave, so he removed his loincloth and
squatted down. The Monsow came then and attacked him
from behind and sucked his blood, and the boy died.

In the meantime his older brother had begun to look for
him, but he couldn't find him anywhere. "Where can he be?
Has he gone on home?" he wondered. After he had looked all
over, he returned and told Momoy, "My brother is lost and I'm
looking for him." She said, "Well, the Monsow has gotten him
and killed him for sure. What you must do is this: Go to your

kinsman's cave and enter it, for he is away hunting now. Take this piece of tule as your weapon, for if you cut the Monsow with a knife he won't die. There is an old woman sitting right in the door of the cave with a knife projecting from each knee—that is the Monsow's weapon. When you enter the cave you will see the Monsow's grandmother sitting there, but don't be afraid. Give her a kick and the knives will drop. Then rub each one with the medicine and replace them, and enter without fear. The Monsow will fight with you, but don't hit him. Just ward off the blows, for the knives are treated, and remove them. Your brother is standing there in a corner, but he is dead. When all the knives are broken, say 'now it's my turn,' and hold the tule stretched between your hands in front of you like this. It will cut him, for he will no longer have his weapons. And cut the old woman with the same tule so that this won't happen again!''

Momoy then told the boy where the Monsow's cave was located, and he left with the reed and the medicine she had given him. He arrived at the cave and entered. The doorway was like a cave, but farther in it was like a road. He saw the old woman sitting there, and he asked, "Where is my brother?" She didn't say a word, and he said, "I'm talking to you, why don't you answer?" Again she didn't answer. He gave her a kick and the two knives on her knees fell off. He put some of the medicine he had brought on each one and inserted them back where they had been. Then he ventured farther into the cave, while the old woman just sat there without a word. He found his brother at last, standing lifeless in a corner, but just then the Monsow arrived home from hunting. He saw the older brother's tracks on the ground and said, "Someone's in my house!" He entered and spoke to the boy, saying, "What are you doing here?" "I'm looking for my brother," the boy replied. The Monsow said, "I'll give you your brother right now!" He went and seized one of the knives that he had hanging on the wall and began to attack the boy, trying to stab him with it, but the boy warded off the blows with his arm and the knife broke. It surely wasn't made of very good steel, for it broke into bits. The Monsow seized a second knife, but it also broke, as did a third and fourth knife. Then the Monsow went to the old woman and gave her a kick and the knives fell from her knees. He picked one up and returned to the attack, but again the knife broke. "Something is wrong—the tip is bad," he said to himself. He grabbed the second knife and tried to stab the boy again, but it also broke. Then the boy took the piece of tule from his belt and said, "All right, uncle, now it's my turn!" The Monsow looked at the tule and laughed. He said, "What can he do to me with that?" The boy stretched the tule between his hands and shoved the sharp edge into the Monsow's mouth and began to saw back and forth with it. The sharp edge of the tule cut right through the Monsow's head. The boy then made another cut farther down, and when he was all through he had cut the Monsow into three separate pieces. Then he cut the old woman into three pieces too, and left the two of them lying there dead. He put his brother on his back and carried him home. Momoy began at once to cure him. She put some kind of medicine on him and revived him.

When the boy had fully recovered, Momoy said, "Don't go out hunting tomorrow or the day after. Let a few days go by." But the younger boy was impatient, and he said, "Brother, let's go hunting again." The older brother liked to hunt and shoot, and so he said, "All right, but don't do what you did last time. Stay with me." They went out hunting and came back with three deer. "Ah, you went very far away, grandsons!" exclaimed Momoy, but they didn't say a word. She began to butcher the deer, although neither she nor they ate anything but pespibata. The youngest boy said, "Tomorrow we'll go to the crest of the hills." His brother answered, "All right, but don't do what you did last time. Stay close to me." The next day they went out, but they didn't find anything, and when they returned Momoy again said, "Grandsons, don't go so far." But the younger boy said, "Brother, tomorrow let's go to the other side of the hills." His brother replied, "No, grandmother told us not to go very far away." "What does grandmother know?" asked the younger boy. The next morning they went out hunting again, and they brought two deer home with them that evening. Momoy warned them once more not to go so far away from home, but the younger boy replied, "Grandmother, we are going to the other side of the hills tomorrow." "You want to leave me already!" she exclaimed, but he said, "No, we'll return. We just want to go over the hills to see what's there." He kept urging his brother to go, saying, "Let's go—I don't think there is any danger—let's go!"

The older brother finally agreed, and so the next morning they started of. They crossed the hills and descended into the valley, but they found no deer or anything, for there were many hunters over there. They came home empty-handed that night. They entered the house and the older brother began playing his flute while the younger brother chatted with Momoy. (The older brother had a flute that he liked to play, which he carried tucked into his belt. He would be walking along, and suddenly he would pull it out and begin playing it.) The younger boy said, "Look, we went across the mountains to the other side and there wasn't anything there—nothing and no one." She answered, "Yes, there are many people over there." "What are people?" he asked. "Well, they're like us," she said. He replied, "Well, I'd like to see other people." She said, "You would see many things, but then you wouldn't return here again. It would be very simple for them to seize you and then you would not see your grandmother again." "But I want to see those people," he said. "And tomorrow we're going to go!" The next morning he said, "Brother, let's go a little farther today than we did yesterday." "No," replied the older boy. "Why not?" "Well, didn't grandmother tell us not to go very far, to stay near here?" "Oh, what does grandmother know about what we'll see over there? She doesn't know, she lives *here!*"

The next morning they asked Momoy for permission to go farther than before, and she replied, "You are leaving already. This will be the last time I'll see you!" But Momoy was very wise and knew many things. She took the older brother to one side and said, "Pox (agave) is your aunt. When you are in trouble call her and she'll help you. Your brother has no sense!" Then the younger brother asked, "Grandmother, why don't you give me a sinew-backed bow too?" She gave him a bow, and they started off. They walked for a while, but all they saw was a small lizard pushing itself up and down on its legs. The younger boy stopped to watch it awhile, but the older boy walked on. Finally the younger boy began to poke the lizard's tail with an arrow, and the tail fell off and began to jump. The boy laughed, and his brother calld him, saying, "Come on, don't pay any attention to that." A little farther on they came across a big lizard that was doing the same thing the other had done, and they both stopped to watch it for a while. The younger boy got out an arrow with which to shoot the lizard, but his brother grabbed him and pulled him away. "Let's go on!" said the older boy. He was angry with his brother and didn't know whether to leave him or not. They finally returned home and told Momoy, "We went farther today, and tomorrow we'll go farther yet." Then the younger boy added, "And you should have seen what I saw!" "I know what you saw, and what it was doing," replied Momoy. "It didn't do anything but push dirt out from under itself with its stomach," said the boy. "It is nunašiš," she told him. "Not very nunašiš—I broke his tail with an arrow!" Momoy replied, "Good, good— and what else did you see?" "I saw a bigger one, only instead of blue and green stripes like the first, it was yellowish and had a very long tail," he answered. "Well, that is the pocoyi. It is very nunašiš," said the old woman. "I was going to shoot it with an arrow but my brother grabbed me and carried me away," said the younger boy.

The next day the two brothers started off again, and this time they went much farther than they had gone before. They walked along, and the older boy played his flute while his brother brought up the rear. The younger brother encountered a little boy playing with a bow and arrow. He would shoot the arrow and when it hit the ground the grass would begin to burn at that spot. The younger brother watched this for a while and then thought to himself, "Let's see if my arrow can start fires too!" He shot an arrow but nothing happened, and he said to himself, "I'll take his arrow away from him!" The next time the little boy shot his arrow the brother ran and picked it up. "Friend, give me my arrow," said the little boy. "I won't give you anything!" replied the brother. He took the arrow and shot it some distance away. The little boy ran and got it but the other boy took it away from him again. "Come on, friend, give me my arrow," pleaded the little boy. "I won't give you anything," replied the brother. "I'm going with my brother now!" The older brother had been watching to see what the younger brother would do, and when he came up to him he said, "Give the little boy his arrow." "No, I'm not going to give him anything!" exclaimed the younger boy.

Just then the little boy grabbed his bow and quiver and came running towards them. "Take this and this and this!" he shouted, and he shot several arrows at them. He wasn't trying to hit them, he was only forcing them towards the fire he had started with his arrow. The older brother didn't say a word to the younger boy. He was furious with him. "Now we're going to be burned up because of this!" he thought to himself. The younger brother called to the little boy, saying, "Here, take your arrow, friend!" But the little boy refused to take it and continued shooting, and they were worried. They were beginning to get blistered from the heat of the fire. Again the younger brother said, "Here, friend, take your arrow and don't burn us!" But the little boy replied, "No, I have others," and kept on shooting at them. The older brother was getting tired, but he wanted to see how much the younger boy could endure. Finally the younger brother said, "Brother, why don't you do something to save us?" "No, you took the little boy's arrow, what can I do?" "Please, brother, help me, I'm very tired!" begged the younger boy. The older boy said, "You're no longer handsome, brother!" They were close to the Pox now, and the older boy said, "Aunt, save us, we've had enough!" Then the Pox opened and they entered, and as soon as they were inside it closed again. (That is why the points of the leaves appear burned: the little boy burned them with his arrows.)

When the fire had gone out the Pox opened once again and the brothers emerged and started home. The little boy called after them, "Tomorrow I'm going to look for you, and I'll get you!" (He had a very evil heart.) The brothers returned home and went silently to their room. The older brother began to play his flute, and the younger boy said sadly, "Things went very badly for us." Momoy said, "Tomorrow the only thing for you to do is to cross the channel, because he's going to be looking for you." The next day she took the older brother to one side and said, "Cross the channel now, for your enemy is going to look for you and the best thing for you to do is to leave! You have an aunt on the other side of the channel. She is the Hap's wife. She is your aunt, and the Hap is your uncle. Look for a canoe that will take you over there." So the boys left Momoy and went to the shore, where they found some men in a canoe who agreed to take them to Santa Cruz Island. They crossed the channel and disembarked, and the canoe returned to the mainland once again.

The brothers didn't know exactly where the house of the

Hap was, so they just started out walking through the hills. They came at last to the crest of the range and looked over, and they saw a smooth plain below them. The older brother said, "There ought to be some houses down there somewhere." They descended the hill and came at last to the Hap's house, where they found their aunt pounding acorns and their uncle away hunting. They greeted the old woman, and she asked, "What are you doing here, when you know very well you'll be killed?" "Well, we were told to come. That's why we're here," replied the older brother. "All right," she answered. She kept on working, making acorn meal. Another old woman came with a pile of baskets in which to put the atole—these were the dishes people used to have—and began to fill them one by one. They placed a big pile of meat on a cleared spot of ground, which was the Hap's table, and arranged the baskets in a ring around it. (The Hap was a great eater. He ate only once in the afternoon, but he ate a *lot*. He would eat the atole, basket and all, and just spit out some of the pieces of the basket.) When the two old women had finished setting the "table," the older brother asked, "How soon will my uncle be coming?" "He'll be here soon," replied their aunt. Then she hid them under a pile of rocks nearby. As she was hiding them she said, "Don't be afraid of him, he won't do anything to you. He will go to sleep with one of you under each arm, and when he's asleep I'll come and put stones in your place. He'll cover the smokehole with hides to prevent your escape, and you'll have to get out some way or other."

In a few minutes the Hap arrived with a load of deer—he was a deer hunter and could cross to the mainland whenever he wanted—and he was carrying the deer and eating at the same time. He dropped his load at the back of the house and sat down to dinner. "What's new?" he asked his wife. "There is no news. Who would be coming here?" she said. The Hap began to look from side to side, and then he asked, "Where are the cʔicʔiwuʔun?" She replied, "No, they didn't come here!" "Don't try to trick me," he said, "they're around here somewhere. Bring them here—I want to see them!" The younger brother heard this and wanted to leave their hiding place, but the older boy restrained him and said, "No, brother, be still!" But the aunt brought them out and the Hap greeted them, poking them here and there and saying, "Good, they are nice

and plump. Fine!" Then he invited them to sit down, and he
began to eat his dinner. While he was eating the younger boy
said, "How very ugly uncle is!" "Be quiet, don't say anything!" warned the aunt. "But he is so ugly," said the boy. The
Hap finished eating at last and said, "Now we'll sleep. I'm
very tired and so are you."

He began to put deer skins over the smokehole of the
house so the boys wouldn't be able to escape, but the older
brother charmed them so that all the arrow holes in the hides
were lined up in a row. Then he took out a bit of feather down
and blew on it, and it rose and covered the hole so that the Hap
couldn't see it. The Hap finished covering the smokehole, and
then he closed the door and fastened it tightly as well. He lay
down with an arm around each boy. "How my uncle stinks!"
said the younger boy. "Hush," exclaimed his brother, "be
quiet!" In a little while the aunt suspected that her husband
was asleep, and she whispered to the boys, "Get up!" They
arose, and she put two large stones in their place. "Now you
must try to get out—I can't open the door," she told them. The
older brother took out another feather and said, "We'll be
going." The boys left through the little hole in the deer hides
covering the smokehole, for they were ʔatiswinič.

The Hap was very tired, and he slept for quite a while
before he remembered the boys and took big bites out of the
two stones lying beside him. He didn't even realize they were
only rocks—what teeth he had!—and he chewed for a time and
then began to spit out pebbles to one side and then the other.
But when he saw the pieces of rock he said, "This is stone! The
boys have gone. The old woman must have let them out!" He
went and asked his wife where the boys were, and she replied,
"How should I know? Aren't they with you?" "Well, they left
me," he said. "I don't know anything. You took them," she
answered. The Hap stood there for a while shaking his head in
anger, and then he said, "Where will they go? I'll follow them
wherever they go. They don't know the trail very well. They
must be close by."

He left the house and followed the boys. They saw him
coming, and the older brother said, "Our uncle is coming now,
he's going to get us." His brother answered, "He won't get
me—I'm going to run fast!" (He didn't know that the Hap
could suck them backwards by inhaling.) The Hap saw the

boys going down a hill, and he began to inhale rocks and trees and everything. The earth was heaving and slipping backwards, and the Hap was spitting out rocks and dirt. The boys climbed another hill and the Hap inhaled again, and once more the earth slipped backwards into his mouth. The younger brother began to get frightened and said, "Uncle is nunašiš! He's going to eat us up!" They descended the other side of the hill and the younger brother said, "I'm tired and scared. How are we going to get across the channel?" His brother said, "Well, uncle himself is going to take us over!" They climbed to the top of a peak and the older boy took out his flute. He took hold of the two ends of the flute and stretched it, and then said, "Do what I tell you and don't be afraid, and everything will be all right. Grab on to one end of the flute and I'll hold the other, and uncle will carry us across!"

The Hap saw them standing on top of the peak, and he said, "Now I'll eat them, I'll eat both of them together! They won't escape!" He came closer, and the older boy told his brother, "Don't resist—when he inhales go towards him." The Hap began to inhale, and as he did so the brothers turned the flute crosswise in his mouth and then sat on the ends, outside the corners of his mouth. The Hap couldn't see them sitting there, and he continued on and swam across the channel carrying the two boys with him. When they had reached the mainland the older brother made a sign and said, "Let's go, now is the time!" They got down, leaving the flute in the Hap's mouth, and he didn't see them leaving. But in a little while he saw them on top of the Santa Inez range here, and he was very angry. He said, "Where do they think they can go where I won't get them? I'll devour them. They've made me walk far enough already!" He inhaled and the earth began to slide and heave, and he spit out rocks and trees and inhaled again. When he reached the spot where the boys had been he saw that they were already on top of another hill. He got even angrier and said, "Now I'll get them and eat them! I won't stop until I do!" He was getting very tired, but so were the boys, for when he inhaled it took strength to get away. And when Momoy had sent them off she had taken their bows, so that they had no weapons.

The younger boy said, "I'm very tired. Do whatever you can to save us!" His brother answered, "Well, our only defense is our kinsman. He will save us." He yelled as loudly as he could, 'Now is the time to help us, we are defenseless!" Coyote heard their call but pretended not to. "Let them suffer a little," he said to himself. The Hap was getting closer all the time, and the younger boy said, "Quick, brother, I'm about ready to give up!" The older boy replied, "Well, I'll call once more and see if we have any luck." So he shouted a second time, "Kinsman, now is the time: save us, we are defenseless!" Now Momoy heard this and ordered Coyote to help them. "Go and defend the poor boys," she said. Coyote replied, "Well, the only way to do it is to kill the Hap, but not just anyone can do that!" "Look, they are tired," she said. "Don't worry, the Hap is an old woman!" answered Coyote. He wanted to let the Hap get as tired as possible before he intervened.

The Hap was following the boys with his mouth open, panting. The older brother exclaimed, "I'm very tired, but they won't help us, we have no defense!" But just then Coyote appeared nearby and said, "Don't worry, boys, I'm right here. Yes, he's an old woman—what can he do?" The Hap was coming along, tired and panting and full of dirt. He looked up and saw Coyote waiting for him, holding onto a tree, with the boys further up the hill. The Hap said, "I'll eat him up, tree and all!" As the Hap approached, Coyote began to cry, saying, "Ah, how ugly the Hap is, how ugly!" The Hap began to inhale, and Coyote shot two arrows into his mouth (the arrows had ʔatišwɨn on the tips). Then Coyote said, "Old woman, you were playing with the boys, but with me it's no game! You have ruined all the land over there, but you won't do it any-more!" He shot another arrow at the Hap's chest, but it wouldn't penetrate, for his skin was too thick—who knows how many skins he had? Coyote exclaimed, "That arrow would have penetrated an oak tree, but it won't go in him!" He quickly returned home and grabbed his flint axe, and then came back and struck the Hap with it. But the Hap's skin was so very thick that it barely made a dent. Coyote kept chopping away, and at last the Hap died. If it hadn't been for Coyote the boys would have been devoured and killed. And they say that the Hap made the gaps in the Santa Inez range when he was chasing the boys, sucking in the land and spitting out rocks and dirt.

sutiwayan ulʔatucʔ

18 MOMOY'S GRANDSON (I) Before the flood, when all the animals were people, Momoy was a very rich widow. She had only one child, a daughter, who grew prettier every day. One day she said to her daughter, "Daughter, when you go to the arroyo to bathe each morning, don't tarry. Just bathe and return home quickly." But the girl paid little attention to her mother, and after bathing she would often sit and watch her reflection in the water. One day as she sat there a man appeared. He was handsome, but his hips and shoulders were unusually thick. He was actually a bear, and he had assumed human form in order to talk to her. He told her that he wanted to marry her, but she did not reply. Then he said, "Don't be afraid." They sat there talking all day, and when it was quite late she said, "I must go now, my mother will be angry." "What can your mother say?" he asked. "You will lack nothing—clothes, money, food of all kinds. During the night I will come to you. But don't be afraid. I am a different kind of person."

When the girl returned home that evening she was sad. Momoy knew everything that happened, for she was part sorceress, and she said to her daughter, "What did I tell you? You didn't obey me." She locked the door, tying it well so that no one could enter. When it was dark that night the bear appeared in his true form, and he spent the night just outside, on the other side of the wall from where the girl was sleeping. In the morning the girl went to bathe in the arroyo as usual, and again the bear appeared in human form and spent the day with her, bringing all kinds of food with him for her to eat. And so it went each day, and Momoy was very sad. And then the girl became pregnant and began to get heavy, and the man failed to appear. For a month he stayed away, but then one day when the girl went down to bathe the bear came and killed her and ate her. Nothing was left. For according to Indian belief a bear cannot stand to see a pregnant woman without killing her.

That evening when her daughter failed to return Momoy suspected what had happened. She took her walking stick and went out, but all she could find at first were some tracks. Finally, far away, she found a little spot of blood on an alder leaf, and she picked it up, crying. "He has done me a terrible injury by killing my daughter," she said to herself. She carried the leaf with the little bit of blood on it home and placed it in a bowl with some water and some of the medicine they used to have in those days—who knows what it was? She stirred the contents of the bowl and then covered it with a big basket. In a little while a sound came from underneath the basket, but she only said "good" and went on about her business. In a little while there came another sound, and she went and uncovered the bowl. There was a tiny little boy in it. She picked him up and wrapped him in some wildcat skins that she had, and then fed him some chia broth. He grew very rapidly: in a short time he was crawling.

He started killing flies and taking them to the old woman. Then he noticed a rat, and he said, "I i i i," for he had not yet started to talk. Momoy said, "My little son, that is edible." Then the boy spoke up and said, "Little grandmother, I want a tiny bow." (He was growing *very* fast!) So Momoy made him a very tiny little bow, with arrows and all, and he began to kill rats. He would bring them to her, and she would skin them and dry the meat, although she only ate pespibata herself. Then he peeped outside and saw a cottontail rabbit, and he said, "Little grandmother, there's another one, but larger." "Yes, my little son, one can eat that, too," she replied. Then he said, "I want a larger bow." "All right," she answered, and she made him one. Now he started killing rabbits and bringing them to Momoy. Then he went out and saw a jackrabbit, and went to Momoy and said, "Little grandmother, I saw one even bigger. It had no tail, but the ears were very big." "My little son, that makes a fine meal," she said. He asked for a still larger bow, and she made it for him. But she said to him, "Little son, do not go too far away—don't go down to the arroyo." "Why does she say that?" he wondered. He went out and killed the jackrabbit, and then all at once he saw a much bigger one. It was a deer. He carried the rabbit home to Momoy and said, "Little grandmother, I saw an even larger animal. It had horns coming out here and extending so far," he said gesturing. "Ah, son, that is a deer and it is very good to eat," she told him. Then he said, "Little grandmother, I want a really big bow." Momoy had many fine bows tucked away under the roofpoles, along with quivers full of arrows, and so she got one down and gave it to him. But when he went out hunting he only killed one deer, and he wasn't pleased. "It's because my little grandmother told me not to go down to the arroyo, where there must be lots of deer," he thought to himself.

He took the deer home and Momoy was content. But the boy said, "Little grandmother, I'm going to get a drink in the arroyo." "No, my little son, there is water here," she replied. "No, I want fresh water," he insisted. She said, "My little son, I don't want you to go to the arroyo." Then he said, "Why is that?" The old woman began to cry, and finally she said, "I will tell you." "That is what I want," he answered. She said, "My little son, have you never wondered why you have no mother? You do have a father—but he is the reason you have no mother." The boy didn't like that and said, "Where does my father live?" "My son, I cannot say where he lives. He is an evil-hearted man." "Aha, fine!" he exclaimed. Then the old woman hastened to say, "You must not go to the arroyo!"

The boy didn't like that at all, but he only said, "Little grandmother, I saw an even larger animal. I want some arrows—arrows with good flint points." "All right," she said, and she went and took some down from under the roof-poles and gave them to him. He left the house and went straight to the spring in the arroyo, where he hid himself and waited. Now the bear always came to bathe at that spring, and in a little while the boy saw him coming. "Ah, that is my father," he thought to himself. "But he killed my mother and I'm going to kill him!" The bear dove in the spring and then emerged from the water, dripping. The boy came out of his hiding place and when the bear turned around he saw him standing there with an arrow on the string of his bow, ready to shoot. The bear rushed at his son to seize and kill him, but the boy retreated as fast as the bear advanced. "No, it's not that easy to catch me!" he said to the bear, and the bear got even angrier. Then the boy shot an arrow, and it went entirely through the bear's body. Then he shot a second arrow, and it went in the bear's mouth and out through his neck, and the bear fell dead. The boy went and looked at him, and said, "Ha! It was you who killed my mother. You are my father, but I have no regrets at all." He grabbed the bear and dragged it down to the spot where they obtained water for the house, and there he propped it up so that it looked as if it were drinking water, but the bear was dead. Then he went home and said, "Ah, little grandmother, I'm very thirsty!" "All right, here is some water," Momoy answered. "No, I want some fresh water," he replied. "This is fresh water," she said, but he said, "No, I don't want this."

So the old woman threw the water out and went to get more, and when she saw the bear, who appeared to be stooping over drinking, she began to scream in fear. The boy was hiding nearby, watching, and he began to laugh. Momoy ran back to her house, frightened, and said to the boy, "My little son, I can't get water because that evil man is there." Then he said, "Little grandmother, don't worry. I am very thirsty." "Don't go, son, your father is there!" He replied, "There is nothing to worry about, for he is dead." "How did that happen?" she wanted to know. "I killed him, little grandmother!" he answered. Then Momoy said, "You have done well. He killed your mother—and I rescued you by means of a little spot of blood." Then she told him everything that had occurred, and added, "Now you can travel around freely, for there is no longer any danger. He was an evil man. Now I am going to dress your hair." She took him into the house and dressed his hair like that of a man, with cʔiwis and cuqeleʔ and all, and she added plenty of money as well. Then she said, "You can now travel about freely, but just don't cross that hill over there." And the boy thought to himself, "I wonder why she doesn't want me to go over that hill?"

The first thing he did the next morning was to go to the top of the forbidden hill and look over, but he had his bow and arrows ready. But there was nothing on the other side of the hill except a village with many people living in it. He sat and watched them for a long time, and he was reluctant to leave. But finally he returned home, and Momoy, who knew everything, said, "My son, don't go there. You are better off by yourself. Bad company isn't good!" And the boy said, "All right, little grandmother, I won't go there again." But the next morning he went straight over the hill to the village. The people there played the hoop-and-pole game all day long, and they asked him to play too, for he was a very handsome boy. There was no other like him. He played first with all the well-to-do men—Xelex and ʔAtimasɨq and ʔAnicʔapapa and the rest—and he was very good. He kept beating them. That afternoon he returned home, and Momoy said to him, "Alas, my son, no good will come of this. It isn't good to be where there are many people." But he had enjoyed himself that day, and the following morning he returned to the village, where again he won. And so it went—every day he won.

Now he no longer returned home. He saw a girl one day he liked, and he married and lived in a house he won. He won all the time, and finally the people were poor and had nothing left to wager. Then one day Coyote decided to intervene in the matter. He said, "Boys, what do you think—what this boy is doing isn't good. I'm the only one who can solve this problem. Shall I do it?" And they answered, "Yes, do it!" Very early the next morning the ksen cried, "It is now the hour to play, boys!" Then Coyote bewitched Momoy's grandson in some fashion, and now he always lost. By the time the sun set that day he had lost everything—his house and wife and all—and he had nothing left. And although he knew that Momoy had lots of money he refused to go and ask her for some, for he was ashamed to see her. He just stood there on the playing field all night leaning on his pole, without moving or eating. In the morning his wife asked him to come and eat, but he said, "Go away! Go back to your house!" He said that because he suspected that it was because of her that he had been ruined. The other players came to him and said that the money was nothing, that they should play some more, but he only said, "No, I don't want to." All day he stood there, and he wouldn't even take pespibata.

For four days and nights he stood there without moving, and he was thinking of leaving and going far away. Coyote began to regret what he had done, and he went to the boy and said, "My son, don't be sad. I am here. If you wish to play, you will win." "No, I don't want to. I'm going away," said Momoy's grandson. Then Coyote said, "If I don't go with you, who knows what might happen to you?" "Good, we will go together," said the boy, "but I have to travel very far." "I know every place there is," said Coyote. "Therefore I'm going with you, so you won't get lost." Then the boy began to sing a very sad song, a song so sad that Coyote cried, and by the end of the third verse he began to turn into a fly. Then they left, with the boy flying along through the air and Coyote walking along below. They traveled far to the north and at last reached Huasna, with the boy arriving first because he was flying. When Coyote arrived he said, "You did well to wait for me.

Now follow me." He found the road that leads to the sky and they started off again, this time with Coyote in the lead.

Now Sun had been watching them, and he told his daughters, "Two people are coming. Receive them well when they arrive." The younger of the two girls kept looking to the north to see them coming, but when they didn't come right away she forgot all about it. There were many little animals there in the house, and in a little while a tiny crow began to sing, "Crow, crow, crow, people are coming." He hopped to the door and said again, "Crow, crow, crow, people are coming!" Then the younger daughter seized a stick and hit the bird. "Who would be coming here? Nobody comes here!" she exclaimed. Then the older daughter said, "What are you talking about? Don't you remember what father said?" The other girl said, "Ah, poor little thing!" She picked up the bird she had hit and cured it. Then she looked outside and said, "Sister, they are coming now." "Didn't father say so?" asked the other daughter. The boy was no longer a fly; he had changed back into a handsome man. The girls went out to meet them, but when Coyote saw their rattlesnake aprons he drew his bow, for he was afraid of the snakes. But the two girls greeted the travelers in a friendly manner and gathered up the snakes in their arms and took the travelers into the house.

Sun's house was very big and was made of pure crystal—xiłiw. There were tame bears and all kinds of other animals inside. Sun's daughters gave them food to eat: chia, piñon nuts, and other kinds of seeds. Coyote said, "I can fill up on this. And look, there's a fat deer!" The older daughter said, "Now, little grandfather, you shall eat indeed!" She seized the deer. "Just don't break the bones, save them," she said. "All right," Coyote replied. They ate and ate, and the deer was completely finished. But Coyote accidentally broke a leg-bone while chewing it. "Here are the bones," he said. The girl took the bones and threw them in a spring of water, and in a short time the deer emerged from the water as whole as ever, but with a leg missing. Then Coyote asked, "What is there to drink?" "We don't drink water," said one of the girls. "What do you drink?" Coyote asked. "Look, here is our water," she said, holding out a bowl. It was full of blood. "I can't drink that—it's blood!" said Coyote. The girl uncovered another bowl, and it was full of pus. "Ugh, I can't drink that—it's filthy!" he exclaimed. She uncovered still another, and this one was full of phlegm. "Aiee, I'm dying of thirst, but I won't drink that!" he said. The girl took out a fourth bowl, and this one contained body fluids. Coyote said, "If I had known that they don't drink water here I wouldn't have come!" Finally the girl said, "Here is another kind of beverage, but we ourselves don't drink it." She pulled out another bowl, a little one, and it was full of miel de jicote. "Ah, that I like!" exclaimed Coyote. "Please save that until I'm thirsty again." By now he had eaten so much that his belly was sticking way out. Momoy's grandson had eaten and drunk everything, saying that he liked it all. He drank the blood and pus and everything. Then Coyote said, "Daughter, it is time for the old man to return. What happens when he comes?" She answered, "First there is fog, much fog, and gales of wind. Then he tumbles rocks in to see what may be inside. But don't worry, we'll protect you."

Just then the fog and wind came, and then tumbling rocks, but each daughter got in front of one of the travelers and protected them from harm. Then there was a thud, thud, as Sun dropped the bodies he had brought with him on the ground. Then the fog and wind stopped, and there was Sun, heating the room with his presence. Coyote spoke up and said, "Ah, old man, you nearly killed me. Those rocks just missed my head!" "No, that's just my custom," Sun replied. He asked his daughters if their guests had been fed, and they said yes. They all sat down and ate then, and it was there that Coyote learned to eat people, while the fly ate silently, his mouth full. When they had finished eating, Coyote said, "Now rest, old one. Tomorrow I will go in your place." "No, you can't," said Sun. "But why not?" Coyote quickly asked. "I know all those places you go, so there is no need to worry!" They argued back and forth for quite a while, and Sun finally agreed to let Coyote go by himself.

Early the next morning when it was time to leave Coyote was ready, and he seized Sun's torch and started off. But he held the torch too low. When he reached Sun's first resting place he held it even lower. Here on this earth people were burning up—and Coyote was laughing. Women were immersing themselves in springs to escape the heat, and the water was freezing. Coyote just laughed. Finally the hour arrived when he was due to return to Sun's house, but he did not appear and Sun had to go and look for him. When he caught up with Coyote, the old man grabbed the torch and said, "People have been burned enough! Let me have this!" "No, I'm doing all right," Coyote replied. "No, you're not," exclaimed Sun. "And you've been gone long enough. You should have been home before now." "But don't you see those travelers on the road? You have no pity for people," said Coyote. "I don't, until they arrive at their destination," said Sun. "I know better than you do." They continued along, arguing, until they reached the end of the trail, and then Coyote got mad and said, "I won't go back to your house again!"

He went off by himself, and then decided to find the Slo?w and see if he could get back down to this earth here. "But how can I find him?" thought Coyote. "I know, I will lie in wait for the Xolxol." He hid in a spot where he knew the Xolxol would pass on its way around the world and waited. In a little while the Xolxol came by and Coyote jumped on him and wouldn't let him go. "Free me," said the Xolxol. "I won't let you go until you lend me your clothing," answered Coyote. "I can't," said the Xolxol. "Yes, you can!" said Coyote. After much argument the Xolxol undressed and Coyote put on his clothing. Then in a very short time he was able to look everywhere in the sky until he found the Slo?w. He returned the Xolxol's clothes to him and then went straight to where he had seen the Slo?w. He arrived and greeted the Slo?w, but the Slo?w never stirred and said nothing in reply. Then Coyote said, "Why don't you hide your face? I know who you are. You are a very bad man. Look at the charnel house you have here. What do I eat? I eat islay and acorns and the other things that people eat. Now that I'm here, I want you to transport me down to that earth down there. I have been here quite a while, leaving my family all alone. And, who knows, maybe you've eaten my wife!"

Coyote was not afraid. He just kept telling lies. And finally the Slo?w got annoyed and said, "I can't carry you down there." "Why not?" Coyote asked. "How could I do it?" the Slo?w wanted to know. "Just stretch your wing down," said Coyote. Finally the Slo?w agreed to try, and he stretched his wing down toward this world and Coyote started running down it. But after he had been running quite a while he got impatient and, thinking that he was almost down, he jumped off the wing in order to arrive sooner. But he was still high in the air, and when he hit the ground he was smashed to pieces and killed. The people here gathered up the pieces and said, "The poor old man! Here he is once again, and he's been gone so long!" The captain ordered the pieces to be assembled and Coyote to be revived. When this was done he jumped up and said that he had been tired and was just resting. He would never admit that he had been dead! Then he told them everything that had happened—and that's how people know. And the fly, Momoy's grandson, remained with Sun and his daughters and never returned to this world. Only Coyote returned.

19 MOMOY'S GRANDSON (II)

Once there was an old woman named Momoy, and she had a grandson, the Yowoyow. The boy cried a lot. The old woman gave him some chia to eat, but the bad boy refused to eat it. Then she gave him some pinole, but he spit it out, and when she tried to give him water he did the same. Then the boy began crawling around after flies, killing them with a little stick, and Momoy said, "Ah, grandson, you're going to be a good hunter." She made the boy a little bow and some tiny arrows and gave them to him. He began to shoot flies with them, and when he had killed enough he took a handful to his grandmother, who said, "Good, grandson, keep on killing them!" She threw the flies away, but he killed more and brought them to her, and again she said, "Keep on killing them, grandson."

Then the boy came to Momoy and said that he had seen a little animal. "Oh, that's a little bird," she said. "I'll make you a bigger bow." She made the bow and gave it to him, and he took it and went outside where the bird was still hopping around. He shot an arrow and killed the bird, and brought it to Momoy. She took the bird and said, "Ah, grandson, you're going to be a good hunter!" The boy went outside again and soon returned, saying, "Grandmother, there's a little animal out there, jumping." Momoy knew what it was, and said, "Ah, that's a squirrel, but if you try to kill it you'll find that it's very smart." He went out and the squirrel was still there, near the cave. The boy shot an arrow and killed it, and took it to

Momoy. "Grandmother, here is the smart little animal," he said. "Ah, grandson, you're going to be a good hunter," exclaimed Momoy. The boy went out once more, but he soon returned and said, "Grandmother, I saw a little animal with big ears." "That's a rabbit," she replied. "But you'll find he's a very quick, smart little animal!" Again the boy went out, and he shot an arrow and killed the rabbit. He took it to Momoy and said, "Here is the very quick, smart little animal." "Ah, grandson, you're going to be a good hunter! Keep killing them, for they're good to eat," she said. He went out again, and when he returned he told Momoy that he had seen an animal with sticks on its head. "Ah, that's a deer," she said. "But that animal is awfully smart and big for a little boy to kill. Take this bigger bow—it's for killing deer," she said. He took the larger bow and left, and he killed the deer and dragged it to Momoy. "Here is the big, smart animal," he told her. "You are a good hunter, grandson. Now I'm going to give you a medicine so that you may be braver and more courageous and manlier," she said.

Momoy took a bowl and put some water in it, then she washed her hands in the water and gave it to her grandson to drink. He drank the water and then began to get dizzy. "I'm sleepy, grandmother!" he said. "Go to bed, and take careful note of what you dream," she said. The boy went to bed and slept for three days, and when he awoke the old woman asked him what he had dreamed. He told her that he hadn't dreamed anything. "Well, grandson, I'm going to wash my hands again," she said. "Grandmother, wash better so that I can sleep longer," he replied. But she answered, "I'm only going to wash up to my elbows." "Grandmother, why don't you take a bath so that I can drink the water and sleep for ten days?" he asked. And the old woman answered, "No, if I took a bath, you'd turn into a devil or die; just up to my elbows is enough." She took the bowl and washed her little arms up to her elbows, and the boy drank the water. "Grandmother, I'm sleepy," he said again. "Go to bed, and pay attention to what you dream," she replied. He went to sleep and slept for six days, and when he woke up he said, "Ah, grandmother, I've slept a long time, but I didn't dream anything. Now what should I do?" "Keep on hunting," she said. "You are a good hunter, grandson!"

The boy went out with his bow into the hills, and he came across a sleeping animal. He returned and told Momoy what he had found, and she said, "Oh, grandson, be very careful with that animal. It is called a bear, and it is very fierce. You couldn't kill him. That animal is very powerful and must be respected." "Well, I'm going to get him,," the boy said. Again Momoy warned him, and added, "It would be best for you to look for your uncle—he can show you how to get the bear!" "And where is my uncle?" he askd. "He is outside there now," she answered. He went outside and saw Coyote, and said, "Uncle, my grandmother says that you can show me how to get that animal up in the hills." Coyote said, "Aiee, nephew, when we go after him, we go after the fiercest and most power-ful one of all!" "Well, I want to get him!" exclaimed the boy. "All right, let's go!" said Coyote.

They reached the place where the bear was sleeping, and Coyote said, "If you grab that animal he will tear you to shreds. The best thing for you to do is to stay hidden here, for if he sees you he will tear you to pieces. And I will go and look the situation over." Coyote wanted to see if the bear was sleep-ing, and map out a way to retreat if the bear should pursue them. He approached the bear very quietly and saw that it was barely dozing. Coyote then began to work his way back to his nephew, turning and twisting through the underbrush. But the boy got tired of waiting, and he went directly to where the bear was lying and grabbed it by the back of the neck like one would a cat. Then he said to Coyote, who was still sneaking around in the bushes, "Uncle, is this the animal you're afraid of?" "Don't let him go!" shouted Coyote. Then the boy picked the bear up and threw it into the bushes where Coyote was, and the bear began chasing Coyote while the boy watched and laughed. Coyote yelled, "Save me, nephew, defend me or the bear will kill me!" Then the boy seized his bow and shot and killed the bear.

He grasped the bear by a leg and dragged him home, and said, "Grandmother, here is the fierce, powerful animal—here it is!" "Oh, grandson, you've killed your uncle! But that's all right. I'm going to make you a quiver from your uncle's skin," she said. "Good, grandmother, good—and do it quickly," he replied. The old woman began removing the bear's skin to make the quiver. The next day the boy said, "Is my quiver

ready?" "Yes, here it is," she answered. The boy took the
quiver and put his bow and arrows in it, and then said,
"Grandmother, what should I do now?" "Continue hunting,"
she replied, 'you are a good hunter." "I want to know where
Liyɨkʔšup—the center of the world—is, grandmother," he responded. "Grandson, how can you get there when you don't
know the way? The best thing for you to do is to find your
uncle and let him show you the way, for he knows how to get
there." "Where can I find my uncle?" he wanted to know.
"There he is over there," Momoy answered.

The boy went and found Coyote, and said, "Uncle, my
grandmother says that you will show me the way to Liyɨkʔšup.
Let's go to the house and get food for you to eat on the trip, for
I don't eat anything but pespibata." "I can go without eating if
you can. I won't eat," said Coyote. "Good, let's be on our
way," replied the boy. And so they left with only pespibata for
provisions, and they traveled along for a while together. Then
the boy said to Coyote, "Uncle, let's see how much of a man
you are." "Do you want to see?" said Coyote. He gave a loud
shout, and before the sound had ended he suddenly appeared
on the opposite hill. "That is all right, but it's really nothing,"
said the boy. He kept walking until he caught up with his
uncle, and then he said, "Uncle, that was all right, but now it's
my turn and I'm really going to travel!" He gave a yell, and
when Coyote looked the boy was already far away in the distance. "Aiee, my nephew has left me behind!" exclaimed
Coyote. He ran and ran, and he finally caught up with the boy,
who said, "Uncle, why don't you yell again so that we can get
there faster?" Coyote agreed and so the two traveled very fast,
leaping from one hill to another until they eventually reached
the village at Liyɨkʔšup.

They went to the house of the wot, where food was prepared and a fiesta held in their honor. Their hosts danced the
bear dance with Coyote joining in, and then the wot said,
"You are tired, for you have come very far. Do you wish to rest
or lie down?" The girls there liked Momoy's grandson very
much, and the prettiest of them went and slept with him that
night. The next morning he got up and went to the stream to
bathe, and then they called him to come and eat breakfast. He
didn't know how to eat; he could eat only pespibata. They
placed ʔilepeš, acorn atole, and meat in front of him and he

couldn't eat it. The wot was insulted, for he had ordered a feast prepared for them and now the boy wouldn't eat a thing. He just pushed all the food to one side and left the house, where he encountered Coyote. Coyote said, "You are shameless. You shouldn't have done that!" "You know very well I don't eat, but they brought me all those things anyway," the boy answered. "It's bad enough not to eat, but it's worse not to say thanks!" Coyote said. "Oh, well, I'm leaving right away with you," said his nephew. "And what about your girls, your sweethearts?" asked Coyote. "Oh, I'll leave them here. If you want them, take them. I'm going," said the boy. Coyote said that he would stay, and the boy said, "Goodbye, uncle. I'll be home tonight."

He left, and that night he was back home at his grand-mother's house. When he arrived Momoy asked, "Did you find what you were looking for, grandson?" "Yes, grand-mother." "And where is your uncle?" "He stayed there in Liyɨkʔšup," he said. "And why did you come back?" Momoy asked. "Oh, I came back because I want to see the islands across the sea." "How are you going to get across the chan-nel?" she wondered, adding: "It would be best to talk to your uncle Hew. He has a canoe, and he could take you over. He is the captain of the boat, and his companion, Mut, is a sailor." "Where can I find my uncle?" he asked. "You will find him down at the beach," she answered.

The boy left and went to the shore, where he found Hew just arriving in his canoe. "Uncle, my grandmother said that you can carry me over to the other side of the channel." Hew said, "Yes, nephew, when do you want to leave?" "Right away," replied the boy. "All right, but first I have to deliver the fish I've brought," Hew said. "All right, uncle, but hurry." Hew delivered the fish, and then said, "Now we're ready, nephew." They got into the canoe and pushed off into the water. Hew asked, "Nephew, will you get sick?" "No, I'm never sick," the boy replied. At last they reached the port at Santa Cruz Island, and Hew said, "Ah, nephew, you will never return!" "Why, uncle?" "Because the wot here, who is called Hap, is very fierce and dangerous," replied Hew. "Have no fear, uncle," said the boy. "I will return, but just in case I haven't come by this afternoon, it will be a sign that I'm dead. But I will return. Don't lose hope."

He got out of the canoe and started off. He reached the village, and Hap saw him and came to meet him. Hap had a horn on his head like a bull or some other animal, and it was with this that he killed people. "Why have you come to my village?" asked the Hap. "What do you want here?" The boy did not answer him, and Hap rushed at him and tried to hook him with the horn, but each time the boy dodged out of the way. Finally the Hap fell to the ground exhausted, and the boy said, "What! They say you are very brave and fierce, but you're not a man—you're an old woman! Men don't act this way!" Then the Hap got up again and said, "Ah, snively boy, I'm going to kill you now! I'm going to make little pieces out of you!" Then the boy seized his quiver, and when the Hap rushed at him again, he hit him such a blow with it that the Hap fell to the ground. He kept hitting the Hap with the quiver until he was dead. Then he cut out the Hap's tongue and left, saying, "I'll return to my grandmother."

He arrived at the shore and found the canoe still waiting for him. "You're still here, uncle," he said. Hew said, "Yes, I've been waiting for you." "Good, uncle. Let's go," he replied. They started of, and then the boy said, "Ah, uncle, didn't you say that the Hap was very brave, powerful and fierce? He isn't a man, he's an old woman! I knocked him down with my quiver. He fell at the first blow!" Hew said, "I can't believe that you could have killed the Hap, for he is the most powerful man in the world!" "But I did indeed kill him, uncle, and here is his tongue!" the boy replied. "Then I believe you. You did kill the Hap," said Hew. "Nephew, here we are, back in our own country." "Good," said the boy. "And how much do I owe you for your labor?" Hew said, "Nephew, whatever you want to give me will be fine." The boy took out his abalorio and began to measure it out. "This is for you," he said, "and this is for your companion, Mut." "Thanks very much for your abalorio," Hew said.

The boy returned home to his grandmother's house, and when he arrived there he said, "Grandmother, here I am." Momoy said, "Yes, and how did it go with you?" "Fine, grandmother. But why do they say that the Hap is so brave, fierce, and powerful when he's no more than an old woman? I killed him with my quiver!" Momoy exclaimed, "Grandson, I can't believe that you could have killed the Hap!" "Yes indeed,

grandmother, I killed him,' he replied. "Here is his tongue!"
"Ah, grandson, you have killed your uncle. That was a bad
thing to do," she said. "Well, it's your fault, for you didn't tell
me that he was my uncle," he replied. Momoy said, "But it is
just as well that he is dead. It's for the best." Then the boy
said, "I'm not going to remain here, I'm going to leave."
"Where are you going, grandson?" "Grandmother, I'm going
back to Liyɨkʔšup," he answered. "Go ahead, grandson," she
said. "And when were you thinking of leaving?" "Right away,
grandmother. Goodbye!" he replied.

He left and started off on his journey, and eventually
reached Liyɨkʔšup. Everyone there liked him very much, and
were very pleased to see him. They liked him so much that
they finally made him wot, and there he remains as wot to this
day.

(In one version of this story the boy goes to Catalina Island
rather than Santa Cruz Island, and the Hap is called Pibitovar.)

20 MOMOY AND THE TUPNEKČ

Momoy was an old woman who lived no one knows
where. One night she suddenly heard a little baby
crying outside her house, and she said, "Who can that be?
Where does he come from?" She went outside to look for him,
but he stopped crying and she could not find him. She went
inside again and lay down on her bed, and then the little boy
began to cry again. "Where are you?" she called. She got up
and looked for him again, but he stopped crying and she
couldn't find him. And so it went all night—the old woman
looking for him and the little boy crying only when she was
inside.

Finally at dawn she found him lying outside kicking the
air with his feet, and she said, "There you are!" She carried
him inside and cleaned him, and then said to herself, "Who
does this child belong to, and who left him here? Oh well, he
will be company for me." She put him in a xʔiʔm and he went
quietly to sleep. When he woke up he began to cry again.
"What can I give him—perhaps he's hungry," said Momoy.
She gave him ʔiʔlepes and water, for there was no milk, but he
wouldn't eat it. He just threw it out. He was like Coyote, he
didn't like it. Next she gave him huxminaš (guata), but he
threw that out too. Finally she went and got some pespibata

and mixed it with water. She stuck her finger in it and put some in the baby's mouth. He sucked on it, and she said, "That's scarce and expensive, but that's what he likes!" She put a little piece of pespibata in his mouth, and he finished it and began to cry for more. So she gave him another little piece, and he lay there kicking and eating his pespibata. The tobacco was just like candy to him. She kept feeding him pespibata, and every time he finished a piece he would cry for more. He wasn't cold or anything—he just lay in the xʔiʔm, kicking and eating pespibata. And he began growing right away, there in the basket.

One day she missed his crying and said, "What has happened to make you stop?" She went to the xʔiʔm and there was the little boy crawling around outside of it on the floor. "Ah, you're a little man now," said Momoy. She brought him another lump of pespibata and went away. In a little while she thought to herself, "I wonder what he's doing now?" She went to look and found the little boy killing flies with his finger. "Ah, you're going to be a warrior, grandson!" she said. She brought him some panocha and more pespibata, and he kept on killing flies. Every little while Momoy would peer inside the basket and see that the little boy was very busy. She began to make a little bow, and an arrow with feathers and a foreshaft. When she had finished them she gave them to him and taught him how to shoot the flies with the little arrows. He was very good at it, and when she went back in a little while he had a small pile of flies that he had shot. "That is how one fights to live," she said. He gave her the flies and she placed them to one side. Like the boy, Momoy only ate pespibata, but not continuously—she just put a little piece in her mouth once in a while. But the boy ate it like it was candy. He went on killing flies, for he was a good shot, and when she went to see what he was doing he would have a pile of flies ready to give her. She would take the flies and give him another bit of pespibata.

He was getting larger all the time, and pretty soon he was as big as the xʔiʔm. Momoy said, "What shall I do with this boy? I'm going to take him out of the xʔiʔm." She put him on the floor outside the basket and went away for a short time, and when she returned he was nowhere in sight. "Where are you now?" she said. She went to look for him, and she finally found him outside in a big bush hunting some little birds. He shot one, but it flew away with his only arrow, and although he looked and looked he couldn't find it anywhere. He returned to the house and told her that a little animal had taken his arrow. "He knows how to talk already!" exclaimed Momoy. She made another bow, bigger than the first, and two arrows, and she gave them to him. He went outside and saw a squirrel, and the squirrel ran and jumped and turned and went "pistuqu, pistuqu." It looked at the boy and must have thought he was a coyote for sure. The Tupnekč saw it—he had never seen an animal like that—and followed it around until he got tired. He returned to the house at last and Momoy asked, "Where were you?" He replied, "Grandmother, you should see the strange little animal out there. He gives a little jump and says 'pistuqutuqutu' and lifts his tail and turns it like this. I'm going to see if I can shoot him with my bow." Then Momoy said, "You can't kill it. If you were a man you could do it, but you aren't a man, you are a Tupnekč." But the boy took the bow and the two arrows and went out without saying a word. He found the squirrel eating seeds, and he hit it in the head and the squirrel died. The boy picked it up and returned to the house. Momoy was watching for him, and when she saw him bringing the squirrel she sat down and said, "You are going to be a warrior, grandson!"

She began to remove the hide while the boy watched. After a while he went and got a piece of pespibata with her permission. "Don't take it all, just take a little bit," she told him. He went outside again and noticed some small birds in a bush nearby. "Those are the ones that stole my arrow. I'll kill one," he said. He began to hunt the birds and shoot them one by one until he had quite a few. He took them to Momoy and said, "Here are those that stole my arrow!" "Fine, fine," said the old woman, and she pulled off the feathers and put the birds and the squirrel out in the sun to dry, so that if Coyote came he would have something to eat (for when Coyote could find nothing elsewhere he came to Momoy to see if she had anything to eat). Then the boy went walking along the edge of the brush and encountered a rabbit. He didn't know what kind of an animal it was. It would raise and lower its ears, then crouch into a ball, and then go on again. While the boy was watching the rabbit, Coyote came along near the house. He was starving, dying of hunger, and he didn't know what to do. He finally said, 'I'll go see the old lady, she'll have something to eat.'' He went down to the house and spoke to Momoy, saying, "Do you have anything I could eat?" "Yes," she replied, and she gave him the birds and squirrel and some acorn atole, and Coyote roasted the dry meat and ate it and atole until he was full. Then he thanked Momoy and left.

Then the Tupnekč arrived and said, "Grandmother, I've seen an animal with big ears and a white tail." "People eat them," said Momoy. "A man could kill it, but not a boy. A good time to hunt it is very early in the morning, when it's eating, and also in the afternoon." The boy thought to himself, "My grandmother doesn't think I can kill that animal, but I will. And not in the afternoon—right now!" He left without saying a word and went into the brush. He began to shoot, first to one side and then to the other, until he had killed four rabbits. He picked them up and carried them home. "Ah, what a hunter you're going to be, grandson!" exclaimed Momoy. She began to skin the rabbits, and the boy left again. He saw a gopher in the field, and he returned and said, "I saw a small animal burrowing in the ground and throwing out dirt. But it's very smart, for it then hides and covers its little door with dirt." "People don't kill that animal," said Momoy. The boy thought to himself, "Well, I'm going to kill him now!" He went out and shot four gophers and brought them home. "You'll be a warrior, grandson!" Momoy said. "This will be for your kinsman, Coyote. He will surely come to eat tomorrow." She began to skin the gophers, and the boy left again. He found some quail and tried to kill them, but he couldn't. They were very smart. He went back to the house and told Momoy, "You should see some little animals that are out there. They have black here and a stripe there, and when one says 'taqaqa qiqiqiqiqiqiqi' they all hide."

Momoy knew what he had seen, for she kept an eye on him and watched over him carefully. She said, "Don't harm them. Leave them in peace. That's a man's job." But the Tupnekc said to himself, "You'll see, I'm going to bring home a lot!" He went out to where there was a clump of trees, and there were some quail high in the branches. He began to shoot at them, and pretty soon he had killed a dozen. He brought them home and said, "Here they are!" "Grandson, you'll be a

warrior for sure," Momoy replied. She removed their feathers
and put them out to dry so that Coyote could eat them if he
came. The boy left, and this time he found some geese eating
grass. He shot and hit one, and then he hit another, and as
they began to fly away he shot two more. He carried the four
geese back to the house and Momoy cleaned them. "I'm going
to give him a sinew-backed bow now, a taʔlip," she said to
herself. She gave him the bow, which she had had stored away
in the house, and he was very happy. He went out, and in a
little while he came across a badger. The badger was very
ferocious and wanted to fight with him. He shot an arrow and
it hit the badger right in the side, and the point came out the
other side. He dragged it home, and when Momoy saw him
coming she said, "You've killed your kinsman!" She skinned
the badger and put the meat in the sun to dry, and she began
to make the boy a quiver out of the hide.

The Tupnekč left once again, and this time he came across
a deer. He shot it and it fell, but then it struggled to its feet and
he had to shoot it again, for the deer is very nunašiš and
strong. The boy picked up the deer and carried it home, for he
was nunašiš too. When Momoy saw him coming with the deer
she stood and looked at him fearfully and said, "Grandson,
you are almost a man now!" She skinned the deer and cut the
meat into strips, which she then hung on a line to dry into
jerky. The Tupnekč killed another deer and brought it back
too, and Momoy said to herself, "He has no sense—he just
goes around killing!" (They didn't eat meat, they didn't eat
anything but pespibata, but still they had everything they
might need stored away—seeds, money, everything.) Momoy
skinned the second deer and put both hides in some water to
soak. Then she scraped the hair off with a rib, while the boy
watched and learned how to make leather. "What are you
going to do with it, grandmother?" he asked. "I'm going to
make you some clothing," she replied. She made him a pair of
pants and a jacket, all in one piece, and she fringed them and
painted them too. The Tupnekč was pleased with his new
clothes. Then he asked, "Where are the little birds that you
dried?" Momoy said, "Your kinsman ate them, and he took
some with him." "Who is my kinsman?" he asked. "You don't
know him," she answered. "His name is Coyote. He's your
kinsman." "How can I meet him? I want to meet him!" said the

Tupnekč. "I think he'll come tomorrow. You can meet him then," said Momoy.

The following day Coyote arrived and asked for something to eat, and the boy said to himself, "He has a tail and ears. He isn't like me: I have no tail, but he does." Momoy gave Coyote some acorn atole and the deer bones, and he asked, "Old woman, where did you get this meat?" She answered, "My grandson is a good hunter." Coyote sat there roasting the bones and eating, and the Tupnekč sat and watched him. He saw how Coyote played with the bones and drank down the atole as though it were water, and he thought to himself, "What a peculiar kinsman!" He watched Coyote go and get more bones and cook them, and he thought he would never stop eating. Momoy came in from outside and saw the Tupnekč sitting there watching Coyote, and she said to him, "Don't sit there watching your kinsman eat!" Then Coyote said, "It doesn't matter. He's just a boy, and very young." Coyote finally got full and left, and the Tupnekč went to Momoy and said, "Grandmother, I hope he comes again, so I can watch him. He is a very strange relative!" "Be careful of him, he is nunašíš," she answered. "He'll come again one of these days."

The boy continued hunting and killing deer, and the old woman prepared the skins for more clothing, because he was growing quite big. One day the Tupnekč was out hunting and he found a footprint on the ground. "Who could be walking here barefoot?" he wondered. He followed the tracks, which were very large, until he couldn't see them anymore. "Who could this be? My kinsman has small feet, but these tracks are large. I'll ask my grandmother." He returned home and entered the house, where he stood quietly as if frightened. "What's wrong? asked Momoy. "What is it that I saw?" he asked. "What did you see?" she wanted to know. He said, "I saw tracks like mine, but without sandles and very big." "It was the footprint of a bear. Be careful, it is nunašíš," she warned. The Tupnekč thought to himself, "I'm going to look for him!"

He left without saying a word and entered the woods where he had seen the tracks. He began to search, and in a short time he found the bear fast asleep with his feet resting on a log. The Tupnekč watched the bear for a while, but he didn't shoot at him because he saw that his arrows were too small. After a time he said to himself, "Now I'll see how much of a man my kinsman is!" He ran all the way home and arrived out of breath, panting, "What's the matter?" asked Momoy. When he had caught his breath he said, "I saw the relative, sleeping. Why is he asleep? You say he's very powerful, but I don't sleep. I go all over, but he's asleep!" He wanted to kill the bear and get the hide for another quiver, for the badger skin wasn't big enough to suit him. Then Momoy said, "You can't do anything to him. It would be best for us to ask Coyote for help. He can kill the bear." "Good!" said the boy. "And when will he come?" "Well, he'll come tomorrow, and I'll ask him," she replied.

The next day Coyote arrived, and he said, "What's new?" Momoy answered, "Well, nothing much, except that this fellow here found a bear, and now he wants to get its hide for a quiver!" She put deer meat and acorn atole in front of Coyote, and he ate the meat without cooking it and played with the bones just as he had done before, and the Tupnekč sat and watched him with great interest. Finally Coyote finished eating and said, "Take it away. I don't want any more now! The bear is powerful—why does he want it?" The boy answered, "Well, I want it and I'm going to get it!" Now Coyote didn't think the Tupnekč was strong at all, and after a while he said, "I'll go, I'll get you the bear's hide. Where is he?" The boy told him, and Coyote said, "Fine. Is he in a thicket?" "Yes," replied the Tupnekč. "He's between a patch of brush and an oak tree." "Have you any flint to cut the brush with to make a trail?" (That was the only kind of axe they had, and they used it to cut down trees.)

Coyote took the axe and the two of them started off. Momoy kept her grandson's bow and arrows, for she was afraid that he might miss and kill Coyote by mistake, but Coyote went well-armed with bow and quiver and knife. They arrived at the spot where the bear was sleeping, and Coyote began to cut a little trail through the brush toward it. The trail wound around a great deal and was very narrow so that if the bear chased them it would have a hard time getting through. The Tupnekč watched Coyote making his trail, and when he got very close to the sleeping bear the boy went straight to the bear and lifted it up by the nape of the neck like a kitten. "Are you afraid of him?" he asked Coyote. Coyote looked at the Tupnekč standing there holding the bear and exclaimed, "He is more powerful than I am, he beats me!" He yelled to the boy to throw the bear as far as he could. But the Tupnekč threw the bear right at Coyote and began to laugh, while the bear began chasing Coyote around and around. At first Coyote had no chance to shoot an arrow at the bear (who was right behind him) but at last the bear got tired and began to lag a little, and Coyote was able to turn and shoot an arrow into the bear's open mouth. The bear fell dead.

Coyote was exhausted. He rested for a while and then began to collect some poles. The Tupnekč watched him for a minute and then asked, "What are you going to do?" "Well, I'm going to take the bear back to the house," Coyote replied. "And what are those poles for?" asked the boy. Coyote explained that he was going to make a kind of stretcher to carry the bear on, and that he would take the front end while the Tupnekč took the lighter back end. "Fine," said the boy. They put the bear on the poles and started off, but in a little while Coyote was about ready to fall over from exhaustion, for his end was just too heavy for him. Then the boy asked, "Are you tired? I'll carry it." "Can you do it?" asked Coyote. "I can do it," replied the Tupnekč. He took off the poles and began dragging the bear away and Coyote just stood there shaking his head. "That fellow beats me!" he said to himself.

Now Momoy had been watching everything that happened, for she had a good view, but when they reached the house she was sitting down inside as if she hadn't seen a thing. The Tupnekč threw down his load on the floor and said, "Here it is—make me my quiver!" Then Momoy said, "Have you no sense at all? You are just killing for the sake of killing. The bear was doing no harm." Coyote arrived and began to at once to skin the bear, saying, "We'll make the quiver right now." He started in with his knife, cutting the hide, and Momoy went and got a small bowl and washed her hands. (They were going to get the Tupnekč intoxicated on the water in which she washed her hands.) She gave the Tupnekč the water and he drank it, and then she laid down a mat on the floor so that he might sleep. He sat down on the mat, but he didn't fall asleep. Momoy asked, "Why don't you go to sleep?" "Grandmother, why don't you take a bath so that I can sleep?"

She got another little bowl and washed her arms up to the elbow, and then gave him the water to drink. He lay down on the mat then and went to sleep, but he only took a little nap. Momoy said, "He's asleep," and went away for a few minutes.

When she returned the Tupnekč was sitting up on the mat, wide awake. She sat down and said, "You have beat me!" (She meant that the Tupnekč was stronger than toloache.) He said, "Bathe, grandmother, so I can sleep!" "No, that is enough," she answered. She went and told Coyote that the boy couldn't sleep. "What are you doing to make him sleep?" he asked. "How many drinks have you given him?" "Two," she replied. "Well, don't give him any more because he has already won. He is stronger," said Coyote. He asked, "Where did the Tupnekč get that strength? It must be natural, because no one knows who his mother or father are. He's going to exhaust us!" He completed the quiver, which was better than the one that Momoy had made from the badger skin.

Now the Tupnekč had a new quiver, and new clothing, and he was already a man. He was very pleased with everything. Then Coyote said, "Tomorrow we'll go out hunting. But tell your grandmother that we are leaving." So the Tupnekč told Momoy what Coyote had said, and the next morning they went out hunting. Coyote killed two deer while his companion killed ten. But Coyote didn't know that the Tupnekč had killed any deer, and so he said, "Here, you have to carry these two deer I've killed." "All right, I'll carry them," replied the Tupnekč. He picked them up as if they were squirrels and they started off. In a short time they came to where the Tupnekč had left his ten deer, and when Coyote saw them lying there in a neat row he thought to himself, "He's going to ask me to carry those!" Before the Tupnekč could say a word Coyote gave a groan and clutched his stomach, pretending to be sick. "I keep getting this pain!" he exclaimed. He pretended to be very sick so that he wouldn't have to carry any of the deer. "Well, if you're sick why don't you go on home? I'm going to carry these deer back," said the Tupnekč. "That is a good idea," said Coyote. "I'll go now."

He left, but after a minute or two he thought to himself, "I wonder how he's going to get those twelve deer home?" He hid in some bushes and watched to see what the Tupnekč would do. The Tupnekč arranged the deer in two piles and then picked them up and started off with six in each hand. Coyote thought, "Wow, I'm afraid of this fellow!" The Tupnekč arrived home with the twelve deer, and when Momoy inquired about Coyote he exclaimed, "What a relative! You say he's a man, but he's nothing. All he can do is skin an animal!" Momoy began to butcher the deer, and in a few minutes Coyote arrived. "What's new?" he asked. "Not a thing, I'm just skinning these deer," she said. "Well, that's why I've come," he replied. So they sat down and skinned the deer, and put the hides in water to soak, and began to roast the meat. Coyote ate the fresh meat and acorn atole—he ate and ate and ate. Finally he said, "Well, I'm going home now." "All right," replied Momoy. "But pass by here from time to time." "I will," he answered. But he left and didn't return for many days, and at last the Tupnekč said, "My kinsman—isn't he going to come back?" "He'll come, perhaps tomorrow. He's going to be near here," replied the old woman.

She stored all the meat inside the house out of sight, and the next day Coyote arrived to eat some dried meat, but there was none in sight. "Where is the meat?" he asked. Momoy replied, "Someone keeps taking it!" "Tomorrow we'll go hunting," said Coyote. The next day he and the Tupnekč left to go hunting, and as they were walking along Coyote saw some bear tracks in the trail. He gave a shout and disappeared suddenly, and when the Tupnekč turned around he saw Coyote coming down a hill some distance away. (When you shout in a canyon it doesn't echo right there; it sounds like someone else shouting farther away.) "All right," said the Tupnekč. "That's nothing, that's all right!" The two met again and went a little further, and Coyote saw another footprint. He yelled once more, and again he disappeared, only to reappear some distance away. "What's wrong with my kinsman?" the Tupnekč said, "Oh, that's what you've been looking at!" They kept traveling higher into the hills. The Tupnekč was looking for deer, not for tracks.

Suddenly they came upon a herd of deer, and the Tupnekč thought to himself, "Now we'll see—this fellow is going to get sick again!" He began to shoot very fast, and he killed five deer before the others fled. "There they go, over there, there they are!" shouted Coyote, and he started after them. The Tupnekč followed after him and shot three more deer.

"This is enough," he said. He picked up the three deer and carried them to where Coyote was standing. "Look, kinsman, this is enough. Why do you want so many?" He carried the three deer over to where the other five were lying, and when Coyote saw how many there were he suddenly began to cry out in pain and clutch his knee. "Well, I'm going to have to go home now, for my knee hurts me badly!" he exclaimed. "Why don't you at least take one home with you?" asked the Tupnekč. "Oh, oh, my knee! Well, I'll try to carry one or two. Please hand me those little ones over there," said Coyote, pointing to the two largest deer of all. "Oh, my knee!" he groaned. The Tupnekč picked up the ten remaining deer and started home, turning around from time to time to see what Coyote was doing.

Coyote picked up the two deer and gave a yell, and when the Tupnekč turned around Coyote was already on top of the hill. "Just look at that sick fellow, how shrewd he is!" exclaimed the Tupnekč. He went on home, and Coyote went wherever he was going. When the Tupnekč got home Momoy asked him where his kinsman was. "He's already gone," he answered. "And he took something with him! He's very, very shrewd. You say he's powerful, but he's nothing. He got sick just now. First he says he always gets a pain in his chest and now it's in his knee!" Momoy answered, "Don't pay any attention to your kinsman." Meanwhile Coyote was trying to figure out how he could come out ahead of the Tupnekč. He thought and thought, but he couldn't decide what to do, and so he didn't return to Momoy's house for many days. Finally he got an idea, and he went to see the Tupnekč and the old woman once again. Coyote said, "Kinsman, why don't we go and see Liyɨkšup?" "Where is that?" asked the Tupnekč. "Oh, over the mountains here," answered Coyote. "There is a village there. Now go and ask your grandmother for permission to go." The Tupnekč was anxious to see new things, and he went to Momoy and told her he was going to Liyɨkšup. "When will you get there, and how will you find it?" she inquired. "Well, my kinsman knows where it is," he said. "No, don't go," she said. But the Tupnekč said, "I'm going to go, but I'll be careful. I'll return." She asked him, "When are you going?" "Tomorrow," he said.

He cleaned his quiver and got everything ready, and in the morning Coyote arrived and asked, "Are you ready, kinsman?" The Tupnekč said that he was ready. Momoy locked herself in the house, for she didn't want to see them go. They started off on their trip. The only thing the Tupnekč took in the way of provisions was some pespibata, but Coyote took some dried meat and chia pinole. They walked and walked, and after a while found themselves in a canyon. Then the Tupnekč asked, "Are we going to follow this canyon or are we going to climb this mountain?" Coyote answered, "We'll walk a little more and then go over the mountain." The Tupnekč remembered how Coyote had yelled when they were out hunting and suddenly appeared far away, and he said to himself, "Now I'll get back at him. He'll see!" He gave a shout and disappeared, and when Coyote turned to look he was already on top of the ridge. "He's beating me. Whenever he wishes he's ahead of me!" exclaimed Coyote. He ascended the ridge to where the Tupnekč was waiting, and then the Tupnekč shouted again and appeared far away on another ridge. When Coyote finally caught up with his companion he said, "Don't walk so fast, you'll get tired! Liyɨkšup is quite far."

They descended the next range of hills and crossed a plain, and eventually they came to a spring at the edge of a desert. "There is no more water after this," said Coyote. "We'll stop and eat." Coyote ate some food while the Tupnekč chewed pespibata. Coyote saw a toad and grabbed it. "Well, that's my companion," he said, and he put it in his quiver. They started on again, and Coyote told the Tupnekč not to shout now. "Why not, kinsman?" "Because someone will answer you if you do," said Coyote. "Who would it be?" asked the Tupnekč. Coyote said, "Well, I don't know who it might be, but someone would answer you." They walked along for a while, and then the Tupnekč gave a shout that was quickly answered from some distance ahead. Coyote said, "Didn't I tell you not to shout?" The Tupnekč answered, "Kinsman, I couldn't help myself, I had to yell!" He shouted again, and they heard someone shout back. "Who is that, kinsman?" he asked. "And where is he?" Coyote said, "Well, he's very close by, that's for sure." "I want to see who it is, I want to see him!" said the Tupnekč. He yelled again, and then listened carefully to the answering shout. In a short time they came to a skull lying on the ground with foxtails growing out of it, and when the Tupnekč shouted the skull answered him back.

The skull was that of another coyote who had died there, and Coyote knew him. He said, "I knew that this old man had died here in Liyɨkšup, and here he is!" The Tupnekč asked, "How can we get him up again?" He was already collecting the bones together. Coyote said, "I'll get him right up." He put his ʔatišwɨn on the bones and they began to shake, and skin began to appear. "Remember!" Coyote said, and he lifted the old coyote to his feet. The old coyote said, "I've slept quite a while!" He began to feel himself all over, and then he said, "What I really want is a piece of fresh fish from the ocean. Do you happen to have some?" "Yes, I brought some with me," replied Coyote. He took the toad out of his quiver and said, "May it turn into a xweteʔet!" (The xweteʔet is a big fish found in estuaries: it resembles a toad and has a round tail with a spine on it.) "Here it is!" he told the old coyote, giving him the fish. The old coyote ate it all and said, "I was quite hungry!" The Tupnekč was very happy and said, "Now I have two companions to pass the time with."

The old coyote began to rub his head and said, "I was sound asleep. I feel very rested. Now, where do you come from?" The told him and he asked them where they were going. "To Liyɨkšup," they said. "And where is that?" he wanted to know. Coyote answered, "Well, I don't know exactly, but we are looking for it." The old coyote said, "If you invite me, I'll go with you." "Fine, let's go. That's why we spoke to you," Coyote said. The old coyote said, "Liyɨkšup is very close to here somewhere, but I don't know just exactly where. I've come from the sky, from ʔalapay, and have been lying here asleep ever since." "Well, how can we find Liyɨk-sup, then?" asked Coyote. "The only way to find it is for you to go that way, and me this way, and if we return at the same time, that's Liyɨkšup."

The Tupnekč began to laugh, listening to the conversation. The old coyote told him to stay there where he was, and the Tupnekč said, "But you are very old, you can't run as fast as my kinsman." "We are equally fast," said the old coyote. He added, "Let's have a race to see who reaches that tree over there first!" He gave a shout and reached the tree ahead of

Coyote. "All right, now return here," called the Tupnekč. They came back and arrived at the same instant. "That's very good," said the Tupnekč. They traveled along for a while, and then the two coyotes shouted and went in opposite directions, but one arrived back before the other. "It still isn't Liyɨkšup," said the Tupnekč, trying to show that he was as smart as the coyotes. They continued along this way the rest of the day, with first one coyote and then the other arriving back first. They never arrived at the same time. The old coyote said, "The village (ʔapanɨs) is here somewhere." "What's a village?" asked the Tupnekč. "It's where there is lots of ʔostus," said Coyote. "And what are they good for?" asked the Tupnekč. "Oh, are you ignorant!" exclaimed Coyote.

When it began to get dark they built a fire, and the two coyotes lay down on each side of it. But the Tupnekč just sat down nearby, eating his pespibata. He didn't know what cold or hunger was. Finally one of the coyotes said to the Tupnekč, "Fool, ʔostus is a very fine thing." "Why is that?" he asked. "Well, it's the remedy for man's heart," said the coyote. Then the other coyote spoke up and said, "Well, that's not true, kinsman." "Why do you say that, when ʔostus is such a fine thing?" the coyote asked. "What is ʔostus?" asked the Tupnekč. "Well, I'll tell you. You make a round hole in the ground and get three or four heads of agave. You put hot rocks in the hole, then some more rocks, and finally you build a fire on top." The coyote stopped and began to laugh and laugh. "And then you come and uncover it, and it is all cooked, and it is very sweet and tasty and fragrant. And that is ʔostus!" The other coyote laughed too, and said, "That's it, and it's very good for the stomach." The Tupnekč said, "Well, if that is ʔostus, fine. You can have it, but it's not for me!" He got very bored with the two coyotes talking of nothing but ʔostus all night.

The next morning they got up and started on again, and the two coyotes kept pushing each other and playing and talking of ʔostus. Finally they saw some houses in the distance, and the old coyote said, "We'll arrive about sunset." They reached the village and were well-received, for the people there knew the old coyote. The girls were quite taken with the Tupnekč, but he paid them little attention—he didn't know what love was. That evening the girls fed them, but the Tupnekč didn't eat anything. He just sat there. After dinner one coyote said to the other, "Let's go look for firewood." They went out, and while they were gone the girls began to flirt with the Tupnekč. When the old men returned they brought wood for the fire, and they began to stir it and fuss around, for they were jealous because the girls weren't paying any attention to them. They didn't want to give the Tupnekč an opportunity of sleeping with the girls. But after a while the two girls and the Tupnekč climbed up to bed and lay down, and the girls began to play with him. They wanted to take his clothes off, but he wouldn't let them. He pushed them away, and one of the girls said, "You're dumb, you don't know anything!" "I know how to make baskets," he replied. "I know how to work and everything! And I can kill deer, too. And you tell me I'm stupid!" "You are stupid," said the girl. Then he said, "I know how to make a x?i?m, and trays, and I can make a quiver, and you say I'm a fool!" The girl exposed herself to him, and when he didn't get on top of her she said again, "You're stupid!"

Coyote put out the fire and said to the old coyote, "I'm going up there myself! I'll take his place, I'll get on one of them!" The bed was very high, with a pole like a ladder leading up to it, and Coyote started up. When one of the girls saw him coming she doubled up her feet and kicked him off the ladder. The other old man asked, "What's wrong?" "Well, she kicked me!" "You know very well that's no way to succeed," replied the old coyote. They began to add wood to the fire and stir it, and it got very hot.

Again one of the girls said to the Tupnekč, "You are a fool, you don't know anything!" He replied, "Why do you say I'm stupid? I know how to make everything, even ?ostus." "You don't know what that is!" she said. "Certainly I know. I know what ?ostus is," he answered. "No, you don't!" "Yes, I do!" he said. "An ?ostus is when you make a hole in the ground and put in hot rocks and grass and three or four heads of pox." The girls began to laugh. He said, "You get more grass and cover it with dirt, and the next day you uncover it. You eat it, and it's very tasty and fragrant." The girls laughed some more, and said, "You're stupid, you don't know anything!" They pushed him and teased him, and said, 'You're very dumb. Your companions are making a fool of you!"

First one girl would push him and then the other, and so it

went all night. At dawn the Tupnekč got up and went outside, and Coyote wanted to climb up into the bed with the girls. But the other coyote said, "No, it's morning. Think of something else!" So Coyote went outside to see where the Tupnekč was. He found him and said, "Well, what should we do now?" The Tupnekč replied, "I am going to leave. You can stay if you want to, but I'm going!" "When are you going?" asked Coyote. "Right now. I'm going to get my quiver and go," replied the Tupnekč. "Why don't you stay with the girls?" asked Coyote. The Tupnekč said, "No, I'm going home to my grandmother and that's it!" He went inside to get his quiver and found the girls asleep. They had slept a little but the other three had been awake all night. He took his quiver and left for home without saying a word. Coyote said, "I'm going too." The old coyote replied, "Well, not me. I'm from here and here I'll stay."

Coyote followed the Tupnekč, but the Tupnekč stayed ahead of him the whole way to the spring. There Coyote stopped and ate some food. On the way up the hill the Tupnekč went slower and waited for Coyote to catch up, and then they went on together. They finally reached Momoy's house, and the old woman was happy to see them. She said that she had thought they weren't ever going to return, and the Tupnekč said that he would always come back. "How did things go?" she asked. "Everything went fine," the Tupnekč said. Then Coyote asked, "Don't you have anything to eat?' She brought out food, and he began to eat and eat, while the Tupnekč ate tobacco. Coyote got full at last and said, "Now I'll go on home and see how things are there." "Go ahead," said Momoy, "but come back in a day or so when you have time."

The Tupnekč began hunting again, and every day he hunted; he had nothing else to do. Then one day Momoy began to ask him why he didn't get married. "Why don't you find a girl to marry? She would keep you company," she said. "Why should I marry? I have more fun talking with my kinsman, Coyote," he answered. But she kept after him every day, saying that he should get married, until one day he said, "I don't like you bothering me like this! I'm going to leave! I don't know if I'll return or not." He left without saying goodbye or anything. He just grabbed his pespibata and went, and I don't know where he is now. He didn't want a wife. And Momoy went on living in her house.

sutiwayan ulʔatucʔ

C.

Coyote's Life and Times

21 COYOTE AND LIZARD
Pio Jose, Juan Estévan Pico's maternal uncle, told Fernando the following Coyote story on two successive evenings. Coyote could scent what anything had in its entrails, and he could make a snake come out from seven feet under the ground. Everyone respected Coyote. As soon as Coyote saw a woman he would say "tsu, tsu," which means a sweet kiss, and he said it so long that it made his snout long.

The first time Coyote met Lizard (he-of-the-flute) was on the beach. Lizard was attracted by the light of poppies on Santa Cruz Island back of Swaxɨl to discover the source of that which lights the world. He saw the serenity of the world and played on his flute. (Just as the bone whistle knows what it is saying, so the four holes of the flute were the voice of the world. The sound meant something to the Indians.) The Lizard played three times, and the fourth time he played Coyote heard him. Coyote had built a fire on the beach and was baking clams when they met this first time. Lizard told Coyote that he had heard of him and wanted to ask him something. "I have been told that you move in the sphere of xutaš, the goddess Earth. Tell me what you have seen, Coyote," said Lizard. Coyote replied, "I once saw the game of gomi played on Xutaš day between Turtle and Hawk. The captain of Xutaš ordered the game to be played. All the world was there."

Coyote then told Lizard what had happened: Turtle and Hawk were to race around the world, for it was a day of Xutaš, and whoever lost was to be burned alive along with his referee. They looked for someone whose judgment was just and found that Coyote himself was the only one fit for the job. Then Turtle selected Coyote as his referee in the name of Xutaš, and Coyote could not refuse. He had to act against his will. Every afternoon for three days Coyote and Turtle went to the starting point, and Coyote watched Turtle's movements and how long it took for him to get his head out of his shell, and so on. On the morning of the fourth day the word was given and the racers started. Hawk rose into the air. Turtle struck the ball and they could only see a streak. Then they saw Turtle going. Hawk got into a strong wind and it completely unnerved him. When they got to where the racecourse turned Hawk was already worn out, but Turtle had no trouble. His ball crossed the line first. Some of the people said that Turtle had won, but others said, "No, wait and see who crosses the line first." Turtle came in first, and Hawk just barely made the line.

Then there was a great argument about who had won the race—Turtle or Hawk—and at last they asked Coyote who had won. He said, "Turtle won, although Hawk is considered the swiftest person in the world." "Why did Hawk lose?" they asked. Coyoted answered, "Hawk was infatuated with a woman, and so he lost." They asked, "How can you prove that Turtle won?" "Hawk crossed the line but his ball hasn't," Coyote answered. (Turtle had a clear conscience. Nothing equals a cloudy conscience for causing ineffectiveness in the world. A clear conscience always works better, for when you have a cloudy conscience you must always be on guard, making sure that things work out in such a way that you are not detected). But the final judgment was that Turtle had lost, for he did not enter the ring at the same time as the ball, and therefore Hawk came in first. So they sentenced Turtle to be burned. He said that as soon as they put him in the fire he would urinate and put it out. When the order was given to burn Coyote as well, he took to his heels. They couldn't catch him—and that was why he was there on the beach now talking to Lizard.

Lizard said, "You aren't safe, for the first time they catch you they'll burn you! You must go in search of qupe, the poppy flower, and take armfuls and present them to Hawk's

bride. Then you will be forgiven." "But I am not familiar with
that flower," said Coyote. Lizard said, "Well, when you see it,
it is as if the sun itself is on the ground, so beautiful is the color
of the flower." Now the two of them had been in many places,
but they had never seen any beauty like that of the poppies on
the islands, and they thought it very promising. But neither
wanted the other to see him dive under the ocean. So Coyote
said, "I am tired of hiding all the time, and you tell me I'm
likely to be burned. Oh well, I might as well be drowned as
burned!" He dived into the ocean and disappeared. Then
Lizard said, "I might as well try it too." He dived into the
ocean also.

Both succeeded in reaching the island, but neither knew
the other was there. When they saw the poppies they said to
themselves, "This is the flower!" Coyote wanted to bring a
plant back with him, but he had no place to put it. But he was
so impressed with the flower that he knew he could describe it
exactly. Lizard, however, was able to put a poppy plant in his
flute. Both Coyote and Lizard returned to this side of the
channel, and when they met again Lizard said, "You disappeared several days ago and we haven't seen anything of
you. Tell me where you have been all this time." When Coyote
told him that he had been over to the islands and had found
the flower he had been told to search for, Lizard said, "What
proof do you have that you were successful?" "Well, I found
everything exactly as you said it would be," Coyote replied. "I
can describe the entire plant to you—its size, color, and every
detail of the flower." When Coyote had finished describing the
poppy Lizard knew that he had in truth seen the real flower,
and he said, "You are safe now. Tomorrow you must go to the
princess and present her with this plant I brought back. And
take your firesticks and a horn of pespibata." (Coyote used to
put some pespibata on his hand and blow it in the direction of
a supposed menace.) "Now take care of yourself, and remember—sometimes the less capable person comes out ahead of
the person who is more capable."

The next day Coyote took the poppy plant that Lizard had
brought back in his flute from the island and presented it to the
princess, saying, "Here is your reflection. I have sought it
throughout the realm of Xutaš, but I didn't find it until a few
days ago. Here is the complete plant." Then the princess told

Coyote, "You are safe now, you are forgiven—but take care, for often the one who is less capable succeeds in obtaining more than he who is more capable." Coyote was very happy when he heard these words, and all the way back he kept saying to himself that he was safe now, and that everything had turned out just as Lizard had said it would. He considered Lizard a person of great knowledge. He had tried to do Turtle all the good he could, but he had just missed being burned. "Sometimes a good deed is repaid with a bad one," he thought.

He came to where Lizard was and told his friend all that had happened. After they had talked the matter over for a while Coyote asked, "Now tell me, what is going to be the result of all this?" "Listen," said Lizard. He began to play his flute, and when he had finished Coyote said, "The sound of your flute is a submission and lament. All will surrender to the power of the world, and thus man will be happy. I am going to leave you a flute song that you can play when you think of me." Then Coyote sang:

q?wɨlmiye, q?wɨlmiye,
čuqile ha!
I'm right on the mark—
Let truth emerge from the conscience of the guilty.

Coyote said, "Don't fear the power of Slo?w, or his laws. If you enter his house with a clear conscience, they will think well of you and take care of you. Remember your advice, that I should take that beautiful flower to the princess. She is pure of heart, without any black mystery, just as it is also pure in the house of Slo?w. The family of Slo?w are of the purest and his sons are the salt of the earth." When Coyote and Lizard were about to part Lizard said, "When you go to a friend's home and meet his daughters, always speak to them in words that are straightforward and pure. Never use words with double meanings." Coyote replied, "If anyone should ask you to play your flute so as to make fun of you, tell them that the flute is yours and that they can go their way. Wherever you live, never entertain anyone with an evil mind, and remember that self-love or ill-founded pretensions possess one."

Then Coyote and Lizard each went his own way, and each got along as best he could—Lizard by means of the powers of

his flute, and Coyote by being able to get along with all the
beings of the world, even the snakes—until they met again on
Xutaš day. "How are you?" asked Coyote. Lizard replied,
"Well, I have followed your advice, and I found things to be
just as you said they were, for I met a man who came close to
surpassing me with less knowledge." Then Lizard went on to
tell his friend what had happened. He had started out all right,
and everything was going fine until this stranger had arrived.
"Hello, are you all alone here?" asked the Stranger. "Yes, all
alone." "How do you pass your time?" the Stranger asked.
"As well as I can pass it," replied Lizard. The Stranger said,
"You are all alone here and unmolested by anyone. You are
lucky. You ought to make things in this place, things that have
never been seen before." Then Lizard remembered the words
of his friend Coyote, that the sound of his flute brought
submission to the power of the world, and so he thought that
he had the true light on life. He said, "Yes, your advice is all
right, but I have seen many things surrender to the power of
the world and I think I'm on the right path."

These words set the Stranger to thinking, and after he had
though a while in silence he said, "I guess you are right, but I
met a man on the road whom I had never seen before, and he
thought differently." Then the Stranger told Lizard that his
new acquaintance had said, "We are liable to meet other
people in the course of our travels who might ask us, 'Where
do you come from?' and my answer would have to be, 'I don't
know.' And if they ask, 'Where are you going?' we must
answer, 'We don't know where we are going.' And if we are
asked who made this world, what shall I say? Perhaps I shall
say, 'Well, we did, for all we know.'" The Stranger replied,
"Well, a lie is very ugly." But the other man said, "Well, I have
traveled for a long time, and you are the first person I've met."
"Yes, that's true," the Stranger answered, "though there is
nothing that sounds as bad as a lie." "That's true, but that's
the way you and I have to live, for in the course of our life we
will find both credulous and incredulous people," said the
man.

The Stranger and his new acquaintance traveled together
for a while, and after some time they reached a village. When
the villagers saw the two men approaching they came out to
meet them with great ceremony. They were given food to eat

and a house to sleep in, and the next day all of the old people in the village came to see them. An old man who had come with the multitude asked, "Where do you come from?" "We come from a land whose name neither of us knows," replied the Stranger. Then the old man asked, "Who was it who made this world?" Before the Stranger could reply his companion spoke up and said, "We did!" "Why did the two of you make it?" "So that many people might live," replied the Stranger's companion. Then the old man asked again, "If you two have made this world, how are we to make a living?" "By gathering the fruits, which are God!"

When the Stranger heard the answers his companion gave to these question, he came to the conclusion that the man was exaggerating his own importance in the villagers' minds and would soon fall from favor, and so he decided to leave and go elsewhere, as politely and prudently as possible. After the Stranger and his companion had been in the village for a little while, each of course had a following. The Stranger made up his mind that before he left he would teach his followers ways of making a livelihood—how to make and use bows and arrows for killing game and for self-defense, how to make those things that are useful in gathering the different fruits given us by the God which is the earth—and he was the first to teach the people that. Before he had left the village the Stranger told his followers, "I have instructed you in everything useful, but remember that there are believers and non-believers. If I show you something that is true, that is useful, believe it; but if I tell you something that is not true and you believe it, you believe in something false."

When the Stranger had finished telling Lizard about his experiences, Lizard decided that the Stranger's words meant submission like the sounds of his flute. Lizard said, "You are right, but you should have told your followers that if strangers came into their midst they should be made to live apart, thereby ensuring peace. Otherwise there would always be turmoil." "You speak very well," said the Stranger. "For the idea must exist before the creation of the soul. You are right—if a stranger should come, place him apart in some nice place where he will be cared for and will not suffer." The Stranger left Lizard and returned to the village, and after he had spent a few days there he once more returned to the place where

Lizard was living. "How were your people getting along?" asked Lizard. "Oh, they were doing quite well, and when I left they showed me respect and were anxious for my return," replied the Stranger. Lizard said, "Well, if you found and left your people well, they may consider themselves fortunate for the basic things you taught them."

Lizard and the Stranger lived together for quite some time, observing the motions of the earth so that they would be useful to future generations. Once Lizard asked, "Do you think we will have an abundance of wild fruits?" The Stranger answered, "I really can't say, for I haven't consulted my astronomy well." Then Lizard said, "I wish my friend Šipiši-waš (Coyote) would come." (Coyote had a way of testing to see whether or not it would be a good year: he would place a leech on a hot rock, and if it didn't die after discharging all the water it had, it was going to be a rainy year.) Then on Xutaš day they met Coyote, and Lizard told him what had happened since the last time they had met. "What has become of your companion whom you met on the road?" Coyote asked the Stranger. The Stranger replied, "I don't know." Then Coyote said, "Well, I can tell you something about him. All of his followers have killed themselves because of his wrong ideas, but you have done well, for you have given your people the right advice, and truth will always predominate the world over." Then he added, to no one in particular, "Nuqaqe qʔwilmiye."

Lizard asked Coyote how he had gotten along, and Coyote said, "I escaped being burned, and Turtle is still alive. All of those born since the day of the race know that Turtle won, for although he threw the ball first and left the starting line last, he was the first one to return to the line with the ball. And what merit would there be in Hawk returning first if he did not bring the ball with him?" Lizard said that the ball was the image, the idea, and was followed by the creation of the soul, the coming into life of those born hereafter. The Stranger said that that was true, for such is the creation of the soul. Then Lizard said to his companions, "Brothers, as long as there is someone to support falsehood, things will not go well in the world." Coyote said to the Stranger, "You have done very well, and now your name is Qʔwilmiye."

(Qʔwilmiye means "I am right on the mark." Lizard's name was ʔEnemeʔme, which means "he sleeps, but his heart is vigilant," and Coyote's name was Sɨpɨsiwas, "he who knows.")

One day Lizard asked Coyote, "What can we do to see things more clearly?" Coyote replied, "Go and look in the mirror of the sea. The clear light of the sun on the sea is a mirror that enables you to see clearly all that is within you. That is all. When you enter that ocean you go to the last resting place. That is the end. One person dies, another resurrects to take his place. We are here in this world looking at the mirror of the sun." The Stranger died, and Coyote and Lizard remained. They discussed the resurrection of their dead companion, and Coyote said that they should observe the next one born to see if he resembled the deceased. He would be a qaliwa, a relative of the deceased (not a real relative, but a person of similar thought or personality). Lizard said, "You are perfectly right. When our blood is strong a son must come forth—what we call a consanguine relative."

(When a child is still in the womb the Indians believe him to be a valiant man already. Fernando once heard a man address his son as kišnuna, and the son answered qʔwaʔyaʔya, "by my grandfather," referring to the relationship. The Indians always gave the derecho [right] to men and not to women.)

Coyote and Lizard were sad over the death of their companion. A third man came along and asked, "What do you miss?" "We miss the sparkling of the sun," they answered. The man went away, and as he was traveling he saw a great stump burning, with sparks flying high in the air. He took a stick and poked the fire, and sparks flew in all directions. He said, "Well, I'll do this again so that the two will see the sparks of the sun." He said that he would sing to make it more effective. He sang:

Qiwuhutipuxyun (four times)
Puxyun (four times)

He wanted his voice (with the aid of the wind) to sound like thunder to Coyote and Lizard. When he had finished singing they said, "What can that be?" The man told them that on the following night they would see the sparks of the sun. And the next night he showed them the sparks of the sun: he pointed at the stars. Coyote and Lizard told each other that the man must be the reincarnation of their departed friend, and that that was the reason that he took so much interest in them. But the fellow had already gone.

(The stars are called the sparks of the sun. The sun snaps his firebrand and it throws sparks.)

22 COYOTE'S COLOR

When Coyote was a man he was very smart in all things. Once he saw a young woman that he liked very much, and since he knew that she always went a certain way, he went and lay down beside the trail and pretended to be dead in order to see what she would do. The girl came along and saw him lying there. She took out her little bowl of paint and a brush and began to paint him an unnatural auburn color. Before she left she told him, "Get up and go to your wife and ask her forgiveness!" When he got up he found that he was no longer his natural color. He didn't dare face his wife again, and so he departed for parts unknown. But his wife's curse reached him.

(A story such as this was told because of its moral teaching.)

23 COYOTE AND SLOʔW'S DAUGHTER

Once the daughter of Sloʔw (Eagle) left Swaxil village on Santa Cruz Island to fish in her canoe. She arrived at the kelp bed and anchored her canoe to the kelp, where she was going to fish. She dropped her line into the water and pulled out some fish. While she was thus fishing, Šipišiwaš (Coyote) happened to look over a cliff on the shore and saw her there. He sat down and watched her carefully and soon recognized her as the daughter of Sloʔw. He said, "How pretty and bright she is!" He began to meditate, and after a little while said to himself, "I am going to get into the water. I shall go and grab the fishhook and remove the bait of that pretty chief's daughter."

Now whenever Coyote saw a pretty woman or heard about a pretty woman he would sing the following formula:

i sari wa (it will continue indefinitely)
i sari wa
i sari wa
i sari wa

yuqire (hurray!)
yuqire
yuqire
yuqire

Coyote was terrible. Whenever there was a fiesta he would always go, and when nearing the village he would hide himself and say this formula, and the people would go out and find him and ask why he said the formula. Now when Coyote saw the eagle's daughter fishing, he sang the formula and then estimated the dive he would have to make and how far he would have to swim to the kelp. Then he backed up, took a deep breath and got his courage up, and with a running jump dived over the cliff. He swam under the water and grasped the girl's hook, and she began to pull on the line. Coyote had not wanted to let go of the hook anyway, but he soon had little choice, for his paw got caught on the fishhook and the daughter of Slo?w kept pulling on the line. He pulled on the cord but he couldn't get free.

She played him for a while, but finally hauled on the line until Coyote's head was out of the water. Coyote laughed and the girl cried, "Aha, you're Coyote! Your head is black and so is your tail. They'll call you Old Man Fish from now on." She let the line slacken so that he dropped back in the water. He was very angry and swam ashore taking her fishing tackle with him. The daughter of Slo?w remained there, hoping someone would come down to the beach and see her, but no one came. She went ashore and sat on a rock. In the middle of the afternoon some birds came and ate the fish she had caught, and she began to think about her home and her father, and she wanted to go home, but she was ashamed to go home for now she had no fish to take with her. And she began to think about Coyote and everything that had happened, and she said to herself, "What bad luck I have! I scorned Coyote, and there is no one else in all the world like him. . . . If I had not rejected him, what a beautiful place the world would have seemed to us. Now Coyote has forced me not to reject him, but I reject

God, I reject the world! What I shall do now is dive alone into the water. In the name of our mother earth I will do this."

All night she sat and thought, and as morning came she arose and plunged into the water, and that portion of her body in the water began to change, to alter. But the water was shallow and she could only submerge the part below her waist, so that half of her body stayed human while the bottom half became fishlike. Certain brilliantly colored shells and fish are all that now remain of that part of her body. And the princess wandered the ocean, never sleeping, until one day she reached the shore of the island called San Nicolas (Xalašat) where she climbed up on the rocks and went to sleep. Now there were some people living on that island, and two boys came along the beach there and found her asleep. They recognized her, of course, but how she had changed! She had the tail of a fish and the breasts of a woman. Her hair was long and very thick, and loosely flowing over her shoulders. The two boys quietly drew back into some rocks and watched her. She finally awoke, sat up, and began to comb her hair and cry. She cried but her heart was dancing. Then she sang a little song, saying:

> Woe is me!
> My love must soften your heart . . .
> Come, my beloved!

The boys returned home and told their grandfather what they had seen. "What did she say as she began to cry?" asked the grandfather. One of the boys sang the song they had heard. Then the old man went back to the beach with them to see for himself. "She who cries is not really crying but singing a song of repentance," the old man said to one of his grandsons. "Now she repents because she is none other than the daughter of Slo?w, she who disappeared from swax̣ɨl. She is called the flower of the world. All of the abalone and fish and the coral snakes in the sea are her offspring. Now our island is called Xalašat." Xalašat is said to mean laurel or victory.

24 COYOTE'S SEARCH Juan de Jesus once told Fernando the following story, continuing it through three successive evenings, for it is quite long.

When Coyote rejected Slo?w's daughter and she dis-appeared, Slo?w told all of the animals to go out in the world and seek her. He appointed a committee of four—Gopher, Turtle, Owl, and Coyote (the grandson of the Coyote who rejected Slo?w's daugher)—to make a special search. Gopher looked in the earth, Turtle in the water, and Owl in the air, while Coyote tramped all over the world to see what he could learn. These four went out incognito, and they had many adventures. Sometimes Coyote would go and lie in the mud and look out to see if people were approaching or to see if he could hear anything. Sometimes he pretended to be deaf or blind, and he feigned anything he thought might be advan-tageous for his purpose.

One day Coyote started out on the road, and he was very hungry. He had not eaten for a long time. He had traveled some distance when he noticed that someone had built a fire beside the road, and when he looked more closely he dis-covered the tail of a roasted salmon sticking out of the ashes. When he saw what it was he was overjoyed. He addressed the fish, saying, "I have to know why you are asleep, buried in this fire! What you have gone through is quite something. Anyone finding you in this condition would be curious. Whose fault is it? Wake up! It's late. Tell me why you're buried!" When he had finished talking he sat down, and as he sat there Xelex came and circled above him three times. Coyote said, "Good, you yourself gave me this fish I've found, therefore I'm going to see what it is!" He grabbed the salmon tail and said, "Wake up! Ah, you won't wake up!" He pulled the roasted salmon out of the ashes and then said, "Xelex gave it to me!" He ate the fish, leaving only the bones and tail, and when he was through he buried the remnants in the ashes again with the tail sticking out. Then he went and lay down under a tree and went to sleep.

While he was sleeping, Frog, whose fish Coyote had eaten, came to get the salmon. He took hold of the tail and pulled it out of the ashes and found only a skeleton left. Frog exclaimed, "Ah, in all the world there is only one person who could have done this—Coyote! But never mind. I won't urinate now, and all the springs will dry up. Coyote will be thirsty, and thus I'll pay him back!" Frog went into his house and tied the door shut, and the springs dried up. Pretty soon Coyote

woke up, and he was thirsty. He went to the stream to get a
drink, but there was only dust where the water had been. He
went to another stream and it was also dry. He sat down and
said to himself, "Ah, the roasted salmon belonged to Frog!"
He hurried off to Frog's house, and when he arrived there he
stood outside the door and shouted, "Frog, give me some
water! I'm dying of thirst!" Frog didn't answer. Again Coyote
shouted, "Frog, give me some water, I can't stand it any
longer!" Frog still didn't answer, and finally Coyote said, "I
give up. Frog, just you wait!" He stepped back a little from the
house and adjusted both his firesticks and his tobacco tubes.
Then he ran up the side of Frog's house and sat down on one
side of the smokehole. He took out his firesticks and built a
fire, and pretty soon Frog's house began to burn. Coyote
climbed down and sat there watching the house burn. In a
little while he heard a report, and he said, "Hiss!" (in imitation
of what he thought was the sound of Frog exploding from the
heat). Then Frog's house exploded into sparks and burned to
the ground, and in a little while all that was left was a pile of
ashes.

Coyote still sat there watching it, and pretty soon he saw
Frog emerge from the heap of ashes, unscathed. Astonished,
he said, "How did you keep from burning?" Frog answered,
"You burned my house, but I dug a hole and urinated in it and
then got in it. That's why I didn't burn. Now cheer up and go
to the river and drink, for I have already urinated." Coyote
went and drank, and when he returned he said, "Frog, tell me
the truth—do you know the fate of the daughter of Slo?w?"
Then Frog answered, "Only you might know, for you are your
grandfather's heir. Cheer up, for you are not to blame for what
you have done to me. Xelex is the one who caused it. He is the
servant of Slo?w. Don't rely on what you have inherited from
your grandfather, or on he who says that he is going to protect
you, for you are now working for Slo?w. Don't cheat or
deceive any poor soul. When there are many of you coyotes
trouble is inevitable. That which all you men seek is called the
flower of the world, the daughter of Slo?w, because she
disappeared, because she repented. Now cheer up, and continue doing your duty. You're going on now. You will meet a
woman; speak to her from outdoors, and there you will meet
your fate."

So Coyote left, thinking about what he was heir to, thinking that he was to have some hardships but that he had received much good advice, and that he would at last be like the light of day. He resolved to harm no one. He would meet a man and he would not talk with him very long before the man invariably gave him something for which he was grateful. The first such man Coyote met asked him where he was going. Coyote said, "I'm just going along this road. I don't know what is ahead, but I'm going to see." The man replied, "It's late now, come home with me and spend the night." Coyote accepted the invitation. On arriving at the man's house Coyote found two old men, three girls and a boy, and his host's wife also there. One old man said to the other, "A man has arrived with my nephew, and he resembles the family that disappeared." The other old man replied, "You're right. Go and talk with him and see what he says to you." So the first old man approached Coyote and said, "You have arrived, I see." "Yes," said Coyote. The old man said, "And what great things or events have you seen in the world?" Coyote answered, "My dear sir, events in the world are all right, but what changes things in this world is love of a woman!" The others overheard this and said nothing. They were speechless.

After waiting for them to speak up and say something, Coyote spoke to the old man who had addressed him, saying, "My dear sir, what events did you notice in the world when you were young?" The old man replied, "It is just as you have said." Then Coyote said, "Well, sir, if you look carefully at this grown daughter of yours, what do you think?" The old man hung his head. "Don't look sad," said Coyote. "Tell me, if you look carefully at your grown daughter, what do you think?" "Yes, it is true," said the old man. "It is the same as then—a man will rejuvenate on seeing a young woman, he will imagine that he is young again." Coyote said, "Yes, what you have said is all right, but you have omitted one thing: it is desire that rejuvenates, not his body!"

Coyote saw that the old man had nothing to say, and he drew closer to them and addressed the one who had spoken to him first, saying, "Did you live in the village of Capwaya?" The old man answered, "Yes, I have been there, and I knew a man who disappeared. I knew the captain of the village, who went to an island and never returned. He was such a good man that we wish to know what became of him. He had a grandson who must have reached manhood by now, and he was as active a man as his grandfather." Coyote said, "What were the good deeds that this man did?" The old man replied, "He was such a good man to both old and young, man and woman. He would always help them with his good advice, and his words were so strong and penetrating that he always brought about a unison of will between man and woman. This often resulted in their marriage. He would go to each of them and say, 'You have reached manhood (or womanhood), and now you should do what is right in honor of your father and mother, to whom you should give rest and peace.' And to those who would not marry he would say, 'You must conduct yourself in a fitting manner so that your aged father and mother may live a quiet life. Remember how your mother and father held you in their arms and how they labored for you. You don't have to hold them in your arms, but labor for them and minister to their wants, so that their last days in this world may be happy.'" "Did you people know that man's grandson?" asked Coyote. "Yes," said the old man. "What was his name?" Coyote asked again. "Aha, before he was born a number of the aged men got together and said that the boy was to have the name Nawaqmayt," replied the old man. Coyote said, "Do you understand what this word means?" "Yes," said the old man. "It is something to be feared. When you hear anything dreadful, you prepare to present yourself at once to Nawaqmayt. And although you might never have seen him, Nawaqmayt could read your mind without talking with you." (These two old men feared Nawaqmayt, but they were talking to him right then, for Coyote was Nawaqmayt!)

The man who had brought Coyote home then asked him if he was tired. "No, but your people are tired," said Coyote. "And if you care for your people, you must see that they rest." The man didn't answer, but he went and told his wife, "That man who came home with me says that our people are tired, and that I must see that they rest." The wife answered, "I'm one of your people and I don't feel tired—although it's true that I am tired at heart, because we have three grown daughters who have arrived at womanhood but are lonesome because we live so far from any neighbors. If we lived somewhere else conditions would be different, and perhaps one or all of our daughters would be married. That is what makes me tired of heart. And so are they. That must be what that man meant when he said your people are tired."

Then the man told his wife, "Now you go over and talk to him and see what he says to you." So the wife went over to Coyote, and Coyote said, "Ah, you did the right thing in coming to me, and your daughters must do so too. They must come to me to learn what they should do." So the three daughters came also. Coyote said, "Your duty is to have consideration for the world, for by doing so we always live, protected by this world." Then he turned to the mother and said, "And it is your duty to advise your daughters to find someone to marry, that they may have someone to protect them, even though he be an old man—for man though old is the shadow, the protector of this world of ours. You have a son, and should a woman ever come here, bid her come in, for she will come here looking for a protector, and if she comes you will find that she is an orphan. When she comes ask her in and let her marry your son, and when she is married and all is well go over to Capwaya village. Now I have told you what to do. Advise your girls well. And tell them that though those old men are old they are well acquainted with the ways of the world. Tell your daughters that they will fare well at Capwaya, and should not place any belief in youthful talk nor in the enjoyment of poppies." (People used to say that poppies were the ruin of girls. Boys would take girls out gathering poppies, and their beauty would overcome them and cause them to yield to the boys.)

After Coyote had given this advice to the mother, he said, "I'm going now." Then he turned to the woman's husband and said, "When that girl comes that I told you about, let her come in and marry your son, for she is the last one left of the village of Capwaya. Treat her well. She is the owner of the village of Capwaya. And tell your daughters to take care of themselves and you too, for you are all going to do well. And tell them to marry those old men, for they are well up in the world, and not to mind younger people." Coyote arranged everything, and the next morning he left.

After he had been traveling for two days he remembered what Frog had said to him about coming to a house where there was a woman, and advising him to speak to her but not to attempt to enter the house. Shortly thereafter he came to Woodrat's house and stopped outside her door. "I have arrived," he called. There was no answer, so he repeated what he had said two or three times. But there was still no answer. Then he remembered that Woodrat liked wild grapes very much, so he sang a song about grapes three times. But there was still no response from Woodrat. He finally got tired of trying to get her to answer, and so he took a stick and began to poke it into the house. While Coyote was getting the stick Woodrat came out of the house quietly and climbed up to the top of it, where she sat and watched him.

Coyote poked the nest for a while, and then he took out his firesticks and started to set it on fire. Still Woodrat didn't come out. He finally sat down and looked up, and there was Woodrat on top of the house. "Ah, you have been making fun of me," said Coyote. He urged her to come down, and said, "I set fire to your house because I was afraid there might be a rattlesnake or something else in there that might harm you!" Woodrat still didn't say anything. Coyote said, "You're laughing at me, making fun of me!" Coyote set fire to some more twigs, and Woodrat jumped to a nearby branch. But she slipped and fell, and Coyote grabbed her before she could get away. He didn't want to eat her there, and so he took her way out on a plain. He preferred to eat her out there in the open. That gave him much pleasure. He held her gently in his mouth, and he thought that he would say to her, "Ha, you thought I wasn't going to catch you, ha!" But as he opened his mouth to say that, Woodrat jumped down and scurried into a nearby hole and that was the last he saw of her.

25 COYOTE VISITS ŠIMILAQŠA

One time Coyote was up north in the Tulare country, and he used his ʔatišwin to change himself into a beautiful woman in order to fool people. He came to the house of Duck, who was a wealthy man, and Duck saw what he though was a pretty girl and said to himself, "I think I'm going to fall in love with this woman!" And he did. "I think I'll marry him," said Coyote. He got all dressed up and they were married. There was all kinds of food there in Duck's house and Coyote ate and ate. After dinner was over Duck said, "Let's sleep together now!" But Coyote did not want to (for they were

both men!) and so he said he was sick. So they had separate
sleeping places that night.

Now Coyote can make himself look just like a beautiful
woman for a little while, but only for a little while, and then he
changes back to being himself again. And when this happened
and Coyote regained his old form, Duck saw immediately that
he had been tricked and he became enraged and chased
Coyote clear out of the village and far down the trail. But
Coyote didn't mind too much for he had eaten very well the
whole time! He journeyed back home to syuxtun, where he
was married to Toad. When he arrived home many of the
people there were just starting out for the Tulare country to
gather seeds, and Toad was going too. But Coyote didn't go, of
course. In the old days, if a person didn't leave after doing
something bad he would be killed. Now Coyote thought they
wouldn't kill Toad if she went to the Tulare country, but they
did. And when everyone returned to syuxtun after their seed-
gathering expedition and told Coyote that his wife was dead,
he wouldn't believe them. He told his sons to go and look for
Toad and see why she hadn't returned.

One of the boys went clear over to the Tulare country and
asked the people there where Toad was, and they told him
only that she was dead. The boy returned and told Coyote
what he had learned, but Coyote still refused to believe that his
wife was dead. "Go and look for her again!" he said. The son
went north once more, and again he inquired about Toad. This
time the people there got irritated and said, "Your father came
and turned himself into a beautiful woman and married Duck,
but he changed back to his real self three days later after eating
all of Duck's food, and so Duck hired people to kill Toad when
she came here!" The son returned sadly home to syuxtun and
told Coyote that Toad had been killed because of what he had
done. This time Coyote believed that his wife was really dead
and he began to cry. He painted his face black and mourned.

The following evening he was sitting in his house when
the figure of Toad appeared suddenly before him. He jumped
up and said, "You've come back! Where have you been?" But
Toad did not answer, for she was a spirit. She just looked
around inside the house and then left. The same thing happened the following night—the spirit came in and looked
around without saying a word and then departed. On the third

night the spirit appeared once more, but this time when she left Coyote followed right behind her, for he knew that now she would be following the road that leads to Šimilaqša and he was determined to go along. (He was able to follow along behind her because he had his ʔatišwɨn.)

They passed first through vast tule thickets in the middle of the sea, and then they crossed the sea, and they came at last to the pole that rises and falls just this side of Šimilaqša. Toad crossed the pole safely and then turned and spoke to Coyote for the first time: "Go out on the log and as soon as you reach the tip jump to this side of the river as I did!" Toad said this because she wanted Coyote to be killed so that they would both be spirits and could enter Šimilaqša together. But Coyote had his ʔatišwɨn, and with this he bewitched the pole so that he was able to cross over safely to the other side and thus reach Šimilaqša.

At first he saw no one there, but he heard the sounds of many people talking and laughing and singing. "They are having a fiesta for my wife!" he thought to himself. In a little while he began to see the spirits of the dead, and they were all singing and dancing, eating and playing games there in Šimilaqša. Coyote began to wander around looking for something to eat, for he was very hungry by this time, but when he tried to pick up a handful of food it was like trying to seize the wind. At last he met Owl, who is the only person alive in Šimilaqša, and said to him, "I'm very thirsty!" Owl offered him some water, but when Coyote looked at it it was already fading away, and so he asked Owl for some real water that he could drink. Then Owl took him to a place where there was a spring of water. There was a huge pinacate leaning over the spring and covering it with its body, and Owl ordered it to move over a little so that Coyote could drink. After he had gotten a drink from the spring the two returned to where the spirits were dancing and singing and eating.

Coyote was very hungry and he kept trying to grab handfuls of the food the spirits were eating, but every time he did so it just faded away in his hand. After a while he got thirsty once more and returned to the spring, but this time he went by himself. The pinacate was still covering the spring with its body, and when he told it to move so that he could drink it never stirred. Coyote got angry and said, "Move over or I'll shoot you!'' The pinacate still refused to move, however, and finally Coyote got so mad he grabbed his bow and shot the pinacate with an arrow. But the water quickly filled with blood and he couldn't drink from the spring after all, so he returned to where the spirits were having their fiesta. The spirits wanted to kill Coyote so that he would become a spirit too, and so they said to him, "We're going to play walpiʔy." That was the name of a game they played there with a long, springy pole. They would pull the tip of the pole down and someone would climb on it, and then they released it and the spirit would be thrown clear to the sea. They thought that when Coyote tried it he would be thrown so far that he would surely be killed, but because he had his ʔatišwɨn he wasn't hurt at all when his turn came. The spirits tried to kill him with other games as well, but each time his ʔatišwɨn kept him from getting hurt. And he returned safely to syuxtun at last, though I don't remember how—I just remember that he did.

26 COYOTE RESCUES XELEX Once upon a time Xelex went fishing in the ocean with the mariners Mut and Heʔw. The three of them went out in a canoe. They were casting out a line when Xelex saw a big seabass. Xelex got his harpoon ready quickly and threw it, but as he did so he slipped and fell into the water. Just then a swordfish (ʔelyeʔwun) happened by and seized Xelex and carried him away. His two companions in the boat were looking all around hoping to see him come to the surface again, so that they could pull him aboard, but though they waited and waited there was no sign of him. Finally Heʔw took some bearings from the mountain peaks so that he could find the spot again, and they returned home sadly to syuxtun.

The wot, Eagle, questioned the comrades about what had happened, where his nephew Xelex was lost, and where he might be. They explained to the chief that Xelex had thrown his harpoon at a seabass and had inadvertently gone overboard with it, and that they had remained there quite a while hoping that he would reappear. Now Coyote happened to be standing nearby listening to all this, and he spoke up and said, "Abandon any hope that he will reappear. They have seized him and taken him away." Then the wot said, "Why is there no hope that my nephew will reappear?" And Coyote an-

swered, saying, "Because there they don't fool around." "Who
are these people that you are speaking about?" asked the wot.
Then Coyote said, "There are people who live in a village
under the sea, just as there are people up here." And then the
chief said, "What shall we do now? We must send someone to
rescue my nephew Xelex and bring him back again."

He?w volunteered to be the one to go and confront the
people under the sea, but the chief knew that only a clever
man could succeed, and so he selected Coyote, although
Coyote protested that he was not the man for the job. "I command you to go," said the wot, "and return with Xelex."
"Well," said Coyote, "do you know exactly where he fell in?"
"Yes," said Mut. Then they asked Coyote when he was
planning to leave. "Tomorrow," he said. "Tomorrow you will
take me to the place in your canoe, but first you must bring me
a lot of tobacco, plenty of pespibata." They brought him great
quantities of tobacco (for he knew that the ?elye?wun were
unaccustomed to tobacco), and finally he said, "Ah, this will
be enough, this will do." In addition to the tobacco he also took
some poison with him made from powdered toadstools; this he
placed in a towonowon fastened to his head. "I'll be well
served by this," he said. "With this I won't be lacking anything
of importance." Last of all he filled his quiver with arrows.
Then the wot asked why he didn't take someone with him,
and Coyote answered that one was enough, that any more
would be a hindrance, saying: "I only want the boys to take me
out in their canoe and show me where Xelex fell into the
water."

The next morning they left bright and early in the canoe,
and after a while came to the right spot. "Here is the place.
Right here Xelex fell into the water and disappeared." Then
the boys asked Coyote how long they should wait there for
him. "If I haven't returned within five days give up hope, for it
will mean that I am dead." But He?w said, "No, we will wait
one more day beyond that for you." "Good," said Coyote, "I
will find you. If you aren't right here I will look for you and
find you." Then he said goodbye to the two boys and plunged
into the water with all of his equipment. He arrived at the
bottom of the sea and began walking slowly along looking
about him. He said to himself, "Now where will I find the

house of the swordfish?" Actually, of course, he knew where it was. After walking quite a while he finally came to the house, but it was closed up tight. He walked all around it but he could find no door to enter by. The swordfish had gone out hunting as they did every day. He walked around the house once more and found eight windows but he still couldn't find the door.

"Well, here is the house," Coyote said, "and I'm being stupid. The door will be on the south side of the house." Then he took out some of his tobacco and began to chew it. He gave a little to the door, and the door liked it very much. "Open, door," said Coyote. "I will give you more tobacco." Then the door opened wide, and Coyote entered the house, while the door closed behind him. When he went a little way into the house he came to the fireplace, and there he saw a very old swordfish lying next to the fire in the ashes. And as his eyes became accustomed to the dim light he saw the body of Xelex hanging from the ceiling, dead. By now Coyote was in the very center of the house, but the old man by the fire did not say a word to him. So Coyote walked around and examined everything the swordfish had there inside their house.

Finally he spoke up and said, "These things are nothing, they are worthless. Our things are much better." By now it was getting late in the day, and Coyote said to himself, "Let them try to seize me, let them come whenever they want. Although I don't know what powers they might have; it could be that they can overcome me." Then he walked over to the fire and nudged the old swordfish with his foot and said, "What powers will your kinsmen have when they come? Will they arrive angry or not?" The old man said, "Well, their powers are nothing to worry about." "Aha, don't mess with me! They aren't going to get their hands on me!" And again the old swordfish said, "Our powers are mere trifles, they are nothing." At this Coyote began to throw pinches of poison from the towonowon into the old fellow's nostrils. The latter immediately began to sneeze wildly from the effects of the powder, and finally gasped, "Kinsman, it is enough, stop!" And Coyote said, "If you won't tell me what they will be like when they come, I will continue." "Then I have no choice but to tell you," the old man said. "But first cure me of this malady." Coyote asked him if they had any water in the house, and the old man said no. "Spit in your hand, then, and rub your forehead and temples with the saliva." The old man did this, and his sneezing quickly ceased.

Then Coyote questioned him again about the arrival of the other swordfish, but the old man gave the same answers as before, and once again Coyote seized his poison and threw some of the powder into the old man's nostrils. The latter began again to sneeze uncontrollably, and finally said again, "Kinsman, stop. Cure me, I cannot stand this malady any longer." Coyote said, "Well, you're going to stay sick just as long as you refuse to tell me what I wish to know." The old man was sneezing like crazy all this time. He didn't want to tell Coyote anything, but Coyote kept throwing pinches of the powder into his nose, and finally the old swordfish could stand it no longer. "Take it away, cure me," he said. "I will speak, and I will protect you from being injured by the others." "Fine," said Coyote. "Tell me and I will cure you."

So the old man spoke up and said, "Well, first of all a strong gust of wind arrives. It is the first thing to come, and it is a sign that they are very close. And then come some poles or clubs, which I think they throw. And that is what you must beware of and hide from, being clubbed to death, for many come at once, not just one." Then Coyote said, "I know very well that there is danger." The old man continued: "And then, finally, after everything else, a mist or fog comes. This mist enters, a white mist, and then disappears, and then a black mist comes, and when that dissipates there are the men with their loads: each one brings his whale." Coyote said, "Good grief, one doesn't fool around with clubs. What can I do, kinsman, to escape these clubs?" "I am going to hide you, and be sure not to stir. They will scold me and I will say there is nothing the matter. But they will be coming any time now."

At this Coyote began to shake with fear. Just then the little man got up from where he had been lying by the fire and said that the other swordfish were almost there. He was cured by this time, for his sneezing had stopped just as soon as he had finished telling what he knew. Now there were some whale hides in one corner of the house, and he covered Coyote completely with these and then lashed them down so that the wind wouldn't move them nor the poles injure him. And Coyote said, "I'm right at home here," and as he turned about

he saw that the edges of the skins all met at one spot and left
him a hole to breathe through. (The swordfish have no bows.
They seize the whales in some unknown fashion, and cut them
up. And the ʔelyeʔwun are fantastic eaters; they devour a
whale as if it were nothing.) Just then a tremendous gust of
wind came and the whole wall of the house shook. "Good
lord!" exclaimed Coyote. Then the wind subsided and it was
calm again. "It's better this way, but it was awfully strong," he
said. A moment later a white mist entered, and Coyote
watched it through the hole in the hides covering him. Then
the white mist disappeared and a black mist entered. Coyote
peeped out and everything was dark. And when the darkness
finally lifted the swordfish were standing there. And Coyote
said to himself, "What kind of men are these? They appear to
be old men, and they have a plume on top of their heads."

Just then one of them grasped a whale, and then another
one joined him, and the two together pulled the whale open.
Then four more took hold of the whale and they all pulled at it
with their hands and teeth. "How strong they are!" Coyote
exclaimed. Then one of the swordfish said to the old man,
"Whose tracks are these? Who has been walking here?" And
the old man answered, "Whose tracks could they be?" "You
are hiding something," said the first swordfish, and the old
man said again, "But who would come here? There is nobody
here, nobody." Then the swordfish began to dine. Coyote,
watching them, saw that when they ate they grabbed the meat
with their teeth and let the grease run down their forearms.
"What hogs," thought Coyote to himself. Then one of the
swordfish said, "Go, old man, and ferret out whoever came
here." And the old man replied, "Go on with your dinner.
Don't be stupid, who would come here?" "But I saw the
tracks!" "I assure you that there is no one here," said the old
man.

They kept eating, but one swordfish persisted in his
questions, insisting that they had a visitor hiding somewhere.
The old man kept denying that there could be tracks or
anything else, but one swordfish finally said that he would not
be satisfied until a search was made. At this point the old man,
seeing that all had eaten, said that someone had indeed come
to rescue Xelex and carry him away. "And who is this man?"
the others wanted to know. Then the old swordfish answered,

"He is an old man like me." "And where is he now?" "He left
to look for you," the old man replied. "Yes, that old man came
for Xelex, and you are going to have to give him up, for if you
don't he will make you all ill. It would be best for you to give
Xelex up to this old man." "Where is this old man now?" the
swordfish wanted to know. "Well, out there somewhere,"
ventured the old man. "And what is this old man going to do
to us?" asked one of the swordfish. Then another spoke up
and said, "No, he's right. It would be best for us to do the right
thing and give him up. That way we will be all right." Then
they all spoke up, saying, "Yes, it is best that we give Xelex
up." "And where is the old man?" one asked again. "Good,"
the old man replied. "If you are sure that you will surrender
Xelex to the old man I will speak to him, for he is almost upon
us now."

Then all the swordfish began to talk at once, saying that
they most certainly would give Xelex up. "Good," the old man
said again. "Now don't hurt him in any way, for others could
come just as he did." And one hastened to say, "No, there is
no danger of that, he need not worry now." Then the old
swordfish arose from his place in the ashes by the edge of the
fire and untied the lashings on the whale hides covering
Coyote, and said, "Behold!" And the other swordfish were
turning every which way, all talking at once to one another.
"Here he is," the old man said, and when they turned around
again Coyote was already standing there beside the old swordfish. "Where do you come from?" they asked. "Well, from my
own land." "And why have you come here?" "I've come for
my nephew, Xelex. And I also come because I was commanded
to do so by the wot, Xelex's other uncle. Incidentally, I have
many friends waiting for me up there," he said, pointing
upwards at a 45° angle. (This, of course, was simply a story to
frighten the ʔelyeʔwun.) "Fine," said one. "And when were
you thinking of leaving?" "Well, as soon as I'm ready," said
Coyote. "And as I'm ready now, I'll be leaving right away."
But the swordfish were determined to kill him some way and
keep him from returning to his own land, and so they said,
"Well, it's not a good idea for you to leave right away. Why
don't you stay three or four days?" "But my people are up
there. . . . Oh well, all right. I am very tired. I'll stay here for
four days and rest."

The swordfish began to pull steaks off of the whale, pulling it apart with their hands and teeth. They made twelve pieces out of the whale, and each piece looked awfully big to Coyote, who was pretty small. "All right," said one of the swordfish to Coyote, "let's eat." Coyote thought to himself, "I don't like the looks of this. I know they're trying to kill me." Now Coyote had his flute there with him. "All right, get ready to dine," they said to him. Coyote adjusted his flute so that no one could see it. "Have some," they said, and thrust a huge whale steak at him. Coyote made it enter the end of his flute so that he did not actually swallow it, giving a high, shrill cry as he did so, and the meat when out through the other end of the flute. A swordfish paused in his eating and thrust still another chunk of whale at Coyote with both hands. And again he said ʔp ʔp in a high, shrill tone and the steak fell through the flute. (He had the flute between his feet in such a way that no one saw it.) The swordfish saw that he was disposing of the meat with very little effort, and so they decided to really attack their dinner in order to surpass him, and to give him so much that he couldn't handle it.

They began to eat furiously, thrusting more and more chunks of whale meat at Coyote, but he kept right up with them, eating, defecating, eating, and disposing of every bit of meat they gave him. But he said to himself, "Tomorrow I'm going to get them drunk so that they won't be able to go out hunting." Finally the twelve pieces of meat were finished off, with Coyote disposing of the last piece in his usual way. "Where is there some water here?" he asked. "I am going to clean myself off." Then he remembered that there was no water, so he sat down on the floor and began to drag himself along as if he were cleaning himself off in this fashion.

The swordfish roused themselves from their torpor, and one said to Coyote, "You must be tired." "Yes, I'll dream well. I haven't slept for three nights because I've been worrying about my nephew," he answered. "Fine, you can go to sleep here in this corner." "Good," he said. He lay down on a mat in the corner, but the swordfish stayed up, sitting around the fire and talking about where they should hunt the next day. And Coyote said to himself, "I don't trust them. I know they are going to try to harm me somehow." The swordfish were sitting there talking about where they should go and what they should do the next day, and finally one said, "Let's take the little old man with us and see if he can keep up with us. Let's see if we aren't superior." And the others agreed: "Oh, we'll carry him far away. He can't travel like we can." Coyote overheard what was said, and said to himself, "I'll go with them tomorrow, but they aren't going to leave me behind. I'll see how fast they are. Everything I see here may be useful, and this trip will show me all the places they travel to."

He pretended to be asleep, but he was actually wide awake. Finally one of the swordfish said to him, "Wake up and let's go, it's time to be off." Coyote said, "Oh, I was sleeping." He immediately arose and bundled up his equipment carefully before leaving it behind and going with them. And so they started off with the swordfish a little way ahead, but no more, and Coyote kept the same distance behind them all the way. And one of the swordfish said to the others, "We will leave him a little farther on. He will tire and stay there. He won't return to the house." They were exerting themselves to the utmost to leave Coyote behind, but he still kept the same distance behind them. They went here, there, and everywhere, but Coyote was always right behind them. Finally they killed a whale to take home with them and started back, with Coyote still following empty-handed, bringing nothing but still coming, for he had taken a lot of tobacco with him and he had been chewing this all the time.

They arrived home with Coyote bringing up the rear. He was very tired and his knees were in bad shape, and he said to himself, "Oh, I feel terrible!" The swordfish ate and invited him to join them, but he said that he had no desire to eat, that he wasn't feeling well. "He's getting so old now that he doesn't want to eat," said the swordfish to one another. Coyote stayed sitting in his corner, groaning, and the ʔelye-ʔwun remained by the fire, thinking. Coyote was thinking that whale meat was not the proper food for him, and that undoubtedly it was what was making him sick, while the swordfish were thinking that he was certainly going to die. By now it was almost morning, and Coyote thought, "Now I'll cure myself." He pulled out the towonowon containing his poison from his ʔolotoc and said, "Now I'll take care of these swordfish before they can leave. I'll cast my medicine on them."

Then he pulled some poison out and began to throw it at the ʔelyeʔwun. The dust entered their nostrils and they began to sneeze. "They have to go, for I'm certainly not leaving. I'm going to rest," said Coyote. The swordfish beat a hasty retreat from the house, sneezing. They were gone the rest of the day, and Coyote took advantage of their absence to get some much-needed sleep. He slept all day at the house of the ʔelyeʔwun. Late in the third day the swordfish killed another whale and started home with it. "Now is the hour that they will surely be coming home," said the old swordfish to Coyote. "Hide yourself in the same way you did before." Once again he covered Coyote over with whale hides and lashed them down well. And in a short time a strong gust of wind came and shook the house so hard it seemed that it would fall down. "Wow, this is bad!" said Coyote. As soon as the wind ceased, the poles entered and pounded on him, but he had so many skins covering him that he wasn't injured. Next of all came the white mist, followed by the black mist, and when this had dispersed there were the ʔelyeʔwun with their catch of whales. "How ugly they are," thought Coyote. They began to eat and he watched them through the little hole in the skins covering him. "How ugly these people are when they eat, what pigs they are, how different from the way we eat our acorn soup with two fingers."

When the swordfish had finished eating they asked the old swordfish lying by the fire where the other little old man, Coyote, was. "He's here, covered up," he said. Then he got up and untied the lashings and took away the hides. Coyote came out and greeted them. They had been talking among themselves, and they wanted to see if he too could catch a whale or bring food home. So they said to him, "Tomorrow go out alone and look for something to eat." He thought to himself that that was just what he wanted to do, go out alone. "Fine," he said. "Tomorrow I'll go out and see what I can find." "Good, it doesn't matter whether you bring anything home or not, but do go out and return in the afternoon," they said. "I'm going to bed now because I'm old, and the last time I got very tired," Coyote replied. And he added to himself, "And now I shall make these people drunk so that they are unable to leave, so that they stay here asleep." And he lay down and pretended to be asleep. In the middle of the night he saw that some were sleeping now, without mats or anything, and there was no one talking or sitting up. So he opened his towonowon and threw powdered tobacco over the sleepers to make them drunk. He threw it as one throws grain to chickens, and it went into their nostrils. It was already getting light out when he grabbed some more tobacco and said, "These people can remain here asleep. I'm leaving." And while they slept there he left, walking away. And when some of them finally awakened and looked at the sun, it was already quite late in the day. Then they said, "It's very late, and the old man will be starting back already." And the old swordfish said, "He is coming now." Then some of them said, "What shall we do if he comes?" Just then Coyote came walking up to the house carrying a gigantic whale that he had caught. The swordfish were there in their house, and suddenly there was a strong gust of wind, and they lay down on the floor and the wind passed overhead. The wind died away, and the poles entered and knocked together, and the swordfish again fell to the floor. Then Coyote said, "Now I'll let loose my arrows." The poles stopped beating, and immediately the arrows came flying, passing just over the backs of the swordfish, and again they hugged the ground, shivering a little from fear of the arrows. Then the flight of arrows ceased and a white mist came, and when it lifted there was Coyote with a whale, a very large whale.

"Well," they said, "he's a very powerful person." Then the old swordfish spoke up and said, "Don't harm him, for he can hurt you worse than you can hurt him." And they stared at him and wondered how he could do so much more than they could, how he could be so strong. And one of them said, "He doesn't seem so very old now." Then Coyote told the swordfish that he was leaving in the morning. "But before you go we must have a race to see who is superior," one of the swordfish said to Coyote. "What will the course be?" he asked. "Will it be from here straight out to there?" he said, gesturing. "Yes," said the ʔelyeʔwun who wanted to race him. So Coyote quietly left the house and traveled along the proposed race course for a while, and then sat down and defecated. He shaped the feces into a coyote-like form, and then addressed it, saying, "You are a coyote like me and you are going to race tomorrow with the ʔelyeʔwun. We are going to run a race." Then he went further on and did the same thing again. "You will get up and run, and run to that point there where the next coyote is, and then it will also run, always just ahead of the swordfish. You will run one way, and then you will run back the same way. But the swordfish will not have such helpers."

The next morning dawned and the eldest of the swordfish said, "Good, we won't have to leave at all, we'll stay here and watch." "Well, I'm not going to run for nothing," said Coyote. "What are you going to wager, what is the prize?" The eldest replied, "Well, if you win, you may carry Xelex off with you, and if you lose, you take nothing away." "All right," said Coyote. Then up stepped the swiftest of the swordfish and said he was ready. "Are you ready?" he asked Coyote. "I think so," said Coyote. The starter clapped his hands three times, and at the third clap the race began. Coyote soon fell behind the swordfish. "Wow, I'd surely lose," he said. He stopped right there and lay down, and his "ally" went on, now out ahead of the swordfish. And on arriving at the next stage the imitation "coyote" rested while the next one continued the race. The swordfish looked ahead and was enraged. "That old man is faster than me!" he exclaimed. And all the time the real Coyote was lying there resting near the starting place. The racers reached the end of the course and started back, the figure of Coyote always in the lead. When they reached the spot where the real Coyote was lying, he got up and continued the race while the coyote "figure" dropped out.

Coyote arrived at the finish line where all the other swordfish were gathered, watching, and he was already tired and red from running. "Well, what do you say?" he asked. "You win," said the eldest. "You win, there's no doubt about it." And Coyote was very tired; he kept getting up and lying down, saying how far it was to the end of the race course and back. "Well, tomorrow I'm leaving with my nephew," he said finally. "All right, you won," said the eldest swordfish. "But tonight we shall have a dance." That night the ʔelyeʔwun began to sing and dance among themselves; there were no guests and no women. And there was no leaping or jumping— they only dragged their feet, dancing and singing in their own fashion around the sides of the house, with the fire burning in the middle. And Coyote sat and watched. "That's not the way we do it," he said at last. "That's nothing!" Just then the dance ended and the swordfish sat down. "Now it's your turn, kinsman," they said to Coyote. "What can I do to please them?" Coyote thought to himself. "I know, I'll throw this poison so they can't see straight or see me clearly." So he threw the poison at them and then began to sing and dance. He sang, he threw out his medicine, and the swordfish watched as he danced, leaping and gamboling after the custom of his country.

Now it happened that there was a little water on the floor, and it seemed to the half-blinded swordfish that he was treading on water. *Cuq cuq cuq* it sounded underfoot, and the swordfish were half-crazy, drunk and almost blind from the medicine, watching in amazement. And they exclaimed among themselves, "This old man always wins, he is always superior to us! Yes, he's surely some kind of devil." Coyote sang louder and leaped higher when he heard what they were saying. Finally he stopped and sat down, and the swordfish sang and danced again, but as before they simply circled around without any fancy steps and repeated what they had done before. "Fine," said Coyote. "But now it's my turn again, kinsmen. Now I'll dance the šutiwɨʔyɨš." And he began to dance and sing, leaping from place to place, and then he suddenly seated himself and began slapping his knees with both hands simultaneously. Finally he leaped up and continued dancing until the very end, when he gave a tremendous leap that carried him clear to the ceiling.

"Wow!" said one swordfish. "Who would think that that old coyote could leap clear to the roof? I couldn't do it!" "All right," said Coyote, "it's your turn again." And once again the swordfish did the very same dance as before, while Coyote watched. And when his turn came he danced the nukumpiyɨš and the swordfish were astonished. By now it was very late, almost midnight, and Coyote said, "It would be a good idea to go to bed now, because I have a long way to travel tomorrow." Then the eldest swordfish answered, "All right. We've enjoyed ourselves very much, and now it's time to stop." So Coyote went and lay down in his corner. Some of the swordfish also lay down while others sat around the fire and talked after their fashion.

When the next morning dawned Coyote said, "Bring me my nephew, because today I have to return. They have been awaiting me for a long time up above." And then he asked,

"Who was it that seized my nephew and brought him here?"
One of the swordfish said that it was he who had brought
Xelex to the house. "Why?" asked Coyote. "Because I happened to run across him and I brought him here. That's the
way things are done here." Then all of the swordfish left to go
hunting, leaving only Coyote, the swordfish who had captured Xelex, and the old swordfish by the fire to settle the
matter and come to whatever agreement they wished.

"All right," said the swordfish, "now what do you want?
Why don't you take your nephew and go?" "Well, I want you
to restore him to life again, to revive him." And the swordfish
answered, "Well, I can't, since I didn't kill him. He was dead
when I found him." Now Coyote was very clever with his
hands, and when he heard this he took a pinch of poison and
cast it into the nose of the swordfish. The latter began to
sneeze violently. And Coyote said, "We're alone here, just the
three of us, for the others have gone hunting for food to make
up for the meals they missed yesterday. They will remain away
for a long time." He kept throwing pinches of poison at the
swordfish until the latter finally cried, "Stop! Take away this
malady, cure me!" And Coyote said, "I can't, you brought it on
yourself." "No, kinsman, cure me! You gave it to me, you're
the one who harmed me this way." At last Coyote said, "Well,
there is only one way to get rid of this malady, and if you don't
do what I wish I'll give you an even worse case of it." "All
right," said the swordfish, "what is it that you want?" "Revive
my nephew and I will cure you." "But I can't, since I didn't kill
him," protested the swordfish. Again Coyote threw the poison, and again the swordfish began to sneeze violently and
couldn't stop. Finally the old swordfish by the fire, who had
been listening to all of this, spoke up and said to the other
swordfish, "Why not come to an agreement so that he can go,
since we all consent to his taking his nephew away?" But
still the younger swordfish refused, and Coyote saw that the
only thing to do was to keep throwing his poison.

The swordfish was feeling awful by this time. His head
hurt and so did his ears. "It would be best for everyone if you
gave up and revived my nephew, and let me be on my way."
At last the swordfish said, "Stop, cure me!" "Only if you
revive my nephew." And the old swordfish also urged him
again to revive Xelex so that Coyote would leave, and finally

the younger swordfish gave in and agreed to do it. Now the
swordfish was also something of a sorcerer. They brought the
body of Xelex down from where it had been hanging, and the
?elye?wun began to massage it, and blow on it, and massage it
some more, talking all the while, and at last Xelex began to
move his hands and feet. Coyote said, "Well, I knew very well
that you were able to do this. Since you killed him, you could
revive him. And besides, he wasn't really dead, he just seemed
to be." As soon as Xelex had fully recovered, Coyote told the
swordfish to spit on his hands and rub his forehead, which he
did, and immediately he began to recover from the effects of
the poison. "Well, there is your nephew, take him and go,"
said the swordfish. "Now you must show me where the canoe
is," said Coyote. And the old swordfish spoke up and said,
"Yes, why don't you go with him and get it all over. You know
just where you grabbed Xelex, and how best to get there." So
the three of them started out on the road, and eventually
reached the spot where Xelex had fallen overboard. "Here you
are," said the swordfish. "This is it." "Good," said Coyote.
"You were to bring us to the canoe, and you have carried out
your part of the bargain."

When they reached the surface there were three canoes
there awaiting them. Coyote and Xelex were each pulled
aboard a canoe, while the swordfish disappeared under the
water without so much as a word. And the canoes started back
for syuxtun, where many people were waiting down by the
beach as the wot had ordered. And the people notified the
chief that the canoes were on their way home. "Are they bringing my nephew?" asked the wot. "Well," the people said,
"two of the canoes have two men apiece, while the third has
only one." Then the wot was overjoyed. "I hope my nephew is
all right," he said. As he was still worried, he waited no
longer, but started for the beach where many other people
were going too. The canoes reached the beach at the same time
the wot did, and he recognized his nephew and Coyote.
"Good, good," said the chief, and the people were also very
happy that Xelex had returned.

The wot hugged his nephew and greeted him, but Xelex
was unable to speak, although he tried, and when the chief
questioned him as to where he had been and what had

happened to him, he was unable to answer. And Coyote said, "Don't bother him now. He's weak from lack of food, and needs time to recover." "Well, I'll take him to my house," said the wot. And so Xelex was taken to the house of the wot, and Coyote went also, for he was something of a doctor. They gave him only ʔilepes to eat, and the next day Xelex could speak a little and asked for some more ʔilepeš. This they gave him, ground up but served uncooked in cold water. Finally he was cured to the point where he could talk as well as ever. So they began to question him, asking him where he had gone, what had happened to him, and so on, and he answered that he didn't know, he could remember nothing, it was as if he had been asleep. And Coyote said, "Well, I don't want that kind of sleep! If it had not been for me, you might still be there, sleeping, but I saved you." And the wot agreed with Coyote and thanked him for what he had done.

Now Xelex was still not strong, and so the chief had him stay there with him. And they gave Xelex's house to Coyote in the meantime, since Coyote had no house of his own. When Xelex was almost fully recovered, a woman in the village fell in love with him and was so shameless in her feelings that one day she entered the chief's house when he was not there, in order to see Xelex. And they began to talk, and then to embrace one another. Just then the wot entered and found them there, and he became very angry and said to Xelex, "Nephew, it would be best for you to take this woman and return to your own house, for I don't like this kind of thing going on in my home." And Xelex answered, "All right, uncle. I'm grateful for your care, but now I have someone else to take care of me." Then the wot sent a messenger to Coyote, telling him to vacate Xelex's house because his nephew was going to marry, and asking Coyote to come and report to him. And Coyote came, carrying only his ʔolotoč with his few possessions wrapped up in it. Then the wot gave Coyote a house of his very own, and so they lived happily for a long time, Xelex with his house and new wife and Coyote with his new house. And one thing is certain: if any enemy should happen by there, he would really have his work cut out for him.

sutiwayan ulʔatucʔ

27 COYOTE VISITS THE ʔELYEʔ-WUN

Once Coyote was walking along the beach near syuxtun, feeling happy and half-drunk, dancing and singing to himself and feeling like one who has drunk toloache. Now there was a house of crystal there in the sea, close to the shore, and in the house there were two women. And the women heard Coyote singing and they began to sing also, making fun of him and his song. At first Coyote did not see the house or the women, and he got very angry because they were ridiculing his song. At first he wanted to kill them, but then he saw that they were women and he wasn't quite so angry anymore. He tried to get into the crystal house, but there was no opening anywhere, the walls were solid. So Coyote gave up trying to get into the house, and instead asked the two women where the house of the ʔelyeʔwun, the swordfish, was. And the two replied, "There is the road that you must follow to reach the house of the swordfish."

Coyote left and traveled along the road they had pointed to. He finally arrived at his destination and found only their servant, a qʔiniʔwi fish, home. "Where are the ʔelyeʔwun?" he asked. "They have gone to hunt whales," was the reply. Coyote began to stroll around and examine everything in the house, and finally the servant told him to be careful because the swordfish were very fussy about their belongings. Then Coyote told the qʔiniʔwi that he was just looking at his grandson's belongings, trying to make the servant think that the ʔelyeʔwun were his descendants. Then Coyote asked about the arrival of the swordfish, and he was told that they arrived in the form of a mist or fog. Just then a mist entered the house and there was a sound of whales being dropped on the floor—you could just hear the sound. The mist cleared away and Coyote saw the swordfish standing there, each with his whale. They looked like old men, with long beards and long white eyebrows growing down over their eyes.

The swordfish saw Coyote and became very angry. They wanted to kill him, but he had bewitched all their belongings and so they couldn't. And Coyote was dodging their blows, dancing here and there until they tired. Then Coyote said, "Now it's my turn!" He tried to bewitch them, but they were evenly matched and so no one was hurt. And so they agreed to let Coyote stay, but secretly they still wanted to kill him. They prepared dinner, cutting their whales into big pieces and roasting them in the ashes of the fire. They took a huge chunk of whale and threw it to Coyote, bewitching it as they did so, but he bewitched it also so that it turned to excrement. Again they took a piece and threw it to Coyote, and again he turned it to excrement. The third time this happened they said, "You aren't eating what we give you!" And Coyote answered, "Why do you eat your own feces? We don't eat excrement at syuxtun!" And the swordfish exclaimed and came to see if it was true, and they didn't know what to say.

That night they went to sleep, and the following morning one of the ʔelyeʔwun came to Coyote and said, "We are all going out to hunt whales now, and whoever fails to catch a whale will be killed." And the swordfish and Coyote left and went out in the sea hunting whales. Each swordfish caught his whale, and Coyote did too. "Whales aren't very hard to catch!" Coyote said to the swordfish. They all returned to the house and had dinner, and again Coyote bewitched the meat and turned it to excrement.

After they had eaten, the swordfish said that they would have a fiesta that night. They put on their cux and feather dancing skirts, and the strongest of the swordfish threw another feather skirt to Coyote. But it was so heavy that it fell to the ground and sank a little into the floor. Coyote said to himself, "How can I wear that?" But he picked it up and shook the dirt off and put it on. Then they gave him a cux and it was also very heavy. "We shall dance now," said the swordfish. "And anyone who can't jump as high as the roof we shall kill." Now the house was big and tall, and there was a smokehole in the middle of the roof. The swordfish began to dance, leaping very high, and jumping here and there. At last they stopped and informed Coyote that it was his turn. So Coyote began to dance and sing. Now while the swordfish had been dancing Coyote had been composing a song using the same tune but with words that referred to "rolling fish in dirty ashes." He made this song up just to get the ʔelyeʔwun angry. When he got to the middle of his dance he said "huy!" and jumped up clear through the smokehole. He came back in through the door and said, "My, your house is so small! My father and I have a house at syuxtun that's *big*. There you say 'huy!' and jump and you're merely in the middle of the house, but here you jump and you're outside, because your house is so tiny!" (Actually, of course, the house was very big.)

At last they all went to sleep, and the next morning the swordfish went out hunting again. They asked Coyote if he wanted to go along, but he said, "No, it would be best for me to stay here. I'm very tired, and I want to rest." Actually he wanted to stay behind because he had seen three fine cʔiwis hanging from the rafters, and he wanted to steal the best one. So the swordfish left, but they didn't go very far, for they suspected what he was planning to do. And Coyote jumped up and seized the rattle and swung it in a circle so that it would make no sound. And he said to himself, "How much will the wot, Eagle, give me for this? I'll sell the rattle to him." He started to leave, but as he did so he shook the rattle a little because he liked it so much, and the swordfish heard the sound. So they commanded a huge wave to form, and it overtook Coyote just as he was about to emerge from the sea, washing the cʔiwis from his hand and carrying it back to the ʔelyeʔwun. And so Coyote lost the rattle that he had stolen.

Once long ago the sea subsided and stayed that way for a while. And the people saw a house exposed opposite ɬueneme, and another one in front of ʔiwayiqʔiqʔ, and still another near syuxtun. The people saw them from a distance but did not approach them for fear of the ocean returning.

The people venerated the swordfish because they sometimes chased whales ashore and thus the people had a lot of meat. They said that the ʔelyeʔwun play ball with a whale, tossing it around. One swordfish would throw the whale far, and another would catch it and throw it back. They said that the projecting sword of the ʔelyeʔwun was his hand. When they threw a whale out on the shore the people were glad for there was lots to eat. The whale belonged to the people who owned the shore just where it washed up.

The ʔelyeʔwun were people. They had a house at the bottom of the ocean, but there was no water inside. They had a fireplace and everything, just as we have here, but there was water all above. Once a Ventureño fisherman looked down into a cove and saw a man lying there on the rocks. His hands and forearms were tremendously big and strong, and so was his chest. He was no bigger than a human being, in fact a little more squat. And on his head was a long bone, his instrument of attack. The fisherman threw a rock and the ʔelyeʔwun jumped far out into the water and disappeared.

28 THE ISLAND GIRLS When animals were still people, Xelex and his cousins ʔAničʔapapa and ʔAtimasɨq started out one day from šɨšačʔiʔ (La Quemada) to go fishing. The three boys were nephews of Sloʔw and were very handsome. They talked and paddled, talked and paddled, and before they knew it they were closer to Santa Cruz Island than the mainland and it was getting late. "Look how far we've come already," they said. And Xelex, who was the oldest, said, "We'd better go to the island and tie up, because if we don't the wind will catch us and we'll be killed."

The people there on the island saw the canoe approaching, and the wot ordered the paxa to go and tell the boys to land without worry. So the paxa went out in his canoe shouting, "Come on, come on, don't be afraid!" When the boys landed the wot went to meet them, for he knew that they were refined and well-to-do. And he ordered dinner to be prepared at once. They ate, and the wot commanded all the girls in the village to assemble because he wished to see them. The girls gathered and there were many of them, but the three prettiest were Otter and Duck and Wildcat. Then the wot said, "Boys, there are many things here to choose from—there is lots of money, lots of food, and plenty of pretty girls." Xelex quickly took a fancy to the dark one, Otter, while ʔAtimasɨq liked Duck and ʔAničʔapapa like Wildcat. That night they slept together as married couples, and the next morning there was lots of food to eat and then they played tokoy on the playing field. That afternoon they played once again with the wot. And so it went. But after five days Xelex said, "I wonder how it's going on the mainland? They must all think we've drowned. Tomorrow we'll leave." And the next morning they ate breakfast and said goodbye. The captain objected to their leaving and said, "Why do you want to go? You are married, and you can stay here forever." "We shall return soon," said Xelex.

"We'll be back in six days." "All right," said the wot. "You lack nothing here, there is plenty of wealth."

The boys left then, and the captain was sad and so were their wives. When they arrived at La Quemada everyone was happy, for they had thought them drowned, and wot Slo?w gave a big fiesta. Their wives were also very happy (for the boys were married here on the mainland also—Qeleq was married to Xutaš, ?Atimasɨq was married to Acorn, and ?Anič-?apapa was married to another Duck). They were beautiful women, and the boys soon forgot the girls on the island. But on Santa Cruz the girls were very sad. They waited day after day, but six days passed and the boys had not returned. Then Otter said, "I'm leaving because my husband hasn't returned." The other two girls said the same. Then Otter ran down to the shore and dived into the water. Duck followed her, and they both swam well. But when Wildcat dived in she almost drowned and had to return to the shore. Otter and Duck arrived at La Quemada and started to look for their husbands.

Now Coyote knew that two pretty girls were coming and he decided to go fishing for them. He was very tricky when he was people! He performed his witchcraft and with his ?atišwɨn he was able to make himself look just like Xelex and deceive the girls. He kept peeping out and watching the girls approach, and when they were close enough he stepped out and confronted them. "My husband!" exclaimed Otter. "No, it isn't," said Duck. "Yes it is!" said Otter. Coyote went to meet them. He hugged Otter and kissed her and took her cloak off. "It's not my husband," said Duck. Coyote seized Duck and hugged her and kissed her. "Who is this? He's not our husband!" said Duck. "Yes he is!" replied Otter. Well, he had them there in his house for three or four days, until Gopher went and found them.

29 COYOTE VISITS THE SKY Slo?w
and Xelex were friends and kinsmen, and they lived at syuxtun where they were both captains. But Slo?w was older and thus was the senior captain of the two. They both had fiancées on Santa Cruz Island. Fox was Xelex's fiancée and Wildcat was the fiancée of Slo?w. They were waiting for the girls to arrive from the island in a boat so that they

could marry them but when the two women reached the beach in their canoe Coyote was there busily shaping boards for a canoe. They spoke to him but he at first pretended that he didn't hear them, that he was old and deaf. They spoke to him again and he finally turned around and they asked him where the houses of Slo?w and Xelex were. Coyote said that he would go and announce their arrival, but he didn't. Coyote had a little house there at syuxtun in which he lived, and he went there instead.

Now Coyote was a wizard and was very smart, and he transformed his house into a very fine place. He put otter skins on the floor and fixed everything up splendidly. Then he transformed himself into a very handsome man, a man even more handsome than Xelex. When he returned and spoke to the girls they thought it was Xelex. He escorted them to his house and they let him, for he was very handsome and they thought he was Xelex. The women entered the house and saw that it was richly furnished. "How aristocratic Xelex's house is!" they said, pleased. As soon as the women had entered, Coyote tied the door shut with long strips of leather, for he had quite a few friends who came to see him.

Meanwhile, Slo?w and Xelex were wondering where the women were, for they did not arrive when they were supposed to. "Why are the girls late?" they asked each other. "And where is Coyote? We haven't seen him!" They began to suspect something was wrong, for Coyote normally went around visiting and talking with people, but now they missed him. People came to Coyote's house and said, "Come over and get your fish guts." (They used to give Coyote fish or deer bowels.) Coyote said from inside, "You're fooling me!" But he finally left his house and went and got the tripe and when he returned he transformed it into fine fish and the whole body of a slain deer, and the girls said to themselves, "How much the people like Xelex!"

People became very suspicious that Coyote was hiding something in his house, for he never left it. He just came to the door and then went inside again, and the door was always tightly closed. At last Slo?w and Xelex sent Gopher to see if Coyote had the two girls in his house. Gopher dug a hole and came up in the middle of the floor, but Coyote saw the earth moving and said to himself, "What is Gopher doing entering my house?" He quickly covered the spot with otter skins so that Gopher couldn't see anything. Gopher returned to the two captains and said that he couldn't say for sure that the girls were there, but that he thought they were for he had felt many otter skins.

Then Slo?w and Xelex said, "Who shall we send now? It must be someone that Coyote will not be aware of." They sent Flea jumping over to Coyote's house, but he knew immediately that Flea was there. Flea did get one glance into the house before Coyote ran him out, and he saw the two girls sitting there. When Flea returned to the captains he told them that he had seen two women, but that he couldn't tell for sure if they were the right ones. They asked him how their faces were shaped, and he replied, "One had a round face and the other a long face." Now they were almost certain that Coyote did indeed have the two women there in his house, and so they sent Louse to make sure. Louse crept in and tasted the two girls. Fox had a salty taste and Wildcat tasted bad. When he saw them he observed that they were already big with child. He returned and told Slo?w and Xelex everything, and they were satisfied now that the two were their fiancées.

Now every year Coyote gave toloache to all the eight-year-old boys in the village, and so they sent word to him that he was to come and do this now. Coyote came and pounded up the toloache hurriedly, for he was afraid they might steal the girls back. He just made up the brew in a big bowl three feet across without measuring or anything, and then said, "Drink it!" While Coyote was administering the toloache, the captains sent Mountain Lion and two other men to Coyote's house to get the girls. Mountain Lion broke the latches that Coyote had tied the door shut with and entered the house. He said to the girls, "What are you doing here? This is Coyote's house, not the house of Xelex!" Both girls were ready to give birth, and he took each one by the shoulders and shook her, and each girl had twelve children. He then took the girls back to the houses of Slo?w and Xelex, and there they remained. Finally he went to Coyote and told him to return home and tend to his children.

Coyote went home and found the twenty-four children lying on the floor. He hurried outside and began chopping, making twenty-four cradles. Then he put each child in a cradle and tied them in. People used to chew mescal and then spit out the quid, and Coyote went all around the village picking up the quids which he placed in a bowl with water to feed the twenty-four babies. The twenty-four children grew quickly, and began to play around the house. They were all boys. The two mothers lived nearby, and whenever they saw the handsomest one (whose name was Weqcum) they would say, "That one is my son!" Weqcum was a good boy but people didn't like him. He was very handsome and he was obedient to his father.

Coyote christened all the boys himself. One was named pop?owmexme?y, and another ?icqoqinacwit (there is a story about this one—he was a bad boy). Other were maqcip?iyp?iynapteleq? ("wiggles his tail"), ?uwustoploqs ("he eats young carrizo shoots"), and ?ese?es ("a web"). These sons of Coyote grew up. He made them bows and arrows and they went deer-hunting. Slo?w and Xelex got very angry and jealous, for the boys were always bringing home lots of deer meat to their father. They were especially jealous of Weqcum, the handsome one, and they began to plot ways of killing him. They told Owl to go at night and poison Weqcum with herbs, for Owl was a noted sorcerer. But Coyote was also a wizard, and he knew all about it. He told Weqcum, "Well, son, they want to kill you, for they are very envious." He hid his son and made an image which he placed in Weqcum's bed, and that night Owl came and threw poison in the bed. The image began to groan, and the neighbors heard it and said, "Listen, Weqcum is dying!" They were pleased. Then Coyote began to cry so that people would think the boy had died.

Slo?w and Xelex were very happy, but the next morning when it was time to go hunting they noticed that all twenty-four sons were there. "Why, I thought he died last night," said Xelex. That night they sent the muhu to kill Weqcum, for they were very envious of Coyote because he had so much food now, whereas before he had always been so poor. But again Coyote put an image in his son's bed, and when the image began to groan the neighbors thought, "Now we have surely gotten him, for the muhu is the shrewdest of all." But when the boys went hunting the following morning Weqcum went too, and so Slo?w and Xelex decided to try something else. They sent Bear to kill Weqcum out in the woods while he was hunting. But Coyote said to his son, "A bear is coming to kill

you, but I am going with you. When the bear comes out of the
brush I want you to shoot me in my navel." When the bear
appeared Weqcum did just what his father had said to do and
the bear dropped dead.

Coyote returned to syuxtun and went around the town
crying out that "broad foot," "he with cracked feet," etc., was
dead. He used many epithets to refer to Bear so that people
would be even more angry. The next day Xelex and Slo?w
decided to send Rattlesnake to kill Weqcum. Coyote, of course,
knew this and told his son where Rattlesnake was waiting. He
went along again, and when they reached the spot where
Rattlesnake was hiding Coyote pointed to the bush where he
was hidden. Then Weqcum said to his other brothers, "Let's
practice shooting at that bush!" They all shot into the bush and
killed Rattlesnake before he had a chance to do any harm.
Coyote ran back to syuxtun and said, "He who bites in the
mountains, flat head that was, he who bites—he is dead." At
last he said that Rattlesnake was dead, but the people said that
now they already knew!

Xelex and Slo?w still plotted to kill Coyote's son. They
decided to give a great fiesta in conjunction with Weqcum,
with the understanding that whoever did not contribute his
share to the expenses of the gathering would be killed. Now
Rat, who also lived there at syuxtun and who was very
wealthy, wanted to get married. When they were busy with
preparations for the fiesta this woman came and asked one of
Coyote's younger sons to go and ask his older brother,
Weqcum, if he would like to marry her. The little boy went and
told Weqcum what she had said and Coyote overheard. "What
does she look like?" Coyote asked. "She is tall and has long
hair, but she isn't very good looking," the little boy replied.
"But she is very rich," said Coyote to Weqcum. "It would be a
good idea to marry her, for then we would have money
enough even to outdo the others in this fiesta." Coyote went
and talked to Rat, and asked her, "Do you want to marry my
son Weqcum?" "Yes," she replied. "But he is involved in
supporting this fiesta," Coyote said. "It doesn't matter," she
said, "I'm very rich." "Well, they are making fun of us, for the
coyotes have little money," he said. "Don't worry, I have
enough to outdo everyone!" she replied again.

So they were married, and Coyote told Xelex and Slo?w to

invite everyone in the village and everyone in the world, and that the fiesta was to last ten days. At this they began to worry. Thunder went around throughout the world inviting everyone to come, even the dead. He invited the swordfish and all the people of the sea, and everyone came. The swordfish came but no one could see them for they were enveloped in fog, and even the dead came, rolling over one another. And Xoy came from the world above. He had never been in this world before. He had the habit of spiraling slowly down through the air and then spiraling quickly when he rose. The fiesta lasted for ten days and everyone was happy but Xelex and Slo?w.

When the fiesta ended Xoy got ready to go, and Coyote decided to go with him to see the world above. Coyote grasped Xoy's legs and they started to rise slowly into the air. Coyote was pleased at first, but Xoy began to go faster and faster and Coyote soon got frightened. He started to let go, but he looked down and saw how far it was and hung on tighter than before. Coyote said, "Xoy, I want to go back, I've changed my mind!" But Xoy didn't answer. Xoy took Coyote through a hole into the world above, and as soon as he saw that it was another world he dropped off and fell on the ground while Xoy kept on spiraling upward through the air. (There are five worlds in all: we live in the middle one, Sun and his daughters live alone in the next, and Xoy lives in the highest world of all.) Coyote didn't know where Xoy had gone to, and he was crying sadly to himself and looking down toward his own world below.

He finally decided to travel to the house that he could see in the distance, and he timed his arrival for midday so that he would get invited to dinner. Just like him! He was surprised to see no other people around anywhere. He reached the house of Sun, and there were lots of wild animals there that Sun kept as pets—lions, deer, bears, and even rattlesnakes. All of Sun's animals were wild, because they had never seen a human being. As Coyote was approaching the house a crow began to sing, saying "There is somebody coming." But one daughter said to the other, "Don't believe crow, he's a story-teller. There are no other people here." Sun's bear wanted to bite Coyote, and he had to dodge around, but the bear couldn't hurt him. Then the rattlesnake tried to get him but he dodged again. Coyote reached the door at last and spoke to the girls, who told him to come in and sit down. He sat down and looked around,

and then said to himself, "What kind of rich people are these?"
For he had always heard that they were very wealthy, but now
he saw no furnishings, not even food. But in a little while they
placed a little food in front of him—a tiny amount of acorn
atole and a small piece of roasted meat. When he saw the food
he said to himself, "What kind of rich people are these to serve
so little food?" He took the food up in his hands and gulped it
down—and when he looked down at his plate there was the
same amount of food still there. He took another gulp and the
same thing happened. Then he realized that this was the way
they ate, and so he ate slowly until he was full. There was still
food left, so he said, "Now you can take your food away."

Coyote talked with Sun's two daughters for a while, and
when he asked them where their father was they replied that
he would arrive in the evening. In the evening Sun came back
from lighting the world. Sun is very proud and he wasn't
pleased to see Coyote there in his house. He pretended to
greet Coyote but in reality he was bewitching him. Coyote
asked Sun where he went, what he saw, and so on, and Sun
replied that he didn't see anything, he just traveled around.

They went to bed and when they got up the next morning
Coyote said to Sun, "I want to go with you when you go
today." Sun did not want Coyote to go with him, but Coyote
begged and at last Sun consented. They started off following
Sun's trail, which consists of a cord stretched around the
world. Coyote was behind Sun when he arose, and he said to
Sun, "Wouldn't it be better to cut that string?" He said this just
to annoy Sun. Sun quickly told him not to cut the cord, for if he
did they would fall to the earth. Later, after they had rested a
while at midday, Coyote begged Sun to let him carry his
firebrand for a while, saying that he had watched Sun carefully
and could carry it properly. Sun was very reluctant to let him
do it, and said that if he made a mistake he could burn up the
whole world down below. But Coyote begged and begged,
and Sun finally consented. Coyote started off all right, but the
firebrand slipped and almost fell, and the world almost burned
up before Sun could get it back.

From then on Coyote just followed behind Sun until he
set, and then they returned to Sun's house by way of the
south. The next day Coyote did not want to go with Sun again,

for he was getting homesick and very sad. He went to the hole in the sky and looked down at the world below. He cried and said, "There is nothing I can do, there is no hope of returning." But just then two eagles came up and said, "What are you doing here, Coyote?" "I'm doing the same thing you are!" he replied, for he always wanted to appear brave. Then the two eagles asked him if he didn't want to return home to his own world, and he said, "Why not?" They told him to get on the back of one of them and they started flying down through the air. Their wing feathers buzzed in the wind and Coyote was envious. "Let me fly too so that I can make that sound. I think I can do it!" The eagle said no, that he would be killed. At last Coyote started to pluck the feathers from the back of the eagle's neck so that he could make wings to fly with, and the eagle got mad and threw him off. When Coyote had fallen halfway to earth the eagle repented and tried to grab him but Coyote was falling too fast and he couldn't catch him. Coyote fell to the ground and was killed.

He remained lying there dead for a long time, until one day Sumiwowo and his brother Six?usus were wandering nearby and the older brother told the younger not to yell, because there was no one around but wild animals. But the younger boy never minded his brother anyway, and so he yelled. And someone answered. It was the dead Coyote, just a pile of broken bones now. "Didn't you tell me there was no one nearby? asked the younger brother when they heard the yell. The two went to the spot where Coyote was lying in a heap of bones, and Six?usus revived him. Coyote sat up and scratched his head and said, "How I've been sleeping!" Now there was another Coyote there who had been going around with the two brothers, and when the Coyote who fell from the sky saw him he said, "You must know a great deal about this world if you are going about with these two. Tell me, how many worlds are there?" Then the other Coyote said, "Well, how should I know?" "If you don't know, what are you doing with them?" Then the Coyote who fell from the sky told the other that there were five worlds in all, and chased him away. "You'd better leave if you don't know anything more than that!" he said. And so he went with the two boys from then on and had many adventures with them.

30 COYOTE AND CENTIPEDE

When animals were still people, the boys used to spend all their time trying to climb a smooth pole in order to see who could do it best, and Centipede always won for he was very good at it. Finally the other boys began to get angry because Centipede was always the winner, and one day they complained to old man Coyote. He agreed to remedy the situation, and after it had gotten dark and everyone in the village was asleep, he went and placed his takulšoxšinaš, his downy cord, around the base of the pole. The next morning the paxa cried, "Boys, now it's time to amuse ourselves with the pole." All of the boys in the village gathered and tried to climb the slick pole, but only Centipede could do it. He started climbing up the pole toward the top, but the higher he went the taller the pole grew, for Coyote was bewitching it.

When Centipede finally stopped and looked down it was already dark underneath him. He said to himself, "What shall I do? I guess I might as well keep on going up." He continued climbing and came eventually to a place where there were very strong winds that almost blew him off the pole. But he traversed this section and came to a place where it was terribly hot. Again he passed this successfully and came again to another spot where there were very strong winds that almost made him lose his grasp on the pole. He looked up then and saw a light far above him—it was the door into the sky. He said to himself, "I'd better reach that place pretty soon!" for his limbs were getting tired. He reached the door into the sky at last and jumped in through it, but as soon as he did so the pole shrank so that he could no longer reach it. He sat down sadly and said to himself, "Where can I go now? I guess I'm stuck here." And as he sat there he heard a buzzing sound that came nearer and nearer. He turned around and looked in all directions. "What can this be?" he thought. Just then a swarm of mosquitoes arrived, but they weren't little like they are here on earth; they were gigantic. They began to sting him and suck his blood, and soon there was nothing left of him but bones—just bones, and nothing else.

Now back on earth Coyote was beginning to regret what he had done to Centipede, and he was sad and unhappy. Finally he told everyone that he was going to go look for Centipede, who had disappeared into the sky and must surely be dead by now. And so Coyote started up the pole, and he passed through the same places of wind and heat that Centipede had traversed earlier. He reached the door into the sky and jumped through it, and as before the pole shrank until it was out of reach. Then Coyote started out to look for Centipede, and he had only gone a little way when he heard someone crying and singing sadly to himself, "Here I sit singing, nothing but bones!" Coyote came up to where Centipede was sitting and said, "Ah, son, how are you?" "Just as I shall always be!" replied Centipede. "Look at me, little uncle!" Then Coyote said "Don't worry, I'll cure you at once." Now in times past they had medicine with which to resurrect people, and so Coyote revived him, although he was now a very ugly color.

"Now let's look for a way to get down to earth again," said Coyote. They left that place where the mosquitoes were and soon reached a safe spot. Then Coyote said, "Wait for me here, I'm going to look for a fellow who will be passing by soon." "All right," Centipede replied. Coyote traveled a little way farther and then sat down and waited. In a little while Xolxol came by on his way around the world. Coyote jumped out and seized him as he was passing by and said, "Give me your clothes and things!" Xolxol refused at first, saying he couldn't, but Coyote assured him that he would return everything very soon and so Xolxol at last gave in and undressed. Now Xolxol was carrying two beautiful, well-made sticks which he rapped together before and behind his legs in order to go great distances at each jump. And Coyote took Xolxol's clothes and sticks and left that spot just as fast as the devil himself. He soon encountered Sloʔw, but he only glanced at him and kept on going around the world. He eventually reached Xolxol again and gave him back his things. "Here you are," said Coyote. "I don't need them anymore."

He returned to where Centipede was waiting and said, "Let's go!" They went straight to where Coyote had seen old Eagle. When they arrived Coyote said to Sloʔw, "How goes it, little uncle? I have come to ask you to do me the favor of carrying us back to our world." "I can't do it," replied Sloʔw. "I could never manage it." Coyote begged so much, however, that Sloʔw began to relent. "How can I carry you?" he asked. "Well, with your wings," Coyote answered. Eagle finally got

annoyed and said, "All right, we'll see if I can do it!" They
climbed on his back and he stretched his wings and flew down
toward the pole far below. Coyote watched as they got lower
and lower, and it finally seemed to him that the pole was
within reach. "This is far enough," he said, but Slo?w said no.
Just then the tip of his wing touched the pole and threw him
off course. Centipede leaped to the pole and was safe, but
Coyote fell clear to the ground and was dashed to pieces.
Centipede climbed down the pole to the ground and told
everyone what had happened. Coyote was lying there dead on
the ground, all in pieces, and Centipede said, "It isn't right to
leave him like this." He collected all of the bones and pieces of
Coyote and joined them back together. And the people said,
"He isn't dead, he will revive." And revive he did—all by
himself. And Centipede stayed just the way he was—sparkling
and shiny, but ugly in color.

31 COYOTE AND HIS SONS Coyote was married to Frog, and they had sixteen children. He was very lazy and very stingy, and never

made any effort to provide for his children. Whatever food he
brought home he ate himself, and it seemed he was always
eating. The children would go and dig cacomites and bring
them home and Coyote ate them all up. He ate so many
cacomites that he began to have diarrhea, and the children
would see cacomites in his excrement. One little coyote would
say to another, "Look, that is one of the cacomites that I dug
up!" "How do you know?" the other would ask. "It has my
mark on it!"

Coyote got sicker and finally he could not get out of bed at
all. Then he called his oldest son and said to him, "Son, climb
to the top of šiyaxšaptuwaš and give three cries announcing
that the wot is dying." "What else shall I say, Father?" asked
the boy. Coyoté said, "Say whatever you want to!" The boy
started up the hill, but he only went a short distance before he
stopped and gave three cries and announced that the wot, he
who makes tobacco, was dying. When the boy returned to his
father's house Coyote was angry and said, "You aren't my
legitimate son. I just slept with your mother as I was passing
by!" He called his second son and told him to climb the hill and
give three cries announcing that the wot was dying, and to add

whatever he wished. The second son went a little farther up the hill and shouted that the wot, the maker of carrying nets, was dying. When he returned Coyote was furious and said, "You're not my son. I met your mother by accident! He who makes carrying nets has money, and I have none!" The third son was given the same directions, and again he went a little further up the hill than the last and shouted that the wot, the basket-maker, was dying. And Coyote said, "Get out of here, you're not my real son! I just met your mother, and you were an accident!"

The fourth son said that the wot, maker of leather, was dying. The fifth son said that the wot, maker of cux, was dying. The sixth son said that the wot, maker of bows and arrows, was dying. The seventh son said that the wot, maker of cordage, was dying. The eighth said that the wot, the fisherman, was dying. The ninth said that the wot, ʔaltomolič (maker of canoes), was dying. The tenth said that the wot, maker of wooden bowls, was dying. The eleventh said that the wot, maker of mortars, was dying. The twelfth said that the wot, maker of abalorio, was dying. The thirteenth said that the wot, maker of beads, was dying. The fourteenth son climbed almost to the top of the hill before announcing that the wot, the good hunter, was dying. When he returned Coyote reproved him and said that a good hunter was a young man, not an old man like him lying there on his back. The fifteenth son climbed slowly up the hill, thinking about the blunders the previous boys had made. He stopped just below the crest of the hill and shouted three times, saying that the wot, hulʔalʔalušʔaqši (he who makes sacrifices at shrines), was dying.

Coyote was still not satisfied, so he called his youngest son to his side and patted him on the back. "My son, climb to the top of the hill and announce that the wot is dying and that those who want to come and see may do so." The last son climbed to the very top of šiyaxšaptuwaš and announced that the wot, hulʔalalʔošuš (he who inspires love), was dying. This pleased Coyote very much, and he asked Gopher to soften the ground for the boy so that he might not hurt his feet coming down the hill. A little while later some of the people of syuxtun began to come to see Coyote, and one of the first to come was Bear. "Who of the captains can I trust now?" he said. And Coyote answered, "True, who can you trust now? I was the only one who could be trusted all the time!" Then he added, "At the same time I'm a little fearful. Could you go a little farther away and cry? Cry over there. Cry because I'm going to die." The bear got up and went a little way away and sat down. Then a flock of geese arrived at Coyote's house, all singing and crying. Coyote said to them, "That's right, cry! For there will never be another wot like me. But the proper way to cry is to bow your head!" And when they all bowed their heads he took a club and began to beat them with it. Half of the flock escaped but the others were killed. Then the bear got up and left, saying, "I thought that was the way it was!" Coyote called his sons to come and dress the geese and cook them. Then he ate them all up without sharing any of it with his sons or Frog.

Frog was infuriated and decided to teach Coyote a lesson. She was queen of the waters, and she ordered the springs to stop flowing and the streams to dry up. "He has eaten lots of geese and he will be thirsty pretty soon," she said. In a little while Coyote called his oldest son and said, "My son, go and get me some water." The boy took a gourd and went to get water, but there was none in the stream where he usually went. The boy then ran some distance up the stream-bed to another place where there used to be water, but that was dried up also. The boy returned and told Coyote that the creek was completely dry. "You didn't go to the creek!" Coyote said. "How could it be dry when there is always lots of water there? You're not my son. I just met your mother and you were manufactured!" He ordered his second son to go and get him water, and the boy went farther up the stream-bed than the first son had gone but still found no water. And again Coyote didn't believe the boy and reproved him. Each of the sixteen sons went farther up the stream than the last, and every one was unsuccessful in finding water.

Coyote was furious. "You're trying to fool me!" he shouted. He got up and went to a place in the creek where they usually got water and dug a little hole there, but it was completely dry. He kept following the stream higher and higher, digging little holes here and there all the way, but there was no water anywhere. At last he reached monušmu, way up the canyon, and he climbed a ridge high above the stream bed. He looked down into the canyon and saw a big flat rock there that glittered, and he thought that it was a pool of water. "Shall I climb down and drink? No, I think I'll climb higher still and jump from up there so that my whole body, ears and tail and all, will drink at the same time."

He finally jumped and hit the rock and lay there for a long time as if dead. His sons told their mother, "Bring the water back again. Father almost killed himself by hunting for it!" But Frog was still angry. Coyote went farther up the stream still looking for water, and Frog released all of the water at once so that it came roaring down the canyon like a flood. He stood in the middle of the stream so that he would get a good drink of it, but there was too much water. He tried to save himself by drawing a crooked line—Mission Creek still zigzags there— but even that did not save him, and the water swept him out into the ocean. He wasn't killed, but he was very sad and so he turned himself into the laxux fish. Coyote's sons were very sad after their father disappeared, and each one turned into something. Weqcum turned into a star, a single bright star seen at night.

32 COYOTE AND QAQ Coyote arrived at mikiw one day and went to a house there. The people asked him what he wanted and he just said, "Blblblblbl," and pretended that he didn't know how to talk. They brought out acorn atole and other things, offering him first one and then another, but he showed them by gestures that he didn't want them. Then he pointed to the pupil of his eye and they understood that he wanted xutaš (chia). They brought him chia and he indicated that that was what he wanted. He pounded it up, nibbling a little as he pounded, so that by the time it was completely pounded up he had eaten it all. Then Coyote went to a second house and did the same thing, and again they brought him chia and he ate it as before.

Coyote came then to the house of Qaq, who was a widow. She already knew what he wanted and brought him chia at once. She offered to take his quiver as a sign of welcome and he let her. Then he made a gesture of spreading hot coals, pointed to the sea, and then made a gesture to indicate fish being split open for roasting on the coals. Qaq said, "No, I'm a woman, not a fisherman. I can't go and get fish." Then Coyote made gestures to indicate that she was to get the coals ready and he would get the fish. He went down to the shore, leaving his quiver at Qaq's house, and there he met his friends He?w and Mut and they gave him a lot of fish. Coyote took the fish back to Qaq's house, and he and Qaq cooked and ate some of them and then set about drying the rest. Now it was getting along toward sunset. Qaq asked Coyote where his home was and he indicated by gestures that he just slept wherever he happened to be. She asked him if he would like to stay there at her house that night and he nodded his head violently and showed he was very pleased with the idea.

After supper they got ready for bed. Qaq was going to spend the night on her bed and Coyote was going to spread a mat on the floor. Qaq began to hunt for fleas on herself, and Coyote howled and kept crying, "Q?ul sq?oso," which is č?umaš and means "there are many fleas." Coyote was beginning to talk now. Qaq thought he was just talking about the fleas and answered, "Yes, there are many fleas here." When Coyote kept howling and saying, "Q?ul sq?oso," she realized that he was having bad thoughts about her and paid no more attention to him. She took all her clothes off, looking for fleas, and Coyote watched her and howled. At last Qaq climbed up on her bed, while Coyote stayed on his mat on the floor. When the fire went out Coyote could stand it no longer, and said that he was going to climb up there with her. (He had already learned to talk—wasn't he a fast learner?) "Well, climb up," said Qaq. They talked for a while after he had climbed into the bed, and then Coyote said, "I'm going to get into the canoe!" "Go ahead," said Qaq, "I'm ready for you!" And so Coyote had intercourse with her, and now he had a home, now he was master of the house.

Qaq had two brothers who were tramps and never did anything; they just bummed around from place to place. Early the next morning they arrived at Qaq's house and were astounded to see Coyote, for they had never before found a man there with their sister. Qaq said to them, "This is your new brother-in-law. You do nothing, but look now!" And she pointed to all the fish that were hung up to dry. She let them know that now she had someone who would look after her very well. She prepared breakfast then, and her two brothers left as soon as it was over. When they were gone, Coyote told Qaq that he needed some money. She pointed to the k?iwis full of abalorio all around the walls (for she was very rich) and told him to take what he needed. Coyote measured off what he wanted on his arm and bit it off and put it in his bag. He told Qaq that he was going to hultomto?mol. "Will you return?" she asked. "Oh, certainly I will," he replied. "How many days will you be gone?" "Three days," he said.

Coyote went to tomto?mol to buy tomol pine boards with which to make canoes. There was an old man there who had the trees all cut and ready to sell. Coyote bought a great pile of wood and paid for it with the money Qaq had given him. By means of his magic power he was able to carry all of the wood in his carrying-net at once, and he arrived home with his load late at night the same day he set out. When he arrived at Qaq's house he didn't knock or call out, but just began fumbling with the door. Qaq was not expecting him back so soon and she thought he was some intruder trying to get in. She called out, "Who is it?" But Coyote didn't answer. Now Qaq had a long lance there in her house, and when Coyote kept fumbling at the door she struck it through the mat over the door. Coyote dodged to one side so that it only grazed his side and gave a call so that she knew who it was. She let him in then and asked him why he had said he was going to be gone for three days and then had returned the same night. Coyote only laughed and said, "Never mind!"

The next morning he started making his canoes. He was a very fast worker. Both a carpenter and a smith, Coyote knew how to do everything. First he made qasɨ for tools, and sharpened them. Then he made two very fine canoes inlaid with shells to give to his friends He?w and Mut. Slo?w was wot at mikiw and Xelex was his nephew, and Xelex went to Slo?w and said, "Look, uncle, Coyote is making the finest canoes for He?w and Mut while those he is making for us are not ornamented at all." Slo?w explained that the two friends had done favors for Coyote. "They helped him out when we did nothing for him." "I still don't like the one he's making for me," said Xelex. Coyote used all of the wood that he had bought in making canoes for the important people of the village. When they were all finished he sent his two tramp brothers-in-law around to tell these people that Coyote wanted them to come to his house. When they were all collected there he presented them with canoes. First he gave He?w and Mut their fine canoes, then he presented Slo?w and Xelex with theirs, and finally he gave the other men their ordinary canoes. Xelex was very envious and said, "He?w and Mut certainly helped him, but it wasn't right not to give the finest canoes to the captains." And he added that the captains should have been the first to be presented with their canoes. Slo? again said, "Never mind."

The next morning Coyote again told Qaq that he wanted some money, and as before she pointed to the shell-money lying around the walls of the house and told him to take what he wanted. He measured it off and put it in his bag. He told Qaq that he was going to toqto?q to get red milkweed. "How many days will you be gone?" asked Qaq, and as before he said, "Three days." Coyote traveled to toqto?q and bought a great load of tok and by his magic power was able to put it all into his carrying-net and bring it all home at once. As before Qaq was not expecting him, and when he started fumbling at the door she took her lance and thrust it through the door. It grazed his side, and he gave a shout to let her know who it was and she let him in. Qaq chided him for acting that way, and said that he must think she was with another man, for he came back the same night when he had said that he was going to be gone for three days. Coyote just laughed and said, "Never mind, it's nothing."

The next morning he started working with the tok. He worked very fast, rolling it into string on his thigh. He made fishing tackle for all the important men in the village, but kept nothing for himself. And as before, he made the best tackle for He?w and Mut. When he had finished his work, he sent his two brothers-in-law around to tell the important people to come to his house. When they arrived he presented them with the fishing tackle, and again he gave He?w and Mut theirs first, then Slo?w and Xelex, and then all the other important men.

After Coyote had distributed the fishing lines Qaq had a child by him, a little coyote. The boy grew very quickly, and was very mischievous. He went around to other houses breaking things all the time, and people were continually coming up to Coyote and saying, "Look, your son has broken my mortar" (or whatever it was). And Coyote would ask, "How much is it worth?" The person would tell him and Coyote would take out his money and pay whatever the sum was. And the little coyote took after his father in making expensive presents to all his friends. He wanted to give everything away and his father let him. All of this used up Qaq's money very fast, and when it was gone she said, "Our money is practically gone." But Coyote and his son kept spending it, and when every piece of money had disappeared she asked, "What are we going to do now?" "We'll turn into animals," Coyote replied. So Coyote and Qaq and their son turned into animals. Coyote went off with his son behind him and Qaq followed them everywhere crying "a, a." She flew along through the trees and Coyote and his son walked and ran along underneath.

33 COYOTE AND BAT (I) Coyote and Bat were friends, and they lived together somewhat apart from the village. They were always hunting and doing things together, and Bat was not misshapen as he is today. It was Coyote who caused it all. Now there was a temescal there in the village, and everyday the people went in and built a fire and sweated, and then came out and jumped in some nearby water to clean themselves off. And they told Bat that it was good for them and cured any ills they had. Bat watched this day after day, observing everything closely, and one day Coyote came and asked, "What are you watching?" And Bat answered, "I'm watching my kinsmen play in the water." "Well, there's lots of water right here," said Coyote. "Why don't we make a temescal also?" "You're right, we'll do it!" replied Bat. So one of them pounded mud while the other brought twigs to mix with it. They put poles around in a circle, leaving a little door to one side. Then they daubed the mud and twig mixture on, and then added more poles to the outside and then more twigs. They put the finishing touches to it and then built a fire inside to harden the mud. "And now it's finished, my friend," said Coyote. "Tomorrow we'll inaugurate our sweathouse."

Now Coyote was very envious of Bat, who was good at everything and who always surpassed his friend in whatever they did. And Coyote thought to himself, "I know I can endure heat better than Bat. I'll surpass him in this!" Now it happened that Bat had brought kindling for the sweathouse the day before, and so it was Coyote's responsibility to tend the fire which they built right by the little door. When they got into the temescal Bat went clear to the back corner while Coyote stayed near the front. And Coyote began to stir the fire and add wood, more and more wood, until Bat was almost suffocating from the heat. And Coyote thought to himself, "I could spend several days in here," for he was sure now that he could endure the heat better than Bat, and he was anxious to surpass Bat at something. Finally Coyote said, "All right, friend, that's enough. Let's leave now." By this time Bat had practically suffocated and wasn't feeling too well. Coyote extinguished the fire, and they went and jumped into the water and washed themselves off. That night at dinner Coyote exclaimed, "How good I feel now, how happy I am! Sweating is certainly good medicine!" Bat agreed, and said that they ought to do it again the following day. But he added, "Today you tended the fire, but tomorrow I'll do it and you fetch the wood. I saw the way you kept the fire going and I'll do the same." Coyote said to himself, "I'll still outlast you, no matter how you tend it." He was feeling very confident.

The next morning Coyote went and got kindling while Bat built a fire. They got into their temescal, but this time Bat stayed by the door while Coyote went back into the far corner. It got hotter and hotter as Bat added wood to the fire, and finally Coyote gasped and pretended to be overcome by the heat. "That's fine! Let's leave!" he said. "No, not quite yet," said Bat. "Just a little longer." And he threw a little more wood on the fire. Then Coyote said, "I can't take it anymore, it's too hot!" And Bat said to himself, "I can endure the heat better than Coyote!" Coyote pretended he was suffocating from the heat and said, "Let's leave, I've had enough!" "All right," said Bat. He put out the fire and they went and jumped in the water. Coyote felt half drunk from the heat, and he complained that his head hurt and he felt sick. Bat, however, was very pleased. His body felt light and he was convinced that the sweating was good for him. That night at dinner Bat said, "Let's go into the temescal again tomorrow." "Go ahead, I feel bad," said Coyote. "You have to come and tend the fire while I fetch wood," said Bat. "That's the rule! One day I tend the fire, the next day you do."

Coyote pretended to agree reluctantly, and so the next morning Bat carried wood while his friend built a fire. Again they got into the temescal, and Bat went clear to the back while Coyote stayed by the door to tend the fire. Coyote had the idea that he really would make things uncomfortable for Bat this time, so he built a very hot fire and kept adding handfuls of dry bark which burns almost like charcoal. The temperature rose higher and higher, and Bat said, "That's fine." Coyote did not reply, he simply put more wood on and moved farther from the fire. Bat could no longer endure the heat, he was burning up, but Coyote stuck to his corner with his back to the fire and pretended to be dozing. Bat got up from where he was sitting, for it was as hot as an oven now, and said, "I've had enough, let's go. Enough!" But Coyote didn't move from his corner, and he pretended to be asleep. And Bat said, "I've got to get out of here!" Now the fire was burning right in the door, and Bat had to go through it to get out, but go through it he did. And that is how he burned himself so badly and got to be the way he is today. Coyote was the cause of it all.

After Bat had left Coyote let the fire burn down, then scattered the coals and left the temescal himself. By this time Bat had returned to the house in bad shape, and when Coyote got out of the water he said to himself, "I don't think it would be a good idea to go back to the house. I'm going somewhere else!" He went and stayed in the village while Bat remained living in the house. And things went along like that for some time until one day another village challenged them to fight a battle. And the wot sent for Coyote and said, "I can't order the people to fight. It would be best for you to take on this war, for they are your enemies." Then Coyote remembered his friend Bat, and remembered that he was a fine archer. "But he was burned and has no feet, he can't travel. But his hands are still all right, and he could shoot a bow. I'll go and see if he'll go with me to fight. If he does, we'll win." And the wot answered, "Well, if you win you will be rewarded." Then he told Coyote that the two opposing sides were to meet at a particular place, and that whichever arrived first was to wait for the other to come.

Coyote left the wot and went to Bat's house. He greeted Bat and explained the situation to his old friend. "But look at me!" said Bat. "I can't walk and it's your fault." Then Coyote answered, "Yes, it was very bad of me to do what I did." "Well, friend, now I suffer a great deal. I have no strength,

and I can't walk or run, so how can I go with you?" And
Coyote said, "Well, I'll carry you on my back, you'll be able to
shoot from there." "Yes, that's not a bad idea," said Bat. "I like
that!" And he asked, "When do we leave?" "Tomorrow
morning," replied Coyote.

Early the following morning Coyote arrived to get Bat,
who had filled his quiver with plenty of arrows and was
already waiting. Bat climbed up onto Coyote's back and clung
there like a leech. "All right," he said. "Let's practice a little
and see how it goes." So Coyote jumped from side to side as if
he were dodging blows. "I like the way you do that," said Bat.
They left and after traveling a while reached the place where
the battle was to take place. The opposing side was already
there, and, as the two approached, the enemy forces saw what
appeared to be a single foe and decided to grab him then and
there. So they began to shoot their arrows at Coyote, and he
was dodging them and leaping from side to side. And Bat did
nothing, he simply clung to Coyote's back and never moved,
and poor Coyote had to jump to and fro to escape the blows
and arrows aimed at him. But the enemy couldn't hit him or
catch him for he was too nimble. He kept dodging here and
there, saying, "Shoot, Bat, shoot! Now is the time to fire!" But
Bat never budged and Coyote began to tire.

The blows were coming hot and heavy and Coyote started
to get worried. He finally pointed to Bat sitting on his neck and
said, "I'm not your foe, he is! He's the one who opposes you!"
The enemy fired at Bat and missed, and Coyote said, "What
bad luck! They're going to win and we'll lose, and all because
my companion won't do anything!" And Bat began to scold
Coyote, saying, "Now you'll pay for what you did, for it's your
fault I'm the way I am!" Coyote began to go around and
around in circles trying to dislodge Bat, and while he was
doing this the enemy was able to get very close. "Now I'm lost
for sure," Coyote said, "Now I'm paying for what I did! Yes,
all is surely lost!" He gave a tremendous leap to one side,
shooting an arrow at the same time, and he shot it with such
force that it landed right in the middle of the opposing forces.
They were frightened and said to one another, "Who is this
man?" Just then Bat also seized his bow and began to shoot,
and they were right in amongst the enemy lines shooting, and
their arrows began to whistle past their opponents' ears. The

enemy fell back in confusion and Coyote followed with Bat shooting all the way.

Coyote had a few minor wounds now, but the two kept shooting and advancing and now there were many wounds on the other side as well, and finally the enemy cried out that they were beaten and began to run away. And so Coyote and Bat won. They sent one of the defeated men as messenger to the wot to tell him the news. And Coyote was dancing along as happy as could be, and he said to Bat, "I will receive lots of food for this victory, and you shall share the reward and we will always be friends! And if any other wars come along I'll carry you into battle and we'll fight together!" They returned to Bat's house, where with some difficulty Bat dismounted from Coyote's back. Then Coyote returned to the village, where the wot gave him a little house of his own and lots of food as a reward. And Coyote in turn took plenty of food to his friend Bat. Later the wot told Coyote, "If our enemies should come again, the two of you must fight once again, for my people here are worthless!" And Coyote agreed to it.

Now it happened that the people in the village that they had fought wanted revenge. They kept telling themselves that it was a disgrace that one man or even two had defeated an entire troop. And so they sent a messenger to the wot declaring war again, and naming a time and place for the return engagement. The wot sent for Coyote and told him what had happened, and Coyote said, "This is bad news, but I gave my promise. I can only go to Bat and ask him to go with me." So he went to see his friend Bat and told him that they had to go to war again. "But I have no arrows left," said Bat. "I used them all up the last time." "I'll get more from the wot," said Coyote. "He has plenty." He went and told the wot what they needed, and the wot gave him lots of arrows and quivers to put them in. Then Coyote went home to sleep, but he didn't sleep very well for he kept thinking, "The enemy are many and I'm only one, and what if Bat does what he did last time?"

The next morning he arose very early and ate a good breakfast. Then he grabbed his bow and arrows, and took some tobacco for provisions. He went to Bat's house and found his friend had already eaten. "Here are your arrows," he said. "Are you ready? It's already late." Bat climbed onto Coyote's back and they started off. When they reached the appointed place the enemy was already there waiting. And all around there were spectators who had come to watch the battle. "It would be a shame to lose now, in front of so many people!" said Coyote. "Let them fire first," said Bat. Then Coyote pointed to Bat (who was such a small and difficult target) and said as he had before, "I'm not your foe, he is!" The enemy began to laugh, shouting that Bat was really grotesque and a sight to see, and they came running to surround them. But they couldn't do it for Coyote fell back dodging from side to side. Then one of them shot an arrow and Coyote said, "This is no game, and I'm it!" And he began to shoot and so did Bat. They shot to this side and that, and Coyote kept leaping here and there, dodging. Their opponents kept trying to surround them but Coyote kept falling back and dodging around, and he and Bat were shooting all the time. The watching spectators yelled and clapped and whooped. First one side seemed to win and then the other, but Coyote was never hit while the enemy received numerous wounds. Coyote was stronger because he had had a good breakfast of meat and sukuyas, and kept chewing tobacco. But he began to get worried and said, "We don't have many arrows left, and then what will we do?" Bat replied, "Don't worry, we're winning!"

The battle raged till almost midday, and then Bat said, "Now is the time to attack!" And every time that one of them shot an arrow it wounded someone, but they were not hit. The enemy didn't dodge while Coyote was continually leaping and jumping here and there. From time to time he would throw some tobacco into his mouth and it gave him new energy and courage. And so they fought on until the enemy finally signaled that they were beaten, and began to retreat. No one had been killed, but there were many wounded. Then Coyote and Bat returned home, and Coyote took his friend to his house. "Tomorrow I'll bring you your reward," he said. "There will surely be plenty of food." Then Coyote went to see the wot, who was very grateful to them for keeping the enemy from the village. And the wot said, "You may have whatever you wish." Then Coyote replied, "Well, I want to take a lot of food to my friend Bat." "Fine, take it," said the wot. And so Coyote took ʔilepeš and chia and all kinds of other foods and carried it all to Bat's house, and when he got there he told Bat, "Here is a little abalorio too. And whenever you need anything, just say so and I'll bring it." He returned home, and the next day the wot sent for him. "You shall marry now and remain here with us in your own house," said the wot. "And I will maintain you and provide you with whatever you may want." And the wot gave him a woman to marry and kept him supplied with provisions, but he didn't forget his friend, and almost every day he went to see if Bat needed anything to eat. And so it went, with the wot maintaining Bat and Coyote, and Coyote happily married in his house.

34 COYOTE AND BAT (II) Bat and Coyote lived together in Bat's house. Coyote kept wishing that it would rain. "Thirty days would be too long for it to rain—ten days would be better," said Coyote to Bat. Finally Bat said, "All right, I'm going to go to sleep. When I sleep it will start to rain, and when I'm sleeping don't talk to me!" He went to sleep and it began to rain. It rained night and day, and finally Coyote got lonely and wanted to talk to Bat. He said, "We have visitors!" But Bat said nothing, and Coyote thought, "What can I do to make Bat speak to me? I know, I'll make a hole in the wall for the rain to enter!" He made a hole in the wall and the water came pouring in on them. He said, "Bat, the water is coming in on us!" But Bat said nothing. Water kept flooding in, and now it was a foot deep. But still Bat didn't speak—he was floating on the water, still sleeping. Coyote thought, "What can I do to get Bat to talk? I know, I'll set fire to the house!" So he set the house on fire, and then said, "Bat! The house is burning down! Get up, Bat!" But Bat didn't get up. He kept on sleeping and got burned. Then Coyote said, "I was stupid—and Bat is burned up. Things are going badly now!"

Bat died, and Coyote decided to hold a wake. "I am going to keep a vigil for three nights, for Bat was a captain," said Coyote. On the third night Coyote was very sleepy. He was swaying back and forth in his drowsiness. Then Bat revived, and he was laughing. Coyote heard the laughter and said, "Who is that laughing?" He looked all around but saw no one. He went back to sleep, and then Bat laughed again. Then Coyote looked up and saw Bat already revived, and he was very glad. Bat and Coyote lived together once again, but Bat's legs and arms grew together because he had been burned.

Bat and Coyote were living there together, and Coyote wished to go to war. He went around through the villages telling lies to the people. Then he went home and told Bat that the people were making fun of Bat by saying funny words like *maqalipʔɨʔl qʔemaqaliphu.* "You're a good man, but you are ugly now that you've been burned, even though you used to be handsome," said Coyote. "I'm very angry now," he went on, lying. "I'm going to go to war!" "I'll help you!" said Bat. Coyote laughed and replied, "How can you help me when you have no arms or legs?" Bat answered, "I can shoot. I'll just sit on your neck." Coyote laughed again and said, "The people would say, 'Here he comes carrying a baby!'" "I can shoot a bow very well," replied Bat. Coyote got some dry yucca stalks and set them up in a circle. Bat got up on Coyote's back with his bow and quiver of arrows, and said, "You run back and forth and I'll pierce every target with arrows." And sure enough, when Coyote stopped there were arrows stuck in every stalk—he hit every one, just as if they had been people. Coyote said, "It's good that we're going, Bat. We'll kill everyone. It's good that we're now going to war!" They prepared arrows and everything they needed. They finished their preparations and started off, and when they reached the village they killed everyone there, all the people.

35 COYOTE AND ROADRUNNER

Coyote and Roadrunner were friends, and they lived together in a cave. Roadrunner would enter a hollow tree and come out and shake his head, and flies would fall from it and he would eat them. He also caught lizards in traps. Coyote would catch gophers and ground-squirrels in traps and bring them home in the evening, and Roadrunner would arrive with some lizards, and that is how the two of them made their living. All went well until one day Coyote thought to himself, "I am going to find out how my friend gets so much even when I am unable to get a single thing."

The next morning Coyote left the cave first and ascended a peak from which he could spy on Roadrunner and see just what he did. In a little while he saw Roadrunner come out of their cave and head straight for a thicket of yellow broom. He took a cux from the thicket and put it on. Then he went straight to a hollow oak and entered, immediately came out again and shook his head, and began to eat the flies that fell from the headdress. After a while he went and set some little traps with which to catch lizards. Coyote, of course, was watching all of this from the peak. In a short time Roadrunner had caught several lizards which he strung on a string to carry home. Coyote watched all of this and then went hunting himself, but he could catch nothing. That evening Roadrunner was already at the cave roasting his lizards when Coyote arrived empty-handed. "Can you give me a lizard, friend? I'm hungry," said Coyote. Roadrunner kept eating and Coyote got nothing. Then Coyote said, "What news have you, what did you see today?" "Nothing. And you?" asked Roadrunner. Then Coyote said, "I saw an old man who entered a thicket of broom and came out with a big head. How funny it was! Then that old man went straight to a hollow oak, and when he came out of that tree he kept shaking his head and flies fell from it and he ate them, dirty fellow. Then he reentered the broom thicket and hid his cux and came out looking very much like you!"

At this, Roadrunner was very irritated but he said nothing. He thought that the following day he would try spying on Coyote to see how he got his game. And so they went to sleep. The next morning Roadrunner left the cave first, climbed the peak, and when Coyote left the cave Roadrunner was watching everything he did. Coyote went straight to a clump of rocks and took out the traps that he kept there, and then descended into a little ravine where he began painting his body with clay. He came out of the ravine all painted up and went to a flat where there were some ground-squirrel holes. He planted the traps and began to sing and dance so that the ground-squirrels would come out to watch, but when they did he didn't catch a single one. He danced until he was tired. Then he picked up the traps and threw them angrily back into the clump of rocks, and descended again into the ravine where he washed off the paint. Roadrunner watched all of this from up on the peak. Coyote then went and gathered some wood and took it back to the cave and built a fire, hoping that Roadrunner would give him a lizard this time for he was very hungry. But when Roadrunner returned he brought nothing with him. And Coyote asked, "What news do you have? What did you see today?" Then Roadrunner said, "I climbed the peak this morning, and saw an old man go into a clump of rocks and come out with some traps. Then he went into a little ravine and came out all painted up. He went to where there were some ground-squirrel holes and planted the traps, and then began to dance and sing. He danced until he was tired and then went and threw his traps into some rocks." Here Roadrunner chuckled to himself. "Then he went back to the ravine, and when he came out the paint was gone and he looked very much like you!"

"Ah!" Coyote exclaimed. "So you saw me!" He went stealthily away and got his bow and arrows and then came back and shot an arrow at Roadrunner, who jumped and dodged. Coyote shot again and missed. Then Roadrunner said, "Now it's my turn!" He also grabbed his bow, but Coyote said, "Don't shoot! Don't shoot!" Coyote became ashamed and laid his bow down. "We can't live together any longer. I'm going to leave," he said. Roadrunner did not reply, and Coyote left the cave and went straight for mikiw which was not far away. Coyote came over a hill and saw the village below him, and he sat down there on the hillside to look things over. The people in mikiw saw him sitting there and Xelex sent another coyote from the village up to look the newcomer over. The village coyote went and talked to Coyote, but he pretended to be dumb, and the first coyote returned and reported that the newcomber was dumb and couldn't talk. Xelex then ordered all the people in the village to go and see if anyone recognized him, but he did nothing but make signs and gesture at the sun as if to say that he had been burnt by the sun's rays. So they took him back to the village and Xelex, the captain, came and looked him over. "This man is crazy," said Xelex. And Sloʔw, the other captain, also came to see Coyote, and said the same thing. "This man is crazy. What are we going to do with him?" asked Xelex. "Send him away. The people don't want him here!" replied Sloʔw. They ordered the village coyote to escort him to the outskirts of the village, and the two went along conversing with one another by means of signs and gestures. When the villager had conducted Coyote beyond the limits of the rancheria, he said goodbye and left him to travel on alone.

36 COYOTE AND THE CHILDREN

Coyote arrived at a village and he was very hungry, but he decided to wait until the middle of the day before entering so that he would be invited to eat. At midday he could smell food cooking, but when he entered the village there was no one anywhere around—just some large and small tarred baskets lying scattered around on the ground. He heard voices on the far side of the village, but when he got there not a soul was in sight. Coyote was enraged. "These baskets scattered around must be the people of this village," he said to himself. He gathered the baskets together and put them on a fire, and at once all of the baskets, large and small, began to cry. Coyote watched the tar on the baskets bubbling, and he was pleased. Finally the crying stopped, and Coyote stuck his hand in some of the tar and painted his forehead with it. Then he left the village and traveled on, still hungry.

After a while he arrived at Dixie Thompson spring and saw some children digging for cacomites. "How can I get their sympathy?" he thought to himself. He cut a lily growing nearby and danced down to where the children were digging the bulbs. The children looked at Coyote and saw that he was very thin. "Why are you so thin, little grandfather?" some of them asked him. "God told me that I'm like a saint, therefore I don't eat much," Coyote replied. Those of the children who were generous said, "Poor grandfather, since you are so skinny eat the bulbs that I've dug up so far." But the children who were stingy didn't want to give him anything. They said, "Coyote, what I've dug is for my relatives only!"

Coyote sat down and watched the children digging, and he ate cacomites until he was satisfied. He bewitched the bulbs so that the good children hardly had to dig at all while the stingy children had to dig very deep for them. When the children had obtained all the cacomites they wanted they went to La Presa to roast them, and Coyote went along too. While the bulbs were roasting Coyote bewitched them again, and when the children uncovered them the ones belonging to the good children were perfectly cooked while those belonging to the bad children were burned. Then Coyote and the good children ate their cacomites, while the stingy children went hungry.

37 COYOTE AND POʔXONO Once there were two deer hunters, Mountain Lion and another man. They went hunting in the mountains, and they found a deer and shot it. They were just beginning to skin it when Poxoʔno arrived. Now Poxoʔno is a man who

wears women's clothing and carries a walking stick which he throws at deer, killing them thus at great distances. And Poxo?no threw his walking stick and it smashed the deer and then returned to him, and the hunters were frightened. Every time they approached the deer to skin it Poxo?no threw his stick again. They finally retreated and left the deer to Poxo?no, who immediately began to eat it. And the two hunters were very sad, for they thought they had seen an apparition and that they were going to die, but they said not a word to anyone about what they had seen.

The next day they again went out hunting, and as before they shot a deer and started to skin it. And again Poxo?no came and threw his stick and frightened them away. They returned home sadly, bringing nothing with them, and Coyote said, "Our chief will die of hunger because of this." And so the two hunters went out once more, and again Poxo?no robbed them of the deer they shot. When they returned to the village Coyote was very angry. "You thought it was a woman, but it's a man! It only dresses like a woman, but you gave it the deer! Well, now I'm going hunting myself!" And Coyote went into the mountains and found a deer and shot it. He took out his knife to skin it, and just then Poxo?no arrived at the scene. "How come you're such a hindrance?" Coyote asked. "You certainly were a nuisance when you were little, and you're still a nuisance now!" And he added, "Leave, or I'll shoot you!" Then Poxo?no said, "I will tip the world from side to side, and if you shoot me the earth will quake." "You can't tilt the world if you're dead," answered Coyote, and he shot an arrow at Poxo?no. There was a quaking of the earth underfoot, and Coyote shot again. Then the earth shook so hard that it seemed to tip over, and Coyote fell down and was frightened. But then Poxo?no fell over dead and things returned to normal. And so Coyote took out his knife and skinned the deer. He severed its neck and feet and put the carcass on his shoulder to carry home. He went directly to the house of the wot, Eagle, and said, "Here is the venison for the captain to eat. And those of you who are laughing about this go and drink romerillo as you would after the loss of a kinsman, for I have killed your woman." The people stopped laughing then, and the wot ate the venison.

38 COYOTE GOES TO WAR

There were three fishermen at Moore's Landing near Goleta, and Coyote was there too. He was singing that he was cold, and the fishermen heard his song. One of them said to him, "Well, if you're cold and hungry, why don't you put on an otter-skin blanket like the Indians do?" Another fisherman threw some fish guts to Coyote and asked him why he didn't eat them. Coyote got very angry and said that he would get the fisherman's guts pretty soon.

Coyote was living at s?axpilil, a large town situated where Goleta is now, and Slo?, Xelex, and Qaq were there also. The three fishermen lived there too. Coyote was very quick to anger, and he got mad because they made fun of him. The next day he prepared to go to war. He went away to the Tulare country to get carrizo for arrows, and he made many arrows. And all night he spent his time making arrows and bows and other weapons. By dawn the next morning he had everything ready. Now usually when they are going to have a war they make a big fire as a signal, but the fishermen didn't know there was going to be a war. Coyote began to shoot at the village. The captain, Eagle, said, "What is wrong with Coyote—has he gone crazy?" He told some men to go and tell Coyote to stop, because he might injure someone in the village. But Coyote paid no attention and kept on shooting, and he killed the men Eagle had sent out to talk with him. The captain was afraid, so he sent the bravest men he had, Qaq and Xelex, who were also captains. But still Coyote paid no attention to them, and the war went on until everyone in the village was fighting. Coyote formed companies of men from Ventura, La Purisima, and the Tulare. At last all were killed, including Qaq and Xelex, and only Slo?w was left, and Coyote. And Slo?w made a motion like he was shooting and said, "I am a captain too, and I can die as well as any." So he escaped.

39 COYOTE AND THE ŠOPO

Once upon a time Thunder and Little Owl were playing a game, and Owl won. Thunder had four šopo which he wagered and lost, and so he sent Coyote to fetch them. So Coyote went and got the šopo, which were all bundled up, and started back with them. Halfway on the return trip he looked at the bundles he was carrying and said to himself, "I wonder what these things are that they ordered me to bring them? I'm going to unwrap one and see." And so he unwrapped one of the šopo, and as soon as he did so it shook itself free of his grasp and began to dance all by itself. Coyote looked at it dancing there, and it was very beautiful to see, and he also began to dance and to sing. Then he said, "I'll unwrap another one and see what happens." He did so, and again the šopo shook itself loose and began to dance, and Coyote danced along with it. Before long all four of the šopo were dancing there on the trail, and Coyote was dancing and singing too. But he finally tired and said to them, "Come now and return to your places." But the šopo did not want to be wrapped up again, and they began to dance here and there, each in a different direction. Then Coyote tried to catch them but couldn't, and at last they disappeared into the hills.

Coyote returned to Thunder and Owl empty-handed, and told them that he had been attacked on the trail by enemies and had lost the šopo. When he heard this Owl became very angry, for the šopo were now his since he had won them from Thunder. And Thunder was worried, for Owl was the stronger of the two. So Thunder said, "I'll repay you with money." But Owl was enraged, for he wanted the šopo and not the money. Then Thunder offered many different things to Owl, but Owl would have none of them. At last Owl grew so enraged that he seized Thunder in his talons, and Thunder began to shake the earth with the force of his thundering, and Coyote was very frightened. And Coyote said to Owl, "If you will release Thunder I will give you mice and everything else I can catch." And Owl quieted down and asked, "What did you say?" And Coyote promised again, "I'll catch mice for you and everything you like to eat." And Owl was pleased by that and released Thunder, and Coyote began to hunt for mice and give them to Owl.

40 COYOTE AND BUZZARD Once
Coyote was traveling, and he was very hungry and very poor. He climbed to the top of a hill and saw smoke, and thought to himself, "I'll go and see who is there." He went to where he had seen the smoke and found the house of Buzzard. "How goes it, bald-headed cousin? he greeted Buzzard. "All right," was the answer. "Are you hungry?"

asked Coyote hopefully. "No," said Buzzard. "But it's the custom always to feed guests," said Coyote. Buzzard reached behind him and got a pestle and a wooden bowl. He put the bowl under his knee and lifted the pestle high in the air and then smashed it down on his knee. Guata showered down into the bowl. Buzzard reached behind him and got a sack and took a bone awl out of it. With this he bored a hole in his nostrils, and a shower of chia fell into the bowl. Coyote took the food and ate it. Then Coyote went over to a spot close to Buzzard's house and made himself a house with his sorcery. He invited Buzzard to come and visit him. Buzzard didn't want to go but he was afraid not to, saying to himself, "He will kill me if I don't go!" Buzzard went over to Coyote's house and Coyote said that he was poor but he would invite Buzzard to eat anyway. Then Coyote took a pestle and a bowl and hit his knee just as Buzzard had done—bang! He reeled over backward. He tried it again, and again he fell over. Then Coyote took an awl out of a bag and began to bore a hole in his nostrils, but all he got was a shower of blood. "Bald-head, it's your fault!" he cried. But Buzzard had already gone.

41 COYOTE'S DREAM

Coyote once dreamed that he saw three men making shell money. He said to them, "You are making money." They responded, "We have been sent to do this work by a man who lives in the west. We have to be attentive, for it we do not pay strict attention we will come to the same end to which we all come and face him who sent us here." Coyote listened attentively to the moneymaker, and when he had finished, he remained silent for a little while, thinking. Then Coyote said, "It is well that you are working, but it is also good if the person for whom you are working has something, for if he has nothing at all there is nothing in it." He thought to himself, "I know, it is Death that has the three working here." Then he said aloud, "Remember that when death comes we have to leave our bones right here in this earth. I am going. I will see you again in front of the man who has brought you here."

42 COYOTE AND QOꝬLOY

Coyote and QoꝬloy were once living together at a time when both were men, and QoꝬloy was continually defecating inside the house. Coyote watched this for a few days and finally said, "I'm going to defecate in here too, since you do it!" And Qoʔloy answered, "But my feces are very good to eat. Try it." Coyote took some of the feces outside as if to throw it away, but instead he tried some and liked it. "Qoʔloy was right, it is good," he said to himself. And from then on he would tell Qoʔloy to defecate in the house because he would carry it out, and when he got outside where no one could see him he would eat it and enjoy it. And this story probably explains why the Indians here used to eat the feces of the crayfish.

43 COYOTE'S SONG

Victorio of Santa Barbara once told Fernando a story that has been a help to him whenever he is depressed. Coyote was on a journey and was feeling sad, but he said to himself, "Why am I sad and lonesome? Am I not the one who has done it all?" So Coyote thought of a song and commenced to sing, pretending to be the one who does everything:

I am traveling—I, I, I
I go around the world—I, I
I cause the mist—I, I.
When I climb the mountaintops
I cause clouds,
I cause the rain.
Long live Coyote!
He will always be.

As long as Coyote continued traveling he sang this song (and so it is repeated at least once). When he tired of his travels he had succeeded in getting what he most desired, which was an acquaintance with the rigors of the world. That is why he went all over and always sang this song. Thus when there is anyone who is dissatisfied with the vicissitudes of life in this world, either because of failure in business matters or because his spouse has left, it is a source of great satisfaction to possess the knowledge that even if he had not journeyed all over the world like Coyote had, if he sang this song he could imagine he had. And now Fernando is receiving fine treatment here at Ventura, and when he goes away it will cause him sadness of heart. He will look back and see how nice he was treated and the singing of this song will give him satisfaction. He has tried this when depressed and it has been a relief to him. And he has been told by his friends that when he goes he leaves an emptiness behind. So Coyote became convinced that the world is social. Life is a dream, and the world is a banquet.

44 COYOTE AT VENTURA The old Indians used to tell the boys that Coyote once went up on the hill back of Ventura and looked out all over trying to decide what it was that he wanted. In doing so he wandered all over the hill and defecated everywhere. That is why the water at Ventura is no good.

45 COYOTE AND TOAD Toad was a widow. For many years she lived alone with her two sons by the hills south of the Santa Ynez River. And Coyote lived quite a bit apart in homomoy. One day he decided that it would be a good idea to leave home and see what he might find. So he crossed the river and came eventually to where Toad was living at ?amaxalamis. He had been traveling for quite some time, so that when he heard someone pounding something in a mortar he was very pleased. "I'm sure to find a family living here," he said to himself. He climbed up a bank and unfortunately he spotted the house. "Ah," said he. "I'll surely find dinner here!" He saw two little boys playing outside, and said to himself, "The widow Toad must live here."

He walked up to the house and greeted Toad and her sons, but he received no reply. "Why are you frightened?" he asked. He began to scowl, and Toad hurriedly said, "Come in and sit down." "I've been traveling and I'm hungry," said Coyote. "Are you going to fix that acorn atole soon?" "No, I was pounding that up for tomorrow," said Toad. He got angry and demanded supper right away, and they gave him acorn atole and islay. Then the two boys went hunting and returned shortly with some birds they had caught. And Coyote demanded that they be prepared for him, and he ate them and gave the others nothing. Then he told the boys to sleep on a mat in the corner, while he got into bed with Toad. She was very unhappy, and he said, "Why are you sad? It's your good fortune to marry a captain, a good man!" Very early the next morning he woke the boys up and told them to go hunting.

"Don't return until you get something," he said. "Be sure you bring something back!" "Let them eat breakfast," begged Toad. "No, no—when they return!" Coyote exclaimed, and ran them out. Then he sat down and ate all the food that she had prepared for breakfast. After he had eaten he told the woman, "I'm going out to see what the boys are up to." When he found them they had caught nothing yet, so he killed them. And back at the house Toad was crying and saying, "What a misfortune that Coyote should find us! We have been doing fine here for years—and now he is going to kill my boys! May he be cursed for coming here!"

Coyote was approaching the house just then and heard part of this. "What are you saying?" he shouted. "You ugly, worthless, misshapen woman!" "Nothing!" Toad answered. But he shot at her and killed her. He left and went to the village of miswaqin, where he told the wot that someone had killed the widow Toad. The wot was angered to hear such news, and he and Coyote and some of the men from the village went to see just what had happened. They found the boys dead from arrow wounds—and Coyote's unmistakable tracks were all around. As soon as Coyote saw them looking at his tracks he fled. Then they found Toad with an arrow still in her body, and they recognized the arrow as one of Coyote's. All of the men were very angry then and they wanted to kill Coyote. And Coyote said to himself, "The best thing for me to do would be to turn into an animal, for they want to kill me!" So he did and that is why the coyote is like he is today—a bad customer.

46 COYOTE AND QUAIL When animals were still people, there was a fiesta at Zaca and all the quail were invited. One family of quail went. Coyote knew how many days the fiesta was to last, and he lay in wait for them on the Zaca grade. When the quail came along he jumped out and killed the wife and little ones. But the father and one little quail hid, and although Coyote looked and looked for them he couldn't find them, and finally he left. Then the quail told his son, "Wait for me here. I am going to inform the people at Zaca what happened to us." He climbed to the top of the hill and gave a shout, and the people at Zaca came out with their bows and arrows. They hunted for Coyote,

but of course they couldn't find him, for he had fled. All they found were his feces. And the quail was crying and very sad.

47 COYOTE AND LARK Coyote married Lark and everything went well for a while. But he brought lizards and moles home to eat, and his mother-in-law (who was also a calandria) was afraid of them. She told him to take them outside, and as he sat there eating them she sat and watched him with her face screwed up, and made insulting remarks about his eating habits. Coyote was infuriated, and when the mother-in-law went to get wood from the arroyo he killed her. When her mother did not return Lark went to look for her, and she was wandering here and there in the arroyo looking everywhere. And at last her mother appeared, but she had become a bird now, a lark just like she is today. She began to sing and her daughter recognized who she was. The bird sang her song over and over, saying, "He killed me! He killed me!" The girl knew what had happened, and she began to cry—and in a little while she too changed into a bird and flew away. And Coyote was very sad when he could not find his wife, but what could he do? He had lost everything.

48 COYOTE AND QƗŠQƗŠ Long ago, when the animals were people, Coyote got to worrying about his poverty, and one day he said to himself, "I'm going to travel around and see what I can find." So he left syuxtun and started across the mountains. He climbed way up on Seneq mountain and rested for a while, looking all around. He saw a place on the plains on the other side of the mountains where there were green trees, and he thought he would go there and see if he could get a drink. Just then he met a pinacate and said, "Well, I'll eat it, it's a good morsel." He ate the pinacate and went a little further down the mountain. Next he found a matavenado. "Ah, how fine!" he said. He ate it and said, "Now I'm satisfied, and I can go farther." He left the hills behind and started across the plains.

Pretty soon he reached the place where he had seen the green trees and found that they were willows and cottonwoods, and that there was a stream of water as well. He sat down under a cottonwood for a while to rest, and then he said, "Now I'm going to drink." He lay down and drank and drank, and when he finally lifted his head he saw that there were big salmon swimming in the water. "Ah, how fine!" he thought to himself. "Now what can I do? Ah, I will bewitch them and see if I can get them out that way!" He began to sing:

> napoy ipqowoč
> čup pqɨtɨwɨcus
> seponowopoʔ

> Jump, salmon, jump
> So you may see your uncle dance!

Then he started to dance, and pretty soon first one salmon and then another came jumping out of the water of their own accord and landed on the bank. Finally he had a great pile of fish in front of him and he was content.

Now Coyote didn't know it, but Qɨšqɨš was up in a cottonwood tree watching everything that he did. Coyote looked at his pile of fish and said, "I'm not even going to waste the entrails—I'm going to use everything!" He looked for stones and firewood, and then he dug a hole and built a fire in it. When it was all going well he put in the rocks to heat. Finally everything was ready, and he put the fish in and covered them up so that they would cook just right. Then he sat down and began to think, "I can't eat that much. I'd better go and purge myself first." He got up and started off, and as soon as he had left Qɨšqɨš flew down out of the tree and began to sample the fish. The bird ate and ate—he dined royally—and before Coyote had even reached his destination the fish were all gone. And poor Coyote walked and walked and at long last reached Tejon, where he drank brackish water to cleanse his stomach. By now he was thin, very thin! Coyote started back, and by the time he returned to where he had left his fish baking he was sweating and half-dead from hunger.

He sat down and groaned, and said, "Where shall I begin? I'll begin here!" He was content, smiling to himself at the thought of all those roasted salmon. He removed a rock from the fireplace and groped around, and then scraped away some dirt, but he didn't see a thing. "They must have burned!" he exclaimed. The Qɨšqɨš was up in the tree again watching, and when Coyote said this the thief burst out laughing and said, "Even licking the rocks, haha! You think they burned. I ate them!" He was hanging head down with joy. Now Coyote lost hope. "I'm going to kill you!" he yelled. He grabbed a sharp piece of flint that was lying nearby and began to saw away at the trunk of the cottonwood tree in which the bird was sitting. Who knows how many days he sawed at that tree before it fell? And just before it did fall Qísquis̆ flew to another tree nearby, laughing. Coyote stayed thin.

49 COYOTE AND WOODPECKER

Coyote envied Pulakak, the redheaded woodpecker, for he had such a pretty red head. He looked up into the tree where Pulakak was sitting and asked, "How is it that you have such a pretty color on your head?" He asked this many times, but the bird never answered. Finally, though, Pulakak got tired of Coyote's questioning, and so he said, "Well, stick a live coal on your head and you'll have a red head too." And sure enough Coyote did it, and he burned his head! And Coyote cried out from the pain, and ran in great leaps down to the creek. And Pulakak watched Coyote from the tree and laughed.

50 THE COYOTES AND THE BEETLE

A coyote was walking along the road one day and he came across a takiɁmɨ, a kind of beetle like a pinacate that also sometimes plays possum. The beetle seemed to be dead. "He's certainly dead," said the coyote. Just then another coyote came along and looked at the beetle, and he said, "It appears that this fellow is dead!" They stood there looking at the beetle, and then they began to poke him here and there to see if he moved. More coyotes arrived at the scene, and pretty soon there was a whole crowd standing around and talking. They blew into the beetle's ears and nose and mouth, and they stuck a finger in his nose in case he was ticklish. They opened his eyes with their fingers and looked in them carefully, and then said, "It's true that he is dead!" And they were thinking that they might as well take some bites from him.

There was one very little coyote there who was young and timorous, and he said, "You're lying, he isn't dead!" "What does he know about it!" the other coyotes replied. But the little coyote insisted that the beetle wasn't dead, and the rest of the coyotes got angry and chased him away. Then they began discussing the situation among themselves once more. "How are we going to divide this fellow?" they wondered. One said he was going to take the whole thigh. Even though it was so little they were still fighting over it! They were pulling and pounding the beetle unmercifully. Then they stopped and talked it over some more. One said, "I'm going to bite his belly. I just want to inhale his body gas, that's all I want!" "Go right ahead!" said the others, glad that he was only going to take a sniff and leave the meat for the rest to tear apart. They said together, "I'm only going to take a little piece of the meat, no more!" Then they all said, "A very little piece!"

The little coyote was still standing some distance away where they had just chased him, and now he said, "What you say about his being dead is a lie—it's a lie!" "Oh, go away!" they yelled back. But the beetle wasn't dead yet. He was groaning now, and half-dead from all the pushing and shoving. The coyotes got ready to eat him, and their captain started to bite the beetle's belly. The captain had a long, rough tongue, and when it touched the beetle's belly he jumped up and hit the captain and all the rest. He chased them down the road, and the little coyote shouted after them, "Didn't I tell you that it was a lie that he was dead? You wouldn't believe me!" And the captain was the fellow who got the beating!

D.

Still More Myths

51 THE STORY OF ʔAXIWALIČ

Once upon a time there was a consumptive by the name of ʔAxiwalič. He kept taking medicine but he got no better. This went on for quite a while. Though he took lots of medicine, he couldn't get well, and he had pretty well given up hope of ever recovering. Now ʔAxiwalič was ʔalʔatiš-winič, a wizard, and he had used all of his power to cure himself, but to no avail. One day he decided to leave home. "I'm just going to go someplace and die," he said. So he started out walking along the beach, following the shoreline, and it got later and later until finally night came.

He stopped and rested, and as he sat there he suddenly noticed a light emerge from a nearby cliff, move around a little and then reenter the rock. And as he sat there wondering about it, the light came out of the cliff again and moved toward him. And he said to himself, "I'll seize it, I'll capture it with my power." And the light came near and he grasped it with his witchery as one might grab a moth with a handkerchief. "Let me go," said the pelepel. (The pelepel is like a youth but shines like a light.) Again it said, "Let me loose! I want to go home!" "I want to go with you," said ʔAxiwalič. "I can't take you," said the pelepel. "You can't get through the small hole." "I won't let you go unless you take me with you," said ʔAxiwalič. They argued back and forth for a long time, but ʔAxiwalič was adamant, and finally the pelepel agreed to take him through the little hole in the cliff.

They entered the hole, and it was like a tunnel. They traveled along it for quite a while, and eventually they reached the end where ʔAxiwalič found himself in a great house. As soon as they entered he released the pelepel, which promptly disappeared. ʔAxiwalič sat down and looked around. There were many animals there in the house with him. There was an old deer lying there motionless, and a beaver with a cloud of hail around his head, and many other deer and birds. They did not say a word to him. And then many more animals entered the house—bears, coyotes, wildcats—all those that walk on four legs. And they defecated on him until his body was covered with feces. Still they did not say a word, and he simply sat there quietly watching. Finally the old deer came and said, "Why are you here?" "I am a sick man, I cannot recover," said ʔAxiwalič. Then the old deer said, "We shall have a fiesta, then we shall bathe you." And they prepared everything they needed for the fiesta, and after it was over they bathed him. And he was cured of his illness and began to eat again.

Then the old deer who had cured him came and said, "We are now going to return you to your own world." And they did, but they returned him by way of a spring rather than through the tunnel the way he had come. And when he reappeared at his old village all the people came and recognized him, and they were overjoyed. "He that we thought dead has returned to us cured," they said. He began to tell them everything that had happened to him, and he was amazed when they said that he had been gone for three years, for he thought he had only been gone for three days!

52 THE STORY OF ANUCWA At

one time there was a village called qasaqunpeqʔen, and the widow ʔAnucwa lived there with her two daughters. She was the sun's first cousin then, when the animals were still people. The older daughter's name was Ponoya. She seldom ate anything but a little tobacco and she worked hard making baskets of different kinds. The younger daughter's name was Šapiqenwaš, and she did very little all day except eat. ʔAnucwa was continually out looking for food because Šapiqenwaš ate everything in the house.

At last ʔAnucwa got very angry and thought to herself,

"The best thing for me to do would be to kill this girl so that I could rest!" That night the mother brought home lots of dry bark and built a roaring fire. After dinner Šapiqenwaš lay down and went to sleep, and pretty soon Ponoya did too. As soon as Ponoya was asleep, ʔAnucwa arose and carefully slipped her arms under Šapiqenwaš and dropped her in the fire. The little girl did not cry out, and she was soon covered over with hot ashes. The next morning ʔAnucwa arose and went looking for food, and when Ponoya woke up and found her sister gone she assumed that she had gone with the mother. But that afternoon ʔAnucwa returned—by herself. Ponoya was very sad. "My sister is dead," she thought to herself. The following day when ʔAnucwa called her daughter for dinner Ponoya said, "No, I'm not hungry, mother."

The next time her mother left to look for food Ponoya began to poke through the ashes of the fire looking for her sister, and at last she found Šapiqenwaš burned and dead. She pulled the little girl from the ashes and placed her in a big bowl. Then she put in some water and threw in some of the medicine that people had then to revive the dead, and in a little while her sister recovered. Then Ponoya said, "Hurry and eat your fill. We have far to go." The little girl ate all the food there was in the house and then said, "Sister, I'm full and I can't eat any more." "Well, let's go, then," Ponoya said. "We have a long trip ahead of us." "Where are we going?" "We have an uncle who lives far away," Ponoya said. "That's where we're going." "All right, but what about mother?" asked Šapiqenwaš. "Well, she is staying here alone," replied her older sister.

The sisters left then for Huasna, for somewhere in that region is the path that climbs up to the sky. And ʔAnucwa stayed behind, weeping and crying day after day and eating nothing at all. She just wept and scratched at the ashes of the fire with a stick. Sun saw her crying thus and pitied his cousin. He threw down two piñon nuts which she seized and ate. But as soon as she had eaten them two more appeared, and so it went until she was full. But at last she was so unhappy that she turned into the kind of small duck called ʔanucwa and flew away. Meanwhile the two sisters traveled very far. Šapiqenwaš was almost dead of exhaustion, for they walked day and night without stopping. But Ponoya had taken her atišwɨin and some tobacco along, and she had tule roots stuck in her hair. She would throw one of these ahead on the trail and her sister would find it, and when Šapiqenwaš picked it up it became several pieces. And Ponoya would eat a little of her pespibata to keep up her strength. But still the road was very long, and finally Sun took pity on them and shortened the road. And he told his daughters, "Two girls are coming— receive them well, for they are my cousins' daughters. I'm going now to look for a place where they can stay." And when Ponoya and Šapiqenwaš arrived at Sun's house they were given a place where he could watch over them, and even now they can be seen as two small stars close to the moon. Ponoya is the larger one, watching over her sister.

53 THE ČIQʔNEQʔŠ MYTH

Once there was a village with only a few families living in it, and in two of these families there was a man and woman who married one another when they came of age. After their marriage, they began to have children, and their first twelve children were all boys. The last, however, the thirteenth, was a girl. The children all grew up, and one day it was discovered that the girl was pregnant. Now the father, although having married quite young, was respected by every- one. So seeing that his daughter was getting bigger every day, it set him thinking, and he concluded that no outsider would have wronged his daughter, for the people all had great respect for him. So he quietly made a hoop or ring of junco such as is used for playing games. He finished it, and the next day he stood his twelve sons up in a line. Getting a cord, he stretched it from east to west between the two stakes in front of them. The daughter he placed to the south, and had her hold a bouquet of feathers in each hand. He said nothing to the boys, but his idea was to discover if one of them was the guilty person.

When everything was arranged, he stood to the west and started to roll the hoop with the idea that if it stopped and fell at the feet of one of his sons, that one would be guilty. He sang a song of divination, and then began to roll the hoop. The hoop rolled clear to the end of the line and did not fall. Again he sang his song and rolled the hoop, and again it failed to fall. While the father sang, the daughter held the feather bouquet in her right hand straight down at her side and the one in her left hand straight over her head. The father threw the hoop a third time and again it did not fall. By now the father was convinced that none of his twelve sons was guilty. But the daughter by now understood what the father was doing, and she then sang a song intimating that if one of the boys was the father of her child, they should never see her again. As soon as she began to sing her song, the father knew everything, and when she finished he sang a song expressing his belief in her innocence and his feeling of shame for not having divined this before. He felt much relieved, but at the same time very ashamed of his suspicions. When the child was born everyone realized it was a phenomenon, but still the father's sense of shame was so great that he finally left, singing:

> I'm going away—
> Don't look for me!

He went away, and his thirteen children stayed at home. When the child was born the brothers called the ʔalaxlapš to come and name him. (The ʔaxlapš was a kind of priest. He could tell whether or not a person would be fortunate in his transactions, and also by the planet of a person what would be his or her fate. He was an anatomist, physiognomist, and astrologer.) The ʔalaxlapš asked who the child's father was. One brother said to ask the child's mother. Then the mother said her baby was a sowing of the clouds. When the ʔalaxlapš heard this, he said to her: "Ah, girl, you were born to be happy. For it is your lot to give birth to this child of the clouds. Name him Čiqʔneqʔš."

When the child, Čiqʔneqʔš, grew old enough to go on errands, there was an old woman in the village who was his grandmother's sister. This old lady was very much inclined to be a sorceress. Čiqʔneqʔš knew about this. One day one of his uncles asked the boy to take this old woman over to his camp on the beach where he was clamming. She was quite old and was blind. Čiqʔneqʔš led the old lady to the camp, which was close to a precipice. Noticing this, the boy left the old woman at the camp and looked over the cliff. He saw there was a cave at the foot of the cliff that would be covered by water at high tide, but which was now dry, and that there were many large rocks scattered around the entrance.

He went back to the old woman and said: "Let's go a little

further." He gave her her cane and led her down the edge of the cliff and into the cave. He told her: "While you're here, I'm going over to the house and I'll return." Then he left quietly. Once outside the cave, he began to pile up stones until the entrance was completely blocked. Sometime later, the uncle noticed that it was high tide and thought to ask Čiqʔneqʔš how the old woman was. "No animal will harm her," said Čiqʔneqʔš. "Is she away from the reach of the tide?" asked the uncle. "Yes," said the boy. Later, another old woman, missing her neighbor, told the uncle: "You had better go and see what Čiqʔneqʔš has done with his grandmother's sister." The uncle went, and not finding the old lady anywhere returned and said: "She is not there." Then the other old lady said to Čiqʔneqʔš: "What did you do with her?" The boy answered: "I put her in the cave." "Why did you put her in there?" "She fooled the world too much by means of her black magic." Then the old woman exclaimed: "You really are a child of the clouds, and only the clouds can punish you. But we must be patient with you, because if the clouds punish you by means of a deluge of water, the punishment will fall on us also."

Everything was peaceful for a while after that. But then one day Čiqʔneqʔš disappeared suddenly, and was gone for several days. When he returned no one would talk to him. They were all afraid of him. When they would not speak to him, he sang this song:

> I have just arrived,
> I have come from far away,
> I am very hungry.
> I am son of the dead,
> And therefore I am hungry.

Finally one of his uncles gave him some food, but it wasn't enough to satisfy him, for he had not eaten since he left. Then Čiqʔneqʔš sang another song:

> There goes one,
> Two,
> Three,
> Four,
> Five.
> Those who went to the West.

The same observant old woman who had talked to him before came and asked him: "Who went to the West?" And Čiqʔneqʔš answered: "Those five that my grandmother's sister killed." Čiqʔneqʔš' uncles would never talk to him after that; only the old lady was not afraid to speak to him. Čiqʔneqʔš remained alone there at the house until finally one day he said to himself, "What am I going to do here? It would be best for me to leave." So he sang a song of farewell to the people of the village, and when he finished the song he was gone.

As he was traveling along one day he met lewelew or yowoyow (the devil). The devil said to him, "Where are you going?" "Just walking along," he replied. "But you are very young," said the devil. "Why are you walking around like this? You'd better get into my carrying-net and I will take you along with me." But Čiqʔneqʔš knew that the devil wanted to deceive him, and he began to sing:

Now I am beginning,
Beginning to make my defense.
I have just put my plant in this soil.
I don't know the end.
I barely put my foot on land.
I come from a great distance (the clouds).
I am the son of all the dead and
That is why I'm hungry.

The devil said to himself, "Where did this creature come from? What am I going to do with this little boy? Where did he come from?" And the devil said to Čiqʔneqʔš: "Do you know that you are under this sun, and that you are seen by means of its light?" And the boy started thinking, "This fellow is trying to get me all mixed up, but I am going to make him cry." So he said to the devil, "Do you know that we all see by the light in which we are?" "What are you trying to teach me?" asked the devil. The boy said, "Just pay attention." Then he began to sing:

What time of day
Do we have to cry?

Čiqʔneqʔš said to himself, "We shall see what this devil wants with me. He wants me to go with him." He told the

devil that he would accompany him. Then he got into the net
on the devil's back and they started off. After they had traveled
for a while Čiqʔneqʔš said, "Where are you taking me?" "I am
going to take you to the kingdom of the fly," answered the
devil. "All right," said the boy. When they got to the kingdom
of the fly the devil said, "What is the name of this place, and of
what is the realm of the fly composed?" And Čiqʔneqʔš
answered, "Xunpes pʔcuwa" (fly palace). The devil said nothing. The boy understood that the devil wanted to get him all
mixed up, so he began to tell the devil all about what the fly
was good for. Čiqʔneqʔš said, "As soon as a fly sees a dead
body he sits down and eats. In the afternoon he gets full, and
lies down near the dead one. In the morning he awakens and
again eats. He finishes eating, and enters the center of the
corpse and defecates. Little flies come out. Now you know
what the fly is." The devil answered, "No, I don't understand.
Continue your story." So the boy said, "Wait and listen! What
the fly defecates are maggots, and soon they are converted into
flies. As soon as they are grown the body is full of flies. They
have no houses, just like the old one" (referring obscurely to
the devil lest he understand it), "nothing more than the wind.
All the sons of the fly are the same as you. All the flies are in
their homes—and you! They kill us and take our homes."

The devil then said to the boy: "Wake up!" Čiqʔneqʔš
replied, "Yes, I am awake. Listen! All the people who have no
homes are like the flies, all the flies and you" (meaning they try
to dispossess people and take over their possessions). Next the
devil said to Čiqʔneqʔš, "Where shall we look?" The boy
answered:

> Here we are going to begin
> Where you come from
> Look to the south
> We are seeing the island of Santa Rosa.
> We begin
> And see the island of Santa Rosa
> There is where it began
> Always it will continue.

Finally the devil went away. He had lost hope of getting
Čiqʔneqʔš all mixed up. Then the boy got to thinking about his
homeland and started back. When he arrived home he found

everyone still living whom he had left. He saluted them with a song:

> Now I am rested
> For people are coming
> Those that came out of hell (on earth)
> Long live the world!

Ciq?neq?š was well received by everyone. They asked him what he had seen, and he answered that the most important thing that had happened to him (and the worst) was that he had had an interview with the devil. He recounted his experiences, and finally the old lady threw up her arms and said, "That's enough! You have conquered the devil, let us make peace." And so they lived in peace from then on.

54 THE DOG GIRL

When animals were people, there was once a family of dogs with many children in it—little dogs. They were poor and got along as best they could. The little dogs grew up, scrabbling for bones to eat, for they were very poor. Then one day one of the children, a girl, climbed a hill and saw a village on the other side. There were many houses and many people, and there was a shinny field where they were playing ball. The people saw her standing on the hill and beckoned to her to come down, but she wouldn't. When she returned home that afternoon and told her mother what had happened, her mother said, "Stupid girl, why didn't you go? They might have given you something!" "Oh, I'll go tomorrow," the girl replied. "Comb yourself first," said her mother.

The next morning the poor girl combed herself and said, "Now I'll go." She left. When she arrived at the top of the hill the people saw her and called out, "Come down, come down." She went down the hill and reached the village. A young man saw her and liked her, for she was a pretty girl. "I want her for my wife!" "Fine," said the mother. She went to the girl and told her what her son had said. The girl replied, "Well, I can't say yes or no. I'll go and ask my mother." They gave her food to eat, and after she had eaten she left.

She arrived home and told her mother what had happened. The old woman said, "Ah, daughter, you've had good luck, very good luck. But one thing I must say: behave well,

very well, and everything will be fine." "All right, mother,"
the girl replied. She combed herself, said goodbye to her
brothers, and then left. She reached the village, and she and
the boy were married. She lived in the captain's house. They
dressed her in fine clothing: she had a many-stranded necklace, a bracelet, earrings, a basket-hat, and an otter-skin apron.
She had everything, and she got along fine with her husband.
But it didn't last, for she was in the habit of eating excrement
lying around outside the house. She had plenty to eat, but she
was a dog and used to it.

One day her husband's younger sister saw her and ran to
the mother-in-law. "Mother, why is my brother's wife eating
filth?" asked the sister. "Be quiet!" exclaimed the old woman.
But the dog girl heard what had been said, and she ran away
into the mountains, crying. When she was high in the mountains she began to sing:

> If only I had worn my bracelet—
> My many-stranded necklace—
> My earrings—
> My basket-hat—
> If only I had brought my apron
> I would be happy.

Having sung this, she went on home. Her mother was surprised. "Why did you get angry and leave?" she asked. The
girl finally told her mother what had happened. She lived at
home ever after.

55 THE STORY OF SIQNEQS Siq-

neqs lived with his family at syuxtun, and one day
his parents went to get islay and left Siqneqs behind
to take care of his baby brother. Before she left the mother said,
"If the baby cries, tie a string to the cradle and pull it so that it
will sway and put him to sleep, and when he's asleep cover
him from the flies." After they had been gone for a while the
baby began to cry and Siqneqs, who was half-witted, tied a
string to the baby's neck instead of the cradle. He pulled on the
string until the baby was dead. Siqneqs thought the baby was
sleeping, so he covered it up as his mother had told him to do.
When his parents returned home that evening he told them
that he had rocked the baby to sleep, and that it was still

sleeping. But when they went to look the baby was dead, and they whipped Siqneqs and buried the baby.

Another time Siqneqs' mother had collected lots of acorns to last them through the spring, and they sent Siqneqs out to look for a cave in the hills in which to store them. But Siqneqs went instead to the beach at low tide, where he found many caves. He returned home and his parents asked, "How did it go?" "Fine," he replied. "There were a lot of good caves there!" So they told him to take the baskets of acorns and store them in the caves he had found. Sometime later when they needed acorns to eat they told Siqneqs to show them where he had put the baskets. They began to worry when he led them not to the mountains, as they expected, but down to the seashore! And sure enough, when they found the baskets of acorns they were full of water and completely spoiled.

Later they told Siqneqs that they were going fishing along the shore, but that he was to go and look for islay. "When you find a place where there is a lot of islay, paint your forehead with white clay so that we can see it from far away. Then we'll come and pick it." And Siqneqs went far up into the hills and finally found a solitary islay bush, and he was satisfied. So he painted his buttocks white, and his parents saw the white color from the shore and climbed all the way up the mountain to where he was. But when they got there they found only a single bush of islay, no more.

Siqneqs did many other stupid things, but his parents always sent him on errands anyway. One time, when his mother went after islay, Siqneqs stayed home. Before she left she told him to make acorn atole just about midday, but he thought she said to throw away the acorns. And so at noon he threw them away one by one. Another time Siqneqs and his mother went to pick islay, and the mother told him to keep a watch out for bears. When she asked him if he saw any bears, he said, "No, only a big fly." Then a bear came and killed the mother. "Why did that big fly kill my mother?" Siqneqs said to himself. He went home and told his grandmother that a big fly had killed his mother. They went to the place and found the woman all torn to pieces. They picked her up and brought her home and buried her.

Another time Siqneqs' grandmother said to him, "You are old enough now to marry, so look for someone about the age of this woman," she said, pointing to Siqneqs' sister. That night he started to get into bed with his sister, and his grandmother said, "What are you doing?" And Siqneqs answered, "Well, didn't you tell me to marry this one?" (In the old days, of course, people would not marry any relative, even a distant cousin.) And the grandmother shook her head and said, "You have to marry someone else, not your own sister!" And even today, when parents scold their children they're apt to say, "That's just like Siqneqs!"

56 THE ABANDONED WIFE Once there was a woman living at Tejon named Puluy, whose husband was a hunter. Each day he went out hunting and when he returned home at night he would bring game for his wife and two sons. But then he fell in love with another woman and began to bring home less and less, giving most of what he got to the other woman. Puluy began to suspect what was happening, and said to herself, "He no longer cares if we eat or not. It may be that he's met another woman. What can I do? I hope he does not forget his sons!" But her husband did not return that night, so they ate what little there was in the house.

The next day Puluy sent the eldest son to find his father. The poor boy left the house and went to where the other woman lived. Now it used to be the custom that the men did all the roasting, and when the boy arrived the father was roasting ducks over a fire. "Sit down!" his father said. Then everyone ate while the boy sat and watched, not saying a word. The ducks were big and fat, and the grease ran down the father's face and hands as he broke the ducks apart and ate them. When the meal was over the father said, "If you want a taste of meat, here it is!" But he didn't give his son a single piece; instead he wiped his hands on his son's body. The boy didn't say a word. They all lay down then and went to sleep, and the boy left, still without saying a word. When he reached home his mother was cooking a little piece of meat she had found. He sat down and she said, "You're in luck, for you can have meat once again. We haven't had any yet, but you can eat again if you wish!" Then the boy spoke up and said, "Why do you think I've had meat to eat? I haven't had a single bit!" "Then how does it happen that you're all covered with grease?" she asked. "The only thing he gave me was the grease that stuck to his hands!" he replied. "Why didn't you tell me!" she exclaimed. "I thought your father gave you something. Don't go there again!"

The following day the father went hunting again and Puluy calculated when he would be returning that evening. Then she told her sons, "Wait for me right here. Gather wood for a fire, I'm just going a little way." She had no sooner left than she turned into a puluy, a heron. She flew along and saw her husband coming loaded down with ducks he had caught in his trap. He didn't see her coming. When she was right overhead she gave a scream (as a heron does) and when he looked up she pecked out his eyes with her beak. Then she gathered up the ducks and carried them home with her. "Now let her children suffer as mine have suffered!" she cried. Her sons were very happy when she returned loaded with the ducks. And the father was dead and could no longer harm them.

57 THE BOYS WHO TURNED TO GEESE   This is not a story, it's an incident that happened long ago, when animals were people. There was a woman with a little boy, and she had remarried, for her former husband had left her for someone else. One day the stepfather went out hunting for ducks and fish, and he brought some home and roasted them, for in those days the men did the cooking. The husband and wife ate the fat ducks while the boy sat watching. They finished eating and cleaned the little boy's mouth and stomach, but they didn't give him anything to eat. The woman told the boy, "Go to your father for food!" The boy got angry and left. He went to look for something to eat—roots or anything else. He finally found some cacomites and ate them.

That afternoon he went home, but his mother said, "Go out and play." The poor boy went out somewhere and lay down to sleep. The next morning he got up and began to dig for more cacomites. He was digging when another boy came along in the same predicament—he was hungry, he had no father, and his mother had remarried. The two boys spent the night in a remote spot, and the next day they dug more caco- mites. Raccoon came along and saw them digging and asked,

"What are you boys doing here?" "We are digging for cacomites," they replied. "Why, don't you have mothers?" he
asked. "Yes, but they don't want us," said the boys. Raccoon
said, "Oh, you poor boys!" He began to dig cacomites for
them. Just then a third boy arrived, and he also had a stingy
stepfather. Raccoon said, "Boys, I'm going to take you someplace else." There is a kind of fruit in the Tejon area similar to
potatoes, and he took them to a place where some of this was
growing and began digging while the boys ate.

Two more abandoned boys came by and saw that Raccoon
was giving the other three boys food. Now there were five
boys. Raccoon said, "I'm going to take you to another place so
you can fill yourselves up." He took them to a place where
there were some tules, and he dug up some tule roots. The
boys ate, and now it was late in the day. Raccoon said, "Go on
home now, boys." "But our mothers don't want us," replied
the boys. "Go ahead—I'm going to watch," said Raccoon. So
the biggest boy went home, but his mother came out with a
stick and said, "Don't come here! Go sleep somewhere else. I
don't want you here!" Raccoon watched all this, and then he
told another boy, "Let's see about you." Again the boy's
mother chased him away. Then Raccoon asked, "Do you boys
want to go and sleep with me? I sleep in the temescal." "Fine,"
they answered. They went to the temescal, and Raccoon built a
great fire and the boys warmed themselves. Then they slept,
for they were content.

The next day Raccoon asked, "Boys, aren't you going
home for your breakfast?" "Oh, no," they said. "Then I'll take
you where there is some ʔaqulpop (chichequelite). He took
them to where some was growing, and pretty soon two more
little boys wandered by. Now there were seven. They ate and
filled themselves, and then the oldest boy said, "Boys, I'm
thinking of going north. What do you think?" The others said,
"Well, where you go, we'll go too." "What about our poor
uncle, Raccoon?" asked the oldest boy. "We'll take him, too,"
said the other boys. "Good, now we'll see how to do it," said
the oldest. He collected some goosefeather down (šoxš) and
put some on the head and shoulders of each boy in turn. Then
they called Raccoon and explained what they were going to do.

"We have given you a lot of work, uncle," they said.
"Now that our mothers don't want us, we're going to leave."

Raccoon was sad. "Uncle, if you want to go with us, we'll take you along," said the oldest. Then Raccoon was content and said, "Yes, why not? I'll go." So they threw down on him, too, and then the oldest boy said, "Follow me, boys. Accompany me, and sing!" He began to sing the following song (in Yokuts):

wilele ho?omoho
ixami hayoqoč?i
ixami hayoqoč?i
iqapapaq? atšripiniyu

papa,
voltéanse pacá, gentes,
voltéanse pacá, gentes,
extend your arms.

The boys were singing and going toward the temescal, but now they didn't touch the ground—they were already in the air. A family lived close to the temescal, and the woman came outside. She said to her husband, "Come and see the poor boys." He looked out and said, "Ah, the poor boys are leaving." The boys went around the temescal clockwise, but now they were flying. Raccoon came along below, walking on the ground.

The boys didn't sleep that night. They sang the whole time. The next day Raccoon took them out to find breakfast, and he was very sad. That afternoon they again returned singing. They covered Raccoon with feather down to see if he could fly but he couldn't. Again the boys flew around the temescal. The neighbor woman saw them and said, "Ah, poor little ones, they are going." Her husband said, "Tell the mother of the oldest boy to come and see what is happening." The woman went to the mother and said, "You are going to be sorry—look at your son!" The mother replied, "What can I do? Let him go!" "All right," the woman said, and she left. All that night the boys sang again, and they told Raccoon, "This is the last time—tomorrow night we're leaving. You can't go with us, though we wish you could." Raccoon was crying, and saying, "What shall we do!" The next day they all went out to find their breakfast, and this time they covered Raccoon completely with down, but he still couldn't fly. The boys returned home singing. They were higher in the air now, and now they were

no longer boys. They were geese. The oldest gave a cry, and
the neighbor woman said, "There come the poor boys again."
She looked out as they flew over, and now they were geese
instead of children.

She ran to their mothers and said, "What kind of hearts do
you have? Go and see your sons!" The mothers went out to
look, and the boys were already high in the air. The oldest boy's
mother extended her arms toward him and said, "Ah, little
son, come down!" But he only climbed higher. She picked up a
long stick and brandished it at him. "Come down!" she cried.
But they kept climbing higher, and now the seven women
were crying. They flew three times around the temescal, and
Raccoon was crying too. The mothers cried below, saying,
"Come down, little ones, come down and eat something!" But
they flew away to the north, and the women followed—that is
why María thinks they are the mothers of the seven Pleiades.

Geese are called merely manoxonox awawaw. But they
cry the same as a little boy. María remembers that there were
many by the Tule. Once they passed over while she was
sewing, crying yéy, yéy, yéy. Brigida was still living then, and
María asked, "Mother, who's crying?" She looked everywhere
but she didn't see a thing. Then she realized it was overhead.
Poor little one, flapping its wings. María began to cry, since
she already knew about this incident. Brigida said, "They are
animals, dumb one!"

58 THUNDER MAKES ZACA LAKE

Zaca Lake was formed when Thunder
sat down there and made a great hole in the
earth. There once was a village at that place, and a man
was eating ʔilepeš there one day when he looked up and saw
Thunder and started talking in an insulting way to him. And
the people said, "Let us get away from here, for Thunder is
someone you have to respect." They fled, and as they looked
back they saw that where Thunder had sat down there was
water, and that the man who had spoken to Thunder had
disappeared. Later, when they had cattle, it was noticed that
cattle near the lake were nothing but skin and bone although
there was plenty of grass. The head of a monster was seen
sticking up out of the lake. No wonder the cattle didn't go near
it! And it is said that in the middle of the lake the water eddies

around and around and there is no bottom to the lake at that point.

59 THE MAN WHO WENT TO ŠIMILAQŠA

At the Tejon about a century ago, when the people there were not yet Christians, the son of a certain rich chief told his mother that he would like to marry a particular girl. The mother said, "Very well, I will ask for her hand for you." In those days the people were different than they are now. The girls stayed at home with their mothers and did not mix with men like they do now, and they never got married without their parent's consent. The boy's mother asked for the hand of the girl and the girl's mother consented, and so the two were married. They had a celebration and lived for quite a while at the house of the boy's mother.

One morning the two ate breakfast and strolled around to get some sunshine, and while walking the wife picked up a little stick to clean her ear with. Her husband was teasing her and accidentally hit her hand. The stick was pushed into her ear and it bagan to bleed, and when she saw the blood she fainted and fell down dead. They had a wake for two nights and on the following day they buried her. The boy did not want his wife to be buried, but his mother said, "She has been dead for two days now." And so they buried her.

The boy went to the funeral and then returned home, but that night he decided to go to the grave to watch over the remains of his wife. He said that even if he died he would follow her. He went at dusk and made a hole near the grave in which to hide, and he stayed there all night watching the grave with only his head sticking up above the level of the ground. The first two nights he spent thus he saw nothing, but he knew she would rise on the third night, and she did. The ground began to move and finally she arose and shook the dirt from her hair. She started north and came back; then she started east and came back; then she started south and came back; and finally she started west and came back. Then she started north again and did not return. Her husband followed. She kept on going. At last she stopped and told her husband to go back because she was not a human being any more but a spirit of the other world. They had a discussion and she finally consented to let him follow her a little further. When dawn came he could see only her heels and what looked like mist, but when evening came again he began to see her more and more clearly until he saw her as clearly as if she were alive.

She told him to go back and said, "You have killed me, and now you are keeping me from my destination." The man replied, "It makes no difference, I will go on even if I perish." He continued to follow her. When they got to the place of the widows she told him that there they had to part. But he did not want to, and so they passed by the land of the widows and kept journeying. After a little while the wife stopped and said, "I don't know what we will do. There is a long pole ahead. I can pass across there but I don't know if you'll be able to." They reached the place, and there was a long pole that kept rising and falling, touching the gate of Šimilaqša and then rising until it brushed the sky. The wife said, "I will hurry and pass the gate. Be careful, there are two animals in the water that will try to frighten you." These animals emerge on each side of the pole and shout, and if a bad soul is passing it falls into the water and perishes but a good soul passes by safely. The wife told her husband that she would try to hold the end of the pole down until he could cross it. The husband looked and saw people standing petrified on the bank on this side, and he recognized some of them as men who had murdered their wives or had done other evil things. And he saw that the water was full of frogs, snakes and turtles with the hands and faces of people. These animals lived on cacomites that grew on the neighboring hill; they would come out of the water and dig for them.

The woman crossed the pole safely and so did her husband. She waited for him, and when he had crossed she said, "You may go this way and I will go the other way. You will come to a very large house of crystal. The old man who commands us lives there, and you can tell him what you want." She went on in one direction and he went in the other. He reached the crystal house where the old man lived, and the old man asked him what he wanted. "My wife died, but I want her back," the husband said. "If you do what I command, you can take your wife home with you. You will be with her for three nights, but you must not sleep with her. You can only talk with her." The sun set and he was happy. He saw a band of people coming and he thought that his wife was among them, but she wasn't. A second band of people appeared, but again she was not among them. A very large band came at last, and this time the wife was among them. She arrived and was very happy. That night the man was very sleepy but his wife told him, "Don't go to sleep." She shook him so that he would stay awake. The following night was the same—they talked and talked, and the man managed to stay awake. On the third day the old man told him, "Do not go to sleep. This time you will get your wife back body and soul." That night the wife said, "Don't go to sleep—I have pity on you." She shook him and pinched him but he finally went to sleep nevertheless, and when he awoke he found only a big log of wood lying next to him. His wife was gone.

Then the old man said, "Now, my son, you have not obeyed my orders. Your wife is no longer in this world, she is a spirit. They are waiting for you at home. Go home, for your mother and father are crying, thinking you dead. But do not tell anyone where you have been, for if you do many people will die. It has taken you several days to reach this place but you will be home by sunset." Then the man lost consciousness, and when he came to his senses he was near home. He waited till dusk to enter the village so that no one would see him arriving. He slipped into his mother's house undetected. When she saw him she asked, "Where have you been?" The boy would not tell where he had been. The next day his friends came around and asked him where he had been, and at first he wouldn't tell them. But at last he broke down and told them everything he had seen. "Now I have told everything that I saw and heard. Now I am going to die, for I was warned that I would die if I told." The mother cried, "My son, don't tell any more!" But it was too late, and he died. He had told the names of all those who were turned to stone or frogs, and the rest, and that is how people know these things. The people at Tejon can tell this story better than me.

60 THE SLIGHTED PRINCESS

Once long ago the people who were considered nobility among the Indians were all invited to a gathering, but a certain princess was not invited. She went anyway, but very little attention was paid to her. However, she said that before she left she was going to express her feelings. So she sang the following song.

> nowwiya qinohonwiya (three times)
> a a aa aa aaaa
> nowwiya qinohonwiya (three times)
> sulxoyoyon mehuq?sisqapu (twice)
> sulquyam hemu huyuwe (twice)
> nowwiya qinohonwiya
> sukquyam wayamcuqele (twice)
> nowwiya qinohonwiya (twice)
> nowwiya ha
> a a aa aa aaaa

> Who is like me!
> My plumes are flying—
> They will come to rest in an unknown region
> Above where the banners are flying.

When she finished singing she said goodbye to everyone and left. Then the two daughters of the two leading men followed her and made her return and be one of their number. Then she stood among them and sang:

> cam susnunal wu?uhun
> ?ispat?islowiwaš
> hiyahiya inowiyahaa
> ?iyiyi ?iyiyi nenšup?
> a a a a aaaaaaaaaaa

> They will be carried
> To the nest of the eagle
> And remain there in joy.
> Joy fills the world.

When she had finished singing this song the princess left, and this time they let her go.

Martina was the one who told Fernando this story. She said that it applied well to him because he was always roaming about being well-received and helped on his way. Fernando said earlier that he had made a solemn vow not to tell this story. Once when he made a vow and broke it he got an awful bump.

61 GAIN IS ALL

A man once played the following song on his four-holed flute:

ci winu hayaya (twice)
winu winu hayaya (three times)

Gain or profit
Will always exist

He was a very close observer, and he began to study the world. He found conflicts that went as far as people killing one another, and the cause of it all was gain. He stopped playing his flute, put it to his ear, and listened to the world. And he heard that all was gain. Then he played the tune again, listened again, etc. And this is all—the hole of the flute is the pathway to thought. After figuring it all out the man concluded that profit is the voice of all. All the time it is a single voice like the humming of the air. Gain is the touchstone of the human heart.

62 THE BOY AND THE SERPENT

There is a place over in the valley somewhere where there is a big river, and people used to catch lots of ducks there. They would make a trap like a house out of woven tules and put a stuffed mud-hen inside. The ducks would enter the zigzag entrance and after a while the trap would be full of ducks. Each man made his own trap, and went every two or three days to check it and remove the trapped ducks.

María's mother Brigida once knew a boy who built several traps at this place but could not catch a single duck. Now there was a spot on the same river called Ašaliw, beyond where the duck traps were located, that was very sacred. No one ever went there. But this boy went to Ašaliw anyway, hoping to shoot some ducks to make up for his lack of success in trapping them. When he got there he shot at a duck but missed, and he thought to himself, "I'm going to have bad luck!" And when he turned around he could no longer see the water. The entire river-bed was filled by the body of a giant serpent with scales as big as baskets. The boy broke his sinew-backed bow and threw it away, and then did the same thing with his arrows. Then he went and touched the serpent with his hand, and he felt it move. He walked alongside it, stroking it with his hand, and then he turned around and walked back. Three times he stroked the serpent's body in this fashion. He took his ʔatiŝwɨn and rubbed it over himself and the serpent, and then lay down on his stomach. For five days he lay there without eating or drinking, taking only pespibata. Finally the snake appeared in human form and told him not to be afraid, and sang a song. The boy went home, and when he arrived there his mother and father already knew that he had met misfortune, and so he was given toloache. Brigida knew this boy personally. How strange! There used to be these places and now they are all gone.

63 THE SERPENT WOMAN The people of Kalawašaq had the custom of playing paʔyas. Once there was a certain man who had the gambling habit bad and lost all the ʔikʔɨmɨš and mucucu his mother had, and his family was poor. On one occasion he had lost everything, and he decided to do away with himself because he was so ashamed. So he took a trail where he knew there were bad animals, and when he reached the place where the lime deposit was located he lay down and went to sleep, not caring if animals killed him or not. But nothing happened to him. He lay there all night and all the next day and all the following night and day too.

About midnight on the third night he thought he heard somebody coming. He said to himself that it must be either a bear or a mountain lion. He lay his head in his arms, and whatever the thing was came up to him and a voice said, "What are you doing here?" He looked up and it said, "Don't be afraid of me—I won't hurt you." He saw that it was a woman who was talking to him. "Don't be sad," the woman said. "I'm not sad," he answered. Then she said, "I have plenty of money and plenty of food to eat. Don't be worried about what you've lost, for it's nothing. Daylight is coming, and I'm going. I will return tomorrow night." Then she left, and in a short while he heard a noise and looked up to see a gigantic snake a foot in diameter crawling away. It was not a woman any longer. The man remained lying there, saying to himself, "I will stay here, inasmuch as I've come. It's my fault for coming here."

The next night he saw the woman approaching again, and she remained there all night talking with him. She told him again not to be worried, that he could go with her to her house which was only a short distance away. She told him not to be afraid, for he would see her as she was. He didn't reply, and as she left she assumed the form of a gigantic serpent that crawled toward the cave. The man could not stand the place any longer, and he returned to Kalawašaq where his mother and her family were living in very destitute circumstances. He told them everything that he had seen. He said that he wanted to die, that he did not want to drink any more toloache, and it came to pass that he did not live very long after that. He died.

That is how people knew that that reptile was living in that place. This happened before the Indians were Christianized. And this serpent that lived in the cave where the lime was dug was the same as the serpent the two workers in the lime pit saw in the sky. It had a special name but María forgets what it was, nor did she ever hear of its origin, but it has been known for centuries that a great reptile lived at that place.

64 THE SEA SERPENT

People used to see the tracks of an enormous sea serpent sometimes. It was the psos ʔi alnuna hee soo, "snake that comes from the water." Four men, or some such number, were thinking of founding a village on the hill or island in La Patera estero, but they did not do it because the tracks of this gigantic snake were reported to the priest at Santa Barbara mission as going up out out of Mission Canyon and past Hope Ranch to that island. The track of this serpent was once seen at Punta Gorda canyon between Carpenteria and Ventura, and an Indian named Juan Capistan (of Dos Pueblos descent) also reported seeing the track of one of these snakes on the beach at Puerto Nuevo on Santa Rosa island. The men who were working with the sheep threw some sheep entrails at that spot and the sea serpent came to eat them.

65 THE OLD WOMAN AND THE LAME DEVIL

The people of Kalawasaq always seemed to have bad luck. A big fiesta was once held at Soxtonokmu as was the custom and the people of other villages were invited to attend. A certain blind old woman lived at Kalawasaq with her daughter and her son-in-law. The husband said, "Wife, let us go to the fiesta at Soxtonokmu. All the ʔalapkalawasaq are going." But the wife said she couldn't go and leave her mother behind for the old woman was blind. So the man said that they should take the old woman along with them. The three started off and arrived without mishap at Soxtonokmu, and the fiesta began. The husband noticed that his wife was talking to other men and he started getting jealous. They had an argument and he told her, "We'd better go home." So they started off with the wife leading her mother by the hand. When they were close to Kalawašaq but had not yet crossed the river, the husband and wife began to argue again and the man got so mad he started thrashing the wife. The old woman was there by the trail with her bundle, but the couple were so upset that they went off and left her standing there.

It got dark and she was still standing there. The old woman said to herself, "I'll stay here by the trail until they come back for me." She stood right in the middle of the trail holding her walking stick in her hand. Pretty soon she felt a hot wind (she was naked, as was the custom). She said to herself that something was going to happen to her. It grew warmer. She heard a sound like a man stepping every now and then. She said to herself, "This is not my daughter, it isn't anyone of this world." But she was not an ordinary old woman—she was shrewd—and she stood up and said, "I will remain here!" She took her staff and held it firmly in her hand.

She heard the fall of a single foot coming, and she thought that it must be the mapaqas ʔasʔil or lame devil who goes around the world. The creature approached the old woman and stood there. Then he gave her a shove, but she didn't budge. "Get away from here," said the devil. He shoved her again. But she said, "I won't move from here!" He said, "Get off the trail. Don't you see that I have to pass?" "Why don't you go around?" she asked, and he shoved her again. She grabbed him by the wrist and began to wrestle with him. She was very strong because of her ʔatišwin. "Let go!" said the devil at midnight, for they were still wrestling. A little after midnight the devil said, "If you let me go I'll give you plenty of money and lots of food to eat." But the old woman replied, "No, I won't let go. I'll hold you until sunrise, so that people can see you and make you ashamed of yourself!" "No!" said the devil. "If you let go you will have many years to live and you will see the world." "No!" replied the old woman.

The daughter and husband, meanwhile, had discovered that the old woman was missing. "Oh, you ungrateful one!" said the wife. "Where is my mother? She must he frozen to death!" They set out to find the old woman and bring her home. At daylight they came to the top of a hill and saw in the distance the old woman still wrestling with the devil. Before they could reach her they saw her fall. A little cloud of smoke left the spot and entered the hollow of an oak. When they reached the place the old woman was lying there on the ground in a faint, but the son-in-law cured her with his ʔatiswɨn.

66 YOWOYOW AND THE BOY

Yowoyow was a nunašiš, a kind of devil. He must have been a big fellow. He carried a basket on his back full of boiling tar, and when he caught a boy he would carry him home in the basket to eat. Once Yowoyow caught a boy and said to himself, "Now I'll have good eating!" He threw the boy in the basket to carry home, and the boy got all stuck up with tar. On the trail Yowoyow passed under a tree, and the boy reached up and grabbed a branch and pulled himself out of the basket. Yowoyow did not notice. He reached home and told his old woman, "Now we'll have boy for supper." But when they looked in the basket the boy was gone. Yowoyow went out to hunt for him, but he couldn't find him anywhere.

E.

Shamans and Other Phenomena

67 BEAR SHAMANS If a man wants to be a bear shaman he kills a bear and pulls the skin off over the head in one piece, cutting the paws and the skin from the head carefully, and fills it with grass to dry. And other men told Fernando that they cut the skin down the back from the head to the tail and stuff it with grass to preserve its shape. Then they make a fine-meshed net of amole fiber and make a kind of shirt to protect the wearer of the bearskin in case of attack by arrows (that is why men sometimes shoot at bears and fail to kill them). Fernando has never seen one of these coats of mail, but Mateo of Ventura told him that there were three cords inside the skin with loops for each of three fingers. The index finger makes the bear walk, the middle finger makes it run, and the ring finger makes it turn. The index and middle fingers together cause the bear to go very swiftly, and if you don't know the combination you are likely to go too fast and bump up against the side of a tree or a mountain or something. These forces are supernatural. The man, of course, would do his part, but he wasn't able to go as fast by himself as he could when assisted by these supernatural forces. The three cords are managed with the left hand and the right hand is then free for dealing blows. Fernando never heard how they entered the skin or how they were dressed. He thinks they had herbs. Pastor once told him, "We are constantly walking on herbs the virtues of which no one knows." The thing must have had many superstitions.

Ustaquio, the old Ventura vaquero, found one of these bearskins on top of sisa mountain and didn't know how to use the strings. If you don't know how to use them you are likely to go over a precipice or anywhere, and before Ustaquio knew it he went to Nordhoff and to the ridge by Kaspatqaxwa where he bumped against the hill and stopped. Then he returned to where he had put the skin on originally, but Mateo said that it didn't take him long to go and return. Mateo also told Fernando that a bear-man hid his skin in a cave somewhere very secretly.

The father of this same Ustaquio was such a bear-man. Ustaquio was wounded one time by a bear and took an oath to kill every bear he saw from that time on. One night Ustaquio's father was going to San Fernando disguised as a bear. The vaqueros went after this bear and lassoed it, but they saw by the way it took the rope from its neck that it was not a real bear. A genuine bear takes the rope off quickly with one paw, but the medicine man disguised as a bear puts both front paws under the lasso and removes it. In those days the men had a straight sword that they carried under the leg piece of the saddle, and when the bear removed the rope from his neck Ustaquio charged it with his sword, and then charged it again. As he began a third onslaught the bear spoke and said, "My son!, don't kill me! I forgive you, for I am at fault. I forgive you all, for people are doing away with bears." But Ustaquio had taken a solemn oath in church, and so he said to his father, "I have taken an oath. You are wounded, and I shall kill you this day." He started to make a fresh onslaught, but another vaquero stopped him and said, "Spare him, he has pleaded with you. You have killed many bears and so have carried out your oath." And so Ustaquio spared his father's life. The old man was carried to Ventura where he died. But before he died he told Ustaquio that he wanted his belongings distributed among the others of the bear belief. There were five of these left, three at Ventura, one at La Purisima, and one at Santa Inez. And when Ustaquio addressed the three old men at Ventura, he said, "This has been my father's will, but I want you to be very careful about what you do, for a bear wounded me and I have taken a solemn oath to kill every bear I come across. So you people be very careful and never come my way!"

At La Purisma they also killed another bear shaman. It was the first time that he had come out to experiment as a bear. The young vaqueros there lassoed him, dragged him around for a while, and finally stabbed him to death. Fernando was shown the place where this happened.

There was an old Indian at Santa Inez who would turn himself into a bear and pull riatas off when he got lonesome, but he never did any harm. These bear doctors ordinarily dressed like any other man, but some other people knew they were bear doctors. Once a Purisima vaquero said to this Santa Inez bear-man, "Your belief in this matter is false, there is no foundation to it. Your courage is brought on by these herbs that you have. I would like to get you out in the open and show you what real courage is. You will see that the actions of a man on a good horse are as quick as thought." Finally the vaquero threatened to lasso the old man then and there and drag him to the priest if he did not agree to meet him in a test of strength. So the old man consented to do it. In the willows in the bed of the river where the road from La Purisima to Lompoc crosses the stream there was a small bare spot, and here the two agreed to meet on a certain night. When the vaquero reached the designated spot it was nearly dusk. His horse had a fine sense of smell, and as soon as they arrived it cocked its ears. The vaquero thought to himself, "The bear is close." He rode to a clump of willows where the bear was hiding and said, "Bear! Have you arrived? Come out! Men never hide from anybody. If you are ready, come out, for nobody is coming now. If you care to try your agility with me, you begin, but if you wish to try my courage and agility, I will attack you." Then the bear spoke up and said, "I will do the attacking." "Then hurry up and get to work!" So the bear attacked, but every time it rushed at the horse, the horse would make a little turn and the bear would miss him. After a while the bear got tired, and the vaquero said, "Do you prefer to be hit with my riata or my tapaderos? All you can do now is wait to be punished by me. You haven't the weight of a real bear. You haven't the strength to bite me. You are like a leaf in the wind." Then he attacked the bear, and at every rush the bear went down under the tapaderos. "Now I will try my riata, and punish you so you won't play spooks anymore."

Finally the bear had had enough, and the vaquero spoke

again and said, "Tell your friends who do this same kind of thing never to dress as bears again. For you people are to blame for a great deal of our suffering and for the fact that we cannot carry out the doctrines taught by the priests. You must promise that neither you nor your friends will do this again. You must not use your herbs." On the way home the vaquero went a roundabout way and stopped in the shadow of some trees in the middle of the Santa Rita plain to see what the bear would do. The bear came loping along, and every time he took a leap there was something in his mouth that made a *hw* sound. As the bear passed the man came out and gave him a final drubbing with his rope. "Never do this any more," he said to the bear. And before he let him go he placed his horse squarely in front of him and asked him what his opinion was of a man on horseback. The bear said, "Ah, a man on horseback is brave and agile, and a thing of power. The horse is the image of man's mind—he knows what the man wants. The only thing he cannot do is speak." Then the bear added, "And a man on foot, too, with his bow and arrows—if he is a man of courage he is a god on earth." Then the vaquero let the bear go.

Some time before the Purisima vaquero had his experience with the old Santa Inez bear shaman, there were three vaqueros who were said to be studying and practicing to become bears. One of these would-be bears decided one day he would have some fun. There was a man coming along the road from Lompoc to Purisima, and this bear appeared and started to climb a tree. The man had a bow and a quiver full of flint-tipped arrows and when he saw the bear he strung his bow with his foot and got ready to shoot an arrow. The bear saw what he was doing and cried, "No, no, no! Don't shoot, it's me!" The man recognized the voice as that of someone he knew and so he didn't shoot.

68 BEAR DOCTORS Wizards or sorcerers would have two bear paws hanging around their necks. They would throw these into a thicket and the paws would have a fight with a wild bear. These men would also get into a bearskin fixed with cords and frighten women who were gathering seeds, or they would go long distances rapidly. They wore bear teeth hanging from their necks.

69 WIYAXAMŠU AND HIS BROTHER

María heard that once long ago there were two men here at Santa Inez who could turn themselves into bears. They would go as far as San Luis Obispo during the night and be home by dawn. At that time the padres were still in power and people were still living at Alayulapu. The two bear men—Wiyaxamšu and his brother—were great bear dancers, but the padres did not allow such dances to take place. The two men were very unhappy about not being able to dance, and one day they decided to ask the people to let them perform secretly. They asked everyone to watch in silence and not make any noise that might attract attention, and the people agreed to their proposal. After dark they assembled quietly in the Canada del Cepo—siyʔap simaʔ or 'house of the jackrabbit'—where the dance was to be held.

Now at this time María's father was a young man, and very mischievous. He and another young man were talking about the dance, and María's father said, "Let's go and watch, and see if it's true that they turn into bears!" "Fine," said the other young man. "But ride a good horse, the best you have, and I'll do the same." They took ropes and everything else they thought they might need and started off. They stopped on the hill above the canyon. There was a fire burning down below for the two bear dancers to dance by, and there were many men and women there watching. The singers were ready with their rattles. "As soon as they stop dancing I'm going to give a yell," said María's father. "No, I'll shout," said the other. "But if they attack me, don't leave me in the lurch—help me!"

After a while the two dancers paused in their dancing, and the two young men on the hill began to yell. The dancers were very angry about the yelling, since they had asked everyone to remain silent. Wiyaxamšu jumped into the fire and threw his arms up, and immediately the flames shot high in the air. The entire area became as bright as day and the two boys on the hill were visible to the crowd below. No one said a word. Wiyaxamšu's mouth had lengthened into a bear's snout, and when he became a person again he remained crouched over. After a while he raised his head and said, "Ah, boys, my heart is sad. I begged a favor of you!" He was very angry. Then María's father said to his friend, "We'd better leave. I'm going to get scolded for this!" He was frightened by now. The two young men left then, and María's father arrived home about midnight, where he found his father still waiting up for him. When he came in the old man turned around and said, "How are you?" "Fine." "Why didn't you let the men dance?" "I wasn't there, papa," he replied. "Then you weren't up above there on the hill, and your companion didn't shout?" the old man asked. "No, papa." "Then you aren't fooling me? You can't defend yourself. You have no ʔatiśwɨn. They will kill you!" the old man said. "Papa, I didn't go there," the boy said. "Yes, you went," his father replied.

He kept scolding his son, and finally the boy gave in and asked, "Who told you?" "I know all that happened," his father said. "Don't think I'm stupid." The boy said nothing. "You think your horse is so powerful. He's nothing, and you along with him!" Then his son said, "It's true that I was up on the hill, but who told you?" "Silence!" replied the father. "Don't ever do that again. Those men aren't like you—and they are very angry!"

Now María's father was a vaquero, and the next day when he went out he rode his best horse. He left with a number of other riders, and as they were riding along they saw a little bear disappearing into some bushes. María's father liked killing bears, and he said, "He won't do any more harm!" He grabbed his rope and rode toward a thicket of scrub oak into which the bear had disappeared. Just as he reached the bushes a huge bear with a sorrel head suddenly emerged from the trees and caught him by surprise. The only thing he could do was to turn and run, with the bear right on his heels. He went up a ridge, and when he turned his horse at the top the bear was very close behind him. The horse jumped a small ravine that was in their path and the bear tumbled into it. But the horse was exhausted by now, and the bear caught hold of its hindquarters and pulled horse and rider down into the ravine. The other vaqueros arrived just in time, however, and roped the bear's feet and head, pulling it off the horse. The young man examined his horse and discovered that its hindquarters were ripped clear to the bone—the flesh was hanging down in strips—and it had very little chance of surviving. He took a knife and disemboweled the bear, and the vaqueros then released it to die.

He arrived home late that night and was surprised to find his father still up waiting for him. When he came in the old man didn't say a word. María's father ate his dinner of meat and acorn atole. The old man built up the fire until it was burning brightly, and then he turned and regarded his son in silence for a while. At last he said, "Ah, boy! Now what do you think? Where is your fine horse?" The young man didn't say a word. "The bears are going to kill you! You think you're a man— you're not a man!" Again there was silence. "If the bear had wanted to, he could have killed you—but there's time enough for that!" The old man kept on scolding his son in this way, but the young man didn't say a word. What was there to say?

Wiyaxamšu died here at the mission. He told his wife, "I'm going to go now. I can remain here no longer. But I'm not going to die. Take care. They can bury me now, and tomorrow they will see my tracks." It was true. He died and they buried him, and the next day his wife and another woman went to the grave and found huge bear tracks on top of it. Now when Wiyaxamšu was a man he burned his feet badly, leaving only claws—and the tracks on the grave showed only claws. Years afterwards two young men from the Tulare country told María that there was a bear over there that was really a man. He stole the very best cattle in spite of everything the American ranchers could do. It must have been Wiyaxamšu, for the bear tracks in the Tulare country had no feet, only claws.

70 THE OLD WOMAN AND THE BEAR

Once at Mištayɨt an old woman and two girls were out gathering barburis. The old woman was a sorceress. A bear (who was really a man) jumped out of some bushes, and the old woman told the two children to come to her. She spoke to the bear and said, "What do you want? Get out of here!" The bear tried to get at the girls. The old woman took her walking stick and pointed it at the sun. Then she thrust it into the bear and burst his skin, and there was a man inside. He had a lot of abalorio inside of the skin. Such men always carry abalorio when they turn into a bear so they can pay people not to betray them in case they get into trouble. The old woman did not take the abalorio but made the bear-man promise never to scare any woman again.

71 SILINAXUWIT
Silinaxuwit was an ʔalʔlat-iswɨnic but he was harmless, although nobody knew it. One day Marina's house caught on fire, and she was standing outside crying. Silinawuwit volunteered to save her things. He loosened his hair and covered his face with it. Then he went slowly into the flames, and it was as if they opened a path for him. He brought all of Martina's things out of the house safely. Now Silinaxuwit was a great talker, prankster, and lover of women. But he suddenly became very quiet and sad, and everyone wondered what was the matter with him. José Ignacio finally asked him, "What's wrong?" Whereupon Silinaxuwit answered, "The time has come for me to go to the bears." They saw him climb the hill and disappear into the mountains. In a little while they followed him, and his tracks became the tracks of a bear. "Then it is true that he is now a bear," they said. He never returned. He was staying with his kinsmen.

72 THE ʔATIŠWɨN OF JUAN MOYNAL
Juan Moynal, Brigida's half-brother, was captain of tinliw village, and very ʔatišwɨnic. Once he and his two brothers and Brigida and their mother were all camping at Tejachapi gathering cʔoyiq, a kind of seed. Many other people were also camped there. And one day Juan came to the children and said, "An epidemic is coming, a very serious one, and many people are going to die. The only way that we can escape ourselves is by leaving at once. Mother is going to die anyway." The children told him that if their mother was going to die they might as well die too. But Juan said, "No, for you have many years yet to live, but she doesn't. Her time has come." The children answered that they would not leave their mother, but that he could go if he was afraid. "No, I will also stay and care for her," he told them. "But there is nothing to be done, for my ʔatišwɨn has said that she is going to die."

Shortly after this people began to fall sick one by one—very sick. And again Juan Moynal's ʔatišwɨn told him, "Take your kinsmen and go, or you will all die. Your mother is going to die anyway." Juan told the children that they must all leave at once, but they refused to go. Then Juan said, "Tonight mother is going to fall ill." And the next morning the mother woke up feeling sick, and again the ʔatišwɨn warned Juan to take the children and go. "There is no hope for her now. Look at her. We must go," he told them. They still refused to leave, but at dawn the next morning the old mother was dead. Juan Moynal again begged them to leave at once, but they would not go until the old woman was well buried and the house and all her belongings burned. Only then did they leave and come to Santa Inez, where Brigida and the two brothers were baptized. But when the epidemic was over Juan Moynal returned home to the Tejon—his ʔatišwɨn told him to.

73 THE CURING OF JUAN MOYNAL

Juan Moynal was the captain of tinliw village in the Tejon region. He had a half-brother named José. Early one morning José went to Juan Moynal's house and offered his half-brother a drink of whiskey. The captain made a remark that showed that he knew what José was doing to him, but he drank the whiskey nevertheless for it was a matter of pride with him not to refuse because of fear. José then took his wife and quickly left the village, never to return. Shortly afterwards Juan Moynal's throat began to swell until it stuck out six inches beyond his chin. It was full of white maggots. Everyone began to shout that the captain was dying. There was a doctor there in the village by the name of Qaq (Alwɨt in the Tejon language). He also had Qaq as his škalukš. When this man heard that the captain was dying he began to run to Juan Moynal's house. There was a crowd of gamblers playing there in the village and Qaq ran right through them shouting wildly for them to make way. He reached the captain's house and succeeded in curing him with his wizardry. This was still early that same morning.

At midday another swelling began to appear on the captain's neck, but this time Juan Moynal cured himself with his own power. That night they told the captain that another ball would soon come out on his neck, so Šapaqay and another little old man said that they would treat him. Šapaqay ordered a fire to be built outside the house, and then they took the sick man and laid him down there by the fire. Šapaqay and the little old man began to dance, accompanied by singers with split-stick rattles. As Šapaqay danced he would lightly touch the sick man's neck with his feather-stick. After a while the little old man said, "It is now my turn. Give me room." Šapaqay kept dancing to one side, and the old man said, "If they will help me, he will live. If they do not help me, he will die. If they come, you will see them!" There were many people watching. Then he cried, "Where are you? I need you now!" He cried this three times, then began to dance violently.

Suddenly María and many of the people who were watching saw two xelex coming in the night, and the birds landed on each of the sick man's shoulders as he lay there on the ground. The two birds kept singing *qeqeqeqeqeqeqeq* and shortly the people heard coyotes sounding right in the middle of the crowd and not far from the dancers. The coyotes were there helping Šapaqay. Finally tears began to run from the old man's eyes, and he said that the sick man would live for many more years. The two xelex then departed. The next day Juan Moynal was better, he was cured.

74 ŠAPAKAY AND COSME Brigida, María Solares' mother, had a brother by the name of Šapaqay who was a famous shaman at Tinliw in the Tejon country. Before Brigida died she asked her daughter to go and see her uncle. He had been setting money aside for María every year, but Brigida told her not to ask for it. So in 1868 María went over to see Šapaqay on horseback, traveling with three others through Cuyama country, and when they got there Šapaqay gave María a lot of money and other things.

Sapaqay was never Christianized. He knew both white and black magic, and he could make a skeleton rise by means of ʔayip. He would run after an antelope and overtake it as easily as a man could catch a little child. Now while María was visiting there at Tinliw, a Tejon man by the name of Cosme (who had been Christianized and lived much of the time at Camulos) sent word to Šapaqay that he did not believe in Šapaqay's practices, and that he would soon be there at Tinliw and wanted to meet him. A Ventureño man by the name of Jesús Tuco was with Šapaqay when this message arrived, and Šapaqay told him to prepare some flicker feathers and to use them when Cosme came in sight. The next day when Cosme came in view Tuco already had a feather under a tray with his knee pressed on it, and when he saw Cosme he raised the edge of the tray and let it flip back and the feather was gone, heading toward Cosme. Cosme staggered but kept on walking straight. Jesús Tuco took another shot with another feather, and again Cosme staggered but kept coming. At the third shot Cosme nearly fell, but managed to keep his feet. Then Tuco shot again and this time Cosme staggered and fell. Then Šapaqay said, "That is enough, let him alone." Cosme was bleeding at the mouth, and Šapaqay ordered that he be given water.

Cosme recovered and he and Šapaqay had a private talk and were friends after that. Later Šapaqay reported that Cosme had said that he wanted to thank him for his reception, and that he wanted to say there in the presence of all that everything said about the magical powers of the Tejon people was true. María saw all this with her own eyes, and later told Fernando about it. They had a big dance then, and Cosme sang for the dance. During the celebration they made María walk three times around a basin of water. The next day after breakfast Šapaqay asked the people what they thought of María, and if they thought it would be a good idea to put her in Brigida's place. They said no, for she was brought up among white people and could not be the same as Brigida, and if she did replace Brigida there might be things for her to do or take care of that would be repugnant to her.

When the women had made this decision, Šapaqay said that since he found himself alone in his wish that María take her mother's place he would retire for good from the magic practices which he had followed so long, out of respect for his sister's death. And he said that in proof of that he would burn all his magic baskets there before them all, and he did so. Then Šapaqay said, "All has ended now—all the practices in which we indulged for our salvation or diversion, for there are few now who believe in them, and the next generation will not endure the hardship and suffering that is necessary to maintain them." And he concluded by saying that he could never again be useful for anything or hold any position. María came back to the coast then and Šapaqay stayed there in the Tejon country.

Now Cosme had it in for Jesús Tuco from then on. Tuco

had a wife, and one day Cosme went to her and said, "Here is a worm, and here is fifteen dollars. When you wash your husband's drawers, put this worm inside." This was at Tejon. A few days later Jesús Tuco felt that there was something the matter with him. He said to his wife, "Go away, don't speak to me anymore, you have poisoned me!" At first she would not confess what she had done, but finally she admitted it and said that she had done it because he had knocked Cosme down with the feathers. One day Tuco took a knife and cut his own thigh open and pulled out a ball. He was seized with an impulse to kill his wife, and so he left there and came over to the coast, where he showed Fernando the wound and told him the whole story. Later Pantaleon told Fernando that Tuco was very sick, and Fernando said that only Cosme or Šapaqay could cure him. A few days later Tuco died.

75 THE DEATH OF ŠAPAKAY Ša-

paqay knew in advance when he himself was going to die. He told his wife, "My days of living are numbered. Listen, when I die don't bury me in the ground. Leave me on top of the ground at the cemetery." Shortly afterwards Šapaqay died and they held a wake for two nights and had funeral ceremonies. Three old women took the body after the second night's wake, and Šapaqay's wife told them, "Have pity on him. Do not bury him, inasmuch as you know his ways. Have pity on him. Do not bury him, just leave him there on top of the ground." The old women obeyed the widow: they left the body on top of the ground and then returned to their houses. The next morning the widow woke up and told her youngest son to run over to the cemetery to see how his father was getting on. The son came back and said that he couldn't find a trace of his father. "He is not there," he said.

Three days later Šapaqay appeared again, and his wife asked him to eat but he refused. She knew that he was ?atiš-winic. He told his wife, "I am going to San Luis Obispo to see my two sisters. I am all right now, and well." He went to San Luis Obispo and several other people accompanied him there. He stayed for two weeks, and when he was about to leave he told his eldest sister, "I'm going away now, and I don't know when I shall return. I may die and then I won't come back again." Šapaqay told her that he was going to leave his necklace of sloʔw and xelex beads with her, and that she would know whether or not he was dead from it. He hung the necklace on a nail in the corner of the room and said, "If that remains hanging I shall still be alive, but if it drops I am dead." Šapaqay and his companions returned to Tejon.

Don Alejandro was an American who was married to a Tejon Indian woman named Šaʔawaqʔum. He had servants and a buggy for his wife whom he kept at the Tejon. Every two weeks they killed cattle they brought from their ranch in the Cuyama. Now Don Alejandro went to San Francisco one time by himself for a vacation, and they killed a beef at his wife's house. Šapaqay's wife told her husband to go over and try to buy four bits worth of meat from Don Alejandro's wife. "I don't know whether she'll sell me meat or not, but I'll go," he said. When Alejandro's wife saw Šapaqay approaching she said to herself, "Here comes that hateful fellow. I'm sure he's coming for meat." She went into the kitchen and Šapaqay followed her. He asked if he could buy some meat, and she refused, saying, "What do you think I am? I have plenty of money. You always come and buy two bits' or four bits' worth only!" Šapaqay said, "Very well. You think you will enjoy eating all your meat yourself!" He returned to his house and threw the money on the table and said to his wife, "It is your fault that I have been put to shame. Now you can go without meat." Then he left and disappeared into the woods.

Šapaqay's wife and little son ate supper alone that night and went to bed. During the night the entire village was suddenly aroused by the yelling of Alejandro's wife, who was crying for help. "Somebody is trying to kill me!" she shouted. She tore up the blanket, tore her hair, and tore her clothes. All night long they struggled with her and all the following day. "I'm dying," she cried. "Call the whole village and divide all my meat among them—the salt meat, the dried meat, the lard, the fresh meat—divide it among all these poor people." She also ordered them to distribute her flour, sugar, and other groceries among the poor because, she said, if this were not done she would die. "I am dying, dying. Divide all my clothes among them. Open this trunk and that, and distribute all this stuff among the poor. I want nothing for myself," she wailed. After her servants had finished distributing everything, even the blankets, it was getting dark. "Now the money, the silver and gold," she cried. Finally she said, "Where is my boy? Kill him! It doesn't matter if only I live. Kill him and bring me his eyes so I can see them!" And the people assembled there and said to one another, "How can we kill the poor boy? If we kill him it will do no good, for she will die anyway. Let's take him out and hide him." But the woman still demanded her son's eyes, and so they finally killed a cat and brought her its eyes. She was almost tearing herself to pieces by that time. She said, "These are not my son's eyes. You want to see me die!" Then she died. Don Alejandro returned from San Francisco five days after she had died.

Šapaqay was out in the hills all during the time the woman was in agony, and the old Tejoneños said that he was the one who had caused this mischief. Šapaqay continued to live at the Tejon until the Americans moved everyone over to Tule River Indian Reservation. He and his wife lived there at Tule for some time, and then one day Šapaqay told his wife again, "I am going to die." He told her that his days were numbered, and told her the number of days he had left. And just as before he said, "Do not bury me in the ground." When the day came that he had designated she woke up and found him dead. They held a wake for two nights, and two old women came to carry the body to the cemetery. Šapaqay's wife said, "Don't bury him!" But the old women had already dug the grave. Many people accompanied the body to the cemetery, where it was left on the edge of the grave, unburied. Halfway back one of the old women undertakers said to the other, "What do you think about this? I have followed this occupation from youth on up, and have never done things this way before. It is a sign of bad luck for us." The other old woman agreed. Then the first old woman said, "I will tell you what we'd better do. After dark, when the widow is in bed, we will go back and bury the body." And this they did. They buried the body, and they had no sooner finished doing so when one of them fell to the ground with a pain in her stomach, bleeding from the mouth and nose. Then she died. And the other woman likewise fell down with the same symptoms and died shortly afterwards.

The widow slept very comfortably that night, and the next morning she told her son to go to the cemetery and see how his father was getting along. In a little while he returned and reported that the two old women were lying dead beside the grave and that his father was buried. If they had not buried Šapaqay he would have revived, but as it was, he went to Šimilaqša, and the necklace that he had hung in the corner of the room in San Luis Obispo fell to the floor. When Šapaqay's sister entered the house and saw the necklace lying on the floor she burst out crying, and her husband came in and she told him that her brother was dead. "Who told you?" he asked. "Do you see this thing lying on the floor?" she replied. "Mice have cut the string," he said. He did not want to believe what she told him, but it was true. And recently two boys from the Tejon came to Santa Inez and said that Šapaqay's son cures people now just as his father used to.

76 THE REJECTED SUITOR There used to be a village at the very mouth of the Cañada de las Uvas at the Tejon, and an old woman lived there who had two powerful stones wrapped in a bundle in her house. This old woman had a pretty daughter living with her. One time a man who had herbs fell in love with the girl and asked her to marry him, but she said no, that she did not want to get married. The man went away, but the next morning he stole up behind her while she was making coiled basketry and put his hands on her bare sides. "What are you doing?" he asked. The girl felt a burning sensation on her sides, and she dropped her basketry and went to her mother. Her mother said, "Let's see." She saw a black spot and said, "My child, you're going to die." The girl's belly became swollen and she died. After her daughter's death the old woman took down the bundle containing the two stones and said, "We are all going to die now!"

She let the bundle drop on the ground. There was a big explosion and it began to rain frightfully. Frogs and black rattlesnakes fell from the sky and there was thunder and lightning. The old woman was going to break the stones by hitting them together, but the people begged her not to. She finally agreed not to carry out her plan. She drank hot water and did the stones up again and all was calm. María's mother, Brigida, saw these two stones. They were plummet-shaped and tapered at both ends. The old woman wrapped each one separately in cloth to make a bundle, and then put each bundle side by side and wrapped them again in rags to make a package two or three feet in diameter. This was put in a carrying net and hung in the old woman's house so that the bottom of the bundle was about six inches above the floor. The stones were called sʔyilyila masoxkon, "trastes del trueño."

77 STOPPING THE RAIN AT TEJON

The old woman at Tejon who had the two charmstones also had a grandson. It rained once during a big fiesta at Tejon and the people called upon that grandson to stop the rain. Everyone contributed ten-cent pieces, abalorio, and everything, and he received it all in his coat. Then the captain ordered that the man be taken to his house, and one fellow said to himself, "I am going to watch and see what he does. They have already paid him and the storm is still going on." When the grandson got to his house he heated some water in a cup and drank it, and soon the sun came out again. The grandson was also a great hunter, and when he was out hunting and it became too hot, he could bring clouds into the sky and make it cooler.

78 THE TWO SOCERERS AT TEJON

If you don't see anything the first time you take toloache, you take some more. Some people see something the first time while others do not. You see everything—even Thunder—and Thunder gives you ʔatišwɨn. Once at the Tejon there were two men who had ʔatišwɨn of Thunder and were very ʔatišwɨnic. There was the father, Qipawaš, and his son Hopono. They did not mingle with other people, but lived somewhat apart on the other side of a little sierra at a place called the "sauzal." They had no friends. Even if they had once had good friends, now that they were ʔatišwɨnic they had no friends at all, and they would kill anybody who came near where they lived. They both wore an ʔatišwɨn of human hair around their necks.

Qipawaš had had a brother who had died, leaving a wife and five-year-old daughter living in the village, and the old man used to take her food at night for a while. The little girl grew up with her mother there in the village and finally married a man who also had an ʔatišwɨn. Now at one time many people used to go to the Cuyama to get sugar carrizo, and the girl decided on one occasion to go along too. The mother did not want the girl to go, for she was afraid that if Qipawaš saw his niece he might kill her, but the daughter was not afraid and wanted to go anyway. Qipawaš and Hopono, of course, did not go with everyone else to the Cuyama, but they did go separately, and one day they appeared on a hill and looked down on the people who were gathering sugar carrizo. The son gave a shout, and everyone heard it and ran, for wizards have no power to go inside a house or into a camp. Everyone left except the niece of Qipawaš and her husband, and she told him that she was going to stay because she was very anxious to see her uncle.

He tried to persuade his wife to leave with everybody else but she refused. The husband said, "Those two have no relatives!" But the wife replied, "I am going to remain here. You can hide over there." The old man and his son arrived with their bows drawn and asked, "Who are you?" "Your niece," she answered. "I'm glad you did not run away with the rest," said Qipawaš. "And why should I run, uncle?" she asked. "You did well. I am your uncle," said Qipawaš. Then the son spoke up and said, "I see you are married." "Yes, my little brother," she answered. "Now that I know you are married, I would be very hurt to learn that your husband had mistreated you," said Hopono. "Therefore it gives me great pleasure to kill you with my own hands!" He shot the girl and she fell dead. The husband was hiding there and saw everything.

Then Qipawaš said to his son, "Since you have killed your first cousin, we will fix the ground where she can be laid." The ground was fixed and they laid the girl down, then they unbound her hair and covered her face with it. They didn't bury her, they just left her stretched out on the ground. The two then left, and as soon as they were out of sight the husband came out of the brush where he had been hiding. He left her body lying there also and returned to the camp, where he told the people, "I have met with bad luck. My wife has been killed. I ask as a great favor that you retrieve her body, for I can't stay here a moment longer. I am going to get revenge and kill the two who killed my wife if it takes every drop of blood in my body!"

He traveled all that day and the following night and reached the Tejon. He went to the house of his mother-in-law and told her everything that had happened, whereupon she began to cry. He said that he was going to get the best sorcerers of the three villages and would return in six days. "Prepare lots of food," he said. His mother-in-law hired lots of women to prepare food, and in three days he returned and told her to get ready, for a large group of people would arrive in three days and he was going to cut the throats of Qipawaš and his son. At dusk on the third day the crowd of sorcerers arrived, and as they approached they made a cry of *ququ ququ ququ*, imitating the cry of the puk (a species of owl). The mother-in-law opened the door, and the most powerful wizards were there. They entered the house and ate supper, talking over their plans and discussing how they were going to catch Qipawaš and Hopono.

They waited until daylight and then started off. The old man and his son were camped in the middle of the willow thicket at the "sauzal" and the group of men completely surrounded them without them knowing it. At daybreak Qipawaš got up and went out a little distance to defecate. As he was getting up one of the crowd said, "What are we waiting for? Why not take a shot at him? If we give him a chance he'll kill every last one of us!" Everyone began to shoot. The first arrow struck him in the eye, and soon every inch of his body was covered with arrows. The arrows were so thick on his body that they held it in the air. The son woke up and saw the crowd and said, "What's happening?" He saw his father's body full of arrows, and he took his own bow and all of his arrows and broke them to pieces. "If I wanted to, I could kill every one of you. But since I don't want to be alone in the world, all of you shoot me now!" They shot at him then, and in a moment his body too was full of arrows.

The day was clear and the sun shone. One of the crowd said, "Why do you leave them breathing, why don't you kill them completely?" So one man went over and cut the ʔatišwɨn from their necks, and as he did so thunder sounded, and that is how it became known that the two sorcerers had thunder charms. And there was a great cloudburst. Frogs and rattlesnakes fell from the skies. One of the men said, "Hurry, we may not be able to get home!" They cut off the head, hands and feet of the old man and his son and put them on a pole. Then they started back for tinliw, where the mother-in-law lived. They had breakfast there, and then held a great celebration in honor of their deed. And that is how people found out that the ʔatišwɨn were connected with the thunder. The ʔatišwɨn which those wizards had were merely necklaces of twisted human hair—*whose* hair, nobody knows.

79 THE GREAT FAMINE

Long ago, before there were white people here, a wizard at San Gabriel caused a great drought and famine that lasted for five years. María's grandfather Estévan and his wife lived through this period. This sorcerer had a tablet or stone on which he painted many figures of men and women bleeding from the mouth and falling down. He took this out into the hills and exposed it to the sun, praying for sickness. For five years there was no rain, and many people died of hunger. The seeds the women had stored came to an end, and there were no acorns or islay. Even the shells along the shore had only sand in them. When the men went out to get mescal only a few came back—the rest died of hunger—and the women put hot water on their breasts so they would have some milk to keep husbands or brothers alive. Finally some other sorcerers spied on the man who was causing all this and saw him going into the hills. When he returned they said, "Let's follow his tracks and see what he has been doing." They followed the tracks and found the tablet or whatever it was with the evil figures on it, and they threw it into the water. Then the drought ended and it rained. How did those people know how to do those things? They were wiser than the Americans in those days.

80 ENCHANTING TREES

At Santa Inez not so *very* long ago, Joaquin Ayala and Tomás got drunk and had a discussion, each one saying that he could ʔaxlapus an oak tree as well as the other. They bet on it, and many people assembled to witness the witchery. Joaquin made a roble rock from side to side by moving his hands from side to side, and Tomás made another roble rock the same way. Thus they both proved that they could šišaxlapus a roble tree in the presence of a large crowd. The people of teqepš were also able to make any tree bend. They were famous for being great sorcerers. A šaxlapus can foretell the future by using the coyote-string and a tray. Most of them are women but a few men are šaxlapus.

81 A PACT WITH THE DEVIL Do some Americans also make friends with a devil? There was such a man at La Purisima long ago, before María's time.

In the old days the people here didn't save their money like they do now, but this man always had plenty of money and he and his wife were always well-dressed. People like that live either ten or twelve years, and this man knew his time was approaching, so he was very sad. His wife said, "Cheer up—come and eat your dinner." "No," the man replied. He went to bed that night without eating. The following day his wife asked him, "What's wrong, are you sick? Why are you so sad, why don't you eat?" Finally the man said, "Why shouldn't I be sad? We've been doing well here. Why shouldn't I be sad? The time has come to fulfill my bargain." "What bargain?" the woman asked. He told her, and she said to him, "Why don't you confess? The padre is nearby—confess!" "I'm going to die anyhow," the husband replied.

Now there was going to be a rodeo here at ʔataxʔic that afternoon, and the woman told her husband, "Since you're so unhappy, why don't you go to the rodeo and get your mind off your troubles?" "Yes, I think I will go," he answered. He ate breakfast and saddled his horse—he had a beautiful big horse—and left for the rodeo. Just as he arrived a white steer jumped out of the herd of cattle and started off. The man went after it. His horse suddenly stumbled and fell, rolling over and crushing the man. They carried him to his house at La Purisima and sent for the padre, who came and said that if the man had sought repentance he would have lived, but that now it was too late. Many people saw this man die. The padre said, "Bury him—there is nothing that can be done."

82 BUZZARD EGGS Sometimes men go into the hills and steal the eggs of the ʔonoq, the buzzard. The buzzard favors the thief in order to get its eggs back, giving him great powers, but the thief dies at the end of twelve years. The devil gets him at the end of that time. A Purisima Indian that María knew was once found dead this way. He had completed his twelve years.

83 VULTURE STONES When the vulture lays eggs in her nest, find the nest and steal one egg. Boil the egg hard and then return it to the nest. Do all this when the vulture doesn't see you. She sits on the eggs and after a while discovers that something is wrong with one of them. She then starts off for the mountains. All this time you are watching carefully. She comes back with a rock and places it right against the egg and the chick hatches at once. As soon as the vulture leaves the nest, you go and take the stone, for with that stone you can get whatever you want. You can get hidden things that are pretty far away, though not too far away.

There was a man who had a stepdaughter by the name of Carlotta who was wealthy in her own right. A man wanted to marry her, but she refused him, and so he sent for someone to come and harm her. The fellow came and dug a hole in the wall and concealed a little bag of poison in it so that it could not be seen at all. Pretty soon Carlotta was sick in bed. Her stepfather, Blas, gãve a fiesta and invited people to come in the hope that someone would be able to discover what was wrong with her. An old man from San Diego by the name of Juan José came and brought with him a stone from the nest of a pajaro pinto. As he entered the room he examined the walls with the aid of this stone. Then he asked for a chair and a crowbar, and when they were brought he got up on the chair and knocked a hole in the adobe and found the concealed sack. He took the bag and immediately threw it into some water. "This is what has caused the illness," he said.

Then he addressed those present, saying, "Do you wish to know the names of the various people of this mission who are harming people? Come with me." They followed him, and in the willows a little way north of there they came across two men making herbs. These two men were discovered by means of the vulture stone. The two men were taken prisoner and they all returned to the house, where Juan José said to all present, "You can either chastise them or burn them." The men were set free after they had solemnly promised never to make herbs again.

84 A TEST OF POWER Once at Saticoy long ago Faustino, Lucio, Manuel, and José María were discussing dangerous animals, and José María was incredulous. He said he believed that there were such things, but that if you didn't disturb them they would not molest you. Then Lucio said that he was not afraid of any of them, because no matter how vicious they were he could stand them off. Now there was an old man there listening to all this (Illuminado, the old pipe-doctor or ʔalšuqlaš at Ventura), and he came up and said, "Young men, never talk like that, never place any confidence in mysterious things. I want to see how you three young men (barring José María) can defend yourselves with those mysterious things you have."

There was a ruined baking oven close by, and there was a young rattlesnake in the mouth of it that Illuminado had undoubtedly seen. He went and caught it and held it out, saying, "You claim that by the aid of these mysterious relics you have in your possession you can save yourself from anything. Now show me which of you can eat this young rattlesnake alive!" Thus he showed them that there was nothing in their claims, for none of them dared answer. Then José María spoke up and said to his three companions, "What is there now in your constant talk that you have this or you have that?" Then he addressed Illuminado and said, "Give me this little animal. They say it makes the world tremble." Then José María took the snake and first bit its head off and swallowed it, and then chewed the rest of the snake down.

It is said that a short time after he ate the rattlesnake his eyes began to bulge out. Then Illuminado said to the other three young men, "Now do something of what you said you could do: save the life of this man." So Lucio went into his room and brought out quiver and bow. Normally they are always careful not to bend the bow on the side where the sinew backing is, but Lucio took the cordless bow and bent it around José María's waist with the sinew inside, and at once the sick man felt great relief and began to sweat freely. After a while Lucio removed the bow, but José María soon felt a second attack coming on and so Faustino was called upon to attempt a cure. Faustino brought a gourd rattle and sat José María up. Then he put the rattle in the sick man's hand and made him shake it three times as if he were going to sing with it. Faustino left him sitting up, and after a while José María began to throw up a lot of slimy stuff, after which he felt refreshed. But then a third attack came, and Manuel took three of Lucio's flint-tipped arrows and bent them about the sick man's waist. After he had left them there for a while he removed them, and the arrows went straight again as if they had never been bent. Shortly after that José María began to vomit blood.

Before the last attack began Illuminado said, "You see, boys, there is no use in placing such confidence in these things. Lucio, whenever you are called upon to use your bow properly, you will be happy. And Faustino, you of the rattle, be happy when it is time for you to sing, but it was never intended that you cure people by that means. Manuel, you become enthusiastic when you see bows and arrows, but these should be made by your own hand. For it has been the rule among us that anything that has been obtained by the use of the bow and arrow cannot be claimed by anyone else, for wherever the arrow strikes, that is the sign of the power of man. Now it is my turn. I am going to do this using something which is the creation of Earth."

He took out his pespibata horn and removed some pespibata which he wet well with saliva. He asked that the dying man be straightened up, and when this was done, he went up to him with the pespibata in his mouth and put it in José María's mouth. Then Illuminado took a mouthful of water and put this in the dying man's mouth also. After a while the pespibata acted as an emetic and José María began to vomit freely. In a short time he felt all right. All this happened at Saticoy at the house of Luis Francisco, seventy years ago, but Fernando knew all the men personally.

85 JOAQUIN AYALA'S DAUGHTER

María has heard of three cases of children being lost—the little girl at Zaca Lake, the two children of Valerio in the Cuyama, and the daughter of Joaquin Ayala at San Marcos. Joaquin Ayala had married María Tomasa, but they had never had any children although she was dying to have some. Finally she said to her old husband, "We are never going to have children. You have plenty of money, why don't you pay those who know and find out how we may have some?" So Joaquin went and talked with an old woman, and he asked her if his wife could have a child. "Yes, she can," was the reply. "How many children do you want?" "I'll ask my wife," said Joaquin. María requested two little girls, and the old woman set to work and somehow cured her. She became pregnant, and finally gave birth to a little girl whom they christened Coleta.

The little girl grew to be quite big—she was talking and running around—and one day they went to San Marcos to pick grapes. They stopped at the house of a friend there, and before lunch Joaquin went up on the hill above the house to talk to the workmen. His wife stayed at the house talking with the women, and the little girl wandered around eating bunches of grapes. She came in once to get more grapes, and her mother asked, "Where are you going?" "No place—just here," replied the daughter. She left the house and wandered part of the way up the slope, dropping grape stems every so often on the way, and finally descended into a canyon quite some distance away. Her mother thought she had gone up on the hill with her father.

At lunchtime Joaquin returned with the workmen, and he asked his wife, "Where is Coleta?" She said, "Didn't she go with you?" "No!" he replied. They started looking for her over toward the river, but of course they didn't find her. It began to get dark, and they gave up hope of finding her that day. Finally someone said that they should consult an old woman who was a šaxlapus, one of those who know where people are. By now the wife was crying and crying, and Joaquin went hurriedly to see the old woman. She said that nothing could be done just then, that it was too late in the day. "Tomorrow," she said. "She is not dead. Tomorrow!" Joaquin and his wife could not sleep all night. María Tomasa cried steadily. Very early the next morning they went to see the šaxlapus, and she said, "Yes, in a few minutes. Let it clear up a little more." In a little while they went to where the girl had dropped the grape stems outside the house, and the old woman told them to find some men to help them. "They should be strong and able to endure running to look for her because she is close to death now," she said.

The šaxlapus then cleared off a spot on the ground right where the little girl had dropped some grape stems. She cleaned off a square area and arranged it carefully, and then said, "Get ready." Joaquin and two men stood by ready to start. The old woman placed a basket (an ʔayakuy) in the middle of the square and then stood to one side. When she hit the basket it flew away from her up the slope and disappeared into the canyon. The old woman told them, "Follow it and look for tracks. Follow it!" They descended into the canyon and found more grape stems that the girl had dropped, and then another cluster of stems a little further on. They couldn't understand how she had managed to travel so far. Joaquin himself finally collapsed from exhaustion. The other two men followed her tracks all the way up the canyon and almost to the top of the mountain before they found her. She had finally come to a big rock that had blocked her path and kept her from going any further, and she was sitting when they arrived. She still had her grapes, uneaten, in her hand.

"Where were you going?" they asked her. "I was following my mother," she answered. They said, "Where is she?" "She went up here, but I can't climb it," she replied. They said, "Your mother is back at the house. You weren't following anything. Come on, we'll take you home." She replied, "No, I'm going to follow my mother!" They carried her back to San Marcos, where her mother and the old woman were waiting. Then the old woman said to Joaquin Ayala and his wife, "Here is your little girl. But she is not going to live. She is going to die. And I will tell you something else: this girl was not born naturally and she will not grow. She has the appearance of a girl, but she isn't. Take her now." The wife took the little girl in her arms and left, crying, and the šaxlapus said to Joaquin, "Your wife will have another child, but the same thing will happen." Joaquin and María Tomasa returned to Santa Inez with their little girl that evening. They arrived home and cooked food and cared for her, but she didn't want to eat anything. Her mother held her in her arms, for she was very weak. About midnight María Tomasa looked at her and saw that she was already half-dead. And later María Tomasa had another daughter, and although she didn't get lost she died very young also.

86 THE LITTLE GIRL IN ZACA LAKE
Once a Santa Cruz Island man dove down under Zaca Lake. Each year at harvest time the priest used to give permission to pick islay for two weeks. There was lots of islay around Zaca Lake, and one year quite a number of families were camped there just where a certain Frenchman has his house now. One woman in the party had a

little girl who was crying and making a disturbance. "Tomorrow morning I won't take you with me," the woman told her daughter. "You are always crying and you don't give me a chance to pick islay." The next morning they ate breakfast and fixed lunches to take along with them. They fixed a lunch for the little girl, and her mother spanked her and left her crying. All the people left to pick islay. The little girl did not eat her lunch, which was placed in a double wooden bowl, but she carried it down to the shore of the lake. On the surface of the water she saw the image of a woman that looked like her mother, and she kept following the image, leaving her bowl off to one side. She left footprints towards the water.

When everyone returned from picking islay they missed her and hunted for her all over. It got dark and the parents were grief-stricken. They found her bowl and the tracks she had made. Then an old man who was there asked, "Why don't you ask the old woman where the girl is?" The little girl's father went to talk to that old woman, a certain very wise old woman, and offered to pay her well if she would tell him where his daughter was. But the old woman said that she would not tell him where the girl was just then because it was nighttime, but that she could say this much: she wasn't dead. The old woman was a šɨpɨš or diviner.

The parents did not sleep that night. The next morning they showed the old woman the girl's tracks and she smoothed them out with her hand. She then took out her string of the kind Coyote had, a Takulšoxšinaš made of red milkweed. That string was powerful—not everyone had one for not everyone understood how to use it. The string had ʔikʔimɨš and feather-down on it. The old woman took the string and made a circle with it to one side of where the footprints had been. Next she took a basketry tray and laid it right side up in the middle of the string circle. She then stood up and said a prayer, after which she slapped the middle of the tray three times with her right palm. The tray arose of its own accord and flew through the air and landed in the water, and then it flew back to the old woman again.

The diviner said that a strong man must be found, one who could follow where the girl had gone. A man from the islands was found who said he would try to return the girl to her parents. He got all ready to go into the water. "Expect me in five days, though I think I'm going to die," he said. He began to swim out into the lake, and then he dived down deep. When he reached the bottom he found land, land just like we have here, and there were trails there. He took the broadest trail, which led north, and followed it for a while. Pretty soon he heard the sound of pestles pounding in mortars, and he thought to himself, "I've reached my destination." He came to a village and he saw many people. But they didn't speak to him, so he sat down and just looked around. He saw a little girl walking around among the people. Four days went by and the man still sat there. Finally a man came over to him and said, "Friend, what do you want?" "The little girl," he replied. Then the man said, "I know what you are looking for. We took pity on her and brought her here. Take her and deliver her to her parents right away, for she is very delicate and will soon die."

The island man took the girl in his arms and started on the return trip. A great crowd of people were standing on the shore here in this world awaiting his return. They saw the waves in the middle of the lake bubbling up, and then the man appeared with the little girl in his arms. He told the mother to come and get the child because she was close to death. The mother took the child, crying, and leaving all of her islay and baskets behind she carried the girl to the mission where they lived. About midnight the little girl fell asleep, and in the morning she was dead.

87 VICENTA'S SONS Valerio, a Santa Barbara or Ventura Indian after whom Valerio Street in Santa Barbara is named, was a notorious bandit. He stole away an Indian woman named Vicenta from Santa Inez and the two of them lived in a cave in the mountains near the Cuyama and had two sons. At the time the following incident occurred, the oldest son was eight and the youngest about three and a half years old.

One day Valerio was out hunting for food for the family, and Vicenta had to go and get water from a spring that was some distance from the cave where they were hiding. She told the oldest boy, "Stay here, I am going for some water." The boy began to cry, saying that he wanted to go with her, but she finally left him and started out with an ʔwak to bring water back in. When she returned to the cave it was already dark, and the two children were nowhere to be found. Valerio returned about midnight and heard his wife crying before he even entered the cave. She told him what had happened. Now Valerio was a great ʔatišwɨinic but he was not an ʔaxlapš, a diviner, so that after hunting for the children until daybreak without success, he told his wife that he would have to go to Tejon and get someone who was an ʔaxlapš to help them.

He traveled on horseback all day and reached the Tejon, then returned that same night with two men from there. "Where did you leave the children?" they asked Vicenta. "Right here," she answered. One of the men cleared off the ground where the children had been left and put the sacred string in a circle on the ground. He then erected an arrow point-down in the center of the circle, and began to pray. Suddenly the arrow rose of its own accord and shot through the air toward the south. "Hurry," the man said, "the children are in that direction, but you must hurry and reach them before they die."

He and Valerio started off in the direction the arrow had gone, and in a canyon some distance away they found footprints. The older boy had evidently been carrying the younger on his back. The men decided that the boys apparently noticed some water in the canyon below and descended the slope toward it. They found a spot where the older boy had dug footholds into the steep slope, and at the bottom of the canyon they found a spot where the sand was still damp from their getting a drink. It was also evident that the boys had eaten some canaigre there. On the other side of the arroyo was a huge sycamore tree with many fallen leaves around its base, and here they found the two boys lying dead from the effects of eating the canaigre and then drinking too much water. The older brother had buried the other boy under the leaves after he had died, and he himself was just breathing his last when the men arrived.

They buried the two boys near the cave where they had lived, and then Vicenta said to Valerio, "I have lived here with you for many years, and you see the result of it all. Now I want to ask a favor of you. Take me to my relatives in Santa Inez and leave me there. It doesn't matter what becomes of me. I don't care if they kill me, I want to go there." Valerio said, "Very well, if you want to be punished, go. If not, you can remain here with me." "No, it doesn't matter if they punish me," she said, "I want to go." So Valerio took her to Santa Inez, and the next day Vicenta went to see the alcalde, Emanuel, the very strict one. She told him the whole story and he in turn told the priests. They ordered her locked up in prison with shackles on her feet. Then she was given twenty-five lashes on her naked back. Each day thereafter she was given twenty-five lashes until her back and buttocks were swollen and bleeding. The priests said, "Let her rest a few days." But when Vicenta heard of this she said, "No, I do not care if I die!"

Her sores were full of worms and she was very ill. She asked to be lashed below her knees and laid down on her stomach. The force of the blows would burst the sores and worms could be seen coming from them. Finally she was so sick that she was excused from further punishment. She had to lie face down all the time. That is the kind of thing that used to happen years ago, but such things do not occur now. Vicenta finally recovered and lived for many years at Santa Inez. Valerio remained in hiding until he was eventually killed near Montecito. He was a great sorcerer and a great burglar, and he could enter houses unnoticed. He left a large treasure in a cave near Santa Barbara when he died.

88 THE ISLAND FISHERMAN There was once a fisherman who lived on Santa Cruz Island with his wife and her aunt, and one day he crossed over to another island. There he fell in love with another woman, and he didn't come home for two or three days. When he did return at last he brought nothing with him—no fish or anything else—and he soon left again. Then the aunt said to the wife, "Listen, don't be stupid. Your husband has another woman and here you are crying. Why cry? Console yourself, your husband will be coming back to you. I will bring him home to you. You are a single woman and there is no one to help you but me, your aunt. But you must do what I tell you. Before morning he will be here, but don't speak to him or it will go badly for *you* instead of him."

That night the two women danced the šutiwɨʔyɨš, and before dawn the husband arrived, trembling with cold. He came in the door and lit a firebrand, but no one spoke to him.

"How are you?" he asked. They pretended to be asleep and didn't answer. He went over to where his wife was lying on her mat and touched her. He gave her a nudge and said, "Are you asleep?" Then he sat down by her side and began to cry. "You are angry with me," he said. "It's all my fault, but I won't do it again." She still didn't say a word. Finally he lost all hope that she would speak to him, and he arose from where he was sitting and seized her in his arms and broke into tears. "Forgive me, I'll never do it again!" he exclaimed. And so the woman won him back again.

89 MARTINA SINGS PEOPLE HOME A woman once went to Martina and asked her to sing songs for the return of her husband. Martina asked the woman to give her something the husband had worn next to his skin. They then went together to the high sand dunes west of qamexmei and Martina sang three times over the article of clothing, after which they returned to Martina's house where she sang three more times—and in three days the woman's husband returned to her. The woman's name was Isidra, and her husband was Fernando's uncle Baltazar.

Another case involved Vicente Borrego, who had been up at Hollister for about a year. His wife went to Martina with an old shoe, which was the only thing she could find. The wife and Martina sang together for three nights, and Vicente felt the influence of this at Hollister. On the third night after the singing he returned and went to his wife bawling like a baby, crying to be taken back, but she would not do it. The point is that one must never take back the person who did the abandoning until he makes a solemn promise never to do it again.

And there was a Spanish woman named Soledad Garcia at Cieneguitas who kept crying because her son had left her. She went to Martina with a pair of old shoes he had left behind, and offered her two dollars to bring her son back. Martina said, "No, I don't want your money." She sang three songs at an hour that suited her and in five days the son returned. Later the woman came and gave Martina three dollars.

Martina herself told Fernando about the following inci-

dents. She was at Santa Barbara one time when an American
woman came and told her that her husband had gone to the
old country and had not returned. The woman had with her a
valise containing her husband's necktie, shirt, and undershirt.
Martina said that she would see if she had any luck, and that
the woman should return the next day. The next morning at
the appointed hour the woman came, and she offered Martina
twenty dollars. Martina refused the money. She asked the
woman if her husband had treated her well. "Yes, but he went
off and left me," was the reply. The two women went over
west of the mouth of the Ventura river where Martina asked
the woman to sit down while she herself went down to the
shore. She walked back and forth from east to west singing a
song three times. Then she returned to where the woman was
sitting and let down her hair and sang the song three more
time, smoothing her hair with her hand. They then returned to
town. Martina said that since the man was far away he would
be back in three months, but that if he had not returned by
then it was because they had had bad luck. But sure enough,
the husband returned and agreed to all the woman said. Then
it occurred to the woman that a friend of hers in the east had
been left by her engaged lover. So she wrote to her friend, who
came here to Ventura, and the two of them went to Martina.
Again Martina sang over her and advised her to wait three
months just as the first woman had. The last that Martina had
heard the lover was here in Ventura.

Once Fernando himself used Martina's formula on a
woman at Santa Inez, named Josefa Garcia, whose husband
had left her. Fernando sang over Josefa three times, and on the
way home that day the woman met her husband, and they
both broke into tears and made up. But Fernando will not tell
the formula that Martina used.

90 RAMON AYALA Ramon Ayala used to
work over at the islands, and sometimes his work
kept him away from home three months at a time.
Once Martina was washing and asked Rita, Ramon's wife, if she
was sad, for it she was she could make Ramon come home. That
night Martina sang and said that Ramon would come home the
following day. Ramon appeared before morning, saying that

the wind had been just right. He arrived at Ventura that very night as if he had been called. This is a true story.

91 THE OLD MEN IN THE SPRING

Once at Santa Inez they wanted to convey water in ditches from the spring of qasaqunpe?qe to the big plain called ?usxaxmu, and they built a dam for this purpose but it always broke. The priest, long before María was born, came in a procession with all the people and said a litany in order to mend it, but prayers were ineffective. Finally the priest went to the spring and looked down into the water with a telescope. There he saw two old men seated with their feet toward one another and their knees half-flexed. When they extended their feet they shut off the water supply. They had long white hair that hung loose down over their faces, which were turned downward. These were called the ?anaxɨxɨ?, the old men, and they were said to be the fathers of the water.

Now a certain Indian said that it would be easy to solve the problem they were having, and the priest said, "All right, let him go ahead and do what he can. He will not be punished if he can get the water flowing properly." The Indian took a basketry tray and put pespibata, chia, and entire live oak acorns in it in little piles. After putting little piles all around the edge of the tray he put little piles in the middle as well. Next he prayed over it. Then he took an ?is?oxšinaš, a painted elderwood stick with feathers on top, and put it and the tray secretly in an earth cave near some live oak roots where the ditch was going to go from the spring. After that there was no more problem, and you can still see the ruins of the ditches.

92 THE ITALIAN FISHERMAN

When Fernando came to Ventura one time about 1864 there was an Italian fisherman there who had in his employ an Indian named Romaldo, an elder brother of José Winai. The two of them went one day to Santa Barbara Island to gather abalone, and after they had gotten as many as they wanted they decided to cruise along the south shore of the island. There was a very small island there, near Santa Barbara Island, and when they reached it the Italian told Romaldo to take the boat in so that he could jump onto the rocks. He climbed up on top of that little islet while Romaldo kept the boat offshore.

Romaldo noticed that the Italian acted very strangely, stooping over and looking down into the rocks. Later the Italian told him of the strange thing he had found. The rock was like an oven, the roof of which had an opening like a window. Sea water would rush in under the rock and the force of it would cause it to shoot up out of the opening at the top when the tide was high. Such a place is called mup. As soon as the Italian got back in the boat he said, "Let's go!" Romaldo noticed that his boss was very sad. When they reached camp the Italian said, "We must load our boat and make ready to leave." The next morning they left for Ventura, and on the way the Italian said, "Romaldo, you don't know the cause of my sadness. I will tell you what I saw there in that cave. I saw the forms of two Indians there in that cave, and I noticed that when the water would rush in they would stand and begin to blow their whistles like the whistlers at an Indian festival here on the mainland. When we go there again we are going to take clothing for those poor fellows!"

When they arrived in Ventura Romaldo went to his mother's house and told her where they had been and what the Italian had seen. Then his mother exclaimed, "Oh, son, now I do believe everything about those Indians who live at Mugu. That is where the exercise of the whistlers originated which is observed at holiday celebrations. I can't keep you from sailing with that Italian if you want to, but I advise you not to because the old Indians used to say that anyone who saw something like that would not live very long." When the Italian was ready to sail again he came to get Romaldo, but Romaldo refused to go with him. Later the Italian moved to Santa Barbara and went into partnership with Frank Harmer and shortly thereafter they were both drowned.

93 THE TWO ʔANTAP An American once went to Santa Cruz Island with a Ventureño boy, and he wanted to go and get abalone at a certain place where they were so thick on the rocks that they were touching each other. The boy objected to this but the man insisted. While they were gathering abalone the American found a cave in the rocks and looked into it. He saw two old

men inside—one had a bullroarer and the other had an elder-wood flute—and they were dancing and singing as do the ʔantap in the naxalyɨkɨš. When the tide came in the cave was covered, but at low tide the old men could be seen in there practicing their ceremony. When the water dashed over them they were unaffected by it, it was as nothing to them. On the way back from the island the American was drowned and the boy returned to Ventura alone. He told his mother what he had seen and she immediately gave him toloache to counteract the effects.

94 TOMÁS MEETS THE DEVIL

Tomás Kola was one of the earliest Indian vaqueros at the Ventura mission. He was once sent to Santa Ana to supervise the sheep-shearing, and after staying there for three days he was returning home when he encountered an old woman, "ʔalʔheleqeč," at San Joaquin canyon. He rode up to her and said, "Where are you going?" but there was no reply. Then he said, "Let me help. I will carry your woʔni home for you." Again there was no reply. Once again he said, "Which way are you going? Let me help you." There was still no answer. He rode along for a little while and pretty soon he forgot all about himself, and when he came to near daylight he was at La Laguna ranch near Point Mugu.

He did not lose his courage, though. The woman was still there, and he rushed his horse at her and tried to lash her, but she never budged. "If you are the devil, he who comes for us, I would like to take you over to the mission," he said to her. He attacked her again, whipping her with his riata. By this time it was daylight. He started home for Ventura, but as he crossed the Santa Clara river he met the old woman again, and this time she spoke to him and said, "I am the devil, I am the one who will have to come for you. Remember that I have taken two of you already." (She was referring to two well-known people who had recently died.) Then she added, "So that you will not treat anyone else the way you treated me, I will make you deaf!" When Tomás reached Ventura he told people what had happened, and later he became deaf.

In his old age he used to say, "Don't harm anyone, even the least creature, for you see what the old woman did to me." This old woman, in the belief of the Indians, would go slowly

around with the wo?ni on her back and a walking stick in her
hand. When she caught a boy she would quickly toss him over
her shoulder into the basket and take him to her home.
Fernando doesn't know where she lived or what she did with
the stolen boys.

95 TOMÁS AND THE OLD WO-MAN

Tomás Kola, an Indian of Saticoy, used
to tell the following story. On several occasions the
Indians noticed bear tracks leading from the cactus field west
of San Fernando up by way of Tapo to Camulos, where they
disappeared by the stream. They couldn't understand it, for
although they followed the tracks they never found any bear.
Once Tomás followed the tracks when they seemed to be fresh,
and he finally caught up with a woman who had a wo?ni on
her back and bearfoot moccasins on her feet. When he overtook her they had a talk and she paid him so that he would not
say anything about it. The woman was like a dwarf. She would
go about the San Fernando mission at night with her wo?ni on
her back.

96 MEETING THE DEVIL AT SANTA INEZ

When María was a little
girl, her grandfather Ignacio used to make her sit
down and listen to his stories, and that is how she knows about
such things as people meeting the devil. Ignacio met him
once—he was a man on a black horse with a new saddle,
dressed in old-fashioned horseman's clothing. It must have
been the devil. When you pass through the Llano Grande you
come to the place they call the Palos Blancos, and that is where
the horseman was seen. In the old days the vaqueros used to
gather horses together there, and the priest had each one guard
the herd for a week at a time. One time it was Ignacio's turn to
care for the mañada, and he went prepared, for every vaquero
had seen the man on the black horse. Ignacio took his rosary
and wore a St. Christopher's medal around his neck, and he
had a relic under his shirt. It was dark by the time he got to
Napamu?, but nothing happened even when he passed Šawla-
lamiš canyon where the horseman was wont to appear. "They
are stories—nothing but lies!" he said to himself.

"Or perhaps tomorrow night, who knows?"

He reached the place where the horses were, and he collected them and began to drive them toward Wahyamuʔ. It was a beautiful moonlit night and he had forgotten his nervousness. But suddenly his horse stopped and whirled around as if frightened, and Ignacio saw a horseman riding from the canyon there, and he said, "Surely that's the black horse!" He got off and tightened his cinch. His horse kept trying to run away. He said to himself, "That is the black horse! But I'm going to speak to its rider." His horse kept turning and trying to get away, but Ignacio kept a tight rein on him. "That's not the devil, that's just someone trying to frighten me," he assured himself. By now the horseman was almost on top of him, and Ignacio was struggling to keep his horse from bolting. "Who are you? What do you want?" he demanded, but there was no answer. The two horses were almost nose to nose, and Ignacio saw that the other rider was wearing the kind of clothing people wore long ago. He could see the buttons shining in the moonlight. His horse was rearing and finally he could hold it no longer. He let the reins slacken and they shot away at full speed. They went through the river like the devil himself, and all the dogs began to bark. In no time at all he was home again, and everyone asked, "What happened?" He said, "I've seen the horseman, but he isn't human, for he wouldn't speak to me." María thinks the devil didn't speak to him because he was carrying his relics.

Ignacio told María about another time when a person here at Santa Inez met the devil. This also happened long ago, when people were still living at the mission. There was a girl here then who used to wander around at night when everyone else was in bed. People told her to beware of the devil, but she paid no attention for she was a little crazy. She had no family—only an old grandmother who cared for her. One night the grandmother and another old woman were sitting up waiting for the girl to return, when they suddenly heard her running toward the house, screaming. "She's coming! Something has happened!" exclaimed one of the two old women. The old grandmother got up and opened the door and the girl fell in, half-dead and unable to speak. The old woman quickly closed the door. Now there was a hole under the door through which cats came and went, and suddenly an arm reached in through the hole—an abnormally long arm—and groped for the girl lying there on the floor. "Look out, he'll surely get you!" the old woman screamed. Now one of the old women was ʔatiš- wi̱nic, and she cried out, "Wi̱p ahiqʔen aqpa!" ("Hit it with my staff!") She hit the arm, and little by little it withdrew until it had completely disappeared. The next day the girl went to confession, and eventually she became a good woman. The devil surely frightened her!

97 THE COYOTE IMITATES PEOPLE

Theodosa once came to the house of Marías grandmother and asked if she could bor- row a digging-stick with which to dig soap-root. After chatting a while she left and climbed up on top of San Isidro mesa, where she started digging. She had gotten about two roots when a tiny little dog who often accompanied her here and there arrived and sat down watching her. Shortly thereafter she looked up and saw a man galloping toward her on horseback, and when he got a little nearer she recognized him as someone she knew well. He approached almost to where she was standing under an oak tree before he stopped and said, "Grab your dog!" "What are you afraid of?" she asked. "He might bite me," the man replied. Teodosa said, "No, he won't bite. He has come with me many times before and has never done anything like that." But the man insisted that she hold the dog, so finally she got him and wrapped him in her shawl. Then the man dismounted and as soon as he did so the dog began to struggle to get loose. "Hold him!" the man said. But Teodosa couldn't stop him. He got loose and began to jump around the man and bite him. She threw her digging-stick at the dog but it did no good.

Finally the man fled with the dog chasing him, and as Teodosa watched he changed into a coyote. He was not a man as he had pretended to be at all. He climbed the hill and stopped, howling, and the dog returned to Teodosa. She came to María's grandmother's house, crying, and the old lady asked, "What happened? Did your husband strike you?" "No," Teodosa replied. Then she related everything she had seen. Some time after this incident she went to Los Angeles with the real man whose imitation she had met on the mesa, and she was killed there. The man himself returned to Santa

Inez, where he fell sick and died also. May the coyote be accursed.

Martina had a similar thing happen to her, too. She was living at that time with a man at qwaʔ (at La Patera), and her husband Narciso was working as a cook for the Noriegas at Santa Barbara. One day she arrived (or seemed to arrive) at the Noriega house to see her husband. She was climbing the steps when she called out to Narciso, "Hold the dog!" Narciso looked at her puzzled, and said, "What is he liable to do?" "Martina" had a red shawl over her head and was carrying some food. She said, "I've got some acorn atole and tortillas for you." "Fine," he answered. "But why are you worried about the dog?" But she came no closer; she stopped some distance away and said, "Hold the dog!" "What's the matter, Martina?" Narciso asked again. The dog, who was very big, began to sniff the air. The figure of "Martina" was very light—for it was really a coyote—and the dress made a swishing sound. The other dogs at the house heard this and came running out, and "Martina" dropped the food she was carrying and fled. Narciso saw that the tortillas were nothing but cow manure. He was very depressed. He asked for his wages that very day and left Santa Barbara and went to qwaʔ to see Martina. He told her everything that had happened, and she said, "Well, we must take toloache." So they both took toloache, and nothing bad happened to them. Toloache is good medicine for things like that.

98 THE BLACK DOG AT SANTA INEZ Benvenuto once killed a beef at his house. It used to be the custom to roast the head and then throw it to the dogs. There was an islander and his wife who lived there at Benvenuto's, and they all had breakfast together and then threw the head out. During the day no dogs came around and the head was untouched, but they showed up after dark. Early in the evening the islander started out to visit some other people and told everyone not to wait up for him, since he wouldn't be back until late. On his way home that night he saw a dog lying with his paws on top of the beef head. The dog's name was Amigo, and his master lived nearby. The dog snarled at him as he passed by and the man

picked up a rock and threw it at him. The dog took his paws from the beef head and looked at the man, who promptly threw another rock at him. Then the dog spoke and said, "Why do you throw rocks at me? I'm eating my breakfast. If you were eating your breakfast and someone threw rocks at you, you wouldn't like it!" The man came home crying and told his wife what had happened, and said, "Get ready to leave. We will go back to San Marcos, where my mother lives." The wife came crying to Brigida and told her the story, and said they were going away. The couple went to San Marcos, and the man's mother gave them toloache to drink. The man got drunk with the toloache and saw the dog again, and the dog spoke to him and said, "Why are you so sad? Don't be sad. I will do nothing to harm you." When the man came to his senses his mother asked him what he had seen. He answered that everything was all right. The dog died at daybreak the same night, and they held a wake over it.

Another time a Ventureño named Ramon was deserted by his wife and took up with a woman named Rosa. He used to visit Rosa every night. After supper one night Ramon put the sheep in the corral and then went to see his paramour, Rosa. It was a moonlit night. He had just reached Rosa's house when he saw a big black dog climbing up the roof of the old Santa Inez Mission to where the bells were hung. Ramon kept walking backwards until he fell into the foundation of the mission, which was steep. He was found there the next day, bruised and injured.

On another occasion, after Captain Moore started a grocery store in that same house, his mother Magdalena wanted to urinate and squatted down by the gate of the cemetery for this purpose. She heard a sound like somebody walking on a board floor. Finally she saw the figure of a dog jump over the gate of the cemetery towards her, and she had a good look at him. It was a very shaggy black or reddish dog. She almost fainted. When she recovered, she saw the dog walking along the wall of the cemetery. She rushed to her husband and said, "A big black dog—I saw it at the gate of the cemetery!" Her husband rushed out with a gun, but the animal had disappeared. That dog is still in existence, and has been seen since. María thinks it must be the devil. That same dog has been seen at Zanja de Cota.

99 SPIRIT LIGHTS

When old Rafael was on his deathbed, María saw a ball of light traveling between the oak in the field and her adobe. This happened for several nights, but the worst was yet to come. One night she went out to throw away the dishwater and she looked up and saw the light approaching. This time it came right toward her, and she threw the dishcloth at it and cried out in terror, "Go away! What do you want here?" As soon as she did this the light changed course and went on down the creek and disappeared. María is sure that it was Rafael's soul. He lived a few days longer and then died. In the daytime such a ball of light appears as a floating white ball. María has seen it.

Once Feliz Carillo's wife Ramona and her young infant were very sick, and María and Josefina saw a ball of light as big as her two fists moving near the house with a smaller ball behind it. Such things are called ʔahašɨš, spirits. Once María passed María Antonia's house and saw María Antonia's husband'looking out at her through the open door. But later it turned out that he hadn't been there at all. Later Clara saw him too. She had exactly the same experience.

Once a Santa Inez Indian named Daniel, a great drinker, died, and his widow moved to another house. The house in which he had died was deserted, but people used to see a light there at night and hear a sound of knocking as if a carpenter were at work, and they would say, "Poor Daniel, his soul is doing penance." People were always talking about these occurrences, and one time an Inezeño named Miguel and his wife Venancia (who was an islander) got into a hot argument about souls returning to this world. Venancia said that after people die they may return again to this world, but Miguel didn't believe her. The next morning Miguel told her that he would go over to Daniel's house and investigate, and Venancia said that she wished he would. That evening he took his prayer book and rosary and seated himself under an oak tree not far from the old house. He took his rosary from his neck and held it in his hand, and began to read prayers from his book. After he had sat there for some time he heard a beating sound and saw a shadow. He looked in the direction the sound was coming from and saw a beautiful bright light that ascended and descended as he watched. Horrified, he turned to go and heard a sound as if someone were following him. It was the soul of the dead man after him. Just as the soul was about to overtake him he remembered that the old Indians used to say, "Step out of the way and the soul will pass by." So Miguell stepped to one side for a minute and then ran home, scared to death. His wife was greatly alarmed when he rushed in that way. He told her what had happened, and she said, "It is true—didn't I tell you?" Miguel believed it after that. That light alarmed people for a long time, but it has not been seen recently.

100 SEEING PEOPLE WHO AREN'T THERE

The Indians here believed (and María thinks it's true) that when a person is near death they are sometimes seen in other places: it is the spirit which has left the body. For instance, you might be either sick or well and asleep at home, and people would see you walking around someplace else. You wouldn't even know you had been there when you woke up. This is a very bad sign and means that you will soon die unless something can be done to prevent it. Certain old men knew how to cure someone who had been seen in another place in this way and could arrange for them to live for many more years. One time people saw Teopista with a canyon. They told her about it and it was arranged that Marcelino should dance the Šutiwɨʔyɨš. Teopista paid him well for doing this. She thus averted a bad fate.

María has twice seen a person who wasn't really there in this way. Once she thought she saw her husband, but he really returned two or three days later. Soon after that he died. The other case involved José Dolores, who used to live just above María. He had been working for Eduardo de la Cuesta for several weeks, coming home every Saturday night only. On Sunday morning María would take him his laundry. One Friday María saw José at his house. He left the house and was seen walking down toward the arroyo with a very dirty shirt on, but when they looked for him later he was nowhere to be found. That Saturday evening he arrived from Eduardo de la Cuesta's as usual, and on Sunday night he suddenly became ill and died.

101 TWO MEN FLY AT SANTA INEZ

At a place a short distance south of Santa Inez Mission there is a bank where they once dug lime for the building of the mission. The priest sent some Indians to dig lime there one time, and ordered others to carry it to the mission and still others to burn it. There were two island men digging lime there at the top of the bank, and the others told them not to talk too loudly or something might happen to them, but they paid no attention. Suddenly they heard a sound like an explosion and everyone looked up. They saw a cloud and in the cloud there was an animal that looked like a serpent. It had a big head with a tuft on it like a quail, but they could not see what the tuft was made of. The two islanders were carried off by the cloud. One finally fell near the mission while the other was carried as far as the Llano Grande.

Now two or three alcaldes had been there watching the workmen, and one of them, a man by the name of Manuel, was very much of a tattletale. He went and told the priest what had happened, and the priest summoned the two men (who were unhurt) and asked them what they had done. They answered that they had done nothing. The priest said, "I would have been very frightened if I had seen that." "We got scared and flew," the two workmen said. The priest said, "I'm a priest, but if I get scared I can't fly!" He admonished them not to do anything like that again, since that was an act of the devil and not of a human being, and they resumed their work.

102 ʔIWHINMUʔU MOUNTAIN

María's mother, Brigida, told her that she had once gone over to ʔiwhinmuʔu as a little girl to pick piñon nuts with some other people. Some of the men were burning brush to hunt jackrabbits and cottontails, and the fire got out of control. They heard a distant cry as someone shouted, "We are burning!" Then a bullroarer sounded and the paxa shouted. A white and a red deer ran out, and then a white cottontail and a red one. Finally the whole region quaked to such an extent that Brigida was swayed from side to side and the piñon nuts spilled out of her sack.

Once when María went to the Tejon, some of the people there were going piñoning and invited her to go along. They camped at the spring near ʔiwhɨnmuʔu—it was the only spring anywhere around. The ridge of ʔiwhɨnmuʔu was right by where they camped and it was loaded with piñon, but it was a sacred place and no one ever touched the nuts there at all. A man by the name of Fernando, an Ineztño, said that that business of people getting scared at ʔiwhɨnmuʔu was nothing. He didn't believe it. One night he got up and went slowly down to the spring to get a drink, waving a firebrand in his hand to keep it burning. The others told him not to go there and to watch out, but he only laughed at them. Just as he stooped down to get a drink he heard a dull sound that was repeated two or three times, and someone said in a deep tone, "There is one at the door, a pauper." Then he heard the whiz of a bullroarer. The other people heard Fernando crashing through the bushes, and they thought it was a bear coming. He said that he believed everything that he had been told now. Soon after the party returned to the Tejon Fernando died and was buried in the cemetery at Tinliw.

103 MARIA'S GRANDFATHER

María's grandfather, Ignacio, was the one who told her the most. He told her to stay in the house from dusk on lest she see a passing soul and have one of the sparks emanating from it fall on her and make her sick. And he told her to get up early in the morning, for he said that if the sun saw her lying in bed he would spit on her and make her ill. Everyone used to bathe before sunrise in the morning, diving under the water three times. This made them healthy. If a person is lazy in the summer and omits the bath, his blood will be warm and he will be bitten by a rattlesnake. But if your blood is cool from your morning bath, the rattlesnake will hiss and give warning.

104 DOG'S TEARS

The Indians never touched the tears of a dog. Juan Estévan Pico used to be very credulous about such things. His mother told him to be cautious and never touch a dog's tears when its eyes are running for if you do you will see all those bad things that dogs see at that time. Her grandfather was from Mugu, and he told her that there used to be many dogs there at one time. It was very common for them to howl at night and weep afterwards, to shed tears. But there was a man there who said that he did not believe any of what they said about a dog's tears. "Well, if you don't believe, go over and try it yourself," said the old men. The man went and got some dog's tears, but instead of rubbing them on his own eyes he rubbed them on the eyes of a little boy. That night when the dogs began to howl, the little boy also began to howl and cry, "They are coming, they are coming!" Just what was coming no one ever found out, for the little boy died in three days and never regained consciousness enough to tell what he had seen.

F.
Good Stories Retold

105 COYOTE AND PINACATE
Coyote met the pinacate, who lowered his head and raised his tail as soon as he saw Coyote. He told Coyote, whom he thought was coming to eat him, that he was looking at the sun, and that he put his head to the ground to hear the people of the other world. "And what do they say?" asked Coyote. "They say that there are three dogs coming to get you!" answered the pinacate. Coyote then shut his eyes as he does when he is sprinting and ran away as fast as he could. When he opened his eyes again he saw that there were no dogs. The pinacate had fooled him.

106 COYOTE AND FOX
Coyote was walking along a trail when he met a pinacate. He made a motion at the pinacate with first one paw and then the other. "Brother Pinacate, I'm going to eat you up!" he said. "And why should you do that, when I'm standing here listening to what they are saying in the other world?" asked the pinacate. Coyote said, "What are they saying in the other world?" "Can't you hear?" the pinacate asked. "They say they are going to hang anybody who defecates on the trail." "Why, I just defecated on the trail!" exclaimed Coyote. "I'm going back and clean it up!" The pinacate said, "Well, you'd better, or you'll be hanged." Coyote ran back up the trail, and the pinacate took the opportunity to hide.

When Coyote returned and discovered what the pinacate had done, he said, "Ah, my little brother has fooled me, but I'll hunt for him!" He looked and looked, but he couldn't find the pinacate anywhere. However, he did find Fox, who was busy catching locusts. Coyote said, "My little brother, I'm going to eat you up!" "Why eat me up when I'm on my way to work? Leave me alone and I'll give you two hens!" "Where are the hens?" Coyote asked. "My boss has lots of them," Fox replied. "Is that true?" Coyote asked. "It's the honest truth," answered Fox. "At dusk, travel in that direction over there and I'll meet you and give you the two hens!" "All right, little brother," said Coyote. When the sun set Coyote started off in the direction Fox had indicated, but after he had walked quite a way he still hadn't found Fox. "He has fooled me," he thought to himself. But he finally found Fox. As soon as Fox saw Coyote coming he ran to where there was a large rock balanced on top of another in such a way that it looked as if it were about to fall. He got underneath the rock and pretended to be holding it up. Coyote said, "Little brother, you're not going to escape me again. This time I'm going to eat you up!" Fox said, "Brother, if you kill me it won't do you any good, for I'm standing here holding the world up. If you eat me you will die anyway! What you should really do is come and hold up this rock for me while I go and get a drink of water. I'm dying of thirst!" Coyote agreed, and he went and put his shoulder against the rock. Fox left, promising to bring Coyote a chicken when he returned.

After a while Coyote said, "Since I'm getting pretty tired, I'll let my body relax a little." A little later he said to himself, "It seems that Fox has fooled me again!" Finally he said, "We'll just have to die!" He let go of the rock and jumped forward to get out of the way, but when he looked back the rock was still balanced there. He exclaimed, "Fox has fooled me, but if I meet him again he won't escape! He might fool me twice, but he can't fool me a third time!" He went hunting for Fox, but he couldn't find him anywhere. Finally, however, he came to a pool of water where Fox was getting a drink, and when he saw Fox he said, "Now, little Fox, you won't escape me. I'm going to eat you up!" "Why do you want to eat me?" asked Fox. "I'm not very big. I wouldn't be enough to fill you up. But there is something here big enough for both of us to fill up on," said Fox, pointing to the reflection of the moon shining on the

surface of the water. "What is that down there?" asked
Coyote. "It's a cheese, a big cheese," answered Fox. "By
drinking the water we can bring it up!" So Coyote and Fox
began to drink water from the pool, but Fox just pretended to
drink. After a while Coyote began to get full. Water was even
coming out of his nostrils. When Fox saw that Coyote was so
full of water that he couldn't get up, he said, "You can lie here
and perish for being a fool! Don't you see that that isn't a
cheese? That's the reflection of the moon. Look up there! Die
there, I'm leaving."

Coyote lay there for a long time and finally recovered. He
said to himself, "Fox, I'm going to eat you up. There isn't
anyplace you can go where I won't find you!" Fox went into a
cactus patch, where he began to remove the thorns from the
cactus fruit and gather them in a bunch. After a while Coyote
came along, and when he saw Fox he said, "Now, little Fox,
you won't escape me this time!" Fox said, "Why do you want
to eat me? Don't you see what I'm doing here?" He gave some
of the cactus fruit that he had cleaned to Coyote, and Coyote ate
them and liked them. "Do you like them?" asked Fox. "Yes,
they're very good," Coyote answered. Fox said, "Well, if you
like them I'll give you all I've picked, but on one condition—
that you eat them with your eyes wide open." Coyote agreed,
and Fox gave him the cleaned cactus fruit. While Coyote was
eating them with his eyes wide open Fox took a bunch of
thorns and threw them in Coyote's eyes. Coyote began to rub his
eyes with his paws, and Fox ran away.

When Coyote left the cactus patch he couldn't see. He
walked along as best he could until he finally fell into a ravine
where there was a pool of water. He drank some water and
washed his eyes until he could see again, and then went
looking for Fox again. "Fox won't escape me this time!" Coyote
assured himself. "I'll surely eat him up." Fox saw Coyote
coming and hid in a patch of cane, and when Coyote passed by
Fox addressed him. Coyote said, "Now, little brother, I'm
certainly going to eat you up!" Fox said, "Why, I'm working.
That's why I spoke to you, so you can help me." "What are
you doing?" asked Coyote. "I'm clearing off a little space
here," said Fox. "There's going to be a big fiesta here, with
plenty to eat. A rich man is going to get married." "At what
time?" Coyote asked. "Just as soon as we finish cleaning up,"

said Fox. "There's going to be plenty to eat. We're going to eat chicken!" Coyote began to pull up cane, while Fox pretended to work. Now there was a fire burning nearby, and after a while Fox said, "There come the people in the fiesta procession." "How do you know?" asked Coyote. Fox said, "Don't you see the smoke? They must be smoking. I'm going to go and meet them and tell them that we have a space all cleaned up, but you'd better hide, for they have some dogs with them. But we shall have plenty to eat anyway, because the people serving are good friends of mine."

Coyote went and hid in the cane, and as soon as he had done so Fox set fire to the cane all around him. Then Fox called to Coyote, "Brother, stay hidden. They are coming now. Don't you hear the firecrackers? But stay hidden, for they have lots of dogs with them!" Fox went and set fire to some more cane, and Coyote raised his head and saw smoke all around. "That must be the smoke from the firecrackers," he said to himself. He stayed hidden in the cane, and pretty soon the fire came and burned him to death. He didn't get to eat Fox after all. Coyote is very smart, and also very stupid.

107 COYOTE AND SKUNK Skunk and Coyote were wandering around looking for something to eat, for they were both hungry. Skunk found a patch of prickly pear cactus, and he knocked down the fruit and ate his fill. Now Coyote had not been able to find anything at all to eat, and he thought to himself, "What am I going to do? I can't find anything at all." Just then he came across Skunk's tracks, and he said, "I'm hungry—I'll force myself to eat him!" He began to follow the tracks. Skunk saw Coyote coming and said to himself, "Here comes another tramp, half-starving." He began to collect a little pile of cactus thorns (he knew already what he was going to do). When Coyote arrived he said to Skunk, "Little brother, I'm going to eat you, because I'm dying of hunger!" Skunk answered, "Kinsman, how can you eat me when I'm working so hard collecting this food to carry back to the village?" "Let me sample some of it," said Coyote. "No, I was ordered to carry it home," Skunk replied. Then Coyote said, "Well, if you don't offer me some I'll eat you!" So Skunk took a knife and cut one of the fruit in half lengthwise and gave it to Coyote. Coyote

was very hungry, and the fruit was very sweet and tasty. He said, "Give me another!" So Skunk gave him three more of the fruit, one after another, and Coyote ate them all. "Yes, this food is very good. Give me that other one," said Coyote. "All right, open your mouth and tilt your head back," said Skunk. Coyote did so, and as he sat there looking up at the sky Skunk threw a handful of cactus thorns in his eyes. Coyote began to rub his eyes with his paws, but the thorns went in deeper, and in a short time he couldn't see a thing.

Skunk left, and Coyote wandered blindly off. He kept walking until at last he fell in a ravine. He said to himself, "I'll follow this and try to find some water." After a time he came to a pool of water. He sat down and began to bathe his eyes, and he finally managed to get all of the thorns out so that he could see again. He said to himself, "Now I'm going to look for Skunk, and I'm not going to give him a chance this time. When I find him I'm going to eat him!" He started off to find Skunk. Eventually he found some tracks and followed them to a spring, and there was Skunk getting a drink in the moonlight. The reflection of the moon was shining on the water. Coyote said, "Now, brother, you won't escape. I'll eat you for sure!" Skunk replied, "You won't get full if you eat me, but look at the cheese there under the water. It's very big!" Now Coyote liked cheese very much, and he thought to himself, "Well, that would be better. This fellow is very small and wouldn't fill me up." So he said, "Little brother, how can we get it out?" Skunk replied, "The only way to do it is to drink the water and dry up the spring. When we get it you can have it all." "Good, very good," said Coyote. He got down and began to drink, while Skunk just pretended to drink. At last Coyote got so full of water that he couldn't walk. He said, "I can't drink any more, brother. I can't even walk!" Then Skunk said, "Well, stay here and die of hunger. I'm leaving!" He left, and Coyote said to himself, "He's done it to me again!"

He lay there all night shaking from the cold, but by morning he was able to move again. "He's hurt me twice, but now I'm surely going to eat him!" he exclaimed. Meanwhile, Skunk had found a wasp's nest in a hole in the ground and had covered the entrance with a rock. Then he sat down near it with a stick in his hand and waited for Coyote. Coyote approached and said, "Now I'm surely going to eat you, little brother!" "Why are you going to do that when I'm sitting here being a teacher?" asked Skunk. "A teacher of what?" Coyote asked. "I am teaching some little boys," replied Skunk. "Where are they?" Coyote wanted to know. "You'll see," said Skunk. He hit the ground with his stick and the wasps began to buzz. Coyote thought to himself, "There are a lot of them!" Then Skunk said, "I'm very thirsty. Take over for me while I go to the stream for a drink." "All right," said Coyote. He thought, "I'll eat the little boys while he's getting a drink!" Skunk left, and Coyote began to dig with the stick. In a short time he had opened the hole, and the wasps poured out and settled all over him and began to sting him. He cried, "What can I do?" He saw a patch of brush nearby, and he threw himself into it and began to roll around. The wasps finally left, and Coyote came out of the brush stiff and sore and swollen all over. He went to the brook and sat in the water until he felt better. Then he said, "Now I'm really going to get him and eat him up!"

Coyote followed Skunk's tracks, saying to himself, "Here goes that nameless one!" He came at last to a patch of cane, and there was Skunk clearing off a small area right in the middle of it. Coyote approached and said, "I'm certainly going to eat you now!" Skunk replied, "Why eat me when I'm working very hard getting ready for a fiesta? There will be lots of chicken and meat to eat. A son of the wot is getting married and there is going to be a fiesta. If you help me I'll pay you and you'll get lots to eat at the fiesta, but if you eat me you won't get full, for I'm really very small." There was a fire burning nearby, and there was smoke rising from it. Skunk pointed at it and said, "Over there some other men are building a road to this place." So Coyote and Skunk worked together for a while and cleared off a fairly large area. "The table will go here," said Skunk. "When the people start arriving they will throw firecrackers to let everyone know. Then you hide, and I'll slip you food." Coyote continued pulling cane and Skunk left for a minute. He got some burning sticks from the fire and started four little fires on each side of the cane-patch, and then returned to Coyote. In a few minutes the cane began to pop from the heat of the spreading fires, and Skunk said, "The people are coming now. Do you hear the firecrackers? You'd better hide now while I go and meet them!" Coyote said,

"There must be many people coming. Those firecrackers are exploding all around!" He hid in the cane and Skunk left through the last remaining gap in the flames.

By the time Coyote realized what was happening he was completely surrounded by fire, and he said to himself, "Ah, my brother has hurt me again, and this time I'm going to die! But I'll do my best." He ran and jumped through the flames, but he burned his feet and scorched his hair and ears and body. He thought to himself, "I'd better leave my brother alone after this or he'll kill me! He's very smart!" His feet were so burned that he could hardly walk, and he said, "The thing for me to do now is fast. I won't eat or drink water, for it's bad for me." He found a willow with drooping branches, and there he fasted and licked his burns with his tongue—it was his medicine. At last he recovered, and he said, "Now I'm going to look for some water." He went down to the shore of the ocean, where an arroyo had created a small fresh-water lagoon, and he found an animal trail that led down to the water. He got a drink and rested for a while, and then said, "I'll go back to my tree now, and tomorrow I'll come again." He found some beetles under some dried manure and ate them, but that was all he had to eat.

The next day a man who lived nearby came down the trail to the beach to see what he might find, and he came across a tiger of the sea lying there on the sand. The man said, "This poor animal! This is not the place for him. He belongs in the ocean! I'll put him back." He picked up the tiger and put him in a sack that he had with him, and put the sack on his back. When he got to the shore he said, "Here is your rightful place. You were on dry land, but now I've returned you to where you belong." He started to take the tiger out of the sack, but the tiger spoke up and said, "Friend, not here—take me out further." The man waded into the water a way and again started to free the tiger, but he said again, "No, not here—out beyond the waves!" The man waded out as far as he could and then stopped, "Well, this is as far as I can go. Here." He began to take the tiger out of the bag, but the tiger had no sooner gotten his head out than he seized the man's hand in his jaws and said, "Now I'll eat you!" The man was frightened. "Why are you going to do that?" he asked. "Why eat me when I did you such a favor, bringing you here from the dry beach?" The tiger replied, "Well, it's like this: a good deed is repaid with evil!" "Well, it's my own fault. I should have left you there, but I didn't."

Now the tiger had the man by the wrist, but the man hadn't finished taking him out of the sack—and there they stood. Finally the man said, "Let's wait until someone comes, and put the case to him. If he says that I should have left you, then go ahead and eat me, but if he says that isn't right, you will lose. Whatever he says we'll do." (As he said this the man was edging back toward the beach little by little.) In a little while a thin old ox came plodding slowly down the trail to get a drink, and the man hailed him. "Excuse me, sir, but can I ask you something?" The ox said, "Let me get a drink, and then I'll talk with you." He went and got a drink, rested for a while, got another drink, and then returned to the edge of the water. "Now what do you want?" he asked. The man answered, "I want you to do us a favor and advise us. Whatever you say we'll do." Then he explained the situation while the ox listened carefully. When the man had finished the ox shook his horns and said, "In the old days, when I was young, my master took good care of me. He gave me food and water and everything. But now that I'm old I've been thrown out, and there are days when I don't eat or drink, and I have to walk very far. I used to do many things for my master, but that is the way it is—a good deed is repaid with evil!" Then the ox said to the tiger, "And so, eat him!"

"All right," said the tiger to the man, "Now I'll eat you!" "No wait, there is someone else coming. Let's ask his opinion," replied the man. The old ox plodded off, and in a little while an ancient horse came ambling down the trail. The man called out, "Good sir, please do us a favor!" The horse replied, "I haven't had a drink for two days. Let me get a drink and then I'll talk to you." He went and got a drink and then rested for a while. Then he drank again and returned to the edge of the water. He asked, "What do you want?" The man explained the situation, and the horse replied, "In the good old days my master took good care of me, and I did many good things for him. He treated me well and gave me food and water and cleaned me. But now that I'm old he's thrown me out, and there are some days when I have nothing to eat or drink. A good deed is repaid with evil, so eat him!" "Good, that makes two in my favor!" said the tiger. "Now I'm going to eat you."

"Well, I guess I'm lost, but let's ask one more person, and if he agrees with the others, then eat me," said the man. In a little while Coyote came limping down the trail to get a drink, and the man called out to him. But Coyote didn't know where the voice was coming from at first, and he turned his head from side to side in a confused fashion. The man thought to himself, "This fellow is sick. I'm lost for sure!" Coyote called out, "Where are you? I'm very old, and I haven't had a drink in three days. Wait a minute!" He went and got a drink and rested for a little while, and then he called again, "Where are you?" "Here in the water," replied the man worriedly. Coyote limped down to the edge of the water and said, "What is it that you want? What's wrong?" The man explained the situation, and when he was through Coyote said, "Ah!" He sat down and began to clean his ears, and then he said, "I'm very old and deaf. Come closer!" The man came closer to the shore, while the tiger protested. "Hm, what is it you want?" asked Coyote again, pretending to be hard of hearing. The man explained once more, and again Coyote said, "I can't hear you, get closer!" The man came still further out of the water over the tiger's protests. He told Coyote again what had happened, and Coyote said, "I still can't hear you, come up here!" The man left the water completely, and again he repeated his story. "Hm, show me just exactly where you found him," said Coyote. They walked over to where the tiger had been lying, and the man said, "I found him right here." Coyote said, "Well, throw him down right there!" When the man had done so, Coyote said, "Now find a good heavy stick." The man went and found a thick, sturdy piece of driftwood, and when he returned with it Coyote said, "Now club him with it. He is shameless and ungrateful! Hit him!"

So the man took the stick and clubbed the tiger and killed him. Then Coyote said, "Well, friend, I'll be going now." The man said, "No, friend, I'm very grateful to you. Let's go to my house and chat a bit." "All right, and what will you give me as a token of thanks?" asked Coyote. "Would you like a couple of chickens?" said the man. "Why not? I'm very hungry and I've been sick, but don't you have anything more?" asked Coyote.

"That is all I have," said the man. "Well, that's all right, that's enough," said Coyote. He accompanied the man to his house, which was surrounded on all sides by a strong fence of thick poles set closely together in the ground. "Wait for me here, I'll bring the chickens out here," said the man. "Fine," said Coyote, and he lay down to rest. The man brought out a chicken and said, "What shall I do with it?" "Free it, and I'll get it," Coyote replied. The man tossed the chicken over the fence, and Coyote caught and ate it. "Now the other one," he said. Again he ran after the chicken and caught and ate it. Then the man asked him, "Would you like another?" "Well, why not?" Coyote answered. So the man brought out a third chicken, and again Coyote chased it down and ate it. The man then went to his house and brought out two hounds that he had there, and he said to himself, "I'm going to run this coyote off so that he won't return!" He asked Coyote, "There are two more chickens here—don't you want them?" "Well, let them go. I'll get them both together!" said Coyote. Then the man let the hounds loose, and when Coyote turned around they were right behind him. He ran away with the hounds after him, and the man laughed and laughed. Coyote got away—who knows where he went?—and eventually the hounds returned to the house. A good deed is repaid with evil.

sutiwayan ulʔatucʔ

108 RABBIT AND COYOTE Once a man had a small garden in which some watermelons were growing, and he had surrounded it with a strong pole fence to keep animals out. But Rabbit had discovered four little gaps between the poles, and during the night he would enter the garden and eat melons. The man noticed that his melons were disappearing but he couldn't figure out who was doing it. "What little animal is eating my melons, and how does he get in?" he wondered. The next morning he walked along the fence, and he finally found one of the little gaps between the poles—and there were little tracks on the ground as well. "Ah, that's where he entered!" he exclaimed. He walked a little further and found another hole and more tracks. "He goes in there, too," the gardener said. He found all four of Rabbit's entrances, and all four had

tracks leading in and out. "How can I catch this little animal?"
he thought. "I know, I'll go to the beach and collect tar, and I'll
make a little tar doll. And that tar doll will catch him!"

The man went down to the shore and gathered lots of tar,
and he made four little human figures like dolls out of it, with
little arms and legs. He placed one of the dolls in each of the
four holes in his fence and then went home. That night Rabbit
came to eat melons, and when he got to the first gap in the
fence he found his way blocked by the tar doll. "There's
someone here in my gate, but I have another gate!" said
Rabbit. He ran quickly to the next hole, but when he got there
he found the tar doll standing there blocking his way again.
"He's already there ahead of me!" exclaimed Rabbit. "But I'll
beat him to the next entrance!" But when he got to the third
gap between the poles the tar figure was already standing
there. "How fast he is. He beat me here!" said Rabbit. "Now
I'll just hit him and run him off!"

He approached the tar doll and addressed it, saying,
"Friend, let me enter my house. I live inside here." But the
doll, of course, didn't say a word. "Come on, my friend, let me
in my house. If you don't get out of my way I'll hit you with
my fist!" But the doll didn't answer, and Rabbit got mad.
"Move or I'll sock you!" he exclaimed. Then he drew back his
fist and hit the tar doll right in the stomach, and his hand got
stuck in the tar. The doll was very heavy and Rabbit couldn't
budge it. "Come on, friend, let me go. If you don't I'll hit you
with my other hand!" Then Rabbit hit the doll with his other
hand and it got stuck also. "Let me go, friend, let me go. If you
don't I'll give you a kick!" he exclaimed. "All right, then," he
said, and he kicked the doll. And now his leg was stuck too.
"All right, I have another leg!" he threatened. "I'll kick you
again if you don't release me!" He kicked the doll again, and
now both hands and both feet were stuck in the tar. The next
morning the man came to see if he had caught anything, and
there was Rabbit stuck fast to the tar figure. "Ah, you're the
thief who has been wrecking my garden and eating my
melons! Now I'm going to take you home and boil you in a
cauldron. You've been destructive long enough!"

The gardener pulled Rabbit loose from the tar and carried
him to his house. There was a cottonwood tree near the house
with a branch that hung down, and the man tied Rabbit's

hands and feet to the limb so that he was hanging upside down above a cauldron of cold water. Then the gardener went into his house, and while he was gone Coyote came by and saw Rabbit hanging from the tree. Coyote asked, "What are you doing there?" "Hush!" exclaimed Rabbit. "But why are you hanging there like that?" Coyote persisted. Then Rabbit said, "Because the man there in that house wants me to marry a girl, and I don't want to! He's trying to force me to marry by threatening me with this cauldron of water, but as you can see, he hasn't built a fire under it yet." Coyote replied, "Well, if you don't want to get married, why not give me the opportunity? I'll get married!" "Well, brother, if you want to, free me, and you can marry in my place!" said Rabbit. Coyote replied, "Good, I'll get married." "Untie me, then," said Rabbit. Coyote climbed up the tree and got on top of the branch with him and then untied him. Then he said, "Don't go yet. You have to tie me the same way!" So Rabbit tied Coyote's arms and legs together under the limb, and then Coyote slipped off the limb until he was hanging upside down underneath it.

Rabbit ran off and hid himself in some brush nearby so that he could see everything that happened. In a little while the gardener came out of his house and approached the tree. "What's this?" he exclaimed. "When I left you were a rabbit. Now you've turned yourself into a coyote! Well, I'm going to boil you right now before you turn into the Devil as well!" He went and got a torch and lit the kindling under the cauldron, and in a few minutes the water began to boil and bubble. Coyote said to himself, "This is a bad situation. Now I'm going to get boiled!" The man cut the rope holding Coyote's hands and feet and he fell. But Coyote made a tremendous effort and just managed to fall to one side of the cauldron of water, although his tail fell in the water and got scalded. He picked himself off the ground and ran away before the gardener could catch him again. He passed close to the patch of brush in which Rabbit was hiding, and as he went by Rabbit yelled, "Ah, Burned Tail!" Coyote said, "I'll eat you for sure, now! Watch out!"

He went into the brush after Rabbit, but though he looked and looked, he couldn't find him anywhere. "I'll get you yet. I'll still eat you!" he said. Coyote kept walking along, looking

for Rabbit, and the next morning he found him. Rabbit was in a
ravine with overhanging sides and there didn't seem to be any
way out. "This is a bad spot to be in," thought Rabbit to
himself. "There are no bushes or anything. This is my only
chance!" He went over to one wall of the ravine (which looked
as if it were about to cave in any moment) and pretended that
he was holding the wall up. Coyote approached and said,
"Ah, brother, now you won't escape!" Rabbit replied, "But
what will you gain if you eat me? This bank will fall then and
you'll surely be killed! I'm holding it up now, but I'm getting
weak from hunger and I don't know how long I'll be able to
last!" Coyote, alarmed, said, "What can we do?" Rabbit
replied, "Well, the only thing to do is for you to take my place
holding it up. You're bigger and you can hold it up better. And
I'll go and get two hens for us to eat." "But you will come
back?" asked Coyote doubtfully. "Of course I'll return!" Rabbit
assured him. "And I'll bring two chickens with me!"

So Coyote took Rabbit's place and Rabbit left, disappearing into the brush. Coyote stood there for a long time waiting
for Rabbit to return, afraid that any moment the bank was
going to fall and crush him. He finally got so tired that he had
to stop. "I'll try to save myself by jumping as far as I can," he
said at last. He gave a tremendous leap, and then he looked
back—and the bank was still there. "Ah, he made a fool of me
again!" he exclaimed. "First he got me scalded, and now this!
I'd better not follow him, though. He would probably get me
killed eventually, and I don't want to die yet!" So Coyote
started off in another direction to the one Rabbit had gone. He
came at last to a stream, and he followed it until he came at last
to a big pool of water. He saw that there were some fish in the
pool, big ones. He watched them for a while, and then he
began to sing and dance. He sang:

Come out, salmon, see your kinsman dance!
Don't you know how to dance like he does?
Why don't you know how to dance?

In a little while some of the fish left the pool and ventured
into the little stream that was flowing out of it. Coyote said,
"The only thing to do now is to grab them before they return
to the pool." So he approached the stream, dancing, as if he
had no intention of harming them. He managed to grab five of

the fish, five of the smaller ones, and he said, "Well, these will do!" He ate two of them right there, for he was very hungry. Then he took the other three fish and started on again, and as he was walking along he saw an old log burning in a field that was being cleared. "Ah, I'll roast my fish," he said. He went over to where the log was burning, and there was no one around. He scooped out a hole with his hands, threw in his fish and some ashes, and then covered everything over with hot coals. He said, "When I return, my fish will be roasted and ready to eat." He left. Now Qusqus (a big bird the size of a hawk) was sitting up in a tree nearby watching all this, and as soon as Coyote left he flew down and began to eat the fish. He ate everything except the bones and the tails, which he left sticking out of the ground just as they had been. Then he flew up to the top of the tree again. In a little while Coyote returned. He grabbed the tail of a fish and started to pull it out of the ground, singing in anticipation of his roasted salmon dinner. (The story ends here.)

109 COYOTE'S STONE STEW

Once Coyote was traveling along and he was very hungry. And he saw a woman and thought to himself, "How can I trick this woman into feeding me?" The woman did not know that Coyote was a great trickster. Coyote thought to himself, "I know! I will tell her that I am going to cook some stones, and she is going to be very surprised!" And so he walked up to the woman and said, "I can make a fine stew out of stones." The woman asked, "How are you going to do that?" And Coyote said, "Well, watch me!" He asked for a frying pan, and he put some rocks in it. Then he asked the woman for a little lard, and then he asked for a little meat, and then a little garlic, and a little tomato and onion, and some salt. And he put each of the ingredients into the pan. And the woman was astonished at Coyote's way of cooking. He said, "That's my way of making stew!" He then ate all of the stew, leaving only the rocks.

110 HERON AND FOX

Once upon a time Heron invited Fox to dinner. Heron made some sipitis and put in in a basket with a long neck because he had a long neck himself. He also served some to Fox in a tall dish. Fox was sitting there wondering how he was going to eat it. And Heron said, "Why don't you eat some?" Fox replied that he didn't feel like eating. He thought that Heron was making fun of him. He thought to himself, "I'll invite Heron to dinner, and fix it so that he can't eat." And in a few days Fox invited Heron to dinner. Fox made a lot of šipitiš and poured it on a flat rock. And Heron was wondering, "How can I eat it with it spread all over the rock?" He couldn't eat it, and Fox finished it all up. Heron went home hungry.

111 THE STORY OF A CAT

There was once a family consisting of a man, his wife and their four sons. The youngest son had a kitten, and whenever it was time to eat he would insist on eating with his kitten. His parents would say that it was disgusting for him to eat with an animal like that, and they would take the kitten away from him, but he always cried and cried and they would have to let him eat with the kitten after all. The other sons would kick the cat or mistreat it, and the mother was always throwing it outside too, but then the boy would cry until they relented. The family was well off, and there was plenty to eat. Then one day the father died, but things went on much the same as always. At each meal Martin, the youngest son, would want to eat with his cat, and every time the others would grab the cat and throw it outside, but the boy would cry and cry and eventually they would have to let it back in. Then the mother died too, leaving the four sons on their own, but again it was just the same: the older boys would kick the cat and throw it out, but Martin would cry for his cat until they relented.

One by one the three oldest sons became sick and died until only Martin and his cat were left. By now the boy was old enough to cook for himself, and his kitten had grown into a big cat, but there was almost no food left in the house to eat. All that there was left to eat were some beans. The boy's clothes were full of holes and falling apart, and everything else in the house was in the same miserable condition. One day the boy got to thinking about the situation and said, "What can we do? We have nothing left now but some beans." He was very sad and he began to cry. Then the cat spoke up and said, "Brother, why are you crying?" The boy replied, "Why shouldn't I cry?

There is nothing to eat but beans, I have no clothes, I don't have anything. Just beans to eat, beans all the time!" The cat said, "Well, don't cry. I'll get you lots to eat, and I'll take on the job of supporting us." The boy looked at the cat in amazement and asked, "How are you going to do that?" The cat said only, "I'm going away for a little now, and you'll soon have plenty to eat."

He left and walked until he came to some houses, and there he stole bread and cheese and anything else he could find. He brought it all back to the boy and said, "Eat!" He left once more and stole some more food to keep them in provisions for a while. And in this way the two of them got along very well. The boy was growing up now and getting to be a young man, and one day the cat began to ponder. He said to himself, "Only the daughter of the king is fit to marry my brother, and that is who he shall marry!" He said to the boy, "Brother, you are going to marry a princess!" The boy began to cry, and the cat asked, "Why are you crying?" "How can I marry when I don't have any clothes or anything? You tell me I'm going to marry a princess, but I have no money—I don't have anything!" the boy replied, and he began to cry again. The cat said, "Aha, brother, just you wait! Follow my instructions and you'll see! What I want you to do is collect all the pieces of glass or broken bottles that you can find." The cat left, and the boy thought to himself, "Why does my brother want pieces of glass? Oh, well, I'll go and do it."

The cat, meanwhile, crept into one house after another, stealing a coin here and a coin there until he had thirty centavos and all the bread and cheese he could carry. He took everything home to Martin, who in the meantime had collected a great heap of broken glass and old bottles. Once again the cat left, and this time he stole four reales in one place and a peso somewhere else. Then he said to himself, "This is enough. This will do." He stole some more bread and cheese and tortillas before returning home. He said to the boy, "Here is a peso and a half—take it and keep it safe, for one of these days it will serve you well." The following day the cat stole only enough for the next day, because he knew he was going to be gone. The next morning the cat said, "Brother, bring me the mare from the pasture." The boy went and caught their mare who was grazing in a little field nearby and brought it to the house. Then he asked, "Where are you going?" The cat climbed up on the horse bareback (for they had no saddle) and said, "I am off to talk to the king, but I'll be back!"

He galloped off to the palace, where he dismounted and tied his horse. He asked the guard for permission to see the king on important business, and was granted an audience. "Good day, Your Majesty," he said. The king thought to himself, "This is no ordinary cat. He knows how to talk!" Out loud he said, "What did you wish to see me about, sir?" The cat answered, "Oh, I have come to ask if I can borrow an armún" (a little box for measuring quantities). "And what are you going to do with it?" asked the king. "Well, I'm going to count some realitos I have," replied the cat. The king thought to himself, "Then this little cat has more money than I! I count my money one coin at a time, while he does it by the measureful. He must have a lot, more than I!" Aloud he said, "Fine, fine!" The cat said, "I don't know if I'll need it all afternoon, but I'll return it when I'm finished." The king had the measure brought and given to the cat, who said, "Good afternoon, Your Majesty." He got back on his mare and left, but the king ordered one of his soldiers to follow him and see where he lived and what he did.

When the cat arrived home he dismounted and turned his horse out to pasture. He told the boy not to come outside or show himself in any way, and as he entered the house he closed the door and the windows carefully so that no one could see in. "Now we're going to work, brother!" said the cat. He spoke loudly so that the king's soldier (who he knew was hiding just outside) would be sure to hear him. The two of them began to fill the measure with pieces of glass and empty it into a box, and each time they did this the glass would make a tinkling sound. "Good heavens!" exclaimed the soldier listening outside. "What a lot of money they have!" All that day the two poured pieces of glass back and forth, until in the middle of the afternoon the cat said, "Fine, that's the amount." And the man hiding outside said to himself, "How rich they are!" Then the cat added quietly, "Brother, bring me five centavos." The boy brought him the coin, and the cat stuck it in a small crack in the bottom of the measure. Then he said loudly, "Now I'm going to return this measure, for I have only borrowed it." He left the house with the measure in his hand,

and the soldier came out of hiding and approached. The cat pretended surprise and said, "Have you come to get the measure?" "Yes," replied the man. "Fine," said the cat. "Here it is, and thank you very much. Tell the king I'm very grateful and so is my brother."

The man took the measure and started off, but after he had gone a little way he opened it and found the coin stuck to the bottom. He ran back to the house and knocked on the door and when the cat answered he said, "Sir, here is a coin that was stuck in the measure!" "Oh, take it," said the cat. "Keep it, and buy yourself a cigar or something." "Oh, they are very rich indeed!" exclaimed the man to himself. He returned to the palace and went to the king, and said, "Sir Cat said to thank you very much." "Did you hear or see anything?" asked the king. "Well, all afternoon they were measuring and keeping count, and measuring and keeping count." "Good heavens!" exclaimed the king. "I count every cent!" Then the soldier said, "And when he returned the measure I found five centavos inside, and when I went running back to return it to him he told me to keep it—and look, here it is!" Then the king said to himself, "My god, they're richer than I am!" The king fretted about it all that night and was envious of their wealth.

Early the next morning the cat said, "Bring me the mare, brother. This time I'm going to get there even earlier than before." He climbed on the mare and galloped off to the palace, where he told the guard that he again wanted to speak to the king on important business. He was admitted and went straight to the king, and said, "Good day, Your Majesty, I've come for the same reason as before, but this time we want to count our ten centavo pieces!" The king was angry when he heard this, and he thought to himself, "That certainly beats me!" The measure was brought and given to the cat, and he started homeward followed by another of the king's soldiers. When the cat reached home he dismounted and turned the mare out to pasture and went in the house, closing the door and all the windows carefully so that no one could see in. And all that day he and Martin filled the measure with pieces of broken glass and poured them tinkling into a box, while the soldier listened outside and marveled at their wealth. Late in the afternoon the cat said, loudly, "It's late, brother, and we haven't eaten. Let's not worry about this little bit that's left. We know about how much there is!" Then in a lower tone he asked Martin to bring him ten centavos, and he took the coin and stuck it to the bottom of the measure as he had before. Then he left the house and encountered the soldier. He pretended to be very surprised and said, "Have you come for the box now?" "Yes, sir," replied the soldier. The cat told him to thank the king for allowing them to borrow the measure.

The man started off on his return trip to the palace but he had gone only a little way when he opened the measure and discovered the coin that the cat had placed there. He hurried back and knocked at the door, and said, "Sir, here is a coin you forgot!" "Oh, keep it and buy yourself a cigar or something," said the cat. The soldier returned to the palace and told the king what had happened. "Did you see the brother?" asked the king. "No, everything was closed up tight," replied the soldier. "But all day long they were counting money there in the house. I could hear them measuring it!" On the following day the cat again asked to borrow the measure, this time in order to count two-real pieces. As before, the king had the cat followed, and all day the soldier hid outside the house and heard a sound as if money were being poured into boxes. And when the cat returned the measure late that afternoon he put a two-real coin in the bottom of it for the soldier to find. Martin said to himself, "I thought we were going to save the money we had, but my brother is throwing it away!" The king's soldier reported finding the coin in the measure, and told the king that he had tried to return it but had been told to keep it for himself. And once more the king was amazed and shaken at the thought of the great wealth the cat and his brother must have.

The next day the cat went as usual to the palace and asked to borrow the measure, saying that they wished to count their four-real pieces this time. Now one of the king's daughters who was very enamoured of money was standing by listening to all this, and when the cat left with the measure she said to herself, "Sir Cat is going to be my brother-in-law!" That day the cat and the boy measured their "money" just as before, and the cat left a four-real piece in the measure. When he returned the measure to the soldier who had been listening outside he said, "Tell the king that my brother is grateful for the loan of the measure, and that someday he will do something for the king in return!" The boy said to himself, "And what can I do for the king?" But he followed the cat's instructions anyway. When the soldier reported to the king that night, the princess spoke up and said, "Father, let them come here so we can see the brother." (She was already in love with the unseen but wealthy brother!) The next day the cat told Martin to fetch the mare as usual, but he said, "This is the last day we are going to have to work!"

He climbed on his horse and rode off to the palace, where he was admitted at once. "Ah, I'm very tired," he told the king. "But what can I do? Please don't get angry. This is the last day I must borrow the measure. We are going to count pesos today. I don't know why my brother doesn't buy one of those measures, with all that money to count! I'm ashamed of coming here so much to borrow it!" The king replied, "Well, that's what it's for, so don't be concerned." The princess herself brought the measure and gave it to the cat, and as he took it he said in a meaningful tone, "Take care!" The girl said to herself, "Sir Cat is going to be my brother-in-law!" The cat returned home, followed by another of the king's soldiers. All day long they measured their "money" while the man hiding outside exclaimed over their great wealth. Finally the cat said, "Brother, bring me a peso." The boy brought him the coin, sadly, and said, "That's the last of our money." The cat put the peso in the measure for the soldier to find, and returned it as usual. That night when the king heard his soldier's story he exclaimed once again, "Good heavens, so much money! I count pesos one by one, not by the measureful. I don't have that much!"

The following day he sent an invitation to the cat and his brother to visit the palace, and the cat told the messenger that they would be happy to come in a day or so. When the man had left, the cat went out to steal what he could, and also to discover anything that might be useful to them in the future. Now on the other side of the hill from where they lived there was a house belonging to a wealthy giant. The giant lived alone in the house for he had neither servants nor family. The cat approached the house quietly on foot, entered it, and went from room to room pretending that he was hunting mice. There was food stored everywhere, and boxes and boxes full of gold and silver. "Our fortune is made!" he thought to himself.

He left the house and started home, thinking all the way, "Our fortune is made. I'm going to return and kill that giant. I'm going to do it all by myself!" Before he reached home he stole some soap and a comb and a piece of ribbon, and as soon as he arrived at their house he told Martin to fetch some water. "Why does my brother want water?" the boy wondered as he went to get some. "Now, take a bath and wash yourself well with soap. You're going to marry the princess!" said the cat. The boy began to cry, and said, "You're making fun of me. I don't have ʔičiʔi or anything!" When the boy had bathed, the cat gave him the comb and said, "Here, comb your hair so you don't have fleas or anything, for you're going to be married." Then the boy began to cry again, and the cat said, "Don't cry. Be brave and everything will be all right. Early tomorrow we are going to the palace, for we have been invited to spend the day there!" "I don't want to go!" cried Martin. "Don't fret, be brave," replied the cat.

The next morning he ordered the boy to bathe again, saying, "Wash yourself well, so you're very clean. For you're going to be married." So the boy took another bath while the cat went and brought the mare from the pasture. "Now climb on the mare and let's be off," said the cat, and they started off on the road to the palace. Now there was a marsh with tules in it alongside the road, and the cat went straight to it and stopped. "Get down and hide yourself behind that rise over there," he told Martin. While the boy was hiding the cat began to daub mud from the marsh all over himself and the horse until he was completely covered with it from head to foot. Then he said, "Brother, stay here. I am going to get you some clothes. Wait here until I return. And if anyone should happen to return with me, hide and don't come out." Then he climbed on the horse and rode on to the palace. The guards saw him coming and said, "Here comes Sir Cat—but alone and in sad shape, for he is covered with mud!" "Let him enter anyway," said the king. The cat arrived and tied up his horse, and said to the guards, "What bad luck! I got stuck in the marsh, and my brother with me. He is covered with mud." He entered the palace and pretended to be very shaken. "Good day, Your Majesty," he said. "Why are you covered with mud?" asked the king. The cat replied, "My brother and I were on our way here, and we were galloping our horses beside the marsh when they suddenly shied. We went shooting into the mud, and my brother went in saddle and all, and he is there still!"

Then the princess came forward and said, "Well, father, why don't you send for a suitcase full of clothing?" "Yes, my brother had good clothing made of the finest wool," said the cat. "All right," the king said. "The least I can do is send some clothing and my own horse and saddle, and I will also send a man with you." "Oh, no," replied the cat. "That won't do! My brother is quite shy. It would be best for me to go alone."

The king agreed to this, and a suitcase full of fine clothing was tied to the saddle of the king's own horse. The cat climbed back on his mare and took the reins of the other horse and rode off to the marsh. When he reached the boy's hiding place he untied the suitcase and said, "Here it is, now get dressed!" The boy took off his old, ragged clothing and the cat went and hid them. Then the boy dressed himself in the fine clothing that the king had sent and looked at himself in a mirror that was fastened to the lid of the suitcase. He looked very handsome indeed. The cat helped him adjust his hat, and then said, "Good, here is a horse. Now mount and let's be off." Back at the palace the princess was getting impatient to meet the cat's brother. "I'm going downstairs to greet them," she told her father. "Don't do that, it isn't proper," replied the king, but she went down anyway when she saw them coming. When they rode up the cat presented her to his brother, while the king paced back and forth on the balcony above. But the king was pleased, for the boy was quite handsome. Then the princess escorted Martin upstairs to meet her father, while the cat remained below with the horses. When he approached the king the boy took off his hat as the cat had advised him to do, and they began to chat. "How are things where you live?" inquired the king. "Fine, fine," said the boy, and he wouldn't budge from that. He said "fine, fine" to everything. "Now I want you to marry my daughter. What do you think of that?" asked the king. "Oh, fine, fine," said Martin. "That's fine!" The king thought to himself, "My future son-in-law is no conversationalist, but he certainly has lots of money!"

The princess was impatient to marry, and she said, "Let's send for the padre now." "Fine, fine!" replied Martin. So the padre was brought to marry them, and when he asked the boy what his name was, he replied, "Martin." "Martin what?"

"Just Martin," he answered. And so the princess and the boy were married by the padre, but the cat stayed out in the field with the mare, pondering what he was going to do about the wedding fiesta. The king had told the cat, "Put your horse in the corral with the others," but the cat answered, "No, she can't eat in there. She'll be better off out in the pasture there." And all during the wedding the cat was worrying about what to do. When the wedding was over they paid the padre and he left, and then the cat came in. The king said, "Now let's celebrate the wedding!" "That's a good idea. I like it," the cat said. The princess was impatient to go to bed, and they ate dinner early. The cat, Martin, and the princess ate at a separate table, and when they had finished the cat said, "Tell your father-in-law that now he should hold a fiesta for three days, and that I will then have a fiesta too." So Martin went and told the king what the cat had said, but he was very sad. "How can we do it?" he thought to himself. "The house will never do, and we don't have a thing!" The king agreed to the proposal and said, "Ah, good, good! What kind of fiesta would you like?" "Well, a royal kind of fiesta," replied the boy. "Whatever you want to do is fine!" "Tomorrow we'll have the fiesta," said the king. The married couple went to bed then—and they had their own fiesta!

The cat had his own room in the palace. The next morning the cat, the boy, and his wife ate breakfast together. Meanwhile the king had had a meal prepared for almost half the town and sent out invitations, and bulls were brought for a bullfight. (That is a game they don't have anymore—to fight bulls, and eat, and dance a little. That is a fiesta.) All the people watched from the grandstand, and the cat and his brother and the princess watched too. But the cat was thinking to himself, "Good heavens, I wish tomorrow would never come! How can I make this turn out all right?" The boy was sad also, thinking to himself, "How are we ever going to match this? Ah, how shamed we'll be!" He was very quiet, thinking, and his wife asked, "Why are you so sad?" "Oh, I'm thinking about home, and here I am!" he replied. The second day of the fiesta was the same as the first, with a bullfight and a feast, and everyone dined royally before going to bed. But the cat spent all his time thinking about how to make it all turn out all right. On the third day of the fiesta the bulls were brought into the arena for the last time, and everyone feasted very well indeed. The king had a band composed of some of his soldiers that played constantly, and the crowd was content. But the cat was pondering, thinking, "Tomorrow it's my turn!" And the boy was the same way. "How ashamed we'll be!" he thought to himself. That afternoon the king said, "Well, that's all. We may have another fiesta like this sometime, but I don't know when!"

That night everyone went to bed and slept soundly except the cat, who stayed awake all night worrying about what to do. The next morning they got up and had breakfast, and by this time the cat had thought of a plan. He said, "Sister-in-law, go and tell your father that I will now throw a small party of my own. It won't be much, but I'll do all I can. He can bring all of his people if he wishes, and his band as well. I'll lead the way." The boy was panic-stricken when he heard this, and when the girl had left he said, "Ah, brother, how shameful for us, and you're inviting everyone to go!" The princess went to her father and told him what the cat had said. "Have him come and talk with me. We will have a conference," said the king. When the girl returned with the message the boy thought to himself, "We are surely done for, we are as good as dead, for we've been living a lie!" The cat went to see the king, and said, "Good day, Your Majesty. What did you wish to talk to me about?" "I wished to talk to you about what you're going to do in response to the fiesta I gave," said the king. "Well, I will lead the way, and you may follow with all of your people," replied the cat. "And this place you are taking us to—is it far?" queried the king. "Yes, it's far enough, I suppose," answered the cat. Then the king said, "I can't take everyone to your house. I'll have to leave half of my people here. And I can't leave today, but I can tomorrow. Today I will arrange everything, and tomorrow we'll go."

When Martin heard what the king had said he was almost trembling with fright. "We're going to die tomorrow, for the king will surely kill us when he finds out the truth!" he exclaimed. His wife came and asked him, "What's wrong, why are you sad?" "Well, I'm thinking of my home, that's what I'm thinking about!" he replied. "Well, my brother-in-law says that we are going there tomorrow," she said comfortingly. The king made all the necessary preparations that day and named the people who were to go with them. The following day they had breakfast, and then the king said, "Now let's be on our way!" So they started off with the cat leading the way on his mare, followed by the band and the crowd of people. Martin and the royal family rode in a carriage. They marched along until at last they reached the old house in which Martin and his family had lived, but the boy was delighted and relieved when they went right on by without stopping. The cat said to the king, "Be patient, Your Majesty, for our destination is just a little further." They climbed a big hill and started down the other side with the band playing from time to time, and there below them was the house of the giant with many cattle grazing the fields around it. Then the cat turned his horse and raised his hand and everyone stopped. He went to the king and said, "Wait here for me. The band can play and you can have some shooting matches in the canyon there. I have to go on ahead to arrange everything, for we've been gone a long time."

The king agreed to the cat's suggestion, and the cat hurried on down the hill to the giant's house. When he arrived, the giant was reclining in a comfortable chair on his veranda. The cat rode up at breakneck speed, dismounted and tied his horse to a post, and then ran up to the giant, pretending great fright. "What's wrong?" asked the giant in amazement. "Well, what is wrong is that they are coming to kill you!" said the cat. "I've come to warn you. Listen, they are playing music up above there, and shooting!" When the giant heard the martial music and the sound of shooting he became very frightened and said, "Brother, can you do anything to save me?" "Oh, yes," said the cat. "That's not difficult. You are very strong. Carry that big rock to the well, tie a rope to it, and then lower yourself down the well. The soldiers will pass by and never see you, and then you'll be safe." "Good heavens, there are many of my enemies, but my brother here has given me good advice!" said the giant to himself. He went and dragged the boulder (which was almost as large in diameter as the well) to the edge of the well and fastened it with a rope so that it wouldn't fall in on top of him. Then he tied another rope to it and began to lower himself into the well. He lowered himself clear to the bottom, for he was afraid of shots from above.

The cat looked up on the hill and saw some of the soldiers

standing there, and he motioned for them to come down. When they did so he gave them an axe he had found and told them to cut the ropes holding the boulder in place. The huge rock rolled into the well (which was quite deep) and fell right on top of the giant. The cat peered over the edge of the well and saw blood on the water, and he knew the giant was dead. He went into the house and opened up some of the boxes of silver coins, and he ordered the soldiers to take them up the hill and cast the coins into the crowd. While the soldiers were doing this the cat went around and asked people who wanted to cook or gather firewood, for as he said, "The house has been empty for a long time." Many people volunteered for various tasks, for the cat promised them that they would be well rewarded. People were going around picking up coins off the ground. Even the king himself was harvesting them, until the cat saw him and said, "You don't have to do that, Your Majesty, for there will be some boxes for you to carry home with you!" Martin was content and happy. "Everything has turned out all right, and my brother has performed a great feat," he said. Then the cat asked, "Now who will bring cattle to butcher, and kill chickens and turkeys?" (The giant had had many chickens and turkeys both.) And that was the fiesta they had—for four days they dined royally on beef, chicken, and turkey. There was nothing to drink, however, for the giant had been a teetotaler.

At the end of four days the king exclaimed, "This is enough. You have given your fiesta one day longer than I did!" "There is a lot left," said the cat, for he knew that there was enough food to last all week. But the king replied, "No, I must go. We shall return home tomorrow. You have done enough." The people were camped all around, for the house was not that large, but still the crowd was very pleased with Sir Cat. He presented the king with a great chest of pure silver. Then he said, "Now, who will stay here with us and look after the stock?" Almost everyone wanted to stay, for there was still plenty of food left. The giant had been very rich indeed. In the end a number of people stayed on as servants. The king said to his daughter, "I'm going back to my town with my people and you are staying here. But you can go with us if you wish and then return whenever you want." But the girl answered, "No, I like it here, and here we'll remain. We lack nothing here. It's

just like home, perhaps even better." The next morning the
king and his people left to return to town, leaving Martin and
his wife and brother living in the giant's house with their new
servants.

One day Martin and the cat were sitting on the veranda
talking, and the cat asked, "Brother, what do you think about
everything that happened?" The boy answered, "Well, I'm
very grateful for what you did and what we have now." "And
what would you do if I should suddenly die—what would you
do with me?" asked the cat. "I will remove your skin and put it
on my bed," said the boy. "Good, that would please me very
much," the cat said. "Yes, indeed, brother, that is what I will
do," promised Martin. The next morning the cat did not
appear for breakfast, and they wondered where he was. A
servant was sent to his room, and when she returned she said
that he was fast asleep. "Let him sleep. He stays awake at
night and he's very tired," said Martin. But at dinnertime the
cat had still not appeared, and the princess said, "Sir Martin,
why don't you go and see where he is?" So the boy went to the
cat's room and when he got there he found him lying stiff in
bed. "He is dead," he said to himself. He called a servant and
said, "Take him and throw him far away down the arroyo!" So
the servant dragged the cat down the arroyo and left him
there. And so the boy did not keep his promise.

When Martin returned his wife asked him what he had
done with the cat, and he replied, "Oh, I ordered that he be
thrown into the arroyo." "Oh, you made a promise and didn't
keep it!" exclaimed the girl. "What does it matter?" he asked.
"He is dead, why not throw him out?" "Because your brother
isn't dead!" she answered. "He's just pretending to be dead to
see if you'll keep your promise!" "Oh, no," replied her
husband. "He's stiff and dead." They ate dinner and went to
bed, and at breakfast the next morning the girl said, "Go and
look and see if Sir Cat isn't in his bed again!" They went to
look, and there was the cat just getting up. They called him to
come to breakfast and he came, but he didn't say a word. He
just ate in silence. Finally at midday he said, "Sir Martin, how
well you kept your promise!" "Oh, I knew very well that you
weren't dead, that you were only playing!" replied Martin.
"That's why I had you thrown out like that." Several days
passed, and then one morning the cat became ill. He said,

"Brother, I'm sick and this time I won't come back. What are you going to do?" The boy replied, "Well, I'm going to do what you asked me to do before." The cat got worse, and one day when they awoke he was lying in his bed stiff and dead. Martin said, "Now I will take off my brother's skin." He skinned the cat and had the hide tanned so that it was soft, and then put it on his bed as he had promised. And there it remained, but the body was thrown out because it was decomposing. They only kept the skin. There they were; there they remained. The cat was smarter than Sir Martin—Sir Martin was useless—but there they remained, and the cat didn't revive again.

sutiwayan ul?atuc?

Appendix

Sources and Comparative Notes

N.A.A. = National Anthropological Archives, Smithsonian Institution, Washington, D.C.

D.L.B. = Department of Linguistics, University of California, Berkeley

1. Informant: María Solares. Location: N.A.A. (Box 137). English text.

2. Informant: María Solares. Location: N.A.A. (Box 5, Fd. 3). English text. The incident of a peon game between Sun and Coyote is cognate to one involving Tihpiknits and Coyote in Chunut Yokuts story (Latta, 1949:240).

3. Informant: María Solares. Location: N.A.A. (Box 137). English text. Stories of similar malevolent beings are common in Pomo folklore as well (see Oswalt, 1964:134-177).

4. Informant: María Solares. Location: N.A.A. (Box 137). English text.

5. Informant: María Solares. Location: N.A.A. (Box 137). English text. The theme of a universal flood is, of course, ubiquitous (see Gayton, 1935a).

6. Informant: María Solares. Location: N.A.A. (Box 5, Fd. 3). English text. A cognate story is "The Origin of Death" (Kroeber, 1907:231); the lizard-hand theme has a wide distribution in California (see Gayton and Newman, 1940:56).

7. Informant: Simplicio Pico. Location: N.A.A. (Box 31). English text. See Note 6.

8. Informant: Fernando Librado. Location: N.A.A. (Box 2). English text.

9. Informant: Fernando Librado. Location: N.A.A. (Box 2). English and Spanish text.

10. Informant: Fernando Librado. Location: N.A.A. (Box 2). English text.

11. Informant: Fernando Librado. Location: D.L.B. (Box 747, Fd. 15). Spanish and English text.

12. Informant: María Solares. Location: N.A.A. (Box 5, Fd. 3). English text. Many of the elements in this narrative have a worldwide distribution.

13. Informant: Fernando Librado. Location: D.L.B. (Box 747, Fd. 3). English text.

14. Informant: Fernando Librado. Location: D.L.B. (Box 747, Fd. 3). English text.

15. Informant: María Solares. Location: N.A.A. (Box 5, Fd. 3). English text. The theme of two brothers who have numerous adventures is widespread in California. There is a possible analogy to this story in DuBois (1904), while the Yokuts story of "The Mischievous Younger Brother" (Rogers and Gayton, 1944:203-204) is probably partly cognate. The theme of a woman with a basket of hot tar is cognate to that in "The Basket-Carrying Ogress, Echo" (ibid.:204), while the theme of the cannibal giant is similar to "Coyote Kills the Cannibal" (ibid.:196-199).

16. Informant: Luisa Ygnacio. Location: D.L.B. English text. See Note 15.

17. Informant: Luisa Ygnacio. Location: D.L.B. Spanish text. See Note 15.

18. Informant: María Solares. Location: N.A.A. (Box 37, Fd. 1). Spanish text. The first portion of this narrative (and no. 15) is cognate to the Yokuts "Mikiti" stories (Kroeber, 1907:225-227; Gayton and Newman, 1940: 67-72), "Falcon Kills Bear and Contests with Guchun" (Gayton and Newman, 1940:23), and the Tübatulabal story of "Blood-clot Boy" (Voeglin, 1935: 211-213). The theme of a loss of gambling skill and subsequent departure is similar to the Wintu "Coyote and Dentalium" (Demetracopoulou and DuBois, 1932:416-424) and the Yokuts "The Prairie Falcon Loses" (Kroeber, 1907:223).

19. Informant: Juan de Jesús Justo. Location: D.L.B. (Box 748, Fd. 5). Spanish text. See Note 15.

20. Informant: Luisa Ygnacio (?). Location: D.L.B. Spanish text.

21. Informant: Fernando Librado. Location: N.A.A. (Box 5, Fd. 1-2). English text.

22. Informant: Fernando Librado. N.A.A. (Box 2). English text.

23. Informant: Fernando Librado. Location: N.A.A. (Box 5, Fd. 1-6). Chumash text with interlinear Spanish and English translation.

24. Informant: Fernando Librado. Location: N.A.A. (Box 5, Fd. 1-1). English and Spanish text.

25. Informant: Lucrecia García. Location: D.L.B. Chumash text with interlinear Spanish translation. This story is based on the famous Orpheus tradition, as is No. 59. See Gayton (1935b) and Hultkrantz (1957) for further data.

26. Informant: Juan de Jesús Justo. Location: D.L.B. Spanish text. A version of this narrative is included as part of "The Prairie Falcon Loses" (Kroeber, 1907:240-242), and "Falcon Captured by Water People" (Gayton and Newman, 1940:81) is also cognate. An unpublished version similar to that presented here was collected by Harrington from a Cahuilla informant.

27. Informant: Luisa Ygnacio. Location: D.L.B. (Box 748, Fd. 1). Spanish and English text. See Note 26.

28. Informant: María Solares. Location: D.L.B. (Box 735, Fd. 2). Spanish text. See Note 29.

29. Informant: Luisa Ygnacio. Location: D.L.B. English text. Coyote's pretense of being Xelex is similar to an incident in the Wintu story "Huik" (Demetracopoulou and DuBois, 1932:461-463). The malicious behavior of Slo?w and Xelex is similar to that in "Coyote's Adventures and Prairie Falcon's Blindness" (Kroeber, 1907:231-240).

30. Informant: María Solares. Location: N.A.A. (Box 137). Spanish and English text.

31. Informant: Juan de Jesús Justo. Location: D.L.B. Spanish text. The incident of killing geese by trickery is similar to the Wintu story of "Why Duck's Eyes Are Pink" (Demetracopoulou and DuBois, 1932:494).

32. Informant: Juan de Jesús Justo. Location: D.L.B. English text.

33. Informant: Juan de Jesús Justo. Location: D.L.B. Spanish text. A version of this narrative, combined with no. 35, has been published as "Coyote and Bat" (Heizer, 1955b:56, 72). It was originally collected by Yates, probably from the same informant or from his father.

34. Informant: unknown. Location: D.L.B. Chumash text with interlinear Spanish and English translation.

35. Informant: Juan de Jesús Justo. Location: D.L.B. (Box 748). Spanish text.

36. Informant: Luisa Ygnacio. Location: D.L.B. Chumash text with interlinear Spanish and English translation.

37. Informant: Juan de Jesús Justo. Location: D.L.B. (Box 748, Fd. 1). Spanish and English text.

38. Informant: Luisa Ygnacio. Location D.L.B. English text.

39. Informant: Lucrecia García. Location: D.L.B. (Box 728, Fd. 12). Spanish and English text.

40. Informant: María Solares. Location: N.A.A. (Box 137). Chumash and Spanish text. This narrative is cognate to the Serrano story of "The Bungling Host" (Benedict, 1926:16-17) and the Wintu story of "Bear and Rabbit" (Demetracopoulou and DuBois, 1932:494).

41. Informant: Fernando Librado. Location: N.A.A. (Box 5, Fd. 1-1). English text.

42. Informant: Lucrecia García. Location: D.L.B. (Box 728, Fd. 12). English and Spanish text.

43. Informant: Fernando Librado. Location: D.L.B. (Box 747, Fd. 10). English text.

44. Informant: Fernando Librado. Location: N.A.A. (Box 5, Fd. 1-6). English text.

45. Informant: María Solares. Location: D.L.B. (Box 735, Fd. 2). Spanish text.

46. Informant: María Solares. Location: N.A.A. (Box 137). Chumash and Spanish text.

47. Informant: Luisa Ygnacio. Location: D.L.B. (Box 728, Fd. 12). Spanish and English text.

48. Informant: María Solares. Location: D.L.B. (Box 735, Fd. 2). Chumash and Spanish text. The salmon-stealing incident is cognate to one in "Coyote's Adventures and Prairie Falcon's Blindness" (Kroeber, 1907:231-240). Also see No. 108.

49. Informant: Lucrecia García. Location: D.L.B. (Box 728, Fd. 12). English and Spanish text. A similar incident is included in "Coyote's Adventures and Prairie Falcon's Blindness" (Kroeber, 1907:231-240).

50. Informant: Lucrecia García. Location: D.L.B. (Box 748, Fd. 1). Spanish and English text.

51. Informant: unknown. Location: D.L.B. (Box 748, Fd. 1). Spanish and English text.

52. Informant: María Solares. Location: N.A.A. (Box 137). Chumash and Spanish text.

53. Informant: Fernando Librado. Location: N.A.A. (Box 5, Fd 1-3). English, Chumash, and Spanish text.

54. Informant: María Solares. Location: N.A.A. (Box 5, Fd. 4). Chumash and Spanish text.

55. Informant: Luisa Ygnacio. Location: N.A.A. (Box 5). Chumash text with interlinear English and Spanish translation.

56. Informant: María Solares (?). Location: N.A.A. (Box 5, Fd. 4). Chumash and Spanish text.

57. Informant: María Solares. Location: N.A.A. (Box 5, Fd. 4). Chumash and Spanish text. Most other Pleiades stories involve girls or wives—this narrative seems to be an interesting exception.

58. Informant: Lucrecia García. Location: D.L.B. (Box 728, Fd. 12). English text.

59. Informant: María Solares. Location: N.A.A. (Box 5, Fd. 3). English text. A version of the Orpheus tradition. See Note 25.

60. Informant: Fernando Librado. Location: D.L.B. (Box 747, Fd. 15). English and Spanish text.

61. Informant: Fernando Librado. Location: D.L.B. (Box 747, Fd. 15). English text.

62. Informant: María Solares. Location: N.A.A. (Box 137). Spanish and English text. Stories involving supernatural serpents are widespread in California (e.g. Oswalt, 1964:145-153, or Uldall and Shipley, 1966:117).

63. Informant: María Solares. Location: N.A.A. (Box 5, Fd. 3). English text.

64. Informant: Fernando Librado. Location: D.L.B. (Box 747, Fd. 15). English text. See Note 62.

65. Informant: María Solares. Location: N.A.A. (Box 5, Fd. 3). English text. See Note 15.

66. Informant: Lucrecia García. Location: D.L.B. (Box 728, Fd. 12). English text.

67. Informant: Fernando Librado. Location: D.L.B. (Box 747, Fd. 10). English text. Stories concerning werebears are common throughout California. A typical example is "Description of a Werebear" (Oswalt, 1964: 205-207).

68. Informant: Juan de Jesús Justo. Location: D.L.B. (Box 747, Fd. 15). English text. See Note 67.

69. Informant: María Solares. Location: N.A.A. (Box 24). English text. See Note 67 and Oswalt, 1964:207-211.

70. Informant: María Solares. Location: N.A.A. (Box 5, Fd. 3). English text. See Note 69.

71. Informant: María Solares. Location: D.L.B. (Box 728, Fd. 10). English and Spanish text.

72. Informant: María Solares. Location: N.A.A. (Box 22). Spanish text.

73. Informant: María Solares. Location: N.A.A. (Box 24). Spanish text.

74. Informant: Fernando Librado. Location: N.A.A. (Box 5, Fd. 1-6). English text.

75. Informant: María Solares. Location: N.A.A. (Box 5, Fd. 3). English text.

76. Informant: María Solares. Location: N.A.A. (Box 5, Fd. 3). English text.

77. Informant: María Solares. Location: N.A.A. (Box 5, Fd. 3). English text.

78. Informant: María Solares. Location: N.A.A. (Box 5, Fd. 3). English text.

79. Informant: María Solares. Location: N.A.A. (Box 137), English and Spanish text.

80. Informant: María Solares. Location: N.A.A. (Box 23). English and Spanish text.

81. Informant: María Solares. Location: D.L.B. (Box 735, Fd. 2). Spanish text.

82. Informant: María Solares. Location: N.A.A. (Box 23). English and Spanish text.

83. Informant: Fernando Librado. Location: D.L.B. (Box 747, Fd. 10). English text.

84. Informant: Fernando Librado. Location: D.L.B. (Box 747, Fd. 10). English text.

85. Informant: María Solares. Location: N.A.A. (Box 137). Spanish text.

86. Informant: María Solares. Location: N.A.A. (Box 5, Fd. 3). English text. The theme of people who live underwater also occurs in the Nisenan story of "Water People" (Uldall and Shipley, 1966:163-164).

87. Informant: María Solares. Location: N.A.A. (Box 5, Fd. 3). English text.

88. Informant: María Solares. Location: N.A.A. (Box 24). Chumash and Spanish text.

89. Informant: Fernando Librado. Location: D.L.B. (Box 747, Fd. 10). English text.

90. Informant: María Solares. Location: N.A.A. (Box 137). English and Spanish text.

91. Informant: María Solares. Location: N.A.A. (Box 5, Fd. 3). English text.

92. Informant: Fernando Librado. Location: N.A.A. (Box 2). English text.

93. Informant: María Solares. Location: N.A.A. (Box 5, Fd. 3). English text.

94. Informant: Fernando Librado. Location: N.A.A. (Box 5, Fd. 1-6). English text.

95. Informant: Fernando Librado. Location: N.A.A. (Box 5, Fd. 1-6). English text.

96. Informant: María Solares. Location: D.L.B. (Box 735, Fd. 2). Spanish and English text.

97. Informant: María Solares. Location: N.A.A. (Box 22). Spanish and English text.

98. Informant: María Solares. Location: N.A.A. (Box 5, Fd. 3). English text. This story is still current on the Santa Ynez reservation (see Gardner, 1965).

99. Informant: María Solares. Location: N.A.A. (Box 24). English text.

100. Informant: María Solares. Location: N.A.A. (Box 23). Spanish and English text.

101. Informant: María Solares. Location: N.A.A. (Box 5, Fd. 3). English text.

102. Informant: María Solares. Location: N.A.A. (Box 24). Spanish and English text.

103. Informant: María Solares. Location: N.A.A. (Box 23). English text.

104. Informant: Fernando Librado. Location: N.A.A. (Box 5, Fd. 1-6). English text.

105. Informant: Fernando Librado. Location: N.A.A. (Box 5, Fd. 1-1). English text.

106. Informant: Juan de Jesús Justo. Location: D.L.B. (Box 748, Fd. 5). English text. The incident of holding up the rock is cognate to "Coyote Holds Up the World" (Rogers and Gayton, 1944:199-200).

107. Informant: Luisa Ygnacio. Location: D.L.B. Spanish text. A version of No. 106, with the addition of the Mexican story of "Repaying Good with Evil" (see Aiken, 1935).

108. Informant: Juan de Jesús Justo (from Lino). Location: D.L.B. Spanish text. The first part of this story appears to be a version of the well-known narrative "The Tar Baby" (see Espinosa, 1930, for further data). However, such stories as the Wintu "Coyote and Stump" (Demetracopoulou and DuBois, 1932:409-411) and the Maidu "Coyote and the Devil" (Shipley, 1963:43-45) raise the possibility of an indigenous source. For the salmon-stealing episode see Note 48, and for the incident of holding up the rock see Note 106.

109. Informant: Lucrecia García. Location: D.L.B. (Box 728, Fd. 12). English text. A version of a well-known European folktale.

110. Informant: Lucrecia García. Location: D.L.B. (Box 728, Fd. 12). English text. A version of one of Aesop's Fables.

111. Informant: Juan de Jesús Justo (from father). Location: N.A.A. (Box 5, Fd. 25). Spanish text. A version of the well-known European folktale "Puss-in-Boots."

Glossary

capwaya—village place name
cenhes heʔišup—wind ("breath of the world")
ciwin—feathered headband
cuqeleʔ—feathered banner (= suqele)
cux—headdress
cʔicʔiwuʔun—great-grandchildren
cʔiwis—rattle
cʔoyinašup—underworld occupied by nunašɨš
cʔoyiq—edible seed

čumaš—Santa Cruz Island (= čʔumaš)

hap (haphap)—a nunašɨš
hew—pelican
humqaq—Point Conception
huxminaš—processed juniper berries (= Sp. guata)

kalawašaq—village place name
kaqunupʔmawa—sun (metaphorical term)
kaspatqaxwa—mountain place name
kišnuna—relative by birth; MB's child
kʔiwis—stone bowl
ksen—messenger; mudhen

laxus—fish species
lewelew—a nunašɨš
liyɨkšup—mythical village ("center of the world")

malaxšišiniš—a nunašɨš ("one that growls, is angry")
makal—bat species
mapaqas ʔasʔɨl—see pakaʔs asʔɨl
maqutikok—spotted woodpecker
masaqsiqʔitašup—mythical serpents ("binding of the world")
maxulaw (mamismis)—a nunašɨš ("one who weeps much")
mikiw—Dos Pueblos village

miswaskɨn—village place name
molmoloqʔiku—First People who became animals after the
          Flood
momoy—jimson weed (*Datura meteloides*)
monsow—weasel
mucucu—a type of small shell bead
muhu—horned owl
mup—cave
mut—cormorant

naxalyɨkɨš—ceremonial enclosure, shrine (= šawil)
nukumpiyɨš—barracuda dance
nunašɨš—animal; dangerous animal; malevolent supernatural
          being

pakaʔs asʔɨl—a nunašɨš ("one-legged one")
paxa—political and ceremonial officer
paʔyas—ring–and–pole game
pelepel—egret, heron; supernatural being
pocoyi—lizard species
pohono—a nunašɨš
pox—agave or yucca species
puk—gray owl
pulakak—redheaded woodpecker
puluy—crane

qaq—raven
qasɨ—abalone species
qilmoy—see sqilmoy
qoʔloy—crayfish
ququ—a nunašɨš
qupe—California poppy
qusqus—bird species (= qɨšqɨš)
qɨšqɨš—see qusqus
qwaʔ—village place name
qʔiniʔwi—fish species
qʔwaʔyaʔya—not translated

seneq—mountain west of Santa Barbara
siliyɨk—dance enclosure at fiestas
sisa—mountain near Ojai
sloʔw—eagle
soxtonokmu—village place name

sqilmoy—type of shell bead
sukuyas—prepared islay
suqele—see cuqele?
sitiwayan ul?atuc?—ending phrase ("they hang up the carry-
      net")
syuxtun—Santa Barbara village
swaxɨl—village place name on Santa Cruz Island
s?axpilil—village place name ("root/sinew, bowstring")
s?yilyila masoxkon—charmstones ("belongings of Thunder")
šaq—tortoise
šawil—ceremonial enclosure, shrine (= naxalyɨqɨš)
šaxlapus—type of shaman; diviner, enchanter
šimilaqša—land of the dead across the sea
šipitiš—acorn soup
šišaxlapus—see šaxlapus
šiyaxšaptuwaš—mountain above Santa Barbara
škalukš—totem animal, spirit (?)
šnilemun—supernatural coyote of upper world
šopo—charmstone
šoxš—feather down
šup—earth, world
šutiwɨ?yɨš—seaweed dance of Santa Cruz Island
šɨpɨš—diviner
šɨšač?i?—La Quemada village ("woodrat's den")

takɨ?mɨ—beetle species
takulšoxšinaš—feathered cord used by shamans
ta?lip—sinew-backed bow
teqeqš—village place name
timoloqinaš—story felt to be true
tinliw—Tejon Ranch village
tišɨpɨš—story told for diversion
tok—red milkweed (*Asclepius* species)
tokoy—a game; stone disk used in game
tomol—plank canoe
towonowon—cocoon rattle or case
tupnekč—child

walpi?y—game played in šimilaqša
wɨp ahiken akpa—"hit it with my staff"
wit—place near šimilaqša
wot—chief

woy—hawk species
woʔni—type of basket
xalašat—San Nicholas Island
xelex—hawk or falcon species
xiłiw—quartz crystal
xolxol—a nunašɨš
xoy—supernatural being; dragnet
xutaš—coffeeberry; earth; chia (?)
xuxaw—coyote (= ʔaska?)
xweteʔet—fish species
xʔiʔm—coiled storage basket

yowoyow—a nunašɨš

ʔahašɨš—spirit, ghost
ʔalampauwauhani—abyss, universe
ʔalapay (ʔalapayašup)—upper world of supernaturals
ʔalapkalawašaq—inhabitants of kalawašaq village
ʔalaxlapš—type of shaman or priest, astrologer
ʔalaxulapu—place name at Santa Ynez Mission
ʔalʔheleqeč—a nunašɨš
ʔalšuqlaš—type of shaman or priest
ʔaltomolič—canoe maker
ʔamaxalamɨš—village place name ("the fiesta")
ʔanaxɨxɨʔ—old men
ʔaničʔapapa—sharp-shinned hawk
ʔantap—member of a religious cult
ʔanucwa—duck species
ʔapanɨs—village, settlement
ʔapɨ—type of shell bead
ʔaqulpop—nightshade species (?) (= Sp. chichequelite)
ʔašixuč—a nunašɨš ("the burner")
ʔataxʔič—place near La Purisima Mission
ʔatimasɨq—hawk species ("the tightly-belted one")
ʔatišwɨn—talisman, fetish, spirit helper
ʔatišwɨnic—shaman; one possessing an ʔatišwɨn (= ʔalʔatiš-
        wɨnič)
ʔawak—type of basket
ʔaxlapus—see šaxlapus
ʔayakuy—type of basket
ʔayaya—place near šimilaqša

ʔayip—mineral (alum?) used as medicine and poison
ʔelyeʔwun—swordfish; undersea supernatural beings
ʔičiʔi—stone used for cracking acorns
ʔikʔɨmɨš—type of shell bead
ʔilepeš—food substance (= ʔilepec, ʔiʔlepes)
ʔisʔoxsinas—feathered pole erected at shrines
ʔitiašup (mišupašup)—world of mankind
ʔiwhɨnmuʔu—Mt. Pinos
ʔɨhɨy—man
ʔolotoč—quiver
ʔonoq—buzzard
ʔostus—not translated (but ʔos = to copulate)

SPANISH WORDS AND PHRASES

abalorio—shell-bead money
alcalde—mission official
amole—soap root (*Chlorogalum pomeridianum*)
armún—small measuring box
atole—gruel, soup
barburis—barberry (*Berberis* species)
batea—tray
cacomites—edible bulbs
calandria—lark species
canaigre—wild rhubarb (*Rumex hymenosapalus*)
chia—*Salvia columbariae*
comal—steatite frying pan
gomi—a ball game
gremio—brotherhood, guild
guata—processed juniper berries
Huasna—place northeast of Santa Maria
islay—*Prunus ilicifolia*
mañada—horse herd
matavenado—Jerusalem cricket
miel de jicote—unidentified food substance
panocha—cake of unrefined sugar
pespibata—native tobacco (*Nicotiana attenuata*)
pinacate—stink bettle (*Eleodes* species)
pinole—ground meal or flour
roble—valley oak (*Quercas lobata*)

romerillo—milkweed (?)
sauzal—willow thicket
temescal—sweathouse
toloache—jimson weed (*Datura meteloides*)
trastes del Trueño—tools or belongings of Thunder

Bibliography

AGINSKY, BURT W.

    1940   "The Socio-Psychological Significance of Death Among the Pomo Indians." *American Imago*, Vol. 1, pp. 1-11. Boston: Dr. Hanns Sachs.

AIKEN, RILEY

    1935   "A Pack Load of Mexican Tales." In *Puro Mexicano*, J. Frank Dobie (editor), pp. 1-87. Austin: Texas Folklore Society.

ANDERSON, EUGENE N., JR.

    1964   "A Bibliography of the Chumash and Their Predecessors." *University of California Archaeological Survey Reports, No. 61*, pp. 27-74. Berkeley: University of California Press.

APPLEGATE, RICHARD

    1974   "Chumash Placenames." *Journal of California Anthropology*, Vol. 1, No. 2, pp. 187-205.

BARRETT, SAMUEL

    1933   "Pomo Myths." *Bulletin of the Public Museum of the City of Milwaukee*, No. 15. Milwaukee: Milwaukee Public Museum.

BASCOM, WILLIAM R.

    1954   "Four Functions of Folklore." *Journal of American Folklore*, Vol. 67, pp. 333-349. Philadelphia: American Folklore Society.

BASSO, KEITH H.

    1970   "'To Give Up On Words': Silence in Western Apache Culture." *Southwestern Journal of Anthropology*, Vol. 26, No. 3, pp. 213-230. Albuquerque: University of New Mexico Press.

BEAN, LOWELL J.

    1972   *Mukat's People: The Cahuilla Indians of Southern California*. Berkeley: University of California Press.

BEAN, LOWELL J., AND THOMAS F. KING (EDITORS)

    1974   *ʔAntap: California Indian Political and Economic Organization*. Ramona: Ballena Press.

BEELER, MADISON S.

    1967   "The Ventureño Confesionario of José Señán, O.F.M." *University of California Publications in Linguistics*, Vol. 47. Berkeley: University of California Press.

BENEDICT, RUTH

    1926   "Serrano Tales." *Journal of American Folklore*, Vol. 39, pp. 1-17. New York: American Folklore Society.

    1935   "Zuni Mythology." *Columbia University Contributions to Anthropology*, No. 21. 2 vols. New York: Columbia University Press.

BERNDT, CATHERINE H.
    1966 "The Ghost Husband: Society and the Individual in New Guinea
          Myth." In *The Anthropologist Looks at Myth*, Melville Jacobs
          (compiler), pp. 244-277. Austin: University of Texas Press.
BLACKBURN, THOMAS C.
    1963 "A Manuscript Account of the Ventureño Chumash." *Archaeo-
          logical Survey Annual Report, 1962-1963*, pp. 133-158. Los Angeles:
          University of California, Los Angeles.

    1974 "Ceremonial Integration and Social Interaction in Aboriginal
          California." In *?Antap: California Indian Political and Economic
          Organization*, Lowell J. Bean and Thomas F. King (editors). Ra-
          mona: Ballena Press.

BOAS, FRANZ
    1916 *Tsimshian Mythology*. Thirty-first Annual Report, Bureau of
          American Ethnology, 1909-1910. Washington, D.C.: Government
          Printing Office.

    1935 "Kwakiutl Culture as Reflected in Mythology." *Memoirs of the
          American Folk-Lore Society*, Vol. 28. New York: American Folk-
          Lore Society.

BOLTON, H. E. (EDITOR)
    1925 *Spanish Exploration in the Southwest, 1542-1706.* New York: Scrib-
          ner's.

    1926 *Historical Memoirs of New California, by Fray Francisco Palóu, O.F.M.*
          Berkeley: University of California Press.

    1927 *Fray Juan Crespí, Missionary Explorer on the Pacific Coast, 1769-1774.*
          Berkeley: University of California Press.

    1930 *Anza's California Expeditions.* 5 vols. Berkeley: University of Cali-
          fornia Press.

BOWERS, STEPHEN
    1897 "The Santa Barbara Indians." Unpublished manuscript, South-
          west Museum, Highland Park.

BROWN, ALAN K.
    1967 "The Aboriginal Population of the Santa Barbara Channel."
          University of California Archaeological Survey Reports, No. 69.
          Berkeley: University of California Press.

CABALLERÍA Y COLLEL, JUAN
    1892 *History of the City of Santa Barbara, California.* Santa Barbara:
          F. de P. Gutierrez

COLBY, BENJAMIN N.
    1973 "A Partial Grammar of Eskimo Folktales." *American Anthropolo-
          gist*, Vol. 75, No. 3, pp. 645-662. Washington, D. C.: American
          Anthropological Association.

COOK, S. F.
    1943 "The Conflict Between the California Indian and White Civili-
          zation." *Ibero-Americana*, Vols. 21 and 22. Berkeley: University of
          California Press.

CRAIG, STEVE
  1966 "Ethnographic Notes on the Construction of Ventureño Chu-
         mash Baskets: From the Ethnographic and Linguistic Field Notes
         of John P. Harrington." *Archaeological Survey Annual Report, 1966*,
         Vol. 8, pp. 196-214. Los Angeles: University of California, Los
         Angeles.
  1967 "The Basketry of the Ventureño Chumash." *Archaeological Survey
         Annual Report, 1967*, Vol. 9, pp. 78-149. Los Angeles: University
         of California, Los Angeles.
CRUMRINE, N. ROSS
  1969 "Capakoba, the Mayo Easter ceremonial impersonator: explana-
         tions of ritual clowning." *Journal for the Scientific Study of Religion*,
         Vol. 8, pp. 1-22. Philadelphia: Society for the Scientific Study of
         Religion.
  1974 "Anomalous Figures and Liminal Roles: A Reconsideration of the
         Mayo Indian *Capakoba*, Northwest Mexico." *Anthropos*, Vol. 69,
         Nos. 5 and 6, pp. 858-873.
DAWSON, LAWRENCE AND JAMES DEETZ
  1965 "A Corpus of Chumash Basketry." *Archaeological Survey Annual
         Report*, 1965, Vol. 7, pp. 193-276. Los Angeles: University of Cali-
         fornia, Los Angeles.
DEMETRACOPOULOU, DOROTHY, AND CORA DUBOIS
  1932 "A Study of Wintu Mythology." *Journal of American Folklore*,
         Vol. 45, pp. 373-500. Lancaster: American Folklore Society.
DOBIE, J. FRANK (EDITOR)
  1935 *Puro Mexicano*. Austin: Texas Folklore Society.
DUBOIS, CONSTANCE
  1904 "The Story of the Chaup: A Myth of the Diegueños." *Journal of
         American Folklore*, Vol. 17, pp. 217-242. Boston: American Folklore
         Society.
DUNDES, ALAN (EDITOR)
  1965 *The Study of Folklore*. Englewood Cliffs: Prentice-Hall.
EHRLICH, CLARA
  1937 "Tribal Culture in Crow Mythology." *Journal of American Folk-
         Lore*, Vol. 50, pp. 307-408. New York: American Folk-Lore So-
         ciety.
ELIADE, MIRCEA
  1959 *The Sacred and the Profane*. New York: Harcourt, Brace.
  1964 *Shamanism: Archaic Techniques of Ecstasy*. New York: Bollingen
         Foundation.
ENGLEHARDT, ZEPHYRIN
  1923 *Santa Barbara Mission*. San Francisco: James H. Barry.
  1930 *San Buenaventura, the Mission by the Sea*. Santa Barbara: Santa
         Barbara Mission.
  1932a *Mission La Concepcion Purisima de Maria Santisima*. Santa Barbara:
         Santa Barbara Mission.

1932b *Mission Santa Inés, Virgen y Martir, and its Ecclesiastical Seminary.*
       Santa Barbara: Santa Barbara Mission.

1933   *Mission San Luis Obispo in the Vally of the Bears.* Santa Barbara:
       Santa Barbara Mission.

ESPINOSA, AURELIO M.
1930   "Notes on the Origin and History of the Tar-baby Story."
       Journal of American Folklore, Vol. 43, No. 168, pp. 129-209. New
       York: American Folklore Society.

FIRTH, RAYMOND
1961   *History and Traditions of Tikopia.* Wellington: The Polynesian
       Society.

FISCHER, JOHN
1963   "The Sociopsychological Analysis of Folktales." *Current Anthro-
       pology,* Vol. 4, No. 3, pp. 235-295. Utrecht: Wenner-Gren Foun-
       dation.

FURST, PETER T. (EDITOR)
1972   *Flesh of the Gods: The Ritual Use of Hallucinogens.* New York:
       Praeger.

GARDNER, LOUISE
1965   "The Surviving Chumash." *Archaeological Survey Annual Report,
       1965,* Vol. 7, pp. 277-302. Los Angeles: University of California,
       Los Angeles.

GAYTON, ANNA H.
1930   "Yokuts-Mono Chiefs and Shamans." *University of California
       Publications in American Archaeology and Ethnology,* Vol. 24, pp.
       361-420. Berkeley: University of California Press.

1935a "Areal Affiliations of California Folktales." *American Anthropolo-
       gist,* Vol. 37, pp. 582-599. Menasha: American Anthropological
       Association.

1935b "The Orpheus Myth in North America." *Journal of American
       Folklore,* Vol. 48, pp. 263-293. New York: American Folklore
       Society.

1946   "Culture-Environment Integration: External References in Yokuts
       Life." *Southwestern Journal of Anthropology,* Vol. 2, pp. 252-268.
       Albuquerque: University of New Mexico Press.

GAYTON, ANNA H., AND STANLEY S. NEWMAN
1940   "Yokuts and Western Mono Myths." *Anthropological Records,*
       Vol. 5, pp. 1-109. Berkeley: University of California Press.

GEERTZ, CLIFFORD
1967   "The Cerebral Savage: On the Work of Claude Lévi-Strauss."
       Encounter, Vol. 28, No. 4, pp. 25-32. London: Encounter Ltd.

GEORGES, ROBERT A.
1968   *Studies on Mythology.* Homewood: Dorsey Press.

GRANT, CAMPBELL
1965   *Rock Paintings of the Chumash.* Berkeley: University of California
       Press.

HALLOWELL, A. I.
1947 "Myth, Culture, and Personality." *American Anthropologist*, Vol. 49, pp. 544-556. Menasha: American Anthropological Association.
HALPERN, A. M.
1953 "A Dualism in Pomo Cosmology." *Kroeber Anthropological Society Papers*, Nos. 8 and 9, pp. 151-599. Berkeley: University of California Press.
HAMMEL, EUGENE A.
1972 "The Myth of Structural Analysis: Lévi-Strauss and the Three Bears." *Addison-Wesley Modular Publications*, No. 25, pp. 1-29. Reading: Addison-Wesley.
HARRINGTON, JOHN P.
1942 "Culture Element Distributions: XIX, Central California Coast." *Anthropological Records*, Vol. 7, No. 1. Berkeley: University of California Press.
HEIZER, ROBERT F.
1952 "California Indian Linguistic Records: The Mission Indian Vocabularies of Alphonse Pinart." *Anthropological Records*, Vol. 15, No. 1, pp. 1-84. Berkeley: University of California Press.

1955a "California Indian Linguistic Records: The Mission Indian Vocabularies of H. W. Henshaw." *Anthropological Records*, Vol. 15, No. 2, pp. 85-202. Berkeley: University of California Press.

1955b "Two Chumash Legends." *Journal of American Folklore*, Vol. 68, pp. 34, 56, 72. Philadelphia: American Folklore Society.

1970a "A Chumash 'Census' of 1928-1930." *Contributions of the University of California Archaeological Research Facility*, No. 9, pp. 23-28. Berkeley: University of California Press.

1970b "More J. P. Harrington Notes on Ventureño Chumash Basketry and Culture." *Contributions of the University of California Archaeological Research Facility*, No. 9, pp. 59-74. Berkeley: University of California Press.

HEMERT-ENGERT, ADOLPH VAN, AND FREDERICK TEGGART (EDITORS)
1910 "The Narrative of the Portolá Expedition of 1769-1770, by Miguel Constansó." *Publications of the Academy of Pacific Coast History*, Vol. 1, No. 4. Berkeley: University of California Press.

HENSHAW, H. W.
1885 "The Aboriginal Relics Called 'Sinkers' or 'Plummets'." *American Journal of Archaeology*, Vol. 1, pp. 105-114. Baltimore: Archaeological Institute of America.
HERSKOVITZ, MELVILLE J., AND FRANCES S. HERSKOVITZ
1958 *Dahomean Narrative: A Cross-Cultural Analysis*. Evanston: Northwestern University Press.
HIEB, LOUIS A.
1972 "Meaning and Mismeaning: Toward an Understanding of the Ritual Clown." In *New Perspectives on the Pueblos*, Alfonso Ortiz

(editor), pp. 163-195. Albuquerque: University of New Mexico Press.

HILL, JANE H., AND ROSINDA NOLASQUEZ (EDITORS)
1973   *Mulu'wetam: The First People.* Banning: Malki Museum Press.

HULTKRANTZ, AKE
1957   "The North American Indian Orpheus Tradition." *Ethnographical Museum of Sweden, Monograph Series,* No. 2. Stockholm: Ethnographical Museum of Sweden.

JACOBS, MELVILLE
1959   *The Content and Style of an Oral Literature.* Chicago: University of Chicago Press.

JACOBS, MELVILLE (COMPILER)
1966   *The Anthropoligist Looks at Myth.* Austin: University of Texas Press.

JONES, W. T.
1972   "World Views: Their Nature and Their Function." *Current Anthropology,* Vol. 13, No. 1, pp. 79-109. Chicago: University of Chicago Press.

KING, CHESTER
1971   "Chumash Inter-Village Economic Exchange." *The Indian Historian,* Vol. 4, No. 1, pp. 30-43. San Francisco: American Indian Historical Society.

KING, LINDA
1969   "The Medea Creek Cemetery (LAn-243): An Investigation of Social Organization from Mortuary Practices." *Archaeological Survey Annual Report, 1969,* Vol. 11, pp. 23-68. Los Angeles: University of California, Los Angeles.

KLUCKHOHN, CLYDE
1949   "The Philosophy of the Navaho Indians." In *Ideological Differences and World Order,* F. S. C. Northrop (editor), pp. 356-384. New Haven: Yale University Press.

1965   "Recurrent Themes in Myths and Mythmaking." Reprinted in *The Study of Folklore,* Alan Dundes (editor), pp. 158-168. Englewood Cliffs: Prentice-Hall.

1968   "Myths and Rituals: A General Theory." Reprinted in *Studies on Mythology,* Robert A. Georges (editor), pp. 137-167. Homewood: Dorsey Press.

KROEBER, ALFRED L.
1907   "Indian Myths of South Central California." *University of California Publications in American Archaeology and Ethnology,* Vol. 4, No. 4, pp. 167-250. Berkeley: University of California Press.

1953   *Handbook of the Indians of California.* Berkeley: California Book Company.

KUNKEL, PETER H.
1962   *Yokuts and Pomo Political Institutions: A Comparative Analysis.* Ph.D. dissertation, University of California, Los Angeles.

LaBarre, Weston
1972 "Hallucinogens and the Shamanic Origins of Religion." In *Flesh of the Gods: The Ritual Use of Hallucinogens*, Peter T. Furst (editor), pp. 261-278. New York: Praeger.

Ladd, John
1956 *The Structure of a Moral Code*. Cambridge: Harvard University Press.

Laird, Carobeth
1975 *Encounter With An Angry God: Autobiographical Recollections of My Life with John Peabody Harrington*. Banning: Malki Museum Press.

Landberg, Leif C. W.
1965 *The Chumash Indians of Southern California*. Highland Park: Southwest Museum.

Latta, F. F.
1949 *Handbook of Yokuts Indians*. Oildale: Bear State Books.

Leach, Edmund
1954 *Political Systems of Highland Burma*. London: G. Bell & Sons.

1967a "Brain Twister." *The New York Review of Books*, Vol. 9, No. 6, pp. 6, 8, 10. Milford: New York Review.

Leach, Edmund (editor)
1967b *The Structural Study of Myth and Totemism*. London: Tavistock Publications.

Lee, Dorothy
1938 "Conceptual Implications of an Indian Language." *Philosophy of Science*, Vol. 5, pp. 89-102. Baltimore: Philosophy of Science Association.

Lessa, William A.
1966 "'Discoverer-of-the-Sun': Mythology as a Reflection of Culture." In *The Anthropologist Looks at Myth*, Melville Jacobs (compiler), pp. 3-51. Austin: University of Texas Press.

Lévi-Strauss, Claude
1967 *Structural Anthropology*. Garden City: Doubleday.

1969 *The Raw and the Cooked*. New York: Harper and Row.

Loeb, E. M.
1931 "The Religious Organizations of North Central California and Tierra del Fuego." *American Anthropologist*, Vol. 33, No. 4, pp. 517-556. Menasha: American Anthropological Association.

1934a "The Western Kuksu Cult." *University of California Publications in American Archaeology and Ethnology*, Vol. 33, pp. 1-138. Berkeley: University of California Press.

1934b "The Eastern Kuksu Cult." *University of California Publications in American Archaeology and Ethnology*, Vol. 33, pp. 139-232. Berkeley: University of California Press.

Makarius, Laura
1970 "Ritual Clowns and Symbolical Behavior." *Diogenes*, No. 69, pp. 44-73. Firenze: Casalini Libri.

MALINOWSKI, BRONISLAW
1953   *Argonauts of the Western Pacific.* New York: E. P. Dutton.
MARANDA, PIERRE, AND ELLI KÖNGÄS MARANDA (EDITORS)
1971   *Structural Analysis of Oral Tradition.* Philadelphia: University of
Pennsylvania Press.
MASON, OTIS T.
1891   "The Natural History of Folklore." *Journal of American Folklore,*
Vol. 4, pp. 97-105. Boston: American Folklore Society.
MAYBURY-LEWIS, DAVID
1969   "Science or Bricolage?" *American Anthropologist,* Vol. 71, pp. 114-
121. Menasha: American Anthropological Association.
MURDOCK, GEORGE P.
1960   *Social Structure.* New York: Macmillan.
NATHHORST, BERTEL
1969   "Formal or Structural Studies of Traditional Tales." *Stockholm
Studies in Comparative Religion, No. 9.* Stockholm: Norstedt and
Söner.
NORBECK, EDWARD
1963   "African Rituals of Conflict." *American Anthropologist,* Vol. 65,
pp. 1254-1279. Menasha: American Anthropological Association.
NORTHRUP, F. S. C. (EDITOR)
1949   *Ideological Differences and World Order.* New Haven: Yale University Press.
OPLER, MORRIS E.
1938   "Myths and Tales of the Jicarilla Apache Indians." *Memoirs of
the American Folk-Lore Society, Vol. 31.* New York: American Folk-
Lore Society.
1946   "The Creative Role of Shamanism in Mescalero Apache Mythology." *Journal of American Folklore,* Vol. 59, pp. 268-281. Philadelphia: American Folklore Society.
ORTIZ, ALFONSO
1972a   "Ritual Drama and the Pueblo World View." In *New Perspectives on the Pueblos,* Alfonso Ortiz (editor), pp. 135-161. Albuquerque: University of New Mexico Press.
ORTIZ, ALFONSO (EDITOR)
1972b   *New Perspectives on the Pueblos.* Albuquerque: University of New
Mexico Press.
OSWALT, ROBERT L.
1964   "Kashaya Texts." *University of California Publications in Linguistics,* Vol. 36. Berkeley: University of California Press.
PEACOCK, JAMES L.
1969   "Society as Narrative." In *Forms of Symbolic Action,* Robert F.
Spencer (editor), pp. 167-177. Seattle: University of Washington
Press.
PIETTE, CHARLES J. G. MAXIMIN (EDITOR)
1946-   "An Unpublished Diary of Fray Juan Crespí, O.F.M." *The Ameri-
1947   cas,* Vol. 3, Nos. 1, 2 and 3, pp. 102-114, 234-243, 368-381.
Washington: Academy of American Franciscan History.

PRIESTLEY, HERBERT I. (EDITOR)
    1937   *A Historical, Political, and Natural Description of California by Pedro Fages, Soldier of Spain.* Berkeley: University of California Press.

REICHEL-DOLMATOFF, GERARDO
    1971   *Amazonian Cosmos: The Sexual and Religious Symbolism of the Tukano Indians.* Chicago: University of Chicago Press.

REICHLER, HENRY, AND ROBERT F. HEIZER
    1964   "The Scientific Expedition of Léon de Cessac to California, 1877-1879." *Reports of the University of California Archaeological Survey, No. 61,* pp. 9-23. Berkeley: University of California Press.

RIVIÈRE, P. G.
    1969   "Myth and Material Culture: Some Symbolic Interrelations." In *Forms of Symbolic Action,* Robert F. Spencer (editor), pp. 151-166. Seattle: University of Washington Press.

ROBE, STANLEY
    1970   "Mexican Tales and Legends from Los Altos." *University of California Folklore Studies: 20.* Berkeley: University of California Press.

ROBINSON, ALFRED
    1947   *Life in California.* Oakland: Biobooks.

ROGERS, BARBARA, AND ANNA H. GAYTON
    1944   "Twenty-seven Chukchansi Yokuts Myths." *Journal of American Folklore,* Vol. 57, pp. 190-207. Philadelphia: American Folklore Society.

SCHOLTE, BOB
    1966   "Epistemic Paradigms: Some Problems in Cross-Cultural Research on Social Anthropological History and Theory." *American Anthropologist,* Vol. 68, pp. 1192-1201. Menasha: American Anthropological Association.

SHIPLEY, WILLIAM F.
    1963   "Maidu Texts and Dictionary." *University of California Publications in Linguistics,* Vol. 33. Berkeley: University of California Press.

SIMMONS, DONALD C.
    1961   "Analysis of Cultural Reflection in Efik Folktales." *Journal of American Folklore,* Vol. 74, pp. 126-141.

SIMPSON, LESLIE B. (EDITOR)
    1961   *Journal of José Longinos Martínez.* San Francisco: John Howell.
    1962   *The Letters of José Señán, O.F.M.: Mission San Buenaventura, 1796-1823.* San Francisco: John Howell.

SMITH, DONALD, AND FREDERICK TEGGART (EDITORS)
    1909   "Diary of Gaspar de Portolá During the California Expedition of 1769-1770." *Publications of the Academy of Pacific Coast History,* Vol. 1, No. 3. Berkeley: University of California Press.

SPENCER, KATHERINE
    1947   "Reflections of Social Life in the Navaho Origin Myth." *University of New Mexico Publications in Anthropology,* No. 3. Albuquerque: University of New Mexico Press.

1957 "Mythology and Values: An Analysis of Navaho Chantway Myths." *Memoirs of the American Folklore Society*, Vol. 48. Philadelphia: American Folklore Society.

SPENCER, ROBERT F. (EDITOR)
1969 *Forms of Symbolic Action.* Seattle: University of Washington Press.

STEWARD, JULIAN
1931 "The Ceremonial Buffoon of the American Indian." *Papers of the Michigan Academy of Science, Arts and Letters*, Vol. 14, pp. 187-207. Ann Arbor: University of Michigan Press.

STIRLING, MATHEW W., AND K. GLEMSER
1963 "John Peabody Harrington, 1884-1961." *American Anthropologist*, Vol. 65, No. 2, pp. 370-381. Menasha: American Anthropological Association.

TEGGART, FREDERICK J. (EDITOR)
1909 "The Official Account of the Portolá Expedition of 1769-1770." *Publications of the Academy of Pacific Coast History*, Vol. 1, No. 2. Berkeley: University of California Press.

THOMPSON, STITH
1929 *Tales of the North American Indians.* Bloomington: Indiana University Press.

TURNER, TERENCE S.
1969 "Oedipus: Time and Structure in Narrative Form." In *Forms of Symbolic Action*, Robert F. Spencer (editor), pp. 26-68. Seattle: University of Washington Press.

TURNER, VICTOR W.
1969a *The Ritual Process.* Chicago: Aldine.

1969b "Forms of Symbolic Action: Introduction." In *Forms of Symbolic Action*, Robert F. Spencer (editor), pp. 3-25. Seattle: University of Washington Press.

ULDALL, HANS J., AND WILLIAM F. SHIPLEY
1966 "Nisenan Texts and Dictionary." *University of California Publications in Linguistics*, Vol. 46. Berkeley: University of California Press.

VOEGLIN, CHARLES
1935 "Tübatulabal Texts." *University of California Publications in American Archaeology and Ethnology*, Vol. 34, No. 3, pp. 191-246. Berkeley: University of California Press.

WHITE, RAYMOND
1963 "Luiseño Social Organization." *University of California Publications in American Archaeology and Ethnology*, Vol. 48, No. 2, pp. 91-194. Berkeley: University of California Press.

WILLIS, R. G.
1967 "The Head and the Loins: Lévi-Strauss and Beyond." *Man*, Vol. 2, pp. 519-534. London: Royal Anthropological Institute.

WITTFOGEL, KARL A., AND ESTHER S. GOLDFRANK
1943 "Some Aspects of Pueblo Mythology and Society." *Journal of American Folklore*, Vol. 56, pp. 17-30. Philadelphia: American Folklore Society.

WOODWARD, ARTHUR

1934 "An Early Account of the Chumash." *Masterkey*, Vol. 8, No. 4, pp. 118-123. Highland Park: Southwest Museum.

YATES, LORENZO G.

1889 "Charm Stones: Notes on the So-called 'Plummets' or Sinkers." *Annual Report of the Smithsonian Institution to the End of June, 1886*, pp. 296-305. Washington, D. C.: Government Printing Office.

1891 "Fragments of the History of a Lost Tribe." *American Anthropologist*, Vol. IV, pp. 373-376 (Old Series). Washington, D. C.: Anthropological Society of Washington.